ANCIENT AND MEDIEVAL HISTORY OF INDIA

ANCIENT AND MEDIEVAL HISTORY OF INDIA

by

H.G. RAWLINSON

BHARATIYA KALA PRAKASHAN
Delhi

First Editon : 2001

Published by **C.P. Gautam**
BHARATIYA KALA PRAKASHAN
3421-A, IInd Floor, Narang Colony, Tri Nagar,
Delhi-110035. Phone : 7153083

ISBN : 81-86050-79-5

Laser Typesetting by :
SHRI BALAJI COMPUTERS
Phone : 7108270

Printed at :
SANTOSH OFFISET, DELHI

Contents

Preface

Indian History, declared *The Times* less than half a century ago, has never been made interesting to English readers except by rhetoric. Since then, the devoted work of a generation of scholars has thrown a flood of new light upon the subject, but the results of their investigations have been chiefly intended for the specialist. English people as a whole have been singularly blind to the signficance of India's contribution to world-culture; there has even been a positive distaste, born of prejudice and apathy, for Indian spiritual and aesthetic values. To-day, when India is once more emerging, with that persistent vitality which has been her characteristic through the ages, from eclipse, it is more than ever incumbent on us to realise the greatness of her past achievements in religion, politics, art and literature. It is impossible to belittle or ignore a culture which gave the world a religious teacher such as the Buddha, rulers like Asoka and Akbar, Kālidāsa's *Sakuntalā*, the superb plastic masterpieces of Sānchī and Borobudur, the Ajantā frescoes, the South Indian bronzes, the Hindu temples of

here in Europe, who have been nurtured almost exclusively on the thoughts of the Greeks and Romans, and one Semitic race, the Jewish, may draw that corrective which is most wanted in order to make our inner life more perfect, more universal – in fact, more human, I should point to India. To write a short book on a vast subject is always a difficult task, involving as it does the inevitable problem of what to select and what to reject. The author's object has been to avoid, as far as possible, a mass of detail and of unfamiliar names, always bewildering to the reader who is not ac uainted with the subject already,and confine himself to those aspects especially signficant or distinctive. The British period, about which much has been already written, has been only incidentally touched upon; the main theme of the book is the history of the Indian peoples.

It is difficult to express obligations to all who have assisted by giving permission to use copyright passages and illustrations, but the author wishes especially to convey his gratitude to the following: – The Secretary of State for India; The Council of the Royal Asiatic Society; The Director-General of Archaeology, India; The Indian Railways Bureau; The Government of ysore; The India Society; The Director of the Victoria

& Albert Museum; the British Museum; the City of Birmingham Museum and Art Gallery; the Oxford University Press; the Cambridge University Press; Messrs. Macmillan & Co.; Messrs. Longmans, Green & Co.; Messrs. George Allen & Unwin, Limited; Dr. Ananda Coomaraswamy of the Museum of Fine Arts, Boston, Mass; The Council of the Young Men's Christian Association, Calcutta; Messrs. Spink & Sons, Limited; and Mr. Arthur Probsthain. The maps and many of the text figures are the work of Mr. C.O. Waterhouse of the British Museum. Miss M. Campbell has prepared the Index. Mr. F. Richter, O.B.E., Secretary of the royal India Society, and Mr. P.D. Mehta have kindly read the proofs. The author is indebted to Mr. K. de B. Codrington, Keeper of the India Museum, and to Lady Hartog, for their kind help in selecting illustrations. To the late Professor C.G. Seligman, F.R.S., the General Editor of the Series, his obligations are not easily expressed in words; Professor Seligman was unwearied in advice and criticism in every stage of the work.

H.G. Rawlinson

Note on Pronunciation

The following hints may be useful for pronouncing Indian names :

a as in c*up*

ā as in father

e as in m*a*te

i as in fit

ī as in f*ee*t

o as in m*o*te

u as in f*oo*t

ū as in b*oo*t

ai as in *might*

ch as in *ch*urch

kh (Persian and Arabic) as in lo*ch*

In aspirated consonants, the *h* is pronounced separately. Thus *ph* is sounded as in *uphill*. There is no sound corresponding to *a* in the English *cat*, and *o* is invariably long. Final *a* is very lightly sounded; *r* is rolled. The following gives the phonetic pronunciation of some familiar words :

Buddha pronounced Boodh

Akbar pronounced Ukbur

Satī pronounced Suttee

Karma pronounced Kurrma

List of Plates

Plates I - XXIII are grouped together immediately following the text on page 420

List of Figures

Fig.

NOTE

Figs. 1-4 are from Sir J. Marshall, *Mohenjo-daro and the Indus Civilization*; Figs. 5, 6, 7, 8, 16, 17, 18, 19, 21, 23, 30, 33, 44, from Moor's *Hindu Pantheon;* Figs. 9-14 from Cunningham, *Sānchī and its Remains*; Figs. 22, 24, 26, 37, 38, 39 from Fergusson, *Indian and Eastern Architecture*; Figs. 28, 29, 31, from Rām Rāz, *Hindu Architecture;* and Figs. 32, 34, 35 from Forbes, *Rās Mālā*. Fig. 42 is from a drawing kindly lent by Dr. A.K. Coomaraswamy. Figs. 36 and 43 are from the India Museum, South Kensington.

List of Maps

Chapter I

Geography and Pre-History

The sub-continent known to western nations by the name of India is, roughly speaking, a gigantic rhomboid, with an area of about 1,575,000 square miles and a population of over 400 millions. This country is peopled by a large number of ethnic groups in every stage of development, from the aboriginal inhabitants of the central forests to the highly cultured men of letters of its universities, speaking a bewildering number of languages, and differing widely in physical appearance and social customs. It would be inaccurate to apply the term "nation" to India. "The people of Intu (India)," says the Chinese traveller, Hiuen Tsang, "call their country by different names, according to the district." Āryāvarta in Sanskrit and Hindustan or Hind in later dialects refer to the Gangetic plain; India was a term originally borrowed by the Greeks from the Persians, who applied it exclusively to the country watered by the Sindhu or Indus river, the inhabitants of which were known as Indians or Hindus. From time to time an Indian Napoleon arose who would temporarily knit this vast congeries of peoples into a coherent whole, and the Mogul Emperors even imposed a single official language, Persians. But it was reserved for her later conquerors to introduce, not only a common tongue, but common political aspirations, the growth of which had been immensely facilitated by the opening-up of communications, the spread of education and the diffusion of western political ideas. This lack of national consciousness is perhaps the main reason why pre-Muhammadan India had no historians. Her vast literature contains no Herodotus or Thucydides, no Tacitus or Livy; the very memory of her greatest ruler, the Emperor Asoka, was forgotten until European scholars at the beginning of the 19th century laboriously reconstructed the story by piecing together the fragments which had survived the ravages of time.

And yet through all this apparent diversity there runs an underlying unity. The conception of a national religion, it has been said, is the only germ to be found in ancient times of the idea of Indian nationality. In spite of all differences of languages, race and sect, from the Himālayas to Cape Comorin, the fundamental principles of the Hindu religion hold their immemorial sway over the vast majority of the population. These may be summed up as the almost universal belief in the authority

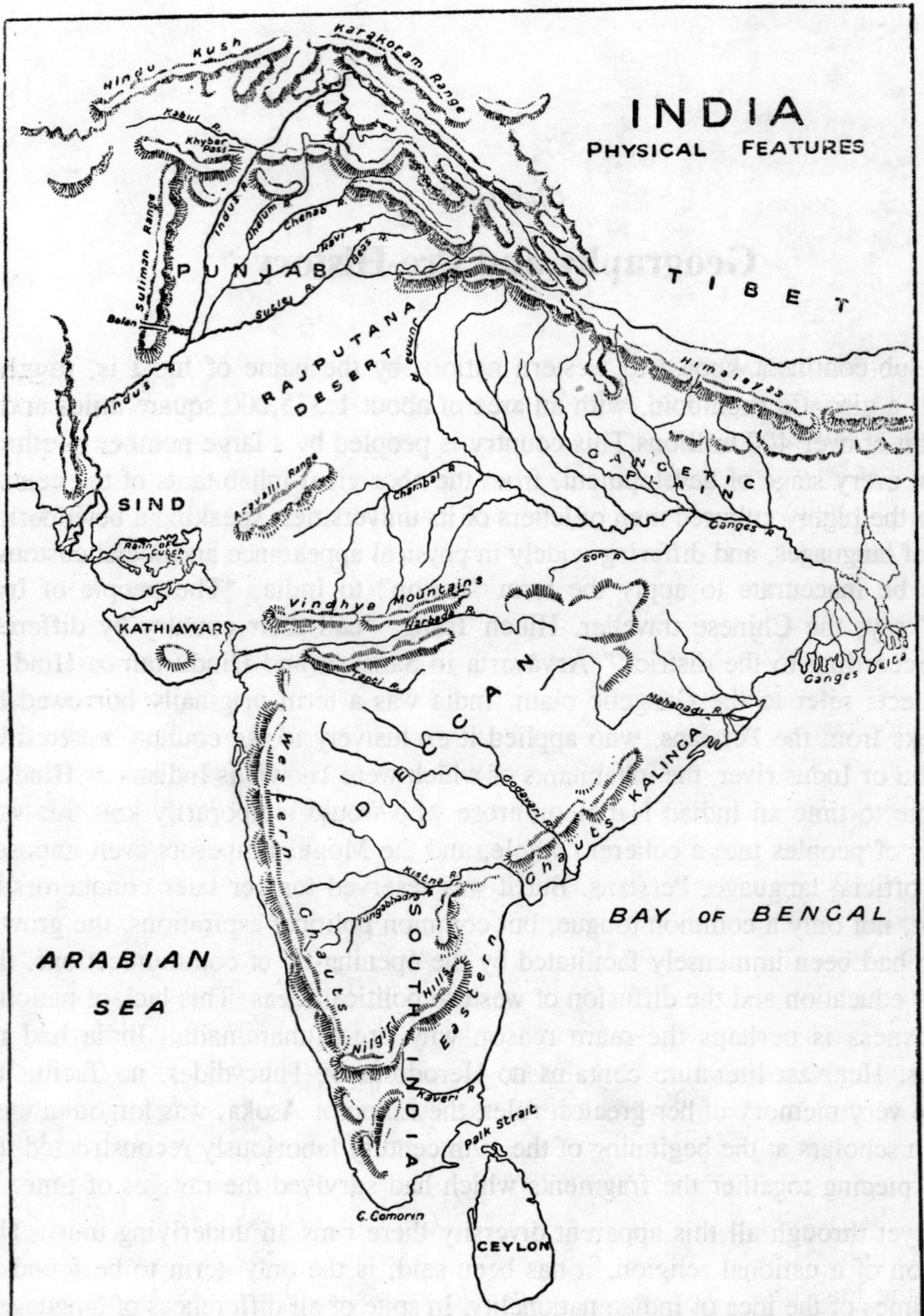

Map 1 : India, Physical Features

of the Vedas and the sacredness of the cow, the worship of the great gods Siva and Vishnu in their innumerable aspects, and the institution of caste. Caste, perhaps, more than any other feature, distinguishes India from the rest of the world.* Its vitality is immense. It has survived the attacks of religious reformers from without and hostile influences from within, and even to-day shows few signs of decay. It is, however, a source of weakens as well as of strength. By splitting the people into a number of water-tight compartments, it has rendered the growth of a national spirit almost impossible, and has been one of the reasons why India has been so largely, throughout her chequered annals, at the mercy of foreign conquerors.

The history of India is to a great extent determined by geographical conditions. To the north, she is shut off by the gigantic mountain-wall of the Himālayas, running along her northern frontier from Afghanistan to Assam for 1,600 miles, and forming an almost impenetrable obstacle to intercourse with the rest of Asia except from the north-west. Here the barrier is pierced where it turns southward by openings through which the Indus and Kābul rivers flow into India. At the north-west angle is the Khyber pass, 3,400 feet above sea-level, with the city of Peshāwar, the ancient Pushpapura, at its mouth. South of this are the Kurram, Tochi and Gumal passes, and the famous Bolān pass. Between the Bolān pass and the sea, the Sind-Baluchistan boundary is formed by the Hālā, Brāhui and Pab mountains; but these are much less formidable than the northern ranges, and there is a gap between their southern extremity and the coast. Through the Khyber runs the road to Kābul. Kābul, again, is the focus of a number of routes, running northwards to Balkh and Central Asia, and westwards to Herāt, Meshed, and Asia Minor, while through the Bolān the road reaches Kandahār, another great meeting-place of ancient routes to Seistan and Persia. All these approaches to India have played a decisive part in her history. By them, from immemorial times, migrating tribes, peaceful traders and conquering armies have poured over the Iranian plateau into the fertile plains lying beyond the mountains.

India falls into four main cultural divisions, each dominated by its river systems. These are the basins of the Indus and of the Ganges, the Deccan plateau, and Southern or peninsular India. Rivers play an all-important part in Indian history, both as a means of communication and a source of water-supply; hence it is not surprising that so many of her earliest inhabitants settled along the banks of the great streams. The westernmost of these divisions is the alluvial plain watered by the Indus and its four tributaries, the Sutlej, the Rāvī, the Chenab and the Jhelum, and hence known as the Punjab, or land of five rivers. South of the confluence of these streams lies Sind, the land of the river Sindhu, the Vedic name for the Indus. A fact of which the historian must not lose sight is the changes which have occurred in the course of time in the beds of the Indian rivers. Flowing as they do through soft, sandy banks,

* See Chapter II, p. 25, ff.

they have latered their channels many times in the course of history. The Sutlej, united with the Saraswatī and Ghaggar, used to form a huge stream – the Hakrā – which flowed through what is now desert land in Bahāwalpur. The Hakrā only dried up in the 18th century. The modern Indus delta is of recent origin. At one time the river flowed into the Rann of Cutch.

The Indus and Ganges basins are separated by the Thar, or Rājputāna desert, and are linked by a narrow corridor running between it and the Himālayas, which roughly follows the course of the Jumna river. This corridor, the ancient Kurukshetra, has been happily named the cockpit of India, for here, owing to its strategic importance, the fate of the country has been decided on innumerable occasions. The Gangetic plain, watered by the Ganges and her great tributaries, the Jumna, the Chambal, the Gumtī, the Gogra and the Son, with innumerable smaller streams, is an immense, fertile tract, with an area of 300,000 square miles and a breadth of 90 to 300 miles. Its vast natural resources and its great waterways have made it the scene of the most striking events in India's history. Along the banks of the Ganges many of the great Hindu empires of the past, with their splendid cities, sprang up and flourished. "Mother Ganges" is, above all, the sacred river of India. Hardwār, where, rising from an icy Himalayan cave she debouches into the plain, and Prayāga (Allahābād) where she joins her 'twin' the Yumanā or Jumna, are places of pilgrimage visited by millions of pious Hindus. Not less holy is the venerable city of Kāsī or Benares, upon her lower banks. Near her mouth she is joined by another mighty river, the Brahmapūtra or "Son of Brahma," which flows through gigantic gorges, from the mountains of Tibet, to pass through Assam and Eastern Bengal.

The southern boundary of the Gangetic plain is formed by the Vindhya mountains and their offshoots. These are sandstone ranges, rising to about 3,000 feet, and formerly clad with dense and impenetrable jungle, the Dandaranyaka or Mahākāntāra of Vedic and Epic days, beyond which the Aryan-speaking tribes found it difficult to penetrate. These ranges form the northern edge of the Deccan plateau. The Deccan, or South Land, is the most ancient part of India, and was once probably linked up with an Austral continent stretching far to the eastward. On the western side, the plateau terminates with the Western Ghauts or "stairs," a steep mountain-wall running roughly parallel with the shores of the Arabian Sea for about 600 miles. This has weathered into a number of flat-topped peaks, easily convertible into almost impregnable fortresses, which were destined to play an important part in the history of the Marāthā nation. The Ghauts shut off the Deccan from the sea, and are pierced by occasional passes, which could only be surmounted in former days by pack-animals. Further south, however, is the all-important Pālghāt, or Gap of Coimbatore, about 20 miles broad, which leads from the Malabar Coast to the plains of the Carnatic. On the eastern side, the Ghauts are much less steep and continuous, and the two ranges terminate in the lofty peaks to the Nīlgiri or Blue Mountains. The rivers of the Indian peninsula, with the exception of the Tāptī and the Narbadā, flow into the Bay of Bengal. The principal streams are the Mahānadī, the Godāverī and the Kṛṣna, with their tributaries. The Tungabadrā, the chief tributary of the Kṛṣṇa, is usually looked upon as the southern boundary of the Deccan. Beyond lies the Tamil country; in the centre are the Cardamon Hills, but for the most part it consists of broad plains, watered by the Pennār and Cauvery rivers. Physical features have tended to isolate Southern India from the rest of the country, and it early developed a culture essentially its own.

Climatic conditions have played a large part in Indian history. The martial races have been chiefly bred in the dry, hilly districts of the north-west and centre and the deserts of Rājputāna, where a livelihood can only be wrested from the soil by intense effort, and, even then, has to be supplemented by raids upon more favoured neighbours; the fertile, low-lying plains of Bengal on the other hand have been inhabited by peaceful, unwarlike cultivators. The destinies of a large part of the peninsula depend to a considerable extent upon the seasonal rainfall brought by the monsoons, currents of moisture-laden air which sweep across the country from the Arabian Sea from June to October. The heaviest precipitation occurs upon the Western Ghauts, where the rain-clouds first strike upon the Indian coast, the southern slopes of the Himālayas north of Bengal, and the Assam Hills. Here the rainfall amounts to over 100 inches in the year; in the Deccan and the Delhi district it amounts to nearly 25 inches, or about the same as London. In Sind and the Rājputāna desert, it is only five inches at the present day. But it must be borne in mind that a series of climatic changes have taken place in Central Asia, including north-western India, which have materially affected the course of history, as they brought about the migration of peoples from the desiccated areas in search of new pastures. Formelry, India was by no means as isolated as she is at present. In what are now the arid wastes of Baluchistan may be seen abundant traces of former cultivation; and Khotan, now a rainless desert, was the seat of a flourishing civilisation as late as the 9th century A.D. Sind, now arid except where it is irrigated, was once densely populated, with an equable climate and a fertile soil. The Indus valley seals exhibit rhinoceroses, elephants and tigers, all inhabitants of well-watered jungles, and unknown in Sind to-day. The Arab historians speak of Sind as an oasis surrounded by deserts, and as late as the 14th century, Timūr lost his horses at Multan owing to heavy rains. Strabo* speaks of the violent monsoon rain of the spring and early summer of 326 B.C. in the Taxila district, which hampered Alexander's operations. Man, by clearing forests, damming rivers and erecting irrigation works, has played his part in bringing about these changes.†

* *Geography* XV, p. 690 ff.

† Deforestation and malaria are two factors which have played an important part in Indian history. See F.J. Richards, *Geographical Factors in Indian Archaeology*, Indian Antiquary, vol. LXII (1933), p. 235 ff.

Peninsular India is more dependent on the monsoon than the plains of the north, where the Indus and the Ganges and most of their tributaries are fed by the periodic melting of the Himalayan snows. The rivers of the centre and south have no such advantages, and dry up when the monsoon rains fail. This formelry led to periodic famines, in which the death-rate was often appalling. These catastrophes are now minimised by irrigation works and by the opening up of communications, which enables the ready transfer of supplies to the affected district. During the rainy season, in days when metalled roads were unknown and rivers unbridged, there was a general cessation from activities. Wandering bands of monks retired to their monasteries and armies went into winter-quarters until the Dasara festival in mid-October ushered in the commencement of the campaigning season.

There is evidence that parts of India have been inhabited by human races from a remote time. Palaeolithic and neolithic remains have been discovered as far apart as Bellary in Madras and Mirzāpur in the United Provinces. In the former district a neolithic potter's workshop has been brought to light. Near Tinnivelly, prehistoric cemeteries covering large areas have been unearthed, and there is abundant evidence of ancient pearl and conch-shell fisheries at the mouth of the Tamraparni river, and of gold-workings, probably of neolithic origin, at Maski in the Nizam's Dominions. At Mirzāpur and other palces, megalithic cemeteries, apparently of the iron age, have been discovered. Rude drawings in red pigment are found on cave-walls in the Bellary and Wynaad districts and other localities. From the evidence, it appears that neolithic man in southern India reached a fairly advanced degree of civilisation. He knew the use of the potter's wheel, and how to cut and hollow out timber and dress skins. He made ornaments of conch-shell, pearls and gold beads. He cultivated crops in jungle-clearings, and had domesticated the dog, ox and goat. In southern India, stone tools were replaced by iron; in the north, copper was employed, and the absence of a bronze age is conspicuous. Finds of copper implements have been made from time to time. At Gungeria in the Central Provinces, a hoard of over four hundred objects was discovered, including shouldered axes, harpoons, barbed spears and swords, and silver laminae.*

Many attempts have been made to present a reasonable conspectus of Indian ethnology, but these have hitherto been hampered by an incomplete knowledge of the distribution of physical characteristics, and even more by a tendency to confuse ethnic type and language. Linguistic terms such as Dravidian and Aryan have been applied to ethnic units. Recently, however, a German anthropologist, Baron E. von Eickstedt,† has evolved a coherent theory of Indian anthropology, which, there is

* *Cambridge History of India,* I, pp. 612-615.

† Von Eickstedt's theories are summarised in L.K.A. Iyer's *Mysore Tribes and Castes* (1935), vol. I, Chaper I. They are criticised in the *Census of India*, 1931, vo. I. iii, p. lxxi.

reason to believe, will with due additions as knowledge advances stand the test of future research. In von Eickstedt's view, there are no Aryans and Dravidians, though there are Aryan and Dravidian languages and cultural usages.

Von Eickstedt considers the oldest stratum, going back to an early post-glacial period, to have been a dark-skinned group akin to the early negroid stocks of Africa and Melanesia. These Indo-Negrids once covered the whole peninsula; they were of two types, the one of smaller stature, more primitive and living in the forest, and the other of higher stature, more progressive and living in the open country. Next after them came another primitive stock, to which the Sakai of Malaya also belong,

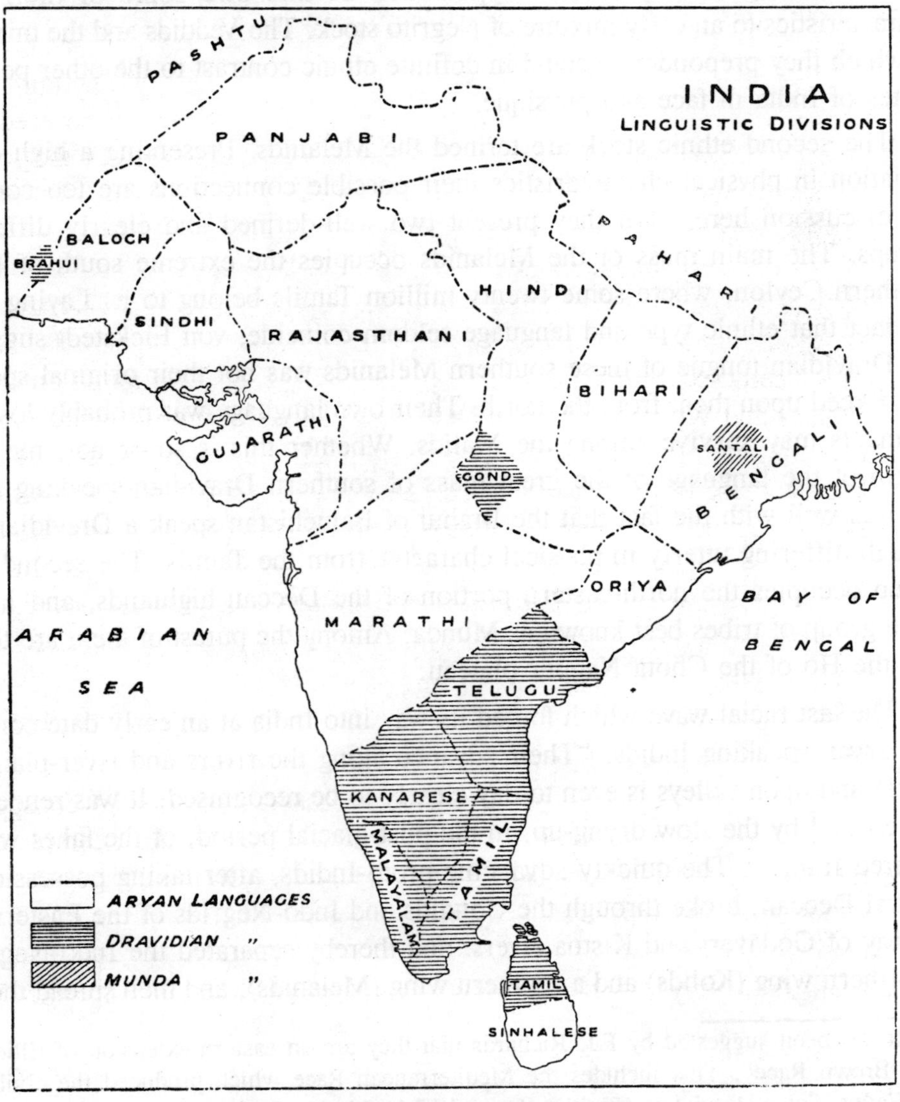

Map 2 : India, Linguistic Divisions

including the Veddas of Ceylon, the Irula of the Nīlgiris, the Panyer of the Wynaad, and many other jungle tribes. They came from the north, interpenetrated and gradually mingled with the Indo-Negrids. Typically they are short, long-headed and rather broad-nosed, with wavy or curly hair, and are sometimes comparativley light-skinned. The many peoples of this ancient and rather primitive stock, related to the Australians, are essentially inhabitants of the forests and of that lovely semi-forest country known as park-land. To these people von Eickstedt gives the name Veddids, taken from one of its best-known members. The Veddids fall into two sub-types, Malids and Gondids. The Malids represent the more primitive type of Veddid. Some Malids have a very dark skin, and it may be that types such as this owe some of their physical characteristics to an early mixture of Negrito stock. The Veddids and the mixed stocks in which they preponderate stand in definite ethnic contrast to the other peoples and castes of India in face and physique.

The second ethnic stock are termed the Melanids. Presenting a high degree of variation in physical characteristics their possible connections are too complicated for discussion here,* but they present two well-defined and clearly differentiated groups. The main mass of the Melanids occupies the extreme south of India and northern Ceylon, where some twenty million Tamils belong to it. Laying stress on the fact that ethnic type and language seldom coincide, von Eickstedt suggests that the Dravidian tongue of these southern Melanids was not their original speech, but was forced upon them from the north. Their own language was probably lost, though remnants may survive among the Malids. Whether this is so or not, the northern origin of the language of the great mass of southern Dravidian-speaking Melanids accords well with the fact that the Brahui of Baluchistan speak a Dravidian dialect, though differing utterly in physical character from the Tamils. The second Melanid group occupies the north-eastern portion of the Deccan highlands, and includes a large group of tribes best known as Munda. Among the purest of them are the Santāl and the Ho of the Chota Nagpur plateau.

The last racial wave which forced its way into India at an early date consisted of the Aryan-speaking Indids. "Their advance along the rivers and river-plains of the fertile and open valleys is even to-day clearly to be recognised. It was rendered even more rapid by the slow dryng-up, in the post-glacial period, of the lakes which had covered Iran. ... The quickly advancing proto-Indids, after taking possession of the central Deccan, broke through the Gondids and Indo-Negrids of the Eastern Ghauts by way of Godāveri and Kistna rivers, and thereby separated the Indo-Negrids into a northern wing (Kolids) and a southern wing (Melanids), and then spread themselves

* It has been suggested by F.J. Richards that they are an eastern extension of Elliot Smith's "Brown Race". This includes the Mediterranean Race which produced the civilisation of Egypt. *Some Dravidian Affinities*, Journal of the Mythic Society of Bangalore, July, 1917.

over the eastern coastal plains." Yet despite the many immigrant waves from the north, the remains of the old Indo-Negrid races of the plains have maintained themselves in the south lands even to the present day; indeed, the last great wave from the north was not quite able to reach this area, so that the North Indids, with associates of other stocks who brought with them their Aryan speech and pastoral culture, only partly succeeded in penetrating Southern India. "For the most part they remained caught in the racial filter of the Deccan, the southern end of which, in Mysore, can even to-day be sharply distinguished from the Tamil South." The distribution of the Indids extends from Central Afghanistan and Baluchistan to the Ganges valley and the Central Deccan. There are scattered groups in the Narbadā valley and Mysore, and other territories occupied by Veddid peoples; in Orissa, Bengal, the Ganges-Jumna-Doāb and other localities, well-marked local types have arisen through the absorption of elements from neighbouring non-Indid groups.

The main body of the Indids now occupy east-central and south-central India The great majority are of the physically smaller and more refined type called "Gracil-Indids" by von Eickstedt, but besides these there is a taller, coarser boned type, found especially among the more northerly groups. This type is distinguished by relatively thick lips and by a strong growth of hair, especially of the beard. These are the "North Indids." They are to be found in the Doāb in the upper social strata and "especially among the military castes, and represent the main body of the population of the entire Punjab, where the Sikhs form one of their most characteristic groups. From here they spread out towards Afghanistan and Kashmir, and are well represented in Rājputāna, where the Rājpūts constitute an extremely well-characterised caste type; they are not infrequently to be recognised in mixed peoples of the Marāthā area, and finally they are also to be found... in Mysore."* Even the Tamil country and Malabar are not quite free from their influence, though in the south only a single people, the Todas of the Nīlgiris, have maintained themselves really pure, an isolated remnant of an old north-Indid pastoral group.

We now come to what may be described as one of the most important discoveries of modern archaeology.† Mysterious seals, bearing pictographic signs in an unknown script, had been discovered at Harappā in the Montgomery District of the Punjab many years ago, but it was not until 1922 that Mr. R.D. Banerji, while working on a 2nd century Buddhist stupa at Mohenjo-daro, 25 miles south of Lārkhāna in Sind, came across the remains of a great prehistoric city belonging to the chalcolithic age. This was excavated under the auspices of Sir John Marshall, the Director-General of

* von Eickstedt, *op. cit.*, p. 38.

† See Sir J. Marshall, *Mohenjo-daro and the Indus Civilization* (1931); L.E. Mackay, *The Indus Civilization* (1935).

Archaeology, with surprising results. The town is well laid out. Its streets are at right angles, running due north and south and east and west. The main street, which is 33 feet wide, has been traced for over half a mile and is unpaved. The side roads are about half this width. The buildings are of burnt brick set in mud mortar. No stone is used and the absence of any kind of ornamentation is conspicuous. The windows and doors open upon the main street, and it was probable that some were several storeys high, with flat roofs. An unusual feature of the houses is the presence of bathrooms, and also of an elaborate drainage system, greatly in advance of anything known in later India. For this purpose, pottery drain pipes and receptacles were laid down, communicating with the street drain or gutter. No temple has been discovered, but a large public bath, 39 feet by 23, has been unearthed. This bath, which was rendered water-tight, is provided with steps leading down to the water,a promenade, and compartments for the bathers. Ingenious arrangements for filling and emptying it are provided. Just to the south of the bathroom is a large building, over two hundred feet long and one hundred feet wide, which may have been the royal palace.

The inhabitants were highly artistic, and the numerous objects found in the course of excavation throw a flood of light upon their social customs and habits. The most numerous are the remarkable steatite seals or amulets, of which large numbers have been collected. Their precise use is unknown, but the fact that they are perforated at the back suggests that they were worn round the neck on a string. They are beautifully carved and glazed; the commonest objects represented on them are a magnificent Brahminy bull, and a "unicorn" (perhaps the urus ox seen in profile), which appears to be eating out of a manger. Tigers, elephants, rhinoceroses, short-horned bulls, antelopes, buffaloes, and the gharial or fish-eating crocodile along figure on the seals, but the absence of the cow and horse are sigfnificant. Many of the seals bear brief inscriptions in a pictographic script which still remains undeciphered. It is probable that they give the names of the owners. Besides the seals, a number of figures in steatite, clay and limestone have been discovered. One of these shows a man with narrow eyes, thick lips and flat nose, a short abundant beard and a clean-shaven lip (Plate I). His hair is confined by a fillet, and he wears a shawl or robe ornamented with a trefoil pattern similar to that found on some of the pottery. Small figuriens of burnt clay, including some charming children's toys in the shape of various birds and beasts, a toy cart, and an animal which moves its head, have been discovered in great numbers. The pottery is fine and varied. It was turned on the fast lathe, and a variety of beautifully shaped specimens have been found, including large storage jars, flat basins with a high foot, and cylindrical and pointed vases. Spouts and handles are very rare. The pottery is usually coated with a slip of red ochre, often so highly burnished that it has the appearance of Chinese lacquer. Very often it is ornamented with a pattern of concentric circles in black, and occasionally with figures of trees,

Fig. 1 : Steatite Seal (Brahminy Bull), Mohenjo-daro

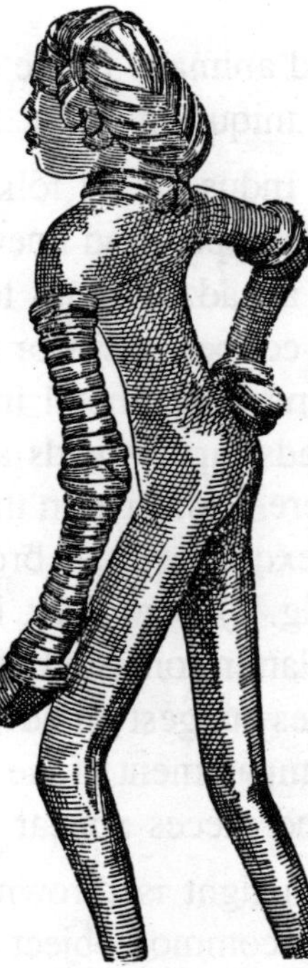

Fig. 2 : Bronze Figure of Dancing Girl, Mohenjo-daro

Fig. 3 : Steatite Seal (horned god), Mohenjo-daro

Fig. 4 : Steatite Seal (goddess, sacred tree and monster), Mohenjo-daro

birds and animals. Some of the pottery is ornamented with clay knobs: this knobbed ware is unique in India. Faience was used for bracelets, statuettes and beads.

The Indus valley folk were skilled metal-workers. They employed gold, silver, lead and copper, and knew how to make bronze. The finest specimen of their bronze work is an adze, about ten inches long, with a socket for a handle. Beakers were made of copper, silver or lead; these were either beaten or cast. Saws, chisels, knives, razors and other metal implements have been discovered, but the weapons (copper spearheads, arrowheads and swords) are of an inferior quality, and suggest that the users were unwarlike in their habits. The *cire perdue* process of casting was practised, and an exquisite little bronze figure of a dancing girl is an almost perfect piece of work (Fig. 2). Jewellery, in the shape of bangles and necklaces, was commonly worn, and the latter consisted of beads of jadeite, lapis-lazuli, amazonite and gold. Weights and scales suggest an advanced state of civilisation. Among amusements, dancing to the accompaniment of the drum, marbles and some kind of game played with a marker board and pieces appear to have been practised.

Much light is thrown by the discoveries upon the religion of the Indus valley. The most common object of worship appears to have been the Mother Goddess, whose cult was spread all over Asia Minor. She is represented in numerous pottery figurines, and on seals and amulets. Another goddess appears as horned, and in association with a sacred pipal tree (Fig. 4). A horned three-faced god, who is represented upon one of the seals in a seated attitude, surrounded by animals, has been identified with the Indian Siva-Mahādeva (Fig. 3), and this hypothesis is strengthened by the discovery of representations of the Lingam, the symbol of Siva. Whether the animals represented on the seals were objects of worship is unknown, but conspicuous among them is the bull, the Nandi of later times, and Siva's vāhan or vehicle (Fig. 1).

Various burial rites seem to have been in use, perhaps by different stocks or tribes. At Mohenjo-daro, the absence of a cemetery seems to point to cremation, but a large burial-ground has been found at Harappā. The ashes were sometimes placed in urns; at other times unburnt bones were collected and buried in jars.

The Indus valley culture was widely distributed. Harappa and Mohenjo-daro are 400 miles apart, and numerous sites have been located all along the Indus, as far as Hyderabad, more than 100 miles to the south; in Baluchistan and the Makran, 150 miles to the west, and as far north as Rupar on the Sutlej at the foot of the Simla hills. Examination of the skeletal remains show that the people were of a mixed race, the Mediterranean being the preponderating type. The skulls agree with those found at Al Ubaid and Kish, and belong to a dolichocephalie people. This, together with some general resemblances between pottery, beads, tools and weapons, suggests that the Indus valley folk were an intrusive stock, who shared a common ancestry with the Sumerians; no doubt they found a more primitive race already in possession of the country when they entered it, and, as usually happens, inter-married with the earlier inhabitants, and to some extent absorbed their customs. Recent discoveries of pottery seem to show that they came by way of the Mula pass and the coastal road which runs through Las Bela and the Makrān and crosses the Hab near Karachi.* But they were no mere immigrants: they developed a type of civilisation which was characteristically Indian. The date of Mohenjo-daro is approximately settled by the discovery of what is undoubtedly an Indus valley seal at Tel-Asmar, in a stratum which may be dated *circa* 2500 B.C. Other finds of Mesopotamian origin in Sind and *vice versa* confirm this. Allowing for the building of the successive cities at Mohenjo-daro, we may perhaps date their arrival at about one thousand years earlier. More we cannot say until a clue is found to the pictographs. This will perhaps be provided by the discovery of a bilingual seal; we shall then be able to decide whether the language spoken in the Indus valley was of Sumerian origin or not.

What caused the downfall of the Indus Valley culture? A variety of explanations have been offered—desiccation, an alteration in the bed of the Indus, epidemic disease, or invasion. We infer from the evidence that the inhabitants were a peaceful folk, whose great wealth must have offered a tempting prey to the wild tribes from the hills, and there are reasons for thinking that Mohenjo-daro was sacked and the inhabitants put to the sword. Groups of skeletons, including women and children, have been found, some in a large room, others at the foot of a staircase leading down to a well, and others again in a street. Their contorted attitudes suggest that they met a violent death, but we must wait for further discoveries to throw more light upon this forgotten tragedy.

* Memoirs, Archaeological Survey of India, No. 48, p. 153 ff.

Chapter II

Vedic and Epic India

We know little about the earlier habitat of the tribes who entered India from the North-West about 2000 B.C., and theories, which located their original home in south-eastern Europe, Central Asia, or even the Arctic Circle, have mostly been abandoned. They were based on the erroneous assumption that identity of language denotes identity of race. These tribes, to which von Eickstedt gives the generic title of Indids, spoke

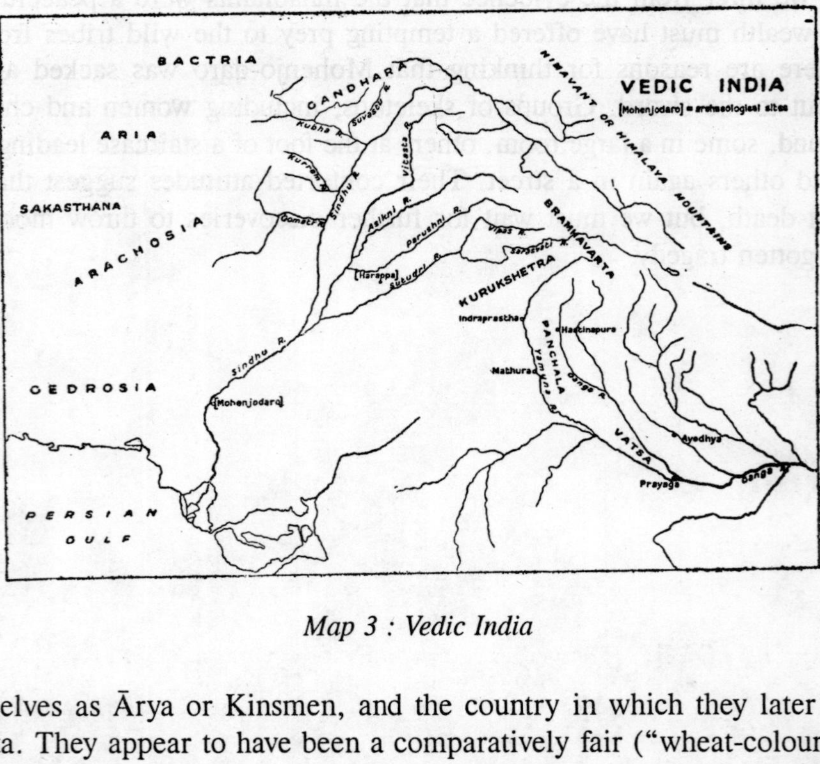

Map 3 : Vedic India

of themselves as Ārya or Kinsmen, and the country in which they later settled as Āryāvarta. They appear to have been a comparatively fair ("wheat-coloured") folk, with long heads, straight noses, well-developed foreheads, and a high facial angle. The relationship of their language to others of the Indo-European stock is clealry shown by the structure of the verbs and nouns, and the names of numerals and fundamental objects. It is interesting to note that islands of Aryan speech have been discovered in various parts of Asia Minor, as far west as at Boghaz Keui in Cilicia, the capital of the ancient Hittites. The kings of the Mitanni in the upper Euphrates invoked Aryan deities to witness a treaty made in 1400 B.C. The Kassites (*c.* 1600 B.C.), dwelling between Irān and Chaldea, used Aryan place-names. The kinship of the Āryan who entered the Punjab with the inhabitants of the Iranian plateau is shown by the close resemblance between their language and sacred books. They came, not like the later invaders, but as immigrant tribes, bringing with them their wives and families, their flocks and herds. Megasthenes, the Greek ambassador who visited Northern India in the 3rd century B.C., says that the people were in old times nomads, "like the Scythians who do not plough but wander about in their wagons."* However, they quickly settled down and learnt to cultivate barley, which is still the staple crop in Afghanistan and the valleys of the Himālayas.† Successive waves of immigrants followed one another at considerable intervals; they retained their tribal organisations and were probably of mixed origin. One of their customs was to employ bards to celebrate the deeds of their kingly leaders and sing the praises of their gods. To these tribal lays, which were handed down from father to son in the families in which they were composed, we owe our knowledge of their life and customs. Collectively they are known as the Rig Veda, and they will be described in the succeeding chapter.

From the mention of the Kubhā or Kābul, the Suvāstu or Swāt (the river of fair dwellings), the Krumu or Kurram, and the Gomatī or Gumāl (the river abounding in cows), it seems that the tribes were at one time settled in Eastern Afghanistan. A later hymn, "in praise of the rivers" (R.V. x. 75), shows them dotted about in various communities stretching from the Kābul river as far as the upper Ganges. It has been conjectured that the bulk of the hymns, which their vivid descriptions of the mountains and the bursting of the monsoon, were composed in the Brahmavarta, the Vedic Holy Land in the Ambāla district, rather than the Punjab. There is no reference in the Rig Veda to the tiger or the rhinoceros, so familiar to the inhabitants of the Indus valley; the elephant, the "beast with a hand," had not yet been domesticated; but the lion, now all but extinct save in Kāthiāwār, was well-known. Rice, destined to become the staple food, is also as yet unknown.*

The new-comers, however, did not enter India unopposed. As they slowly advanced in an easterly direction, impelled, perhaps, by pressure from later arrivals, they came into conflict with the earlier inhabitants. They are described as short in stature, swarthy

---

* Arrian, *Indika*, Chapter VII.

† The hymns of the Rig Veda (VII. 67, 10; X. 134, 2) contain references to reaping barley (*yava*), which show that at the time that they were composed, the tribes had passed from the pastoral and nomadic to the agricultural stage.

* Rice is first mentioned in the Atharva Veda (iv 34-5, etc.).

and noseless, with ugly features and voracious appetites. They practised phallic rites, which filled the Aryan-speaking tribes with abhorrence, and they are contemptuously spoken of in the Vedas as Dasyu or slaves. There is evidence, however, that the Dasyu, though shorter and less warlike than their opponents, were probably more civilised. They dwelt in castles and strong cities in considerable luxury, and were credited with magical powers. We do not know who these Dasyu were, but Haddon remarks that from the descriptions given of them in the Vedas might be compiled a fairly accurate anthropological definition of certain Veddid tribes of to-day.†

The first duty of the tribal leaders was to drive back the Dasyu, the enemies of the "Aryan colour," and this they did with the ferocity of the American pioneers in their struggles against the Redskins. The Vedic hymns constantly refer to the wars between Divodāsa, the ruler of the tribe of the Bhāratas, and the Dasyu prince Sambara. Gradually, however, the contest became less fierce. The Aryan-speaking conquerors intermarried with the Dāsīs or female slaves whom they had captured, and the offspring formed a mixed race, who adopted many of the customs of their mothers. The tribes were constantly at war among themselves, like the Rājpūts of later days, and they even made alliances with the Dasyu against their foes. As time went on, the Indo-Aryans, like the Normans in England, became absorbed in the population of the country, though they left behind them indelible traces of their influence. The very considerable divergencies between the religion of the Vedas and later Hinduism cannot be accounted for merely by development; they are due to the pre-Aryan element which came to the surface in the fusion of the two cultures.*

The Vedas throw a flood of light upon the social organisation of the Aryan-speaking tribes. The unit was the family, which inhabited a common dwelling, shared its possessions and worshipped at a common hearth. The head of the family was the father, a real "despot" (*dama-pati*) or house-lord; the *patria potestas* over his wife, his daughters, his sons and their families was almost absolute. At his death, the property was divided. Women held a high place in soicety; the wife was mistress of the house, shared in the sacrifices, and ruled over the slaves and female members of the family. A Vedic marriage hymn (R.V. x. 85) shows how lofty was the ideal of wedlock. The wife was addressed in the following terms :

Free from the evil eye, thy husband hurting not,
Kind to our beasts, be friendly, full of energy,
Bear heroes, love the gods, and live in happiness,
Bring welfare to our bipeds and our quadrupeds.

---

† *Races of Man*, p. 4.

* See E. Gilbert Slater, *The Dravidian Element in Indian Culture* (1924). The author holds that Hinduism is mainly Dravidian in origin, and considers caste to be a Dravidian institution (p. 150 ff.)

The bride was adult, and child marriage was not practised. Polygamy seems to have been unknown, and marriage was regarded as a sacrament. The bridegroom, taking the bride's hand, repeated the verse (R.V. x. 85), "I clasp thy hand for happiness, that thou mayest reach old age with me thy husband."

At the conclusion of the wedding ceremony, the husband pointed out to his wife the star Dhruva, and exhorted her to be steadfast as it was. The wedded couple departed to their new home in a car decked with flowers and drawn by white bulls, bearing in a pot fire from the husband's family hearth. The wife's duties were to grind the corn, prepare and cook her husband's food and wait upon him at meals, clean the pots and pans, smear the floor with cowdung, and above all to bear him a son to carry on the family rites. At about eight, the boy was duly invested with the sacred cord of consecrated *munja* grass, tied over the left shoulder and under the right arm. The officiating priest whispered in his ear the Gāyatri *mantra* or formula (R.V. iii. 62, 10)

Tar Savitur varenyam Bhargo devasya dhīmahi:
Dhiyo yo nah prachodayāt.

"Let us meditate on the excellent glory of the Sun, the God: may He enlighten our understanding." He was now initiated as a "twice-born," and entered upon the duties and responsibilities of his caste.

A group of families constituted the village (*grāma*) which was the unit of organisation. Here they dwelt with their serfs and servants, their flocks and herds. The village was, like the Indian village of to-day, a little republic, with its headman and hereditary officers, and its stretch of common pastureland. Oxen were used for ploughing and drawing carts. The wealth of a man was reckoned by the number of cows he possessed. Sheep, goats, oxen and dogs were domesticated. Horses were probably only kept by the wealthy and were harnessed in chariots rather than ridden. Barley (*yava*), various kinds of millet, wheat, lentils and sesamum, were cultivated, thus providing both winter and summer crops. A primitive kind of irrigation came early into use. Ploughing, sowing and reaping, dairywork, tanning, spinning wool and weaving and dyeing cloth, working in wood, copper and gold, and making hoes, plough-shares and other agricultural implements were, then as now, the usual village occupations. Silver and iron were apparently unkonwn. Meat, including the flesh of the cow, was consumed at weddings and other festivals; otherwise, as to-day, no doubt the diet normally consisted of parched barley, unleavened cakes, vegetables, *ghī* or clarified butter and preparations of milk. An intoxicating beverage, distilled from grain and known as *sūra*, was drunk.

Houses were constructed of wood, with mud walls and thatched roofs, and the clay floor was strewn with grass. Clothing was usually made of wool or skins, a skirt being worn round the loins, and a shawl or cloak over the shoulder. The hair was carefully dressed and combed, and ear-rings and necklaces were worn.

The Indo-Aryans were inveterate gamblers, and a pathetic hymn in the Rig Veda (x. 34) describes the unhappy plight of the ruined gamester:

> My wife rejects me, and her mother hates me,
> The gamester finds no pity for his troubles.
> No better use can I see for a gambler,
> Than for a costly horse, worn-out and aged.

The hymn ends with an excellent piece of advice:

> "Play not with dice, but cultivate thy cornfield,
> Enjoy thy riches, deeming them sufficient;
> There are thy cows, there is thy wife, O Gambler!"
> This counsel Savitar the noble gives me.

Chariot-racing was a favourite sport of the higher classes, and other amusements were archery and hunting. Dancing was also popular. The drum and a number of string and wind instruments were used; music is one of India's most ancient arts. Listening to bardic recitations at festivals and sacrifices was another favourite recreation.

The head of the Indo-Aryan tribe was the Rājā or King. The King, surrounded by his nobles (*rājanya*), and mounted in his chariot, led his people in war. The nobles, like the Homeric Greeks, wore armour, and fought from chariots with bow, sword and spear; the commons went on foot and used axes, lances and slings, or threw rocks. The king's power was not absolute. As with all the Indo-European peoples, he had to win for his acts the approval of the popular assembly (*sabhā*) consisting of the males of fighting-age, who, no doubt, ratified his election in the first instance. The king was the administrator of justice; the punishment for murder was the payment of blood-money, which varied according to status of the victim; the fine for the slaughter of a man of high rank might be a hundred cows, paid to the dead man's relatives. The death penalty does not appear to have been inflicted. Thieves were put in the stocks, and an insolvent debtor might be sold into slavery. Minor cases, criminal and civil, were doubtless settled by the village council according to custom. An important person was the family priest (*purohita*), who, like the Brahmin of later days,was the king's councillor. He composed hymns in praise of his patron's exploits, and invoking the favour of the gods upon him. For this he was munificently rewarded; many of the Vedic hymns were composed for the purpose of praising the generosity of the royal patron to his bard.

The rudiments of the caste system may be traced in the later Vedas. The division into three classes or social groups (*varna*), the Brahmins or priests, the Kshatriyas or warriors, and the Vaisyas or cultivators, goes back to very early times. A similar classification existed among the Iranians, and traces of it are found in early Greece and Rome; it is based upon a natural distribution of functions. To these the Indo-Aryans added a fourth class, distinguished by its colour; these were the Sūdras or serfs, the descendants of the aboriginal inhabitants, who were not admitted within the pale of Aryan society. The origin of the "four Varnas" or groups of castes is allegorically described in a late Vedic hymn (R.V. x 90) which tells how, when Purusha, the Primeval Man, was sacrificed, the Brahmins arose from his head, the Kshatriyas from his arms, the Vaisyas from his thighs and the Sūdras from his feet. But in Vedic times, the rigid barriers between the castes had not yet arisen. The Kshatriya could become a priest and *vice versa*; the King, though a warrior, exercised certain priestly functions. The author of one of the hymns (R.V. ix. 112, 3) says: "I am a composer of hymns, my father is a physician, my mother grinds corn on a stone. We are all engaged in different occupations." Caste-exclusiveness started with the Brahmins, who claimed a monopoly of religious rites. The lower orders imitated their social superiors by forming similar exclusive groups, founded to a great extent on occupation. Occupational castes resembled the guilds of medieval Europe, except that they could not be recruited from without. But castes arose in a number of ways; one was from mixed marriages, which is the explanation given by the authors of the Dharamsāstras. In later times, reformed religious sects, such as the Jains, Lingāyats and Sikhs, tended to become castes, as did groups of people migrating to distant parts of the country, or foreign tribes like the Gūjars on admission into the fold of Hinduism. The claim to form a national or military caste is made by peoples with strongly marked individuality like the Rājpūts or Marāthās.

Thus the caste system has many blended aspects, racial, religious and occupational. A caste is defined by one of the greatest authorities on the subject as "a collection of families or groups of families, bearing a common name which usually denotes or is associated with a mythical ancestor, human or divine; professing to follow the same calling; and regarded by those who are competent to give an opinion as forming a single homogeneous community. A caste is almost invariably endogamous in the sense that a member of the large circle denoted by the common name may not marry outside the circle; but within this circle there are usually a number of smaller circles, each of which is also endogamous."* A man must marry within his caste, but outside the *gotra* or clan to which he belongs.† At present the four original Varnas

* Sir H. Risley, in *Imp. Gaz. of India* (1908), I. 311. The problem of the origin of caste and the conflicting theories on the subject are examined in Chapter VI of that work. V.A. Smith (*Oxford History of India*, p. 35) regards the grouping of the castes (*jāti*) into the four orders (*varna*) as a later priestly fiction.

† A *gotra* (literally "herd"), like the Latin *gens*, is a group descended from a common ancestor, usually a Rishi or legendary saint.

are split up into thousands of water-tight castes and sub-castes, which constitute a phenomenon unique in the history of civilisation. The members are not necessarily debarred from any particular trade, excepting such as involve cremonial defilement, or any set of beliefs within those accepted by all Hindus, such as the acceptance of the authority of the Vedas and reverence for Brahmins. But every caste has its own *dharma* or set of rules, violation of which involves a number of penalties, or even expulsion. Caste for the Hindu is part of the Divine Order of the Universe; a man's caste is determined by his conduct in a previous existence.

The Aryan religion consisted in the worship of the Devas or Shining Ones, celestial beings who dwelt in the firmament. Of these, the chief was Dyaus-pitar (*Ζεύς*, Jupiter), the Sky Father, though he later gives way to Varuna, the god of the "wide expanse" of sky and ocean. Varuna in some of his aspects resembles the Hebrew Jehovah. He is the omniscient ruler of the universe, the guardian of religion and morality.

Whoever moves or stands, who glides in secret,
Who seeks a hiding-place, or hastens from it,
What thing two men may plan in secret council,
A third, King Varuna, perceives it also.

Although I climbed the farthest heaven, fleeing,
I should not there escape the Monarch's power;
From Heaven his spies descending hasten hither,
With all their thousand eyes the world surveying.

Whate'er exists between the earth and heaven,
Or both beyond, to Varuna lies open.
The winkings of each mortal eye he numbers,
He wields the Universe, as dice a player. (A.V. iv. 16)

With varuna are associated other celestial deities – the Sun under his various names (Sūrya, Savitri, Mitra), who drives daily across the sky in his seven-horsed chariot, and his beautiful consort, Ushas (Aurora, *'Ηώς*), who inspires some of the loveliest of the Vedic hymns (Fig. 5). Issuing from the gateway of the East, like a bride adorned for her husband, she looks down upon the tribes of men, going about their daily work:

Now Heaven's Daughter has appeared before us
A maiden shining in resplendent garments.
Thou sovran lady of all earthly treasure,
Auspicious Dawn, shine here to-day upon us.

In the sky's framework she has gleamed with brightness:
The goddess has cast off the robe of darkness.
Rousing the world from sleep, with ruddy horses,
Dawn in her well-yoked chariot is arriving. (R.V. i. 113)

Fig. 5 : Sūrya, the Sun God

Most popular of all, however, appears to have been Indra, the Indian Thor, the ideal warrior, who rides in his war-chariot, armed with the thunderbolt, helping his worshippers in their battles against their foes the Dasyu, and quaffing huge cups of the exhilarating soma-juice which they offer to him. His chief exploit was the slaying of the dragon Vrita, who had shut up the kine, the storm-clouds which bring rain to the fields, in the mountain-caverns.

Other gods, who fall into a somewhat different category, are Agni and Soma.

Fig. 6 : Agni, the Fire God

Agni (Ignis) is the Sacred Fire (Fig. 6), burning upon the family hearth, and summoned from heaven by the priest with his fire-sticks. His duty is to convey from earth to heaven the sacrifices of pious worshippers. Soma was the juice of a plant known to the Indo-Aryans before they separated from the Iranians. It grew upon the mountain-sides and from it was prepared, accompanied by elaborate ritual, an intoxicating drink, which was consumed sacramentally and offered to the gods.* It

* Soma has been doubtfully identified as a plant of the *Sarcostemma* or *Asclepias* genus. It has been suggested that it was *bhang* or Indian hemp, still widely used as an intoxicant.

is Amrita, the nectar of immortality, and a whole book of the Rig Veda is devoted to hymns in praise of it. Its exhilarating effects were supposed to exalt the participator to the gates of heaven. Soma was mystically identified with the moon, who controls vegetation, and whose cup is for ever filling and emptying, as he waxes and wanes. These are only a few of the many inhabitants of the Vedic pantheon, which is peopled by numerous celestial beings, most of them personified natural phenomena. Rivers, too, were worshipped, and their praises sung by the Vedic seers.The gods protect men from the demons of drought, disease and famine, and give them rain in due season, sons and daughters, flocks and herds and crops. They are benevolent and truthful, rewarding righteousness and hating lies, deceit and dishonourable dealings. In later Vedic literature, a deeper and more philosophical note begins to creep in. The gods are only aspects of the One who underlies all phenomena. "The True is One, though the wise call Him by many names." (R.V.I.64). And behind all the gods lies Rita, the Moral Law, unswerong and changeless, the *Aviaγxn*) of the Greeks, which even they cannot violate or alter. These "obstinate questionings" find their final expression in the magnificent Creation Hymn (R.V. x. 129), the earliest specimen of Indo-Aryan philosophical thought:

Nor Aught nor Nought existed; you bright sky
Was not, nor heaven's broad woof outstretched above.
What covered all? What sheltered? What concealed?
Was it the water's fathomless abyss?
There was not death – yet was there nought immortal;
There was no confine betwixt day and night;
The only One breathed breathless by itself,
Other than It there nothing since has been.
Darkness there was, and all at first was veiled
In gloom profound – an ocean without light –
The germ that still lay covered in the husk
Burst forth, one nature, from the fervent heat.

Who knows the secret? Who proclaimed it here?
Whence, whence this manifold creation sprang?
The Gods themselves came later into being –
Who knows from whence this great creation sprang?
He from whom this great creation came,
Whether His will created or was mute,
The Most High Seer that is in highest heaven,
He knows it – or perchance even He knows not.*

---

* Max, Müller, *Chips from a German Workshop*, I. 78.

The Vedic gods, unlike those of the Greeks and later Hindus, were never very clearly anthropomorphised. It is true that they have some human attributes; they eat, drink, drive their chariots and consume offerings, but as is said of one of them, "his sound is heard, but his form is unseen." No temples and no images form part of Vedic worship. The ritual was performed on a cleared and levelled space of ground, which was spread with the sacred grass and served as an altar. The sacrificial fire was kindled with the fire-stick, and nearby was the stone Soma-press. The fire was fed with clarified butter; milk, grain and cakes were offered, and on occasion, rams, oxen and horses were sacrificed. The Soma was pressed with elaborate ritual, diluted with milk, and drunk. Meanwhile, the officiating priest (*hotri*) chanted verses from the Veda, while a host of assistants or servers performed their offices. The rites, simple at first, became more elaborate and stereotyped as time went on. The ritual had to be carried out with meticulous care, as a slip would render the sacrifice invalid, and it was made the subject of profound study by the Brahmin families whose duty it was to perform it.

At death, the body was carried to the funeral pyre, accompanied by the wife and relatives of the deceased. In the right hand of the corpse was laid his staff if he were a Brahmin, his bow if he were a Kshatriya, his goad if he were a Vaisya. His wife sat beside him, until she was called away with the words, "Rise up, O woman, into the world of the living."* The pyre was then kindled with fire from the family hearth, and the hymn for the dead, "Go forth, go forth, upon the paths of old" (R.V. x. 14), was chanted. While the flames consumed the body, the relatives sat and discoursed upon pious subjects; they then returned homeward in procession, the youngest leading. The bones were collected, washed and buried in an urn. Vedic ideas of life after death were as vague as those of the Homeric Greeks. The soul departed to "the fathers," where it was received by Yama, the first man to die and now King of the dead, and rewarded or punished according to its deeds. As in the Homeric poems, the spirit of the pious warrior reposes under shady trees, quaffing the heavenly Soma with the gods to the sound of music. On the other hand, the unchaste, the liar and the unrighteous are hurled into a bottomless pit.† The later doctrine of transmigration had not yet appeared.

The two great Indian epics, the *Mahābhārata* and the *Rāmāyana*, give us a vivid

---

* From this it may be inferred that the old practice of immolating the wife with her husband had been generally discontinued. It survived locally, however; it is mentioned in *Ahtarva Veda* XVIII, 3, I, and was revived later. The widow of a man who died childless might contract a Levirate marriage with her brother-in-law.

† For the fate of the righteous after death, see R.V. ix. 113, x. 154, and for the unrighteous R.V. iv. 5, 5, and ix. 73, 8 (Muir, *Metrical Translations from Sanskrit Writers*, p.335 ff, and passages there quoted.)

picture of life and manners in the post-Vedic age. The *Mahābhārata* or great story of the sons of Bhārata, which has the unenviable distinction of being the longest poem in the world, consists in its present recension of 100,000 couplets. The original kernel was about one-fifth of this. At the time it was composed, the Indid peoples had pushed eastward, and were settled in the Doāb between the Ganges and the Jumna. Here, in the Kurukshetra, or country of the Kurus, on the banks of the Ganges, was the town of Hastināpura, the capital of the blind old king Dhritarāshtra, with his hundred sons, the Kauravas, and his five nephews, the Pāndavas. Jealousy between Duryodāna,the eldest of the Kauravas, and his cousins, leads to the banishment of the Pāndavas, who set out to make their fortunes. They reach the court of the King of the Panchālas, whose daughter, Draupadī, is holding a *swayamvara*, or Maiden's Choice, and all the young princes from far and near have assembled. Arjuna, one of the Pāndavas, wins her hand in the archery-contest. Draupadī becomes the co-wife of the five brothers,* who now return and found the city of Indraprastha (Indarpat near Delhi), on the banks of the Ganges. But the wicked Duryodana tempts Yudhisthira the eldest to a gambling match, in which the latter stakes and loses all that he has, including his kingdom and Draupadī herself. Once more the brothers retire to the forests, but this time it is to plan revenge. A civil war breaks out between the cousins, to which tribes from the confines of India are summoned. The Kaurava host consists of armies from such distant places as Eastern Bihār and Bengal on the one hand and the Punjab on the other; the allies of the Pāndavas are from Agra and Oudh, Rājputāna and Western Bihār. This, if historical, is interesting, for it shows how widely the Indid tribes were now diffused in Upper India.† For eighteen days the battle rages, and the greater part of the epic is occupied with a descrition of the fight and the prodigies of valour shown by the heroes on both sides. In the end the Kauravas are all slain, and Yudishthira is installed as king of Hastināpura. In the final scene the five brothers give up their royal state, and accompanied by their co-wife Draupadī and their faithful dog, set out for the Himālayas. Reaching Mount Meru, the Indian Olympus,they are admitted into Indra's heaven.

The great epic reaches its sublimest heights in the description of the little band setting out on its last quest, though an English translation only gives a faint idea of the austere grandeur of the original:

Then the high-minded sons of Pāndu and the noble Draupadī

Roamed onwards, fasting, with their faces towards the East; their hearts

---

* This solitary instance of polyandry in Sanskrit Literature is very striking. It has been suggested that the Pāndavas were a Himalayan tribe admitted into the Hindu fold. For Mongoloid elements in Northern India see V.A. Smith, *Oxford History of India*, p. xii.

† This list, like the Catalogue of the Ships in the Iliad, was no doubt inserted or added to by tribes who wished to claim a respectable ancestry.

Yearning for union with the Infinite, bent on abandonment
Of worldly things. They walked on to many countries, many a sea
And river. Yudishthira walked in front, and next to him came Bhīma,
And Arjuna came after him, and then in order the twin brothers.
And last of all came Draupadī, with her dark skin and lotus-eyes,
The faithful Draupadī, loveliest of women, best of noble wives.
Behind them walked the only living thing that shared their pilgrimage,
The dog. And by degrees they reached the briny sea. Then with souls well-disciplined.
They reached the northern region, and beheld with heaven-aspiring hearts
The mighty mountain Himavat.*

The *Rāmāyana*, which appears to be a later and more artificial composition, is assigned to a sage named Vālmiki. In its latest recension it consists of 24,000 couplets, and describes the fortunes of Prince Rāma of Ayodhya, the capital of Kosala or Oudh on the Gogra river. Rāma is driven into exile by the jealousy of his wicked stepmother Kaikeyī, who wants the throne for her son Bharata. Rāma, with his wife Sītā and his brother Lakshmana, goes to the forest, where they spend their time in deeds of knight-errantry, and warring with the Rākshasas or demons (no doubt the aborigines of the primeval forest). At last Rāvana, the demon-king, tempts Rāma away in pursuit of a magic deer, and in his absence, abducts Sītā, whom he carries off to the island of Lanka (Ceylon). Rāma and Lakshmana, helped by Hanumān, the king of the monkeys, go in pursuit of Rāvana, and the monkey-hosts cast mountains into the sea to make a passage. Rāvana is slain, and Sītā's chastity is vindicated by the fire-ordeal (Fig. 7). Rāma and Sītā are crowned at Ayodhya amid great rejoicings.

It is impossible to say to what extent the epics are founded upon dimly-remembered historical events. Probably, like the Iliad and the Odyssey, or the stories of Arthur and Charlemagne, they have a background of actual fact, and are idealised accounts of the struggles of the tribes in their advance along the Ganges valley into the Madhya Desa or Middle Country. But their influence upon subsequent Hindu literature and thought have been immense. Like the Homeric poems, they are the fountain-head from which subsequent poets and dramatists have drawn inexhaustible stores of material. The *Mahābhārata* is looked upon as both a "fifth Veda" and as a Dharmasāstra or Canon of Morality. Rāma has become an incarnation of Vishnu, and in the mouth of Krishna, the king of the Yādavas and Arjuna's charioteer, is placed that wonderful philosophical poem, the *Bhagavad Gītā* or Song Celestial. The heroes and heroines–Arjuna the typical Hindu warrior, Draupadī and Sītā, Damayantī and Sakuntalā, and Sāvitrī, the Hindu Alcestis, are the Hindu ideals of manhood and womanhood.

* Monier-Williams, *Indian Wisdom*, p. 413.

Fig. 7 : Scene from the Rāmāyana

The epics describe a state of society which has its parallels in the Homeric Age of Greece. The Indo-Aryans are living in numerous kingdoms dotted about the Ganges valley; the more remote outposts are clearings in the great forest covering the slopes of the Vindhyas, and inhabited by "demons," the aborigines who are their traditional foes. They are now city-dwellers. The city is surrounded by battlements and moats; it is laid out in squares and the streets are watered and lighted. The ruler is the king or Rājā, who dwells in a palace in the heart of the town. The palace is a spacious building, with a durbar hall, a court of justice, a gamblimg room, and a cockpit for wrestling and bear-baiting. The king is surrounded by his councillors and warriors; he is no autocrat and is guided by their advice. A bad ruler may be deposed or even put to death. He spends his time in fighting, hunting, and gambling. The cow is now regarded as sacred, but meat except beef is eaten and strong drink is taken. Polygamy is practised and 'nautches' are a favourite form of recreation. Chivalry is as characteristic a feature of the Indo-Aryan price as of the knights of medieval Europe: hospitality and the right of sanctuary are sacred obligations, and neither a kindess nor an injury is ever forgotten. The greatest glory is death in battle, which ensures eternal fame in this world and the next. "Sweet it is to die in battle; the path to heaven lies in fighting." "Glory is to be preferred to life."* But the warrior

* *Mbh. VIII 93.55 and 56.*

must fight fairly; the Kurus reproach the Pāndavas because one of the latter intervenes in a duel on the battlefield to help a friend who is being worsted. The hero Bhisma says, "with one who has thrown away his sword, with one who has fallen or yielded, with a woman or one who bears a woman's name, or with a low-born fellow—with these I fight not." Woman occupies a high place in Epic society. When the princess comes of age, the princes are invited to a Maiden's Choice. Games and tourneys are held, and she casts a garland round the suitor upon whom she bestows her hand. The wife shares her husband's perils. In the *Rāmāyana*, when Rāma is banished to the jungle, Sītā says:

> My mother often taught me and my father often spake
> That her home the wedded woman doth beside her husband make
> As the shadow to the substance, to her lord the faithful wife,
> And she parts not from her consort till she parts with fleeting life.
> Therefore let me seek the jungle where the jungle rangers rove,

Fig. 8 : Indra

† R.C. Dutt's translation (London, 1899), pp. 41-2.

Dearer than the royal palace, where I share my husband's love!†

In the *Mahābhārata*, the wife is described as "half the man, his truest friend, a perpetual spring of virtue, pleasure and wealth ... A sweetly speaking wife is a companion in solitude, a father in advice, and a rest in passing through life's wilderness."*

Priests occupy subordinate position in the epics. There is no church, but there are several rival schools of thought and ritual. The family chaplain, as in Vedic times, holds an important position, and his greed for fees is notorious. Sacrifices are numerous and costly, the most important being the *asvamedha* or horse sacrifice, which was celebrated on the king's accession with elaborate ceremonials and lasted for many months. The most popular god was Indra, the warrior's deity (Fig. 8); but the Vedic gods are receding into the background, and are being superseded by the Hindu pantheon, Brahma, Vishnu and Siva, Ganesa and Hanumān. The position of the common people is only lightly touched upon. They follow the king to battle in an ill-armed and undisciplined rabble, the real fighting being between the nobles in their war-chariots. They are mainly engaged in agriculture, but in the towns a mercantile class is springing up. Among the city-folk of Ayodhya who go to welcome Rāma on his triumphant return are the chief merchants, gem-cutters, weavers, armourers, sawyers, glass-makers, workers in ivory, cooks, incense-sellers, goldsmiths, wood-workers, shampooers, physicians, lamp-makers, wine-sellers, washermen, tailors and actors.† Slaves—aborigines, captives of war and debtors—perform the menial tasks. They have no legal status, but there are indications that they were not badly treated on the whole, and had opportunities to redeem themselves.

* Monier-Williams, *Brahmanism and Hinduism* (1892), p. 389.

† *Rāmāyana,* Trans. Griffiths (Beanres, 1895), p. 917.

Chapter III

Vedic Literature, the Rise of Buddhism and Jainism

Our knowledge of the Indo-Aryans is derived from the Vedas. The word Veda (from the word *vid*, to know) means Wisdom, and orthodox Hindus regard the Veda as eternal, and revealed to the Rishis or seers. The Vedic hymns have come down to us in three recensions: the Rig, the Sāma, and the Yajur Veda. The Rig Veda (from *rik*, a stanza) is the oldest. It consists of 1,028 hymns, now grouped into ten books. They were mostly in praise of different gods, and were intended for recitation by the *hotri* or chief priest at the sacrifices. The tenth book is evidently much later than the rest and is more philosophical in character. The Sāma Veda consists of verses from the Rig Veda arranged in the form of a hymn-book for the use of *udgatri* or chanter; the Yajur Veda, on the other hand, is interpolated with prose passages or prayers to be recited by the priest who performed the manual acts. Besides these we have the Atharva Veda, which is on a different plane; it contains some fine hymns, but it consists principally of spells and magical formulae.

The Vedic hymns were handed down from father to son in the families of the Rishis who composed them. They were regarded as a jealously-guarded secret, to be preserved at all cost from profane ears: the revelation of the Veda to a Sūdra would bring untold disaster. For this reason they were never committed to writing. In one of the hymns, the pupils learning to repeat the Veda after their teacher are comically compared to frogs heralding the bursting of the monsoon by their croaking.* The learned Chinese traveller I-tsing, who visited India between A.D. 671 and 695, says: "the four Vedas, containing about one hundred thousand verses, have been handed down from mouth to mouth, not transcribed on paper or leaves. In every generation there exist some intelligent Brahmins who can recite 100,000 verses."†

When the creative period of the Vedas came to an end, and the hymns assumed their final form, a number of prose treatises called Brāhmans were added. They contain instruction in ritual and explanations of meanings, often conveyed by

* R.V. vii. 103.

† *Buddhist Religion*, Trans. J. Takakusu (1896), p. 182.

mythoiogical stories. At the time they were composed, the Indid tribes had moved eastwards as far as Kosala (Oudh) and Videha (Bihār). Side by side with the Brāhmanas are other treatises, the Aranyakas or Forest Books, and the Upanishads, theosophical works containing mystical speculations for advanced students. As a kind of appendix to these came the Sūtras, so called because they consist of aphorisms strung together. The Srauta Sūtras give elaborate rules for the performance of the Vedic sacrifices; the Dharma Sūtras contain the beginnings of Hindu law, and the Grihya Sūtras deal with domestic ceremonies to be performed at the time of marriage, birth, the investiture with the sacred cord, and similar occasions.

From the Brāhmanas we learn that the life of the Brahmin was divided into four stages. After his initiation, he went as a novice to the *āsrama* or monastery of his Guru. Here he remained for ten or twelve years, studying one of the Vedas, with its commentaries, together with grammar, phonetics and ritual. He lived a life of poverty and chastity, begging alms, waiting on his teacher, and tending the sacred fire. He then married, and devoted himself to bringing up his family. When he felt old age creeping on, he retired to the forest, and passed the third and fourth stages of his life in religious meditation and preparation for death. Even to-day these customs are not entirely extinct. There are schools where the Vedas and their commentaries are still committed to memory, and pious Hindus still renounce the world at the approach of old age. In 1886, Gaurishankar Udayashankar, the Prime Minister of the State of Bhavnagar, after a distinguished career, became a Sannyāsi or ascetic on retirement.*

The period of the Upanishads (*c.* 800-600 B.C.) was one of profound religious discontent. The old beliefs were in the melting-pot; the later Vedas show a growing desire to probe into the origin and destiny of man, and there now arose a new religious philosophy, with a number of element quite foreign to the spirit of the earlier hymns. The first was a feeling of pessimism. Life is an evil, and the main object of religion is *moksha* or *mukti*, a way of release from its trammels. The second was the belief in a World Soul, Ātmā, of which all individual souls are a part :

A motion and a spirit, that impels
All thinking things, all objects of all thought,
And rolls through all things.

The Ātmā permeates the human body, as a lump of salt, to use the favourite simile of the authors of the Upanishads, permeates a bowl of water. In the *Chhāndogya Upanishad*, the sage Uddālaka orders his son to throw a lump of salt into water, and return in the morning. The boy does as he is bid, and the father says: "Take out the salt which thou didst put into the water in the evening." The boy is unable to do so,

* L.S.S. O'Malley, *Popular Hinduism*, p. 210.

and the father orders him to taste the water. He obeys, and finds that the salt, though invisible and intangible, is still there, permeating the fluid. "Even so," says the father, "That Reality is here in this body, though thou dost not perceive it. That atom, which forms the essence of the Universe, That is the Truth, That is the Soul. That art Thou (*Tat twam asi*)."*

Thirdly, there was the doctrine of metempsychosis. The later Hindu thinkers, like the Orphic schools in Greece, were not content with the belief that the soul after death passes to an endless Elysium. They found a solution in the theory that the soul undergoes a long series of "wanderings" (*samsāra*) from body to body, until at last it finds release in re-absorption in the World-Soul. The theory is set forth in its earliest form in the *Chhāndogya Upanishad*. Having gone to various regions, the spirit on its return becomes mist or cloud or the herbs eaten by men and animals, and through them it is reborn in their offspring. He whose conduct was good in a previous birth is reborn as a Brahmin, Kshatriya or Vaisya; the evil-doer is reborn as "a dog, a hog, or a Chandāla."†

A man's life on earth is determined by his actions (Karma) in his previous existence. "Just as he acts, just as he behaves, so he becomes," says the *Brihadāranyaka Upanishad* (IV. iv. 5); as fast as the clock of retribution runs down, it winds itself up again, as Deussen puts it.

One method by which evil Karma, accumulated in past lives, could be exhausted, and release obtained, was the practice of penances, which often assumed grotesque and painful forms. From them, probably, was developed the practice of Yoga, a method of "yoking" the mind by means of intense concentration, the assumption of certain postures, and controlling the breath. These practices were systematised into a formal ἄσκησις or discipline by Patanjali, the author of the Yoga Sūtras. It was claimed that the Yogi acquired abnormal powers, and there seems to be little doubt that Yoga goes back to a stage of belief when there was no distinction between the priest and the magician.

Even more important is the Sānkhya school of philosophy, traditionally ascribed to Kapila, with its boldly materialistic outlook; it is a complete departure from the theosophical speculations of the Upanishads. Only a few of its leading tenets, however, can be indicated here. The doctrine of the Ātmā is rejected. Matter and individual souls are both eternal and real. Matter has three qualities (*guna*), goodness, passion

* *Chhāndogya Upanishad* vi. 13. Translated in *Sacred Books of the East,* Ed. F. Max Müller, Oxford, I. 104.

† A Chandāla, the offspring of an illicit union between a Brahmin woman and a Sūdra, ranks lowest of all in the social scale.

and darkness.* From the combination of these in varying proportions, the phenomenal world arises. Soul is, on the other hand, undifferentiated; perception and sensation asrise from the subtle body, formed from Karma, which causes the soul to migrate from birth to birth. Rebirth is due to ignorance. Once this is dispelled, the Karma of former lives drops away, and the soul returns to its undifferentiated condition. The Sānkhya system had immense influence on suceeding literature and thought, both within and outside India. It has been traced both in the earlier Eleatic and the later Gnostic schools of Greece, and the oldest Sānkhya manual was tranlsated into Chinese in the 6th century A.D. The two great religious reformers of whom we shall now speak, Vardhamāna Mahāvīra and Gautama Buddha, were born in a Sānkhya atmosphere, and this had a marked effect upon their doctrines. These two teachers had much in common. Both belonged to the Kshatriya or warrior caste, and led revolts against the priestly tyranny of the Brahmins, who represented to the common folk that salvation was only to be won by the performance of a complicated ritual, known to themselves alone. Both employed Prākrit, the language of the common people, for their teaching, in place of Sanskrit, the language of the priests. Buddha has been called the Indian Luther, and there are some parallels between this movement and the Protestant Reformation in 16th century Europe. Both ignored the Vedas and caste-distinctions and taught that salvation, *i.e.*, release from future births, could only be obtained by Right Faith, Right Conduct, and Right Action. Both founded congregational and monastic religions; their followers lived in communities, begging their daily bread and practising the virtues of charity, benevolence and simplicity, never stealing, coveting, or telling untruths, and above all abstaining from taking life in any form. But Jainism is more extreme than Buddhism. Vardhamāna, its founder, practised extreme asceticism, while Gautama followed the "middle path." The Jains considered that suicide under certain circumstances was justifiable, which was quite repugnant to Buddhist ethics. One Jain sect actually went stark naked, while the Buddhist monk was content to wear the yellow robe of the beggar; the Jain looked upon all nature, even lifeless objects, as animate,† and took the most elaborate precautions to prevent the accidental death of even the smallest animalculae, whereas the Buddhist merely refrained from taking life or flesh-eating. The fate of the two religions is also curiously dissimilar. Both went through many vicissitudes; from time to time, under royal patronage, they rose to postions of great importance,

* *Sattva, rajas, tamas*.

† See, for instance, the *Acharanga Sutta* (*S.B.E. XXII*) where it is stated that there are living souls in particles of earth, fire, water and air. So Wordsworth (*Prelude* III.49) says :

> To every natural form, rock, fruit or flower,
> Even the loose stones that cover the high-way,
> I gave a natural life.

until they were finally overthrown by the revival of Brahminism. But Buddhism, extinct in the land of its birth, has become the religion of the greater part of Asia, while Jainism, which does not aspire to be a world religion, is confined to India, where it still flourishes.

We know little about Vardhamāna, afterwards called Mahāvīra, the founder of Jainism. He belonged to the royal family of Vaisāli and was probably born in 599 B.C. His mother was of the Lichchavi clan, and his kinsfolk observed the rules of an older reformer, Pārsva by name, who lived about two centuries earlier. He married and had a family, but when thirty years old, he handed over the rulership of his state to his brother, and forsook the world. For twelve years he lived the life of an ascetic, wandering about among the primitive tribes on the Bengal border. At the age of 42, while sitting in deep meditation, he attained enlightenment.

> "Omniscient and comprehending all objects, he knew all conditions of the world, of gods, men and demons; whence all come, where they go, whether they are born as men or animals, or become gods or hell-beings; their food, drink, doings, desires, and the thoughts of their minds; he saw and knew all conditions in the whole world of all living beings."*

For the next thirty years he was engaged in preaching his doctrine; during the rainy season he stayed at various cities of Bihār, inlcuding his birthplace, Vaisālī. His work was hindered by schisms, especially that started by a former disciple, Gosāla. He probably died in 527 B.C., at the age of 72, in the little town of Pāwā near Rājagriha in the Patna district. Some centuries after his death, the Jain church was divided into two sects, the Svetambaras, or wearers of white robes, and the Digambaras or "sky-clothed," *i.e.*, naked. We shall speak in other places of the subsequent fortunes of Jainism, the part it played in the civilisation of Southern India, and the temples with which the Jains crowned the peaks of Gujarāt and Kāthiāwār. The language of the Jain scriptures is the ancient Prākrit dialect of Bihār, known as Ardha-Māgadhī. As time went on, the Jains, like the Buddhists, began to recognise and worship previous incarnations of their founder, who were known as Tīrthakāra or "ford-makers." Images of these were installed in temples and worshipped as gods. Owing to its rigorous views, Jainism has never been the religion of large masses of the people, and to-day the Jains are a small but wealthy community, dwelling mostly in Gujarāt and Rājputāna. Their extreme opinions on the subject of taking life in any form have closed the door of many professiosn to them, and they are usually merchants and bankers. Many Jains have spent large sums in endowing animals hospitals for the care of aged and sick beasts and birds of all kinds. The Jains to-day regard themselves as a reformed Hindu sect, and employ Brahmins to perform their domestic ceremonies.

---

* *S.B.E.* XXII. 201.

Gautama Sākyamuni, the sage of the Sākyas, was born, probably in the year 563 B.C., the son of a petty chieftain named Suddhodana, at Kapilavastu on the Nepalese border, one hundred miles north of Benares, and within full sight of the snow-crowned Himālayas. The spot was afterwards marked by the Emperor Asoka with a column, which is still standing. The Sākyas formed one of the many little tribal republics which were afterwards swept away in the advancing tide of empire which presently absorbed all the smaller states of Northern India. The tribesmen, who probably had a good deal of Mongolian blood in their veins, transacted their affairs in a common mote-hall. They lived in villages on the edge of their rice-fields; these were mere clearings in the Great Forest which covered the foot-hills all round them, and was the haunt of robbers and runaway slaves.

Gautam ain due course married his cousin Yasodharā, who bore him a son, Rahula. At the age of twenty-nine he determined to abandon the world. "In the days before my enlightenment, when I was as yet but a Bodhisattva, I bethought me that a hole-and-corner life is all that a home can give, whereas a wandering mendicant is as free as air; it is hard for the home-keeping man to follow the higher life in all its completeness and purity and perfection; come, let me cut off hair and beard, don the yellow robe, and go forth from home to homelessness. So the time came, when I was quite young and with a wealth of coal-black hair untouched by grey and in all the beauty of my early prime—despite the wishes of my parents, who wept and lamented—I cut off my hair and beard, donned the yellow robe, and went off from home as a wandering mendicant."* This was the Great Renunciation. For a time he studied under two learned ascetics of Rājagriha, but they failed to satisfy him. Then he practised austerities and penances until he nearly died. At one time he was on the point of collapse, when his life was saved by a village girl, who gave him a draught of milk. But he was still as far as ever from his goal. For six years he wrestled in vain, when one day, while sitting in profound meditation under a *pipal* tree at Bodh Gayā, he received Bodhi or Illumination. On the site now stands the Mahābodhi temple. The Buddhist Scriptures tell us that at this crisis he was assailed by Māra, the Prince of Darkness, who sought in vain by all manner of terrors and temptations to shake him from his purpose.

After remaining in the same spot for some days, enjoying the bliss of deliverance, Gautama, or rather Buddha, the Englightened One, as he must now be called, hastened to Benares, and here in the Deer Park he preached his first sermon and "set the Wheel of the Law rolling." The text of this discourse has come down to us: "Sorrow; the cause of sorrow; the removal of sorrow; the way leading to the removal of sorrow." All existence is sorrow. This sorrow is caused by the thirst of the individual for

* Chalmers, *Further Dialogues of the Buddha*, I. 115.

existence, which leads from birth to birth. It may be quenched by following the Eightfold Path – Right Understanding, Right Resolve, Right Speech, Right Action, Right Living, Right Effort, Right Mindfulness and Right Meditation. Buddha was deeply touched by the pessimism of his age. Existence is an evil, from which an escape must be found. Like Mahāvīra, he thought this deliverance lay in a practical way of life, attainable by all, and not in the abstract Right Knowledge of the privileged few. Where Buddha differed from his contemporaries was in his view of the Ātmā or Ego. This, he declared, was not an entity, but an aggregate of qualities or tendencies; "a transitory manifestation of a collection of phenomena." What persists after death is not the Ego, but Karma, the result of our deeds. It is this which is reborn. Later Buddhist philosophers compare rebirth to the lighting of one candle from another. The light is at once the same and yet different. By following the Eightfold Path, Karma will be at last extinguished. There will be nothing left to be reborn, and this is Nirvāna, or the blowing out of the flame. "After the dissolution of the body, neither men nor gods shall see him." Buddha would have agreed with the declaration of the great western philosopher, so nealry his contemporary, that "if death is the absence of all sensation, like the sleep of him whose slumbers are unbroken by any dream, it will be a wonderful gain."* On the subject of God he is silent. Karma is the moving force in our lives. What a man sows he must reap. Sacrifice and prayer are idle things. In the gods, the innumerable spirits of earth and air and sea, Buddha, like any other Hindu of his time, believed. But they are as much in need of salvation as mankind; later Buddhists regarded them as the Buddha's satellites. These metaphysical subtleties, however, Buddha doubtless kept for his inner circle of disciples. To the world at large he preached the necessity of kindess to all living things, purity of heart, truthfulness and charity, abstention from covetousness, fault-finding, hatred and violence, as the highway to salvation, which lay open to all, from the highest to the lowest, irrespective of caste.†

After the Buddha's sermon in the Deer Park, disciples began to flock to him. At the end of three months there were sixty, including the beloved Ānand, the companion of all his wanderings. The little band then started on their mission, preaching as they went from village to village. Princes and Brahmins, merchants and husbandmen, hermits and outcasts, noble ladies and repentant prostitutes joined the community. A life-like picture of a typical day in the life of the Master has come down to us. Rising at dawn, and donning their yellow robes, he and his disciples would go from door to door, begging for their food from pious householders, for they subsisted

---

* Socrates, *Apology* XXXII. Socrates was born in 469 B.C.

† The Buddhist Ten Commandments are – not to kill; not to steal; not to commit impurity; not to be false in language; not to be double-tongued; not to use bad language; not to use fine, glozing speech; not to covet; not to be angry;not to take heretical views.

entirely on charity. Returning home, they ate their meal in common, regardless of caste. The heat of the day was spent in rest and meditation. In the evening the villagers assembled and the Buddha would preach to them "in a manner suitable to their understanding." Religious discourse and the solution of difficulties occupied the time until the first watch of the night, when all went to rest. During the rainy season, the monks retired to one of the retreats which had been presented to them by piosu donors, and spent the time in study and preparation for their work. A favourite resort was the Jetavana monastery, which was built in a park at the city of Srāvastī, now Seth Mahet in Oudh, given to the Buddha by a wealthy merchant of the name of Anāthapindaka, and here many of his discourses were delivered. One of his first visits after his Englightenment was to his ancestral home. His son was converted and his wife became one of the first of the newly-founded order of Buddhist nuns.

For forty-six years the Buddha travelled far and wide, in the states of Kosala and Magadha. Amongst his patrons was Bimbisāra, king of Magadha,and according to one story, he sternly reproved his son, the parricide Ajātasatru, for his father's murder. Sometimes he met with violent opposition; an attempt was made to assassinate him, and he was greatly troubled by the rivalry of his cousin, the heretic Devadatta. During his travels he visited Vaisālī, where he gave dire offence to the nobles, by preferring a meal prepared by the dancing-girl Ambapāli to their sumptuous banquet: "Were you to offer all Vaisālī and its subject territory, I would not give up so honourable a feast."

The story of his death is told with great pathos and simplicity in an old narrative, the *Mahāparanibbana Sutta* or Book of the Great Decease.* The Buddha was now eighty years old, worn out with toil and travel. At a village near the little town of Kusinagara, in the Gorakhpur district, about 120 miles north-east of Benares, a poor smith named Chunda had prepared a dish of pork for him. The food was tainted, but the Master, with his usual courtesy, partook of it rather than hurt the feelings of a humble follower, though he forbade his disciple to follow his example. Then he continued his journey, but after a few miles a sharp attack of dysentery came on, and in great pain he lay down to rest in a grove of Sāl trees. Feeling his end to be approaching, he called his disciples together and urged them, if they had any doubts or difficulties, to lay them before him. "Be ye lamps unto yourselves. Be a refuge to yourselves. Hold fast to the truth as to a lamp. Look not for refuge to anyone besides yourselves."†

* *Sacred Books of the East*, vol. xi.

† Mrs. Rhys Davids, *What was the original gospel in Buddhism?* p. 38, translates the passage as "Live ye as those who have the Self as lamp, the Self as refuge, the Law as lamp, the Law as refuge, and no other." She regards the later pessimistic nihilism as amonastic accretion unknown to the Buddha.

The faithful Ānanda, heartbroken at the prospect of losing his life-long friend and teacher, went aside and burst into tears. The Buddha sent for him, and gently reproved him. "Enough, Ānanda! Do not let yourself be troubled: do not weep! Have I not already, on many occasions told you that it is the very nature of things most near and dear unto us, that we must divide ourselves from them, leave them, sever ourselves from them? Whatever is born must be dissolved." A postulant named Subaddha came begging to be admitted to the Order; the disciples would have turned him away, but the Buddha called him to him and received him. Another characteristic act of thoughtfulness for others was to send a message to Chunda, begging him not to reproach himself. "Then the Blessed One addressed the Brethren and said: 'Behold now, brethren, I exhort you saying, Decay is inherent in all component things! Work out your Salvation with diligence!' This was the last word of the Blessed One." He

Fig. 9 : Steatite Reliquary from Sānchī

passed into Paranirvāna, "from which there is no return," without recovering consciousness (483 B.C.).*

After his death, the brethren solemnly cremated the Buddha's body. A dispute arose over his remains, which were distributed among his followers and were enshrined as relics in mounds of brick, known as stūpas or dāgabas, in many parts of India. It was necessary that the Master's teachings should be preserved uncorrupted, before the lapse of time should make those who had heard forget them, or remember them imperfectly. Accordingly 500 disciples met at the Satapanni Cave near Rājagriha,

* V.A. Smith, *Early History of India*, Chap. II, Append. C. gives reasons for preferring an earlier date (623-543 B.C.)

and all the Buddha's precepts were collected, learnt and recited by the whole gathering. The language was an early Prākrit dialect of Bihār, afterwards called Pāli or "text" by the monks of Ceylon, to distinguish it from the commentaries which were in Sinhalese. Thus the Buddhist canon was formed. The sacred books were divided into three Pitakas or "baskets," consisting of the Vinaya, dealing with the

Fig. 10 : Buddhist Triratna or Three Jewels (The Buddhist, the Law and the Order).

daily life and discipline of the Order; the Suttas, stories and sayings; and the Abhidamma, or higher philosophy of Buddhism. It is the second of these which appeals most strongly to the student to-day. It contains what are probably authentic records of the Master's sayings, Buddhist texts and psalms of great spiritual beauty, and the Jātakas, a series of charming folk tales of how the Buddha,in previous existences, did deeds of charity and benevolence to all creatures. About a century later, a second Council, held at Vaisālī (376 B.C.), caused a serious dissension. A band of heretical monks, who chafed at the severe simplicity of the rules of the Order, demanded certain relaxations or indulgences.

> "They broke up the old scriptures and made a new recension, attached new meanings to new words as if spoken by the Buddha, and destroyed much of the spirit by holding to the shadow of the letter."

In 240 B.C., however, the canonical books were finally settled at a Council held at Pātaliputra under the patronage of the Emperor Asoka.

The Buddha expressly disclaimed either divine birth or supernatural powers. He worked no miracles. He repeatedly warned his hearers that salvation lay in their own hands alone. The most that he could do was to show the way. His immediate disciples stricIty followed the Master's teaching. The earliest sculptures carefully refrain from depicting him in bodily form. His presence is indicated by symbols – the empty throne, the Wheel of the Law, or a pair of footprints.* But as time went on the historical Gautama became, to all intents and purposes, a divine being, to be worshipped in temples by prayers and offerings, and was looked on as only one of an endless series of incarnations, past and future, sent down to earth for the salvation of the human race.

A few extracts from early Buddhist literature may serve to illustrate the lofty ethical teaching of the Buddha:

"Hatred does not cease by hatred at any time; hatred ceases by love." (*Dhammapada* 5.)

"Let a man overcome anger by love, let him overcome evil by good. Let him overcome the greedy by liberality, the liar by truth." (*Dhammapada* 223.)

"All men tremble at punishment, all men love life. Remember that you are like unto them, and do not cause slaughter." (*Dhammapada* 130.)

"Not to commit sin, to do good, to purify the mind, this is the teaching of the Buddhas." (*Dhammapada* 183.)

"This is called progress in the discipline of the Blessed One, if one sees his sin in its sinfulness, and refrains from it in the future." (*Mahāvagga* IX, 1, 9.)

"Not by birth does one become an outcast, not by birth does one become a Brahmin. By deeds one becomes an outcast, by deeds one becomes a Brahmin." (*Sutta Nipātā* 27.)

LEADING DATES

(Approximate)

B.C. 1200-1000	Period of the older Vedic Hymns.
1000-800	Period of the later Vedic Hymns.
800-600	Period of the Brāhmanas.
600-200	Period of the Sūtras.
599-527	Vardhamāna Mahāvīra, the founder of Jainism.
563-483	Siddhārtha Gautama, the founder of Buddhism.
483	First Buddhist Council.
376	Second Buddhist Council at Vaisālī.
300	Schism between the Svetambara and Digambara Jain sects.

* In early Buddhist iconography, a lotus flower symbolises the Buddha's birth; a Bodhi-tree, the Englightenment; the Wheel of the Law, his first Sermon; and a stūpa, his Nirvāna. J. Ph. Vogel, *Buddhist Art* (1936), p. 15, *note*.

Chapter IV

First Contacts with Persia and Greece

By the end of the Epic Period, the tide of Indid invasion had definitely receded in an easterly direction. The original settlements in the Punjab were cut off from Āryāvarta, and are scarcely mentioned in later literature. Orthodox Hindus regarded the Punjab as non-Aryan and unholy. The tribes in the Punjab, however, remained in touch with their Iranian kinsmen on the other side of the mountains, with whom they had many common characteristics, ethnic and linguistic. Persians and Parthians appear to be mentioned in the Vedas.* The old Persian and Vedic languages are closely allied, the most marked difference being that the Vedic sibilant becomes an aspirate in the language of the Avesta, the sacred literature of ancient Persia. Thus the Soma, the juice of the plant used by both in their sacrifices, is Haoma in old Persian, and Sindhu is Hindu. Curiously enough, the old Persian gods tend to be looked upon as evil spirits by the Hindus and *vice versa:* the word Asura, applied by the Persians to the highest god (Ahura Mazda) comes to mean a demon in classical Sanskrit, while conversely Indra appears as a demon in the Persian scriptures. This may be due to the religious reforms of Zoroaster (660-583 B.C.), which swept away much of the old mythology. Iran, however, continued to exercise a definite cultural influence upon India, even after the fall of the Persian Empire.

The outstanding event in Western Asia in the sixth century B.C. was the rise of Persia. In 612 B.C. an army of Babylonians and Medes overthrew Nineveh, the Assyrian capital. In 550 B.C. the ancient Medic line was deposed by the Persians, and Cyrus (558-530 B.C.) became ruler of a great kingdom. In 538 B.C. Cyrus overthrew Babylon, and laid the foundation of the Iranian Empire, which Darius Hystaspes (522-486 B.C.) extended from the Indus to the Mediterranean. Apparently Cyrus overran Gandhāra, a term which later denoted the Peshawar and the Rawalpindi districts, but then probably included Kābul. The annexation of the Punjab was left to Darius, who about 516 B.C. sent a Greek mercenary named Scylax of Caryanda to explore the Indus.† Scylax, starting at a city named "Caspapyrus" (Kāsyapapura), a

* Parsavas (R.V. x. 33, 2); Parthavas (R.V. vi. 27, 8).

† Herodotus IV. 44.

frontier city of Gandhāra, sailed down the Indus to its mouth, and thence, probably coasting along Southern Arabia, up the Red Sea to Arsinoe, the modern Suez. The voyage took two and a half years. Scylax, like most ancient voyagers, took his time, creeping along from port to port, and halting for long periods to wait for the monsoon winds. After this, says Herodotus, Darius conquered the Indians and made use of this sea. The voyage of Scylax first brought India into touch with Greece and the western world. The Greeks knew the race with whom they thus came into contact as Hindus or Indians, the people of the Indus: the Indians spoke of the Greeks as Yavanas (Yonas) or Ionians. Herodotus describes India as the vastest of all countries, populated with various tribes, speaking different languages and in different degrees of civilisation, and bounded on the east by a limitless desert of sand.

Herodotus mentions the Indian satrapy as the twentieth in the Persian Empire, paying the enormous annual tribute of three hundred talents of gold-dust, over a million pounds in modern currency. This was aluvial gold, collected by washing from the rivers of Dardistan in Kashmir. Herodotus has preserved curious travellers' tales of the gigantic ants which guarded the gold mines, presumably the fierce dogs still seen in villages in these regions.* India was one of the subject nations which sent contingents to swell the gigantic army mobilised for Xerxes' invasion of Greece in 480 B.C. The Indian contingent consisted of infantry and cavalry, under the command of a Persian general named Pharnazathres. The infantry soldiers were clad in cotton, and armed with cane bows and iron-tipped arrows. The cavalry were mounted on horses, but their chariots were drawn by wild asses.,† Fortunately, perhaps, for the Greeks, no elephants were included. During the next century, India was in close touch with Persia and, through Persia, with Greece. In the early Buddhist books we hear of long vogyage made by Indian merchantmen. One Jātaka story of about the 5th century B.C. relates how some Indian merchants who made periodical voyages to Bāberu (Babylon) took with them a performing peacock.‡ The peacock is first mentioned in Greek literature about this time as the "Median bird." Greek mercenaries served in the Persian army, and Greek officials were employed in the Imperial court and in the satrapies. At no period were conditions more favourable for the interchange of ideas.§ Many attempts have been made to trace resemblances between early Greek and Indian philosophy. The parallels between Orphism and Buddhism are certainly very close. Both sects lived in monastic communities, abstained from taking life or eating meat and believed in the doctrine of metempsychosis. Pythagoras, who was born about 582 B.C., is credited with having wandered as far as India in search of knowledge. "It is not too much," says Garbe,

* Herodotus III, 97. The story of the ants arose from the Sanskrit term "ant-gold" (*paipilika suvarna*) used for alluvial gold.

† *Ibid*., VII. 65.

‡ E.B. Cowell. *The Jātaka* (Cambridge, 1907) III. 83.

§ Rapson, *Ancient India* (Cambridge, 1914), pp. 88-9.

"to assume that the curious Greek, who was a contemporary of Buddha, and it may be of Zoroaster too, would have acquired a more or less exact knowledge of the East, in that age of intellectual fermentation, through the medium of Persia. It must be remembered in this connection that the Asiatic Greeks, at the time when Pythagoras still dwelt in his Ionian home, were under the single sway of Cyrus, the founder of the Persian Empire."* Eusebius preserves a curious story, which he attributes to Aristoxenus the musician, a pupil of Aristotle, about certain Indian philosophers who found their way to Athens and interviewed Socrates.† They asked Socrates what was the object of his philosophy. Upon being told that it was an enquiry into human affairs, the Indians burst into laughter, saying that no one could enquire into human affairs, if he were ignorant of divine ones. This story, if true, may explain the many points of similarity to Indian philosophy in Plato. In the vision of Er the Pamphylian, with which the *Republic* closes, are clearly stated the Hindu doctrines of reincarnation and Karma, "each soul returning to a second life, and receiving the one agreeable to his desire." The Myth of the Cave in Book VII is an equally clear exposition of the Vedānta doctrine of Māyā, the illusory character of the objects of the senses. Plato's division of his ideal polity into three orders—Guardians, Auxiliaries and Workers—is reminiscent of the Indian Varnas, Brahmins, Kshatriyas and Vaisyas. It is difficult to believe that these may be accounted for merely as coincidences.‡

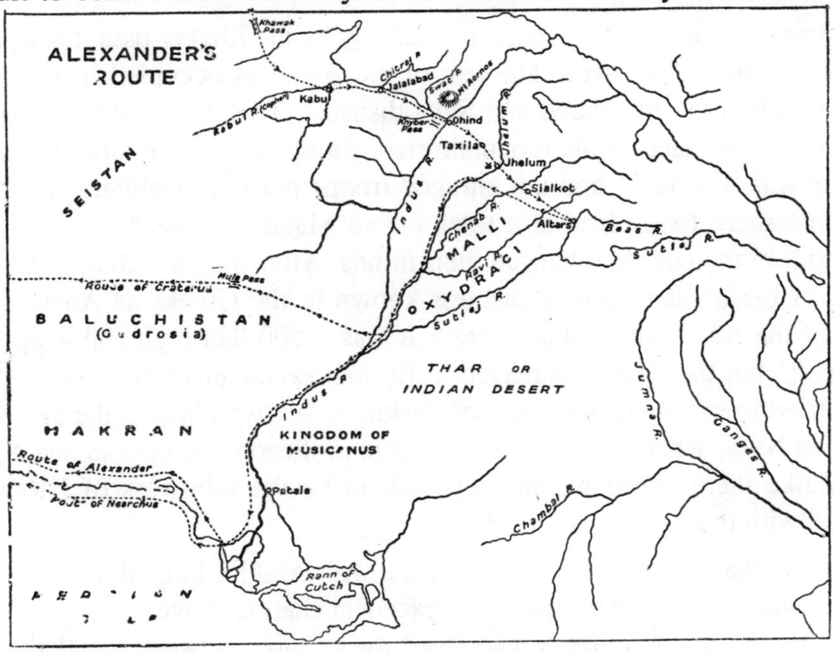

Map 4 : Alexander's Route

* Garbe, *Greek Thinkers*, Eng. Trans., I 127.

† *Praeparatio Evangelica* (*c.* A.D. 315), XI. 3.

‡ B.J. Urwick, *The Message of Plato* (1920), p. 29 *et passim*.

In 334 B.C. Alexander the Macedonian set out on his expedition for the conquest of the Persian Empire. In 331 B.C., at Gaugamela on the Tigris, an Eastern contingent under the Satrap of Bactria, including Indian hillmen, together with a small force of elephants, took part in the disastrous battle which decided the fate of Persia and its unhappy monarch. It would be beyond the scope of this work to follow Alexander's eastern campaign in detail. In 330 B.C. he captured and destroyed the imperial capital of Persepolis. In the winter of the same year he reached Seistan, and established an important outpost at the great meeting-place of the highways of Western Asia, which he named Alexandria of the Arachosians, and which is now known as Kandahār. In the following year he crossed the passes into the Kābul valley, and founded a post known as Alexandria-under-Caucasus, near the modern Charikar, about 30 miles north of Kābul. Using this as a base, he undertook a strenuous campaign for the reduction of Bactria and Sogdiana (Balkh and Bukhāra). He entered the ancient Iranian town of Balkh, "the mother of cities," and was horrified at the customs, especially that of exposing the dead to be devoured by vultures and dogs, which he found being practised there. In May 327 B.C., as soon as the snows were sufficiently melted, he returned to Afghanistan by the lofty Khāwak pass, 13,000 feet high, and established another fortified post which he named Nicaea, perhaps the modern Jalālabad, guarding his communications.

He appears to have entered India, not actually by the Khyber pass, but by following the course of the Kābul river. The rest of the year was occupied in fierce fighting with the tribes in the Malakand and Swāt districts. This involved the storming of a number of almost inaccessible mountain strongholds. At the capture of one fortress, Alexander was wounded, and the enraged troops put the inhabitants to the sword. Another massacre took place at a town called Massaga, where the garrison, after offering to join the Greeks, changed their minds. After this, the chief exploit was the storming of the great mountain fastness known to the Greeks as Aornos, near the junction of the Kābul and Indus rivers.* It was 7,000 feet high and supposed to be impregnable, but the Greeks managed to fill in a ravine protecting the summit. The garrison tried to escape under cover of darkness, but were put to the sword. Near a place called Nysa, where ivy and vines grew in profusion, the Greeks met a fair tribe, strangely like themselves, whom they took to be the followers of Dionysus, and fraternised with them.

Alexander was already in communication with Āmbhi, king of Taxila,who saw in an alliance with the foreign conqueror an excellent chance of overcoming his neighbour and rival, the Paurava monarch who ruled the country between the Jhelum and the Chenab. Accordingly, in February 326 B.C. the Macedonians crossed the Indus in

* For the identification of Aornos, see Sir Aurel Stein, *On Alexander's Track to the Indus*, Chapter XX.

the neighbourhood of the modern Ohind. It was a momentous day in Alexander's career, and he may have felt that he was on the threshold of a New World. The crossing was celebrated by games and sacrifices and feasting, for which purpose the rājā sent 3,000 oxen and 10,000 sheep.

Soon after this he entered Taxila (Takshashilā), the capital of Gandhāra. Taxila, we are told in the Jātakas, was a famous university town. Here sons of the upper classes went to study "the three Vedas and other accoplishments," medicine and other subjects. The descriptions of the Greek historians are confirmed by recent excavations on its site, which lies about 20 miles north-west of Rāwalpindi. Taxila stood in a fertile valley near the mouth of the Khyber pass, and so was a natural halting-place for traders and travellers from all parts of Asia. Here the Greeks saw many strange customs. One was a marriage-market, where those who were unable to dispose of their daughters in marriage owing to poverty exposed them for sale, a crowd being assembled by the sound of conch-shells and war-drums. The dead were burnt, or thrown out to be devoured by vultures, and polygamy was practised. Wives burnt themselves on the pyres of their deceased husbands; they did this of their own accord, and those who refused were held in disgrace.* This description, which comes from the pen of Aristobulus, one of Alexander's companions, contains many points of interest, and shows that even at that date Taxila was a cosmopolitan town and the meeting place of many races. The marriage-market was Babylonian,† and the practice of exposing the dead to vultures was Zoroastrian. The reference to widow-burning indicates that it survived in these remote districts though discountenanced in the Vedas.

Another sight which greatly impressed the Greeks was that of fifteen ascetics, on the outskirts of the city, sitting naked and practising almost inhuman penances. They reminded Alexander of Diogenes the Cynic, with whom he had a famous interview at Athens. He sent an officer named Onesicritus to enquire into their beliefs, but they informed him that to try and explain Hindu philosophy through an interpreter was like making water flow through mud. One of their number, whom the Greeks called Kalanos (Kalyāna), was persuaded to accompany Alexander to Babylon, where he burnt himself to death on a pyre. He and his companions may have been Jains of the Digambara or naked sect.

After thoroughly resting his men, Alexander continued his march in an easterly direction. On the banks of the Jhelum, not far from Chilianwala, where the fate of the Punjab was destined to be settled many centuries later,‡ he found his way barred by the Paurava monarch, with a huge host, composed of the traditional "four arms"

* Strabo, *Geography,* XV. i. 62.

† Herodotus I. 196.

‡ For the actual site of the battle, see V.A. Smith, *Early History of India*, p. 78. Authorities differ between Jhelum town, or Jalālpur, further downstream.

of the Hindu army, cavalry, infantry, chariots and elephants. It was now the beginning of July, the rains had set in, and the river was in spate. To attempt a crossing in the face of such formidable opposition was an impossibility, so, on a dark and stormy night which covered his movements, Alexander, while diverting the enemy's attention by feint attacks, slipped across the river with a picked force of all arms at a point about 20 miles away. The Indian chariots, which were detached to meet the Greeks as soon as the crossing was reported, stuck in the mud and were easily defeated, and the rain hampered the Indian archers by wetting their bowstrings. The Indian army now changed front to meet the attack; the infantry were drawn up in dense masses, with 200 elephants, "looking like towers in a city wall," distributed at intervals along the front line. In the midst, on a richly caparisoned war-elephant, sat the Paurava prince, a giant over six feet high. As so often happened later, the clumsy Indian host was no match for its more mobile opponents. The Greek mounted infantry rode round it, pouring in showers of arrows, which stampeded the elephants, causing them to retreat, "like ships backing water," to use Arrian's picturesque phrase, and trample upon the troops behind them. In the midst of the confusion, the Macedonian cavalry charged home and, at the same time, the infantry drawn up on the further bank began to cross. The slaughter was terrible. The Paurava, though wounded, fought to the last. At length he was persuaded to dismount and was led into his conqueror's presence. "How do you wish to be treated?" he was asked. "Use me as a king (*βασιλιxῶς μοι χεησαι, ϖ Ἀλέξανδεε*)." the Kshatriya answered. "And when I said 'as a king,' everything is contained in that." He was restored to his kingdom as Alexander's viceroy.

Alexander now heard rumours of the kingdom of Magadha, which was vaguely called that of the Prasii or Easterners. He was told that it was only eleven days' march across the desert, and the Nanda King who occupied the throne was a worthless ruler, the son of a barber, who had obtained his throne by a base intrigue with the wife of his predecessor, whom he had murdered. He was anxious to advance and conquer it also; but on the banks of the Beas, his weary soldiers mutinied, and refused to go further. Deeply mortified, he built twelve immense altars to mark the furthest spot he had reached, and prepared to retrace his steps. It is said that for many years Indian kings used to worship there on crossing the river. The site is now irretrievably lost, mainly owing to an alteration in the course of the stream. It was probably not far from the modern Gurdāspur.

Alexander, being foiled of his original plan, now decided upon another. He determined to follow the old route of Scylax down to the mouth of the Indus, annexing the country he passed through, and exploring all possible means of communication with Western Asia both by land and sea. A fleet of about 2,000 vessels was prepared on the Jhelum, and booty, stores and non-combatants embarked upon it. The troops were drawn up on either bank. Early in the cold weather of 326 B.C., after pouring out libations to the gods, Alexander gave the order for the huge armada to set out on its way to the sea, the Indian onlookers dancing and singing "in their barbaric manner." The passage down the Indus was severely contested by the inhabitants at more than one point. The Mālavas and Kshudrakas (Malli and Oxydraci) formed powerful tribal republics, settled in the country between the Rāvī and Chenab rivers. In storming the capital of the Mālavas, which has sometimes been identified with Multān, Alexander was severely wounded, and the infuriated army, getting out of control, put the garrison to the sword. The inhabitants then submitted, and sent the conqueror presents of chariots and shields, bales of cotton, tortoiseshell, and 100 talents of "white iron." These gifts give us an indication of the prosperity of the country and the advanced state of its civilisation. In what is now the Sukkur district, the Greeks found a singular country, the inhabitants of which dined together in public and were remarkable for their longevity. Musicians (Mushaka), the king of this state, submitted, but was afterwards induced by the Brahmins to rebel. Peithon, the officer in charge of communications, exacted a terrible punishment from the king and his evil counsellors, putting them to death and exposing their corpses. In July 325 B.C. Alexander reached the town of Pātala, at the head of the delta.* Here he started to build a great port, with walls and dockyards. While it was in process of construction, he undertook a reconnaissance down to the sea. Reaching the open water, he offered sacrifices to the ocean. He now made preparations for his homeward march. The Punjab was divided into three provinces. The northern province was under Philip, son of Machatas, with his capital at Taxila, commanding the Khyber pass. He was afterwards killed in a mutiny, and was succeeded by Eudemus. The country between the Jhelum and the Beas was already under the charge of the Paurava Prince, and Peithon, son of Agenor, was governor of Sind. Beyond the Indian frontier, Alexander's father-in-law, Oxyartes, was ruler of Afghanistan, with his capital at Alexandria-under-Caucasus, commanding the northern approaches to India. It was impossible for the whole army to return by the same route, in view of the barren nature of the country and the lack of water and provisions. Alexander divided it into three parts. The first, under Craterus, with the sick, elephants and heavy baggage, was to go by the Mūla pass and across Baluchistan. Alexander himself was to proceed along the coast, through the Makrān, while Nearchus took the fleet home by way of the Persian Gulf. The homeward march started at the end of September 324 B.C., as soon as the monsoon permitted ships to sail. Alexander's troops suffered in crossing the Hālā Range, but at last both forces arrived at Susa, after a march of over 500 miles, in April-May, 325 B.C. Here they were joined by Nearchus, who had experienced many novel and exciting adventures in the Persian Gulf before reaching the mouth of the Tigris.

* This is located by V.A. Smith near the modern Bahmanābād.

A little more than a year after this (June, 323 B.C.) came the news of Alexander's premature death at Babylon at the age of 33. The vast empire which he had founded was shaken to the core, and at once began to split up. Mutinies broke out among the veterans in the military posts along the banks of the Indus. The viceroys departed for Asia Minor to take part in the scramble for power, and by 321 B.C. Greek rule in the Punjab was at an end. This was mainly due to the exertions of a young Indian named Chandragupta, whose fortunes will be described in the following chapter. So ended Alexander's brief and meteoric conquest of the Punjab. It had no immediate effect, and passed off like countless other invasions, leaving the country almost undisturbed. No mention of it is to be found in contemporary Indian literature. But Alexander was no mere casual raider, like Tamerlane or Nādir Shāh, intent on nothing but plunder. A pupil of Aristotle, he conceived it to be his mission to westernise the East. He came with historians and scientists in his train, to keep a careful record of his discoveries. His work was intended to be permanent. At various points along his route, he established a chain of fortified posts, to keep open his communications. Many of these survive to-day. He meant the Indus to be the great military and commercial highway of his Indian provinces and, had he lived, there is little doubt that a second Alexandria would have sprung up at its mouth and, in all probability, the Punjab would have been hellenised like Asia Minor or Egypt.

LEADING DATES

B.C. *c.* 612	Overthrow of the Assyrian Empire by the Medes and Babylonians.
660-583	Zoroaster, religious reformer of Persia.
558-530	Cyrus, King of Persia: conquest of Gandhāra.
522-486	Darius, King of Persia: 516 B.C. Exploration of the Indus by Scylax.
330	Battle of Arbela: Overthrow of the Persian Empire by Alexander the Great.
B.C. 327	Alexander crosses the Hindu Kush.
326	Crossing of the Indus: battle of Jhelum (July): erection of the altars. Return journey commenced (October).
325	Defeat of the Mālavas (January). Nearchus reaches the sea: Alexander commences his march through the Makrān.
324	Alexander reaches Susa (May).
323	Death of Alexander at Babylon (June).
322	Revolt against Greek rule in the Punjab.

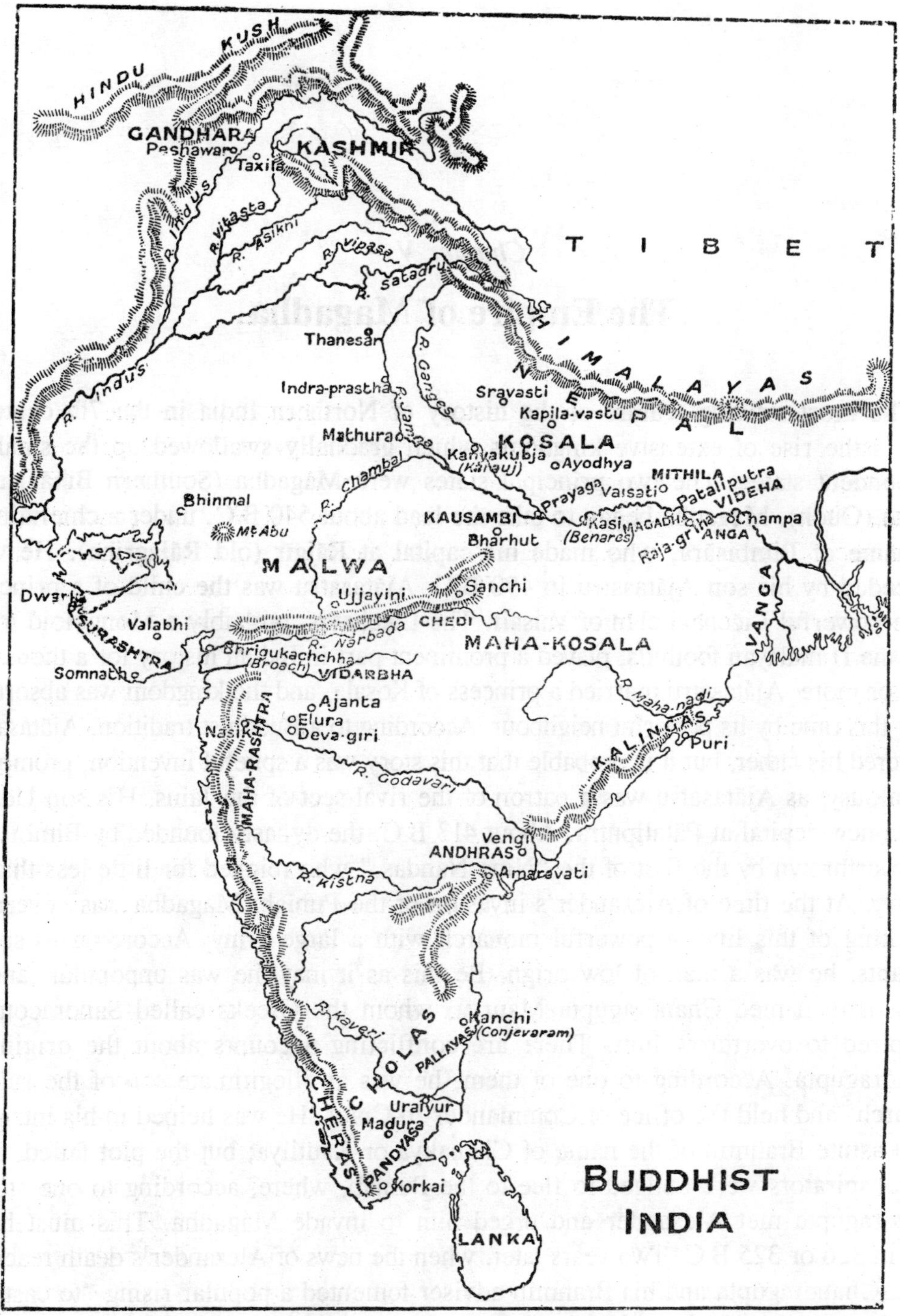

Map 5 : Buddhist India

Chapter V

The Empire of Magadha

The most striking feature of the history of Northern India in the 7th century B.C. is the rise of extensive kingdoms which gradually swallowed up the smaller independent states. The two principal states were Magadha (Southern Bihār) and Kosala (Oudh). Magadha began to take the lead about 540 B.C. under a chieftain of the name of Bimbisāra, who made his capital at Rājgīr (old Rājagriha). He was succeeded by his son Ajātasatru in 490 B.C. Ajātasatru was the child of a princess of the powerful Licchavi clan of Vaisālī. The Licchavis, probably a Mongoloid tribe from the Himalayan foothills, played a prominent part in Indian history for a thousand years or more. Ajātasatru married a princess of Kosala, and the kingdom was absorbed about this time by its powerful neighbour. According to a Buddhist tradition, Ajātasatru murdered his father, but it is probable that this story was a spiteful invention, prompted by jealousy, as Ajātasatru was a patron of the rival sect of the Jains. His son Udaya built a new capital at Pātaliputra. About 413 B.C. the dynasty founded by Bimbisāra was overthrown by the first of the "Nine Nandas," who reigned for little less than a century. At the time of Alexander's invasion of the Punjab, Magadha was governed by a king of this line, a powerful monarch with a large army. According to some accounts, he was a man of low orign. Be this as it may, he was unpopular, and a young man named Chandragupta Maurya, whom the Greeks called Sandracottus, conspired to overthrow him. There are conflicting accounts about the origin of Chandragupta. According to one of them, he was an illegitimate son of the ruling monarch, and held the office of Commander-in-Chief. He was helped in his intrigue by an astute Brahmin of the name of Chānakya or Kautilya; but the plot failed, and the conspirators were obliged to flee to the Punjab, where, according to one story, Chandragupta met Alexander and urged him to invade Magadha. This must have been in 326 or 325 B.C. Two years later, when the news of Alexander's death reached India, Chandragupta and his Brahmin adviser fomented a popular rising "to cast off the yoke of servitude from their necks, and slay their masters," which put an end to Greek rule in the Punjab. He then collected an army, and in about 322 B.C., returned to Magadha, defeated and killed the Nanda King, and occupied Pātaliputra. A Sanskrit historical drama, the *Mudrā Rākshasa* or *The Minister's Seal*, written about seven centuries later, gives a vivid picture of the palace-intrigues by which the revolution was brought about.

In 305 B.C. Seleucus Nicator, who in the partition of Alexander's Empire had become ruler of Western Asia, tried to reconquer the Punjab. Chandragupta defeated him, and compelled him to cede extensive territories in the Kābul, Herāt and Kandahar districts and Baluchistan, which brought the western boundaries of Magadha up to the Hindu Kush. In return, Seleucus received 500 elephants, which proved to be of great use in his wars against his Greek rivals. This friendly understanding was cemented by a marriage alliance between the two rulers, and was further strengthened by the despatch, about 302 B.C., of an ambassador named Megasthenes to the Court at Pātaliputra, where he resided for a number of years. Megasthenes was no stranger to the East. He had been employed under Sibyrtius, satrap of Arachosia (Kandahar). He wrote a detailed account of India; the original has unfortunately perished, but copious extracts are preserved by later writers, and particularly in the 15th book of the Roman geographer Strabo (A.D. 23). It was the standard work on India for the Greeks.* With it, we step from darkness to light; we have to wait for six centuries before a foreign traveller again lifts the curtain upon ancient India. Other sources of information supplement the account of Megasthenes. One is the earlier narrative of Nearchus, Alexander's Admiral, also known to us only in extracts. Another is a treatise entitled the *Artha Sāstra* or Manual of Politics, discovered some thirty years ago in a South Indian library, and traditionally ascribed to Kautilya himself.

Chaṇdragupta's capital, Pātaliputra (or Palibothra, as the Greeks called it), on the site of the modern Patna, is described by Megasthenes as a splendid city, standing on the northern bank of the Son. It was the shape of parallelogram, roughly nine miles by two, and was surrounded by a broad, deep moat, which received the drainage and was connected at its two extremities with the river. The city wall was a massive timber palisade, with drawbridges, towers and gates at regular intervals. The town itself was well planned and laid out, with inns, gaming houses, theatres, race-courses, and meeting-halls for guilds and religious sects. There were handsome bazaars where indigenous and foreign goods were displayed for sale. The streets were crowded with a busy and many-coloured throng of men and animals. The houses were two or three storeys high, and as they were mostly wooden, elaborate precautions were taken against an outbreak of fire. In the heart of the city was the royal palace, which stood in the midst of a walled-in park, with ornamental trees, tame peacocks and pheasants, and lakes full of sacred fish.

---

* The quotations which follow are from J.W. McCrindle, *Ancient India as described by Megasthenes and Arrian* (1877).

The palace, like many buildings in Burma, Kashmir, and other parts of India today, was built of wood exquisitely carved; the pillars were plated with gold and silver, ornamented with designs of vines and birds. The king lived in great state. "In the Indian royal palace," we are told, "there are wonders with which neither Memnonian Susa in all its glory, nor the magnificence of Ecbatana can hope to vie." Chandragupta, like most usurpers, went in daily fear of his life, and his unpopularity was enhanced by his oppressive government. "He himself oppressed with slavery the people whom he had delivered from external domination."* He took elaborate precautions against assassination. He never slept twice in the same bed, and all food and drink were carefully tested in order to guard against poison. No one could enter the palace precincts without a permit, and an army of spies and *agents provocateurs* was employed to watch what was happening in the city, and no methods were considered too unscrupulous for getting rid of enemies of the state. He was surounded by a host of slave girls, who cooked and served his food, tended to his wants, massaged his limbs and entertained him with dancing and music. A bodyguard of foreign Amazons kept watch over the palace day and night. Chandragupta seldom went abroad except on festal occasions, when he rode in solemn procession through the streets in a litter on the back of an elephant. "Then comes a great host of attendants in holiday dress, with golden vessels, such as huge basins and goblets six feet broad, tables, chairs of state, drinking vessles and lavers, all of Indian copper, and many of them set with jewels, such as emeralds, beryls and Indian garnets; other bear robes embroidered in gold thread and lead wild beasts, such as buffaloes, leopards and tame lions, and rare birds in cages." The Amazons lined the streets, keeping the spectators at a safe distance. "It was death to come inside the line of women." At the time when the King washed his hair, a solemn durbar was held, at which the nobles were required to attend and offer the customary tribute.

Chandragupta worked hard. Roused at dawn by music, he rose, and after bathing and religous observances, he visited the Law Courts and Hall of Audience. He received ministers, heard the reports of his spies, and attended to his correspondence. He then retired during the heat of the day for rest and food; the evening was spent in inspecting his troops and fortifications and in recreation. Hunting was a favourite sport, and drives were arranged, in which large numbers of beasts were slain. Animal fights and gladiatorial displays were held, and also public chariot races, in which horses and oxen took part. Both nobles and people betted heavily on these races. Chandragupta maintained an immense army, which, in the traditional Indian fashion, consisted of elephants, chariots, cavalry and infantry. When mobilised it is said to have been 600,000 strong, but as in all Oriental armies, a proportion may have been camp-followers and attendants. Chandragupta placed his chief faith in his elephants

* Poplum quem ab externa domination Vindicaverat, ipse servitio premebat. *Justin*, XV, 4.

and chariots. The latter may be compared to armoured cars; they carried archers, and the skill of the Indian bowman was proverbial. The army was under an elaborately organised War Office, divided into six boards and charged with keeping the arsenals and armouries in a state of constant readiness for war. Their practical efficiency is demonstrated by the fact that Chandragupta was able to defeat the Greek veterans under so famous a general as Seleucus.

The Empire was divided into three provinces, each under a Viceroy, usually a member of the Royal Family. The provincial capitals were at Taxila, Ujjain and Tosali. Under the Viceroys were divisional commissioners and under them again were the district officers. They were well paid: a high officer of state received the equivalent of 4,000 rupees a month. As to-day, the lower ranks of the Civil Service contained a host of petty officials. The main source of income was the tax on the land. Megasthenes rightly observes that all land, then as now, belonged to the state. There was no private ownership in the soil. The assessment, we are told, was one-fourth the value of the crops. The greater part of the country was under irrigation and bore two crops a year. If Megasthenes can be believed, famines were almost unknown.* Irrigation received special attention; an inscription at Gīrnār in Kāthiāwār bears witness to the care bestowed by successive Viceroys on an artificial lake and dam constructed there. Megasthenes records that the district officers, as to-day, "measure the land and inspect the sluices by which water is distributed into the branch canals, so that everyone may enjoy his fair share of the benefit." These officers were also in charge of mines, timber and forests. Forests must have been much more extensive than at present, and were inhabited by wild tribes. A part of the forests was reserved for royal hunting grounds, and for the breeding of elephants, which were a royal monopoly. Towns, however, were numerous, and the whole kingdom was connected up by an excellent system of roads. Milestones and rest-houses were erected at intervals, and couriers maintained a postal service on these highways. The chief was the great Royal Road, which ran from Taxila to the capital, linking up all the principal towns. Another trade-route ran from Pātaliputra through Prayāga, Bharhut and Vidisa to Ujjain, an important trading-centre, whence roads diverged northwards to the mouth of the Indus and southwards to Bhrigukaccha or Broach.

The civil administration was bureaucratic. The ruler was assisted in his duties by his ministers, who took charge of various portfolios. Local self-government is no novelty in India, and Pātaliputra, and doubtless other cities as well, was administered by a municipality consisting of six boards of five members each. The first dealt with trade. It fixed rates of wages and safe-guarded the rights of artisans, who enjoyed the special protection and patronage of the state. The second did the work of a Foreign Office or Consulate. It examined carefully all visitors leaving and entering the capital,

* J.W. McCrindle, *Ancient India as described by Megasthenes and Arrian*, p. 32.

stamped their passports, saw that they were properly accommodated, and provided medical attendance when they were sick. If they died, the board provided for hteir burial and forwarded their effects to their relatives. The third board was concerned with the registration of births and deaths, and maintained a census for taxation purposes. The fourth, fifth and sixth boards were in charge of commerce. The fourth regulated sales and stamped weights and measures. Merchants had to purchase a licence from it in order to trade. The fifth board saw that old goods were not palmed off as new, while the sixth was concerned with the collection of a tax of one-sixth on all sales. Any evasions of the tax, if detected, were drastically punished. Besides these committees, the municipality as a whole was responsible for public works of all kinds. They had to see that refuse was not left on the roads, and that the drains were kept clean. They were charged with the duty of ensuring that the fire-brigade was in constant readiness and the curfew duly sounded and observed.

Justice was administered by civil and criminal courts. Cases were heard by three judges, who were advised by Brahmins acquainted with the law, but no doubt most civil cases were settled in the traditional Indian manner by *panchayat* or juries of the caste-fellows of the litigants. Nearchus tells us that "the laws were preserved by oral tradition, and not in books." Criminal law was terribly severe. The death-penalty was exacted for a number of crimes, including injury to artisans and evasion of dues to the State. Maiming was inflicted for offences such as perjury, and torture and trial by ordeal were used in order to ascertain the truth. Brahmins, apparently, enjoyed the benefit of clergy.

Trade was evidently in a flourishing condition, and a cosmopolitan crowd of merchants from various parts of Europe and Asia could be seen in the bazaars of Pātaliputra. Goods from Southern India, the Golden Chersonese, China, Mesopotamia and the Greek cities of Asia Minor were exposed on the stalls, and like everything else in the Mauryan Empire, their sale was strictly regulated and controlled. "Silks, muslims, the finer sorts of cloth, cutlery and armour, brocades, embroideries and rugs, perfumes and drugs, ivory and ivory-work, jewellery and gold (seldom silver): these were the main articles in which the merchant dealt."* Nearchus noted that they were wonderfully clever at imitating European goods of all kinds: similar remarks were made by European travellers in the 17th century. The *Artha Sāstra* gives elaborate Shipping Regulations, and no doubt there was a considerable amount of coastal trade; Indian merchant vessels crossed the Indian Ocean to the mouth of Tigris and to Aden. There was a famous overland route from Taxila to Balkh: from there, Indian goods were carried down the Oxus to Europe by way of the Caspian and the Black Sea. It is a curious fact that with all this highly developed trade, the Mauryas never developed a regular coinage of their own. Athenian "owls" and Persian darics were freely

* Rhys Davids, *Buddhist India*, p. 98.

circulated. The only indigenous Indian coins known to us are very crude. They are usually square in shape, the silver ones being cut from strips and the copper ones from bars. They were then stamped by means of a punch with marks showing their value and the mint from which they were issued. The standard coin of this type appears to have been the *pāna*, worth about a rupee or somewhat less in modern currency.

Megasthenes made careful enquiries into the popular reglion and philosophy of the Hindus. They worshipped, he tells us, Heracles, Dionysus, and Zeus Ombrios. The chief centre of the worship of Heracles was at Mathurā; hence he may be identified with Krishna, the charioteer of the epic hero Arjuna, and king of the Yādavas, whose birthplace was Mathurā. It is interesting to note that he is already the god of a local cult. Dionysus is probably Siva, and Zeus Ombrios is Indra, who releases the rainclouds and causes the thunder. It is significant that no mention is made of images or temples. He gives an interesting account of the Brahmanical schools, with their strict system of discipline, and of their teaching, and notes its resemblance to Greek philosophy:

> "In many points their teaching agrees with that of the Greeks – for instance that the world has a beginning and an end in time, and that its shape is spherical; that the Deity, who is its Governor and Maker, interpenetrates the whole: that the first principles of the universe are different, but that water is the principle from which the order of the world has come to be; that besides the four elements, there is a fifth substance (*ākāsa*, ether) of which the heavens and the stars are made; that the earth is the centre of the universe. About generation of the soul, their teaching shows parallels to the Greek doctrines, and on many other matters. Like Plato, too, they interweave fables about the immortality of the Soul and the judgments inflicted in the other world and so on."

Besides these, there were the "Sarmanes" or mendicant ascetics, who lived mostly in the jungle, wearing clothes made of bark, begging their food, and abstaining from cohabitation and wine. Some of them practised fortune-telling, necromancy, and healing by spells, very much as is the case to-day. Women could join the mendicant orders, and suicide was permitted and even admired. Curiously enough, egasthenes makes no specific mention of the Buddhists or Jains. The caste-system was strictly enforced. "No one is allowed to marry outside his caste, or exchange one profession or trade for another, or follow more than one business." But a man of any caste could enter the religous life. Megasthenes gives an attractive picture of Hindu society. He devides it into seven "classes" (*γεννέαι*). First came the Philosophers and Brahmins, who performed the public and private sacrifices and acted as diviners and astrologers. Like the Roman augurs, they had to declare the auspicious days for undertakings, and if anyone's prediction proved to be false, he was dismissed. Every year the King held great assemblies of Brahmins, at which those who had produced works of merit were rewarded. This custom went on through the ages, right down to the Peshwas of Poona in the eighteenth century. The second class was the agriculturalists, harmless folk, who seldom left their villages and went on ploughing even when contending armies were fighting at a little distance. India is a country of self-organised villages, and the grouping of the villages into states and empires left their inhabitants little affected, so long as their customs and rights were not interfered with.

The third class was the herdsmen, shepherds and hunters. They destroyed the wild animals and vermin, and trapped and tamed elephants on behalf of the Government. The fourth class was the artisans, a highly privileged group, who were under the special protection of the government, and enjoyed many immunities in return for their services to the State. The fifth was the military class. The immense standing army of Chandragupta gave employment to a large number of men; the soldiers were well paid and supplied by the War Office with horses and equipment, which had to be returned after use. "When not engaged on active service, they spend their time eating and drinking. They are maintained at the King's expense, and hence they are always ready, when occasion calls, to take the field, for they carry nothing of their own with them but their bodies." Sixthly came the inspectors, a branch of the Civil Service specially employed by the Emperor. They travelled from one end of the Empire to the other and submitted confidential reports upon the work of the local officials. While they were on circuit even the meanest subject could appeal to them if he had a grievance. They carried on a complicated system of espionage, and were especially on their guard against plots in the army. For this purpose they used the courtesans of the City. Service in this department especially appealed to adventurous youths. Seventhly and lastly came the Royal Councillors. To them belonged the highest posts of government, the tribunals of Justice, and the general administration of public affairs. They were doubtless Brahmins. "Some Brahmins," says Nearchus, "enter political life and attend the King as councillors, while others devote themselves to philosophy." The Brahmins in Hindu India, like the clergy in medieval Europe, were the power behind the throne.

Megasthenes tells us that a noble simplicity was the predominant Indian characteristic, and this is confirmed by other Greek travellers. "No Indian has ever been convicted of lying." In signing contracts, witnesses and seals were considered to be superfluous and houses were left unguarded.* In the whole of Chandragupta's

* Another foreign traveller, Hiuen Tsang, some nine centuries later, confirms this. Colonel Sleeman, who spent his life among the Hindu peasants, says: "I have had before me hundreds of cases in which a man's property, liberty and life depended upon his telling a lie, and he has refused to tell it." (*Journey through Oudh*, II. 68-9.) Marco Polo says that the Brahmin merchants were famous for their honesty, and "would not tell a lie for anything on earth." Yule II. 363.

camp of 400,000 men, there were no conviction for thefts exceeding 200 drachmae (£8). They were not litigious.

Cotton (tree linen) was the usual material for clothes; the people liked bright colours and jewels, and carried umbrellas to protect themselves from the sun. The staple food was "rice boiled after the manner of porridge," and upon it were placed seasoned meats, dressed in Indian fashion—surely the earliest description of curry and rice. A spirituous liquor, like the 'attrack' of to-day, was distilled from grain, and doubtless 'toddy' was brewed from the sap of various palms. Women were well treated, and wives had their dowries as their private property. A husband could be punished for cruelty, and offences against women were severely dealt with. If a wife bore no children, the husband could take another, and widows could re-marry. In the Punjab, which was more old-fashioned and less progressive than the capital, the practice of holding a Maiden's Choice was still in vogue. Nearchus states, somewhat crudely, that in Taxila, girls were put up as the prize of victory in a boxing-match: the victor obtained his wife without paying a dowry. Voluntary *suttee* was permitted, but was confirmed to the warrior caste, and the widow who refused to burn herself was looked on with contempt. An account has been preserved of a case which occurred among some Indian mercenaries in Irān in 316 B.C. The widow of the dead leader went to the pyre exultant, "crowned with fillets by the women who belonged to her, and decked out splendidly as for a wedding." On reaching the spot, she distributed her ornaments among her friends. She was helped on to the pyre by her brother, and lay down beside her husband. As the fire seized her, no sound of weakness escaped her lips. The Greeks thought the custom savage and inhuman.* Modern social legislation was anticipated by provision for the families of soldiers and workmen, and for orphans. Megasthenes says that slavery, so prominent a feature of Greek society, was unknown, but here he seems to be wrong. A mild kind of domestic slavery was apparently in vogue; slaves were usually prisoners of war, insolvent debtors and members of the lower castes. They could purchase their freedom. The people were fond of amusements, and processions and circus entertainments were provided by the Court. Acting, dancing and pantomime shows were popular, and companies of strolling players toured the country. Caste-feasts were held, and the capital was illuminated for public festivals.

In 298 B.C. Chandragupta died or abdicated his throne; according to one storey, he became a Jain monk and retired to Sravana Belgola in Mysore, where he committed suicide. Of the long reign of his son Bindusāra we know little; his surname Amitraghāta seems to imply that he was a great conqueror, and he probably extended the Maurya Empire south of the Vindhyas as far as the Pennār river, adding to it a

---

* McCrindle, *Ancient India as described in Classical Literature* (1901), p. 202 ff.

fourth province with its capital at Suvarnagiri, "Golden Rock," perhaps near the ancient gold-fields of Maski in the Raichur district, where the southernmost inscription of Asoka has been discovered.* Bindusāra maintained friendly relations with his Greek neighbours. Ambassadors from Antioch and Alexandria continued to visit Pātaliputra; a Greek admiral explored the Indian coast; and the Greek and Indian monarchs maintained an amiable correspondence.

Asoka succeeded to the throne in 273 B.C. He was Viceroy of Ujjain at the time of his father's death, and at first had some difficulty in asserting his claims. He was not corwned until four years later. We are fortunate in knowing more of Asoka than of any early Hindu ruler, from the fact that he embodied his principles of government in a number of edicts, graven on the rock or on pillars and recording his own words. In 261 B.C. Asoka determined to round off his empire by the conquest of Kalinga or Orissa, one of the last of the independent states, situated on the Bay of Bengal between the Mahānadi and Godāvarī rivers. The country up to modern times has been a wild one, with impenetrable forests haunted by wild tribes, unfordable rivers and a scarcity of roads. The Orissans,who had a language and culture of their own, and a considerable army, stoutly resisted this wanton invasion of their land, and a war of extermination ensued. 125,000 people, Asoka tells us, were carried away captive; 100,000 were slain, and many times that number perished. In defiance of all rules, Brahmins and ascetics fell by the edge of the sword. This was the last of Asoka's annexations to his empire, which now stretched from Mysore to the Himālayas, and from the borders of Assam to the Hindu Kush. Shortly after, he fell under the influence of a famous Buddhist teacher named Upagupta of Mathurā, and was converted. He contemplated with horror and remorse the butchery for which he had been responsible. "If a hundredth, nay, a thousandth part of the persons who were then slain, carried away captive or done to death were now to suffer the same fate, it would be a matter of remorse to His Majesty."† He resolved to forswear war, and to govern in the light of one law only, the *Dhamma* or Law of Piety laid down by the Buddha. "The reverberations of the war-drums became the reverberation of the drum of the Law." "The only true victory is that effected by the Law of Piety," and he earnestly adjures his sons and grandsons to bear in mind, if ever they are tempted by the lust of empire, the worthlessness of conquest by force. "The conquest of the Law," he assures them, "is alone a conquest full of delight."

As time went on, Asoka became more and more religious. He had entered the Buddhist order as a lay brother: he now became a monk, and determined to use the Civil Service inaugurated by his grandfather to propagate the Law through his dominsions. "Everywhere in my dominions, the Commissioners and the District

* V.A. Smith, *Early History of India*, 4th edn., p. 172, *note* I.

† The Edicts are translated in V.A. Smith, *Asoka* (1920), p. 149 ff.

Officers every five years must proceed on circuit, not only to execute their ordinary duties, but to give instruction in the Law." The Secret Service of Chandragupta was now mobilised into a body of "Overseers of the Law," whose duty it was to report upon religious progress in all quarters of the Empire. In order that the people might clearly understand what was expected of them, edicts were engraved on rocks or on pillars set up in places where they were most likely to attract the attention of the passer-by. These were erected at various places as far apart as Peshawar, Kāthiāwār, the Nepal frontier, Orissa and Mysore. "The Law, wherever pillars of stone or tables of stone exist, must be recorded, so that it may long endure." The Law, as enjoined by Asoka, was stricity practical and suited to the popular understanding. No mention is made of metaphysical subtilties. It consists of compassion, liberality, truth, purity, gentleness and saintliness of life, "hearkening to elders, reverence to the aged, and seemly treatment of Brahmins and ascetics, of the poor and wretched, yea, even of slaves and servants." These virtues will bring the only true happiness, "in this world and the next." Asoka's first thought was for the comfort and well-being of his subjects. On the main roads, shade-trees were planted, wells dug, and hospitals erected for men and animals. No mention is made of schools, but it is obvious that education, as in most Buddhist countries, must have been widely diffused by the monasteries; otherwise the edicts would have been of little avail. The harsh laws of the reign of Chandragupta were as far as possible relaxed. Jails were thrown open on the anniversary of the Emperor's coronation. Prisoners under sentence of death were given a respite in which they could lodge an appeal, and were visited by pious men, who would prepare their souls. Governors were given wide latitude in granting pardons. One of Asoka's chief reforms was to carry into practice the Buddha's law of *ahimsā*, kindness to all living things. He gradually and progressively stopped the slaughter of animals, setting the example himself. The royal hunt was abolished. Killing for the royal kitchens was cut down. Animal sacrifices were forbidden and a close season was introduced for various beasts and birds.

One of the Emperor's chief concerns was to inroduce complete religious toleration. There were to be no wars of religion in his empire. He warns his people of the evils of schism and deprecates the habit of exalting one's own views at the expense of others. Though a convinced Buddhist, he extends his patronage to Brahmins, Jains and other sects with complete impartiality. A characteristic action was the construction of the costly caves at Barābar for the naked ascetics of the Ajīvika sect founded by Gosala, the rival of Mahāvīra.

Unlike his grandfather, who ruled by fear, Asoka was anxious to make the foundation of his government the love and willing obedience of his subjects. He wished to be regarded as the father of his people. "Just as a man, having made over his child to a skilful nurse, feels confident and says to himself, 'The skilful nurse is eager to care for the happiness of my child,' even so my Governors have been created for the welfare and happiness of my country." Especially tender is the royal compassion towards the poor jungle-folk, who lie outside the pale of the Hindu community. Every effort is to be made to win their confidence and prevent them from being oppressed. "The root of the whole matter lies in preservance and patience."

Fig. 11 : Asoka Capital

The Emperor set a high standard for his officers, but he practised what he preached. He took no holidays. "At all times, when I am eating, or in the ladies' apartments, or in my private room, or in the mews, or in my conveyance, or in the pleasure-grounds, everywhere the persons appointed to give information should keep me informed about the affairs of the people. ... I never feel satisfaction in my exertions and dispatch of business. Work I must, for the welfare of all the folk." One of the many activities he undertook was a pilgrimage to the Holy Places of Buddhism and the erection of pillars on the sites of the Master's birth, first sermon, englightenment and Parinirvāna (Fig. 11). Another was the dispatch of missionaries to distant nations, in order that they too might share the benefits of the Law. Asoka had the true missionary spirit. He dispatched preachers to Gandhāra and Kashmir, to the Deccan and the Tamil countries, and, further afield, to Ceylon and Burma, and to his Greek friends, Ptolemy Philadelphus of Egypt, Antigonus Gonatas of Macedonia, Magas of Cyrene and Alexander of Epirus.* The names of the missionaries who went forth to these distant lands are preserved. Whether the yellow-robed evangelists ever actually reached Antioch or Alexandria we do not know, but there is no doubt about the sources of the mission to Ceylon, which was already colonised by emigrants from north-eastern India. It was led by Mahinda and Sanghamitta, the King's son and daughter, who took with them a branch of the sacred Bodhi Tree and planted it at Anurādhapura, in the centre of the island. The Sinhalese king Tissa was converted with all his court, and to-day Buddhism, extinct in the land of its birth, flourishes in its purest form in that beautiful island.

The mssions of King Asoka are amongst the greatest civilising influences in the world's history; for they entered countries for the most part barbarous and full of superstition, and amongst these animistic peoples Buddhism spread as a wholesome leaven.

"The history of Ceylon and Burma, as of Siam, Japan and Tibet, may be said to begin with the entrance into them of Buddhism; and in

* It is important to note that the only years when all these monarchs were reigning simultaneously are 261-258 B.C.

these lands it spread far more rapidly and made a far deeper impression than in China with its already ancient civilisation. As to-day Christianity spreads very rapidly amongst the animistic peoples of Africa and the South Sea islands, exerting a strong influence and replacing superstition and chaos by a reasoning belief in One God and an orderly universe; so Buddhism in these eastern lands has exerted a beneficent influence by putting Karma, the law of cause and effect, in the place of the caprice of demons and tribal gods and a lofty system of morals in the place of tribal custom and taboo.

"The Buddhist missionaries, moreover, brought with them much of the culture of their own land. It seems clear, for instance, that it was Mahinda who brought into Ceylon the arts of stone carving and of irrigation which his father had so successfully practised in India; and the Ceylon Buddhist of to-day thinks of his religon as the force to which his country owes the greatness of her past history. ... Not far from the ruined city of Anurādhapura a lovely rocky hill rises out of a dense sea of jungle, and here is the rock-hewn 'study' and the tomb of the great and gentle prince Mahinda, who about 250 B.C. brought Buddhism to Ceylon."*

Asoka did much besides this for the propagation of Buddhism. In one of his edicts, he gives a list of his favourite passages of the Scriptures and recommends them as being particularly suitable for study. A Buddhist Council, under the presidency of Upagupta, was convened at Pātaliputra, and sat for nine months. At this Council sectarian disputes, which were dividing the order, were settled, and the canon of the Buddhist scriptures was definitely closed.

In his later years, Asoka seems to have become a recluse, retiring to a monastery and leaving his kingdom to his son. He died in 232 B.C. His reign of forty years is without a parallel in history. He found Buddhism a local sect; he made it the official creed of his empire. He has been compared at various times to Marcus Aurelius, Saint Paul and Constantine. But no Christian ruler has even attempted to apply to the government of a great empire the principles of the Sermon on the Mount, or to announce, in a public edict addressed to his subjects, that "although a man does him injury, His Majesty holds that it must be patiently borne, as far as it possibly can be borne." Two hundred and fifty years before Christ, Asoka had the courage to express his horror and remorse at the results of a successful campaign, and deliberately to renounce war as a means of policy, in spite of the fact that his dominions included the unsubdued tribes of the north-west frontier, and was able in practice to put an end to cruelty to man and beast, and establish complete religious toleration throughout India. Asoka fulfilled Plato's ideal of the state in which "king are philosophers, and philosophers kings."

* K.J. Saunders, *The Story of Buddhism* (1916), pp. 76-9.

But Asoka's great experiment did not long survive him. We know little of his successors. His grandson Dasaratha appears to have followed in his footsteps, but soon after this a reaction, doubtless fomented by the Brahmins, set in. In 185 B.C. the Mauryan dynasty came to an end. The last ruler was murdered by his commander-in-chief, Pushyamitra, who founded the Sunga dynasty, and marked the return of northern India to Brahminism by celebrating the *asvamedha* or horse-sacrifice. He is said to have cruelly persecuted the Buddhists.

By this time the empire of Magadha was fast disintegrating. Invaders from the north-west had overrun the Punjab, while in the east the people of Kalinga, under a prince named Kharavela, shook off the yoke and attacked their rulers. About 73 B.C., the Sunga rulers were succeeded by a short-lived dynasty, the Kānvas, who were overthrown by the Āndhras of the Deccan in 28 B.C. Centuries later, the Chinese pilgrim, Fa Hian, gazing awestruck on the ruins of Asoka's vast palace in the now deserted capital of Pātaliputra, declared them to be the work "of no mortal hands."* No human agency, he was convinced, could have reared the mighty walls and gates, piled up the stones, and decorated them with such delicate carving and intricate inlaid sculpture work.

MAURYAN CULTURE

The inscriptions on Asoka's rock and pillar edicts and the contemporary Buddhist reliquaries are the earliest extant examples of Indian writing, but they are the work of expert calligraphists, and could only have been executed if the art had already been practised for a long time. It is, indeed, impossible to imagine that Chandragupta's elaborate bureaucracy could have been carried on without written records and accounts. Religious literature, it is true, was handed down orally; Brahmins committed the Vedas to memory, and we are told that if a Buddhist community required a certain text they borrowed a learned monk who knew it by heart, as we borrow a book from a library. The Buddhist canon was not written down until the reign of the Sinhalese monarch Vattagamini, in 29 B.C. But frequent mentions of letters are found in the Jātakas, where they are spoken of as being written with a stylus on a leaf of a talipot palm, and Nearchus, Alexander's admiral, says that Indians used for the purpose "fine tissue closely woven" (σινδόνες λίαν χεχεοτημένοι). Hence we may conclude that writing was employed for business purposes long before it was utilised for literature. The inscriptions, written as they are in the current vernacular and not in Sanskrit, would have been useless unless reading and writing were widely diffused. The characters are in the Brāhmi script, which is the parent of the scripts used in various parts of India to-day. It is generally supposed that it is derived from a north Semitic source such as that which appears upon the Moabite Stone (*c.* 890 B.C.).

* Beal, *Buddhist Records of the Western World*, I. lv.

The recent discovery of the Indus valley seals has led some scholars to suppose that the origin of the Indian alphabet may be traced to them, but this hypothesis appears to be extremely doutbtful. Another script, of Aramaic origin, and known as Kharoshthī, was in vogue on the North-West Frontier and, as Aurel Stein's discoveries have shown, in Central Asia, and was employed for the edicts inscribed in these districts.

Asoka was a great builder, and appears to have introduced the practice of using stone instead of wood. The palace at Pātaliputra, for long the wonder of Chinese pilgrims, has now disappeared, save for a few scanty remains unearthed by the archaeologists. His extant monuments are all marked by the "noble simplicity" which Megasthenes considered to be an Indian characteristic. The principal surviving remains are the stūpas, the pillars, the rock-inscriptions, and some early cave dwellings. The stūpa or dāgaba was originally a burial ground, erected over the ashes of a departed chieftain. Buddha was of the Kshatriya caste, and, as we have already seen, at his death his ashes were divided among his followers and enshrined in mounds of this kind. Running round the stūpa was a raised platform for perambulation, and this was surrounded by a wooden rail to keep off intruders. Asoka erected a vast number of stūpas to enshrine relics of the Buddha and Buddhist saints. The most famous of these is the Great Stūpa at Sānchī near the ancient city of Vidisā or Bhīlsā in Bhopāl State, though none of Asoka's actual work is now visible; it has been subsequently encased in sandstone blocks, while a stone railing, obviously imitated from an earlier wooden original which it probably replaced and, still later, four highly decorated gateways, have been added. The stūpa itself is at present 56 feet high, with a diameter of 121 feet; the "umbrella," a symbol of royalty which originally crowned all stūpas, has recently been restored* (Fig. 12).

Another stūpa, which once stood at Bharhut, about 95 miles south-west of Allahābād, has disappeared, but portions of the railing, bearing figures in low relief, have been preserved (Plate IIIa). A "Buddhist rail" of the same period is at Bodh Gayā. The carvings in low relief on the railings and gateways of these stūpas are charming examples of indigenous Indian art, imitated, no doubt, from earlier work in wood and ivory. It is significant that one of the panels at Sānchī is the gift of "the ivory workers of Vidisā". These sculptures were the work of generations of pious donors, and they must have taken many years to complete. Their principal object is to illustrate incidents in the lives of the Buddha for the edification of pilgrims visiting the spot. Incidentally they throw a food of light upon the everyday life, customs and dresses of the time. Nothing could be more fascinating than these naïve and wholly

* Sir J. Marshall, *Guide to Sānchī* (1936). The Great Stūpa is surrounded by a number of smaller stūpas, pillars and temples of every period from the 3rd century B.C. to the 7th century A.D., after which, apparently Vidisā was abandoned. (Plate II.)

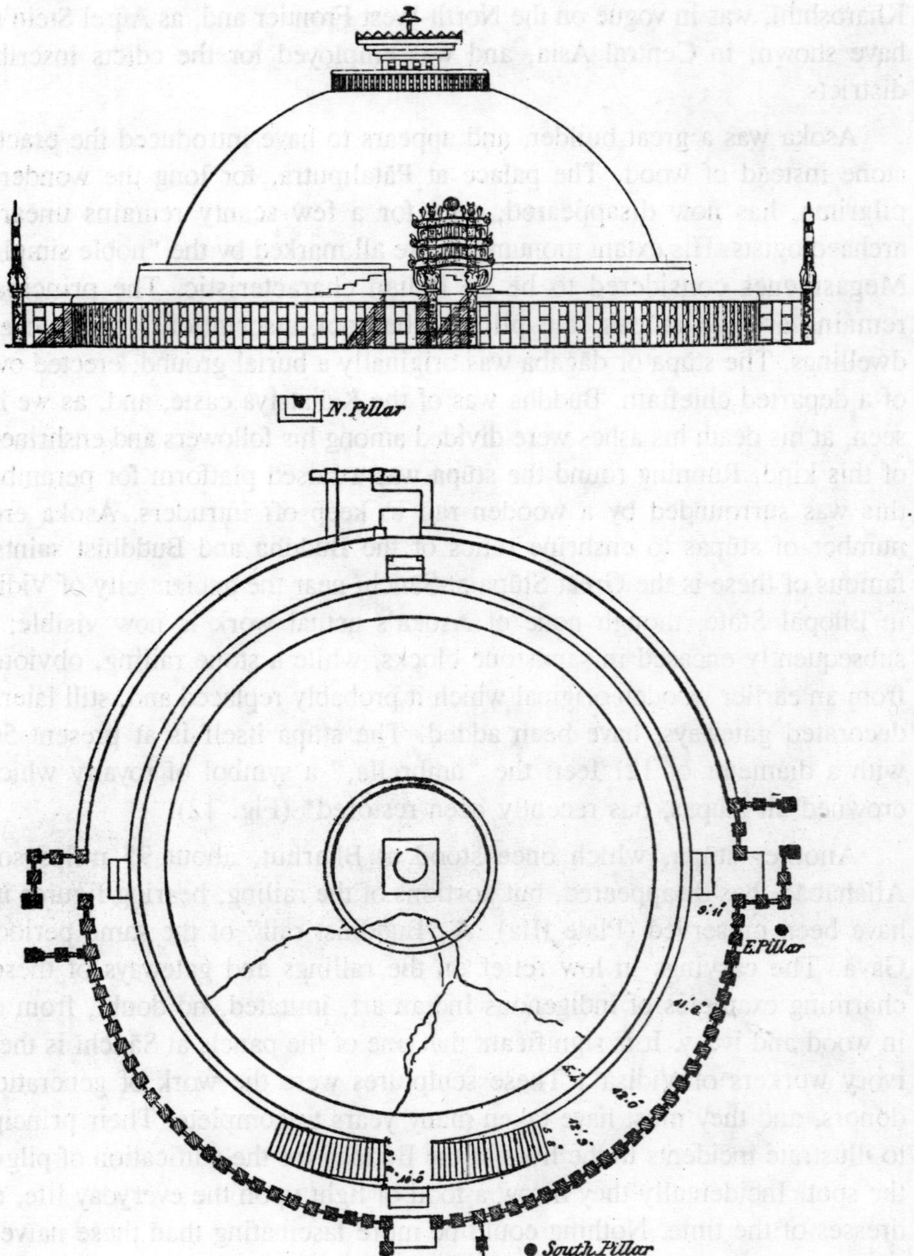

Fig. 12 Plan and Elevation of the Great Stūpa, Sānchī

delightful peeps into early India. "The main interest," it has been said, "is neither spiritual nor ethical, but altogether directed to human life; luxury and pleasure are represented, interrupted only by death, and these are nothing but practical facts, endorsed by the inherently sensual quality of the plastic language"* (Fig. 13, 14). The earliest and most primitive are the sculptures from Bharhut, and the work culminates in the gateways at Sānchī, with their realistically modelled elephants and the beautiful flying dryads of the brackets. These gateways were erected, as an inscription tell us, during the reign of an Āndhra king, perhaps in the first century B.C. (Plate IV).

Fig. 13 : Panel from Gateway, Sānchī Stūpa No.2. "Gift of the lute-player, Vadyuvāhanikaya."

Asoka's pillars fall into a different category. They were the work of royal workmen, and the Emperor took special delight in their erection to mark spots which he wished to commemorate. They are huge tapering monoliths of hard sandstone, forty or fifty feet in height, and must weigh at least fifty tons. We gain some idea of the skill of Asoka's engineers in moving these enormous columns from their quarry at Chunar to their destinations, when we read of the almost superhuman exertions required to shift two of them to Delhi and to erect them there about fifteen hundred years later. Thousands of workmen were employed, and elaborate carriages, boats and elevating apparatus had to be constructed. These pillars are burnished till the surface is almost like glass, and their high polish so deceived later travellers that they thought they were made of metal. They were surmounted with a bell-capital, an abacus and a symbolic figure, usually a lion. The most striking of these capitals is the one found at Sārnāth, with its four magnificent lions upholding a *dharma chakra* or "Wheel of the Law", which was first set in motion at this spot. The abacus is decorated with realistic figures of bulls and horses in bas-relief. Sir John Marshall speaks with profound admiration of "the masterful strength of the crowning lions, with their swelling veins and tense muscular development," and goes

* A.K. Coomraswamy, *Indian and Indonesian Art* (1927), p. 27.

so far as to declare that both bell and capital are "masterpieces in point of both style and technique—the finest carvings, indeed, that India has yet produced, and unsurpassed by anything of the kind in the ancient world." (Plate IIIb.)

The Indian monastic communities were in the habit of retiring, during the rainy season, to a permanent abode for rest and meditation. This led to the excavation of vihāras or monasteries from the hillside for their accommodation. The earliest of which we know was the group constructed by Asoka and his grandson Dasaratha for the Ajīvika sect in the side of the Barābar hills near Gayā. These are tunnelled out of very hard gneiss, and the walls are brilliantly polished. The whole undertaking must have involved skilled labour of the highest quality. The doorway and façade of one of them, known as the Lomas Rishi cave, with its horseshoe arch and ribbed porch, clearly betrays it to be a copy from a wooden model, probably the earlier

Fig. 14 : Domestic Scene, Sānchī Stūpa

wooden hermitages in which the monks were housed. Of the other works of art of Asoka's time, mention must be made of certain colossal stone statues in the round, which have been discovered at Parkham near Mathurā, Besnagar and Patna.* Specimens of jewelry, and of reliquaries in steatite and rock crystal, show that the Mauryan workman was equally proficient in the minor arts as in sculpture and architecture.

* These may belong to an earlier period. See V.A. Smith *Early History of India*, 4th Edn., p. 34, *note* 2.

Although the Mauryan Emperors were so closely associated with their Greek contemporaries in Asia Minor, there is scarcely a trace of Greek influence in their art or culture. Persian influence, on the other hand, is marked. It was to the stately civilisation of their Iranian kinsmen and neighbours that Indians turned for an example. Chandragupta in his youth visited Taxila, the capital of the Persian Satrapy, and Greek travellers naturally compared his court, with its elaborate ceremonial, to that of Susa or Ecbatana. It was from Persia that Asoka borrowed his sermons in stone; and their similarity in tone to that of the valedictory address of Darius at Naksh-i-Rustam has been noted. The idea of excavating rock-hewn vihāras may have been suggested by the tombs of the Achaemenian kings. Asoka's columns with their bell-capitals show clearly their Persepolitan origin. But whatever India borrowed she assimilated and made her own, and Indian art, in the Mauryan and subsequent periods, reached a standard of technical and artistic perfection unsurpassed, save perhaps in Athens, anywhere in the ancient world up to that time.*

LEADING DATES: THE EMPIRE OF MAGADHA

(1) *Saisunāga Dynasty (650-413 B.C.)*

B.C. *c.* 642	Sisunāga.
540-490	Bimbisāra.
490-459	Ajātasatru.
458-435	Darsaka.
435-413	Udaya.

(2) *Nanda Dynasty*
(Nine rulers *c.* 413-322 B.C.)

(3) *The Maurya Dynasty (322-185 B.C.)*

B.C. 322	Accession of Chandragupta Maurya.
305	Invasion of India by Seleucus Nicator.
302	Megasthenes comes as ambassador to Pātaliputra.
298	Death or abdication of Chandragupta: accession of Bindusāra.
273	Accession of Asoka.
269	Coronation of Asoka.
261	Kalinga War: Asoka's conversion to Buddhism.
259	Despatch of Buddhist missionaries.
257-6	Publication of the Rock Edicts and Kalinga Edict.
250	Mission to Ceylon.
240	Council of Pātaliputra.
232	Death of Asoka: accession of Dasaratha.
185	Death of Brihadratha, the last Mauryan ruler.

* For Persian influence on Mauryan culture, see D.B. Spooner, *The Zoroastrian Period of Indian History*, J.R.A.S., 1915.

(4) *Sunga Dynasty (185-73 B.C.)*

B.C. 185 Pushyamitra. Brahmanical reaction.
175 Invasion of Magadha by Menander.
73 End of dynasty.

(5) *Kānva Dyunasty (73-28 B.C.)*

B.C. 28 Overthrow of the Kānva dynasty by the Āndhras of the Deccan.

Chapter VI

The Second Contact with the West : The Rise of Mahāyāna Buddhism

The break-up of the Empire of Magadha had the usual repercussions on the North-Western frontier. The control of the central power being relaxed, insurgent tribes begun once more to pour through the passes into the Punjab, and the Land of the Five Rivers again becomes the chief centre of activity. In 250 B.C., while Asoka was still reigning in Pātaliputra, two important events occurred in the West. Almost simultaneously, Diodotus, the governor of the Greek colony at Bactra or Balkh, and a chieftain named Arsaces in Parthia, south-east of the Caspian Sea, threw off the yoke of the Seleucids and set up independent kingdoms. Subsequently the Greek rulers of Bactria crossed the Indian frontier and occupied Gandhāra. At first they issued coins of a purely Greek character, some of which may be ranked among the finest specimens of the coiner's art in the ancient world. The noble portraits of Dometrius (*c*. 190 B.C.) wearing his elephant-head headdress, and Eucratides (*c*. 175 B.C.) in a *kausia* or sun-helmet of a singularly modern pattern, are especially notable. As time went on, however, they became more and more Indianised. They issued coins square in shape, and bearing on the reverse legends in Brāhmī or Kharoshthī characters. It was these bilingual coin-legends which gave Prinsep the clue to deciphering the Asoka inscriptions. The only surviving monument of the Indo-Greek dynasties is a pillar, once surmounted by a Garuda, a mythological bird, the *vāhan* or vehicle of the god Vishnu, which was discovered at Besnagar in the extreme south of the Gwalior State in 1909. It bears the following inscription in Brāhmī characters:

> "The Garuda-column of Vāsudeva (Vishnu), the god of gods, was erected here by Heliodorus, a worshipper of Vishnu, the son of Dion, and an inhabitant of Taxila, who came as a Greek ambassador from the Great King Antialcidas to King Kasiputra Bhagabhadra, the Saviour, then reigning prosperously in the fourteenth year of his kingship."

This inscription is full of interest; it shows that by this time the Greeks born in India had become so completely Indian that they were actually received into the fold of the Hindu religion. The greatest of the Indo-Greek kings of the Punjab was Menander and we are fortunate to know more about him than any of his contemporaries, owing to the fact that he was converted to Buddhism by the Buddhist doctor Nāgasena, and his conversion is made the subject of a famous dialogue, *The Questions of Milinda*. From it we learn that Menander was born at the village of Kalasi, not far from "Alasanda of the Yonas" (Alexandria under Caucasus). His capital was at Sāgala, the modern Siālkot, which is described in glowing terms :

> "There is in the country of the Yonakas a great centre of trade, a city that is called Sāgala, situated in a delightful country well watered and hilly, abounding in parks, gardens, groves and lakes and tanks, a paradise of rivers and mountains and woods. Wise architects have laid it out, and its people know of no oppression, since all their enemies and adversaries have been put down. Brave is its defence, with many and various strong towers and ramparts, with superb gates and entrance archways, and with the royal citadel in its midst, white-walled and deeply moated. Well laid out are its streets, squares, cross-roads and market-places. Well displayed are the innumerable sorts of costly merchandise with which its shops are filled. It is richly adorned with hundreds of almshalls of various kinds and splendid with hundreds of thousands of magnificent mansions, which rise aloft like the mountain-peaks of the Himalayas. It streets are filled with elephants, horses, carriages, and foot-passengers, and crowded by men of all sorts and conditions – Brahmins, nobles, artificers, and servants. They resound with cries of welcome to the teachers of every creed, and the city is the resort of the leading men of each of the different sects. Shops are there for the sale of Benares muslin, of Kotumbara stuffs, and of other cloths of various kinds; and sweet odours are exhaled from the bazaars, where all sorts of flowers and perfumes are tastefully set out. Jewels are there in plenty, and guilds of traders in all sorts of finery display their goods in the bazaars which face al quarters of the sky."*

Menander himself was a scholar as well as a soldier. "As a disputant he was hard to equal, harder still to overcome; the acknowledged superior of all the founders of the various schools of thought. As in wisdom, so in strength of body, swiftness, and valour, there was found none equal to Milinda in all India. He was rich too, mighty in wealth and prosperity, and the number of his armed hosts knew no end." He was wont to relieve the cares of state by holding philosophical arguments with learned Brahmins and others, of whom he invariably got the better. In the end,

* *Sacred Books of the East,* vol. XXV, pp. 2, 3. It is possible that memories of Menander and Sāgala inspired the wonderful descriptions of the royal city of Kusāvati and its king, Mahā-Sudassana, "a king of kings, a righteous man who ruled in righteousness, an anointed Kshatriya," in the *Mahā Sudassana Sutta* (*Sacred Books of the East,* vol. XI). Such stock descriptions of the Ideal City are, however, not uncommon in Buddhist and Jain literature

however, the sage Nāgasena visited the city with his disciples, "lighting up the city with their yellow robes like lamps, and bringing down upon it the breezes from the heights where the sages dwell." Menander, accompanied by five hundred courtiers, went to interview Nāgasena. In the arguments which follow, the Buddhist doctrine of the impermanence of the Ego is expounded, and Menander is converted. An interesting feature of the *Questions of Milinda* is the Socratic method of dialectic employed by Nāgasena, which gives it the air of a Platonic dialogue.

Menander was a great warrior, and made an attempt to conquer the kingdom of Magadha, now very much shrunk from its former size and greatness. The Yavana horsemen overran the Middle Country, and all but succeeded in capturing the sacred horse, which the Sunga King Pushyamitra had released to wander over the country in preparation for the horse sacrifice,† but the Greeks were recalled by troubles which broke out in their own country and retired. Menander's date is probably 180-160 B.C. He issued some fine coins, one of which bears the Buddhist Wheel of the Law. According to one legend, he was regarded as an *arhat* or saint, and after his cremation his ashes were distributed as relics, like those of the Buddha. The Greek rulers of the Punjab were in the end overwhelmed by invading Saka tribes from Central Asia. These Sakas or Scythians, who had long been a menace to the Persians, pushed southwards by other tribal movements from the north-east, overflowed the Greek kingdom of Bactria, and occupied the valley of the Helmand, which is still known as Seistan (Sakastan). Entering the Punjab, probably by the Bolān pass, they gradually superseded the local Greek rulers. They set up principalities at Mathurā, Taxila and other centres. The use of the Persian titles Satrap and Great King of Kings, suggests that they were feudatories of the Parthian King Mithradates the Great (123-88 B.C.) whose rule extended almost as far as the Indus. The Parthians played an important part as intermediaries between Greek and Indian culture, as the excavations of the Parthian city of Sirkap in the Taxila area clearly show. One of the Indo-Parthian or Saka princes of Taxila, known to the Greeks as Gondopharnes, is of especial interest to us because, according to the apocryphal *Acts of Thomas*, the Apostle Thomas came to his court to preach Christianity. There was formerly a great deal of doubt whether Saint Thomas ever visited India, but recent researches tend to prove that the legend is founded on historical fact. Bartholomew and Thomas were sent to preach the gospel in the East. Thomas probably reached Taxila by the well-known sea-route from Alexandria to the mouth of the Indus. He was hospitably received at the court of Gondopharnes, for Taxila was a cosmopolitan centre of culture and accustomed to

---

† For Pushyamitra, see p. 80. The horse-sacrifice was offered by a king who claimed the title of *chakrawartin*, or universal monarch. To capture the horse was to challenge this. Pushyamitra, doubtless, revived the custom in order to celebrate the return of Magadha to orthodox Brahmanism.

give a ready hearing to teachers from strange countries. His missionary labours were, however, interrupted by the Kushān invasion, and Thomas was compelled to flee. He retraced his steps to the mouth of the Indus, and thence took boat to Muziris, the Roman colony on the Malabar coast, touching at Socotra on the way. Here he arrived in A.D. 52 and founded the Church in Malabar. Twenty years later he transferred his labours to the East Coast, and was martyred by the Brahmins. His relics repose in the Cathedral dedicated to him at Mylapore near Madras.* Gondopharnes is a corruption of the Persian Vindapharna, Bringer of Victory. In the Armenian version of the story, this becomes Gathaspar, from which is derived Gaspar, the name given to the second of the Magi who visited the cradle of the infant Jesus. A powerful Saka dynasty also sprang up about this time at Ujjain. Its rulers, Rudradāman, Rudrasena, etc., were known as Great Satraps, and assumed Hindu names. Their kingdom comprised Mālwā, Kathiāwār, Kacch,and Gujarāt, and they intermarried with the Āndhra rulers of the Deccan. This dynasty maintained its position until A.D. 388 when it was overthrown by the Gupta Emperor Chandragupta II. Another Saka dynasty, known as the Kshaharātās, ruled for a short time at Nāsik in the Konkan, until it was absorbed by the Āndhras.

Meanwhile a nomadic horde, known as the Yueh-chi or Tkharians, was displaced by the Huns from the territory between Kansu and the Great Wall, in 174 B.C.† They moved westwards, entering the territory between the Jaxartes and the Oxus, and driving the Sakas before them. In 126 B.C. fresh tribal movements from the north compelled them to travel southwards, and they occupied Bactria. Here they settled down the lost their nomadic character. In A.D. 48, a section of the Yueh-chi, the Kushāns, finding Bactria too cramped, broke off from the main body, and under a chieftain named Kadphises or Kadapha, entered Gandhāra, and overthrew the last Greek monarch, Hermaeus. The Kushāns gradually reduced to subjection the various petty Greek, Parthian and Saka kingdoms, and built up an extensive empire, including the Punjab and Sind, Northern Gujarāt and part of Central India. Kadphises tried to extend his influence northwards over the Pāmirs, the ancestral home of his clan, but an expedition sent for this purpose was disastrously defeated by the Chinese. Subsequently, the Kushāns greatly expanded their territories to the east, and it is thought that the so-called Saka era of A.D. 78 commemorates the conquest of Northern India by a monarch known to historians as Kadphises II.

The greatest of the Kushān rulers, and the only one of whom we have any personal knowledge, is Kanishka. His date, like that of all the Kushān rulers, has been the subject of a lively controversy, but he probably ruled from A.D. 120 to 162. His

* J. N. Farquhar, "The Apostle Thomas in Southern India." *John Rylands Library Bulletin*, 1927, p. 20.

† P. Masson-Oursel, *Ancient India and Indian Civilization* (1934), p. 43.

capital was at Purushapura or Peshāwar, and soon after his accession he sent a great military expedition which annexed Kashmir and a part of Chinese Turkestan, including Kashgar, Yarkhand and Khotan. It is said that Kanishka compelled the Chinese authorities to surrender hostages, who dwelt for some years at the Emperor's capital, where they were granted special quarters and other privileges. The Kushāns, like the Moguls, looked upon Central Asia, and not India, as their homeland. Like all Central Asian folk, they detested the heat of the Indian plains, and retired to Kashmir or Afghanistan for the hot weather.

The coins, as well as some remarkable statues dug up at Mat near Mathurā, give us a clear picture of these monarchs. They were big, burly men with long beards and prominent features : they dressed in long, padded coats and wore riding-boots and spurs.

To what extent Kanishka's empire extended eastwards is uncertain. The Saka Satraps of Ujjain were apparently his feudatories, and it must have included most of the territory west of the Ganges as far south as the Narbadā river. Kanishka assumes the titles of *Shāonānoshāo*, or King of Kings, *βασίλευς, Καῖσαe,* and *devaputra,* the last being the Chinese *t'ien tzu,* Son of Heaven; and his coins reveal that he ruled over a veritable *colluvies gentium,* Indo-Greek, Zoroastrian, Buddhist and Hindu, who were settled in Gandhāra, the meeting-place of the Central Asian trade-routes. The language of the Kushāns was apparently Tokhāri, which they wrote in modified Greek characters.

The Kushāns were on excellent terms with Rome. In the first century A.D. the boundaries of the two empires were less than 600 miles apart, and the Romans were anxious to cultivate their friendship, hoping to capture the silk trade with China from their rivals, the Parthians. When Trajan became Emperor in A.D. 99 a Kushān monarch (probably Kadphises II) sent an embassy to Rome to congratulate him. The ambassadors had a flattering reception, and were given the high compliment of senators' seats in the theatre. The Kushān rulers struck gold coins in imitation of those of the Roman Emperors, of the same weight and fineness as the Roman *aureus.** They kept us a brisk trade with the Roman colonies in Asia Minor, which went on almost uninterruptedly for the next two centuries: the goods went partly by the overland route through Balkh, and partly by sea from the port of Barygaza (Broach, at mouth of Narbadā River). From Barygaza travellers would to go the head of the Persian Gulf, up the Euphrates to Thapsacus and then across the desert to Antioch. A caravan route, running through the famous city of Palmyra (Tadmor in the

* The Roman *aureus* was current all over the East. A well-known story is related by the travellers Kosmas Indikopleustes (6th century A.D.) of a Persian and Roman who met at the court of a Sinhalese monarch. The Persian talked volubly of the greatness of his country. The Roman merely produced an *aureus* and bade the king compare it with a Persian *drachma*.

Wilderness) connected Antioch with the prot of Berenice on the Red Sea. An Alexandrian sea-captain who visited the Indian coast about A.D. 80 wrote an interesting guide-book entitled *Periplus Maris Erythraei,* in which he speaks of the immense volume of trade in condiments, spieces, unguents and silks which left the ports of Gujarāt and Sind, in exchange for Roman *aurei*, Greek wines and "choice girls for the royal harems." Syrian and Alexandrian travellers and merchants must have been a common sight on the coast and at towns like Broach, Ujjain and Peshāwar. "Videtis gentes populosque mutasse seds," says Seneca. "Quid sibi volunt in mediis barbarorum regionibus Graecae artes? Quid inter Indos Persasque Macedonicus sermo? Atheniensis in Asia turba est."* Among these perhaps may be reckoned the famous miracle-monger, Apollonius of Tyana, who is supposed to have paid a visit to Taxila, of which his biographer gives a romantic description, in the first century A.D.

The most important event of Kanishka's reign was his conversion of Buddhism. Buddhism made a stronger appeal to the chieftains from beyond the border than Hinduism, with its innumerable and vexatious caste-restrictions and, according to a well-authenticated story, Kanishka was converted by Asvaghosha, a learned Brahmin from Ayodhya, who had himself become a Buddhist convert. Asvaghosha was one of the many scholars from distant parts of India who flocked to Kanishka's court, and made Peshawar a renowned centre of Buddhist culture. He was extremely versatile, a philosopher, writer, dramatist and musician, and did much to reconcile Buddhism and Hinduism by writing on Buddhist themes in polished Sanskrit. He was the author of one of the earliest Indian dramas of which we know, a Buddhist play in nine acts dealing with the conversion of the saints Sāriputra and Maudgalyayana, two of the Buddha's earliest disciples, at Rājagriha, fragments of which were recently discovered at Turfān in Central Asia. He was also the author of the *Buddha Charita,* a poetical history of the Buddha containing highly ornate passages of great beauty, which are among the first examples of the Kāvya or artificial epic, and were imitated by later writers like Kālidāsa.

Kanishka was duly instructed in the mysteries of his new faith by his preceptor and was puzzled by the numerous Buddhist sects and their conflicting interpretations of the scriptures. In imitation, therefore, of his predecessor Asoka, on whom he appears to have modelled himself, he determined to call a Council to settle these difficulties. This, the fourth and last General Council of the Buddhist Church, met at Kundalavana Monastery in Kashmir, and was attended by 500 monks from all parts of India, but not, however, Ceylon, under the presidency of the learned Pārsva. Other celebrated scholars, including Asvaghosha, Visvamitra and Nāgārjuna, took part in its deliberations. The Council sat for six months. Elaborate commentaries on the

* *De consolatione ad Helviam,* Ch. VI.

scriptures were drawn up, and a Buddhist encyclopedia, the *Mahā vibhāsa*, was compiled. Eventually, as the Chinese traveller Hiuen Tsang informs us, "Kanishka rājā ordered these discourses to be engraven on sheets of red copper. He enclosed them in a stone receptacle and, having sealed them, he raised over it a stūpa with the scriptures in the middle." Here they probably still remain, awaiting the fortunate archaeologist who has the good luck to unearth them.

Kanishka's Council at Kashmir marks the beginning of a new epoch in the history of Buddhism. This was the rise of the Mahāyāna or Northern Church, which differs as much from the primitive Buddhism of the Hīnayāna, or Little Vehicle of the South, as Medieval Catholicism does from the simple creed of the Christians of the first century. The change was partly due to attempts of learned Brahmin converts like Asvaghosha to reconcile Buddhism with Hinduism. But it was due still more to the fact that in North-Western India a number of new influences—Greek, Christian, Zoroastrian and Central Asia—had crept in.When Buddhism became the religion of the foreign invaders from the northern steppes, it entirely lost its original character. Buddha ceased altogether to be a dead teacher, and became a living Saviour God, incarnate, like Rāma or Krishna, for the salvation of the human race. The theory of Avatars or incarnations, which was being applied to Vaishnava Hinduism and Jainism, was adopted by Buddhism. The historical Gautama was regarded as merely the latest of a series of incarnations of the Adi Buddha or Primeval Spirit, and fell more and more into the background. Parallel to the human Buddhas were the Dhyāni or Spiritual Buddhas, each with his own Paradise, and the Bodhisattvas—exalted beings who have reached Buddhahood, but who deliberately decline to enter into Nirvāna in order that they may devote themselves to saving mankind. These deities are now unknown except in sculptures in the land of their birth, but have survived in China and Japan, and their scriptures have mostly come down to us in translations made by Chinese scholars. The most important of the Dhyāni Buddhas is Amitābha or Āmida, "The God of Boundless Light," who has a large following in China and Japan. He dwells in a glorious "Western Paradise," which is the subject of many poetical descriptions, and there he will remain until the whole human race has found salvation through faith in him. Salvation by faith in the religion of the Amidists takes the place of the austere doctrine of salvation by works preached by Gautāma, which is admitted to be altogether impracticable for the ordinary man of the world. The believer who takes in faith the name of Āmida will be born again in the Western Paradise, and will there under more propitious conditions reach the enlightenment unattainable on earth. Among the Bodhisattvas, the most important are Avalokitesvara, "the God who looks down," Manjusri, and Maitreya, the coming Buddha who is yet to be born. Of the Mahāyāna Scriptures, the most noteworthy is the *Saddharma Pundarīka* or Lotus of the Good Law, of about A.D. 200. In this Buddha declares that he is "repeatedly born into the world of the living," and says :

"I am the Father of the world, the Self-born, the Healer, the Protector of all creatures. Knowing them to be perverted, infatuated and ignorant, I teach final rest, myself not being at rest."

To what extent Buddhism and Christianity mutually reacted upon one another in the first two centuries after Christ affords interesting matter for speculation. Reference has already been made to the intimate intercourse between India and Western Asia, and at Alexandria, the great meeting-place of Eastern and Western thought, Indian scholars were a common sight. The *Questions of Milinda* talks of a voyage to Alexandria as an ordinary occurrence, especially for Buddhists, who were not bound by the caste restrictions of Hinduism. Dio Chrysostom (*c.* A.D. 100) speaks of Bactrian, Scythian and Indian residents in Alexandria. Clement of Alexandria (*c.* A.D. 200) knows a great deal about Buddhism. "There are," he says, "some Indians who follow the precepts of Buddha (*Boῦττα)* whom by an exaggerated reverence they have exalted into a god." They believe in transmigration and worship "a kind of pyramid (stūpa) beneath which they believe the bones of some divinity lie buried." Plotinus the Neoplatonist, and Bardesanes and Basilides the Gnostic writers, all went to the East for instruction in philosophy. The resemblances between the Gnostic doctrines and Mahāyāna Buddhism are well-known, particularly those between the *Pistis Sophia* and the *Saddharma Pundrīka.* Many curious parallels between the birth-stories of Jesus Christ as related in the Gospels, and of Buddha as told in works like the *Lalita Vistara* and the *Buddha Charita,* have been observed, though it is impossible to say whether these themes were carried by Buddhists to Palestine, or by Christian Missionaries like St. Thomas to India.* The climax was reached in the 9th century A.D., when, in the famous romance of *Baalam and Josaphat,* by John of Damascus, the Buddha figures as a Christian prince.

Kanishka's empire, enriched as it was by the trade of Europe and Asia, was wealthy and prosperous to an almost unheard-of degree, and he was a liberal patron of art. His capital at Peshawar was embellished by many magnificent buildings. In particular he erected a lofty wooden tower, over six hundred feet in height, in order to shrine certain relics of the Buddha. It consisted of fourteen storeys, and was crowned by an iron pinnacle, surmounted with a number of copper-gilt umbrellas. This tower must have represented the transitional stage between the Indian dāgaba and the Chinese pagoda. Its sides were adorned with numerous images of the Buddha, and it was many times restored. It was still standing in the 6th century A.D., and foreign visitors to India regarded it as one of the wonders of the world. The site was excavated in 1908 and in the relic-chamber was found a small copper-gilt reliquary, not quite eight inches high, of a Greek pattern. On the lid are figures of the Buddha and two Bodhisattvas, while the casket itself is decorated with figures of Kanishka, Buddha,

* Rhys Davids, *Hibbert Lectures* (1881), p. 93; Max Müller, *Last Essays* (First Series), p. 251.

the Sun and Moon deities, and Amorini bearing garlands. An inscription in Kharoshthī proclaims to be the work of "Agesilaos, overseer of Kanishka's vihāra." (Fig. 15.) Near the tower stood a large monastery, which was munificently endowed by the emperor and was long looked upon as the leading seat of Buddhist learning in North-Western India. Remains of three separate cities have been excavated on the site of the ancient Taxila. Beneath the Bhir mound to the south was the old Hindu city visited by Alexander, where Asoka must have dwelt as viceroy. In the centre, on the spot now known as Sirkap, was the Bactrian and Parthian city, while to the north at Sirsukh was found the new capital built by the Kushāns. The site contains a Kushān palace, which appears to be of an Assyrian pattern, and on the neighbouring site of Jandial

Fig. 15 : Kanishka's Relic Casket.

a building has been discovered which has been identified as a Zoroastrian fire-temple. It has Ionic columns and pilasters. At Chu, a stūpa has been unearthed, which is decorated with some striking Buddha figures of the Gandhāra school.*

The Kushāns, being foreigners, felt none of the puritanical scruples of the early Buddhists against the portrayal of the Master in human form. These had already begun to vanish as Buddha came to be regarded as a god. For the purpose of embellishing their buildings, they employed Graeco-Roman craftsmen from Asia Minor, like the Agesilaos already mentioned, who probably found their way to Gandhāra through the Parthian Empire.† These sculptors evolved a hybrid school of art, in which the whole range of Imperial Roman imagery was used to portray events from the Buddha's life, and the Buddha himself repeated the type of an early Imperial toga statue. The most important centres of the Indo-Greek or Gandhāra School are at Jalālabād, Hadda and Bamiyān in Afghanistan, the Swāt Valley, and the Peshawar district. The earlier Gandhāra sculptures, both in relief and in the round, are usually of grey slate : these are more purely Greek in type than the later stucco examples. The Buddha, while usually retaining his essential characteristics, is stylistically Hellenic: his features are Greek rather than Indian, and he wears his monastic robe treated like classical drapery. Plate V, representing a Buddha from Takht-i-Bāhi, near Peshawar, *circa* A.D. 300, is a fine example of the later Gandhāra type. In some examples, representing him before his enlightenment, he appears standing or sitting in European fashion, with a moustache and jewellery, like an earthly prince. In the bas-reliefs, Corinthian capitals are introduced as *motifs,* and Zeus, Apollo and other Greek gods are adapted to suit Buddhist mythology. The Gandhāra school flourished, roughly speaking, between A.D. 100 and 300, the age of the Antonines, and it had many points of contact with Palmyra and other Hellenistic centres of culture in Asia Minor. The Guides' Mess at Hoti Mardān, and the museums at Lahore and many different cities of India and Europe contain numerous examples of these reliefs in the Indo-Greek manner, illustrating scenes from the life of the Buddha and other Jātaka stories. These, together with stone and plaster statues, must have been turned out in large numbers to decorate the stūpas and other religious edifices of the Kushān Kings.

The researches of the French archaeologists have established that a later school, which Sir John Marshall has named the Indo-Afghan school, distinct from Gandhāra but reviving its traditions, sprang up in Eastern Afghanistan, and reached its zenith at the time of the Han invasions in the sixth century A.D.

At the same time, a purely indigenous school of contemporary art, lineally descended from that of Bharhut and Sānchī, appears to have flourished at Mathurā,

* Sir J. Marshall, *Guide to Taxila* (1921).

† *The Western Aspects of Gandhara Sculpture,* by H. Buchthal, Proceedings of the British Academy, 1945.

Bhītā, Besnagar, and other centres. Mathurā was a place of particular importance, both religious and secular. Fa Hian, writing three centuries subsequently, says that it contained twenty Buddhist monasteries, with upwards of three thousand inmates. Excavations have also revealed the presence of a number of Jain vihāras. It was here that the worship of Krishna developed, and Ptolemy calls it *H Μόδουεα τῶν θεῶν*. It was probably a provincial capital, and at the neighbouring village of Mat stood a chapel of the Kushān Kings. Mathurā was a centre of intense artistic activity, and statues from its studios, carved in the characteristic local red sandstone, were exported to Srāvastī and Sārnāth, and many other sacred sites all over northern India. It was formerly the custom to attribute to foreign influence the innovation of making representations of the Buddha, Mahāvīra and the Hindu gods, but it is now generally agreed that this must be traced to the indigenous artist of Mathurā rather than to Gandhāra. The earliest known Buddha image of the Mathurā school is theh colossal statue in red sandstone found at Sārnāth, dedicated by the Friar Bāla in the year 3 of Kanishka. These statues revolutionised the artistic history of Northern India, as local artists began to imitate them, and a school deriving its inspiration from Mathurā gradually grew up. The Vedic religion was, it is true, aniconic, but the lower orders, whether Hindu or Buddhist, clung to their animistic beliefs, and had no doubt continued to make rude images in clay, terracotta, wood and other perishable materials of the godlings they worshipped—yakshas, nāgas, tree-spirits, the mother-goddess, the *lingam* and the *yoni*—uninterruptedly since the days of the Indus valley civilisation. The Buddha figure must have been produced simultaneously, probably early in the first century A.D., in Gandhāra and Mathurā, in response to a demand created by the internal development of the Buddhism which was common ground in both areas, in each case by local craftsmen, working in the local tradition.* Here something may be said of the chief characteristics of the classical Buddha figure. The Buddha is represented with the signs of physical perfection which distinguished him at birth—the curling hair, long ears, the protuberance (*usnisā*) on the skull, the mark (*urnā*) between the eyes, and the lucky signs on the palms and soles of the feet. He is seated in a yogic pose (*āsana*) on a lotus or 'diamond' throne, in the posture in which he received Illumination: the feature are calm and expressionless. Each gesture of the hands (*mudra*) has a special significance. His Buddhahood is symbolised by 'calling the earth to witness,' with the hand pointing downwards. Preaching is signified by the hands 'turning the Wheel of the Law'; meditation by the hands folded in the lap. The right hand is raised in the attitude of 'warding off fear' (*abhaya mudra*), and the first and middle fingers are joined to denote discourse. The Buddha wears

---

* Coomaraswamy, *Indian Origin of the Buddha Figure* (Boston, 1928). A. Foucher, *Beginnings of Buddhist Art* (1917), p. 113. It is interesting to note that one of Kanishka's gold coins bears a standing figure of Buddha with the inscription in *ΒΟΔΔΟ* Greek characters.

the monastic robe of the order: in some examples the right shoulder is bare. As time goes on, the folds of the robe became fainter and fainter, until the Buddha appears clothed in transparent drapery, every contour of the figure beneath showing clearly. Another feature of later Buddhist iconography is the nimbus or aureole, which appears to be of Iranian origin. Small and plain at first, it gradually increases in size and is edged with tongues of flame.

Kanishka's long and prosperous reign of nearly half a century came to an end in about A.D. 162. A strange legend is related of his death. It is said that the people grew weary of his insatiable ambition. "The king," they said, "is greedy, cruel and unreasonable: his campaigns and continued conquests have wearied the mass of his servants. He knows not how to be content, but wants to rule over the four quarters. The garrisons are stationed in distant frontiers, and our relatives are far from us. Such being the situation, we must agree among ourselves and get rid of him. After that we may be happy." As he was ill, they covered him with a quilt and smothered him.

He was succeeded by his sons Vasishka and Huvishka, who had probably been provincial viceroys during their father's lifetime. Huvishka's coins exhibit the same religious eclecticism as those of Kanishka. He was a patron of Buddhism and endowed a splendid Buddhist monastery at a city bearing his name in Kashmir. The lası Kushān king of whom we know anything is Vāsudeva; his Hindu name, and the fact that most of his inscriptions are found at Mathurā, suggest that he had been deprived of part of his realms by foreign conquerors, perhaps the Sassanians of Persia, who rose to power at the beginning of the third century A.D.

The Kushān period is one of the utmost importance in the history of Indian culture. During this period "nascent Christianity met full-grown Buddhism in the academies and markets of Asia and Egypt, while both religions were exposed to the influences of surrounding paganism in many forms, and of the countless works of art which gave expression to the forms of polytheism. The ancient religion of Persia contributed to the ferment of human thought, excited by improved facilities for international communication and by the incessant clash of rival civilisatins."* Buddhism itself was transformed from a highly individualistic philosophy of life into a world religion, and spread along the Central Asia trade routes, through Khotan, were India and China meet, to China itself. It was a time of intense artistic and literary activity. Buddha and the Hindu deities appear for the first time in human guise, and Indian art, by virtue of its contact with Hellenistic Asia, acquires a fresh impetus. New literary forms come to light: the drama and the court epic make their appearance and classical Sanskrit is evolved. The Kushān period is a fitting prelude to the Age of the Guptas.

* V.A. Smith, *Oxford History of India* (1922), p. 134.

LEADING DATES

(Approximate)

B.C. 250	Revolt of Bactria and Parthia.
200	Greek Kings from Bactria invade the Punjab: Demetrius, Eucratides, Pantaleon, Agathocles, etc.
174	Migration of Yueh-chi from China.
180-60	Menander, Greek King of Siālkot.
130-58	The Sakas expel the Greeks from Bactria : Saka rulers in the Punjab, Maues, Azes, etc. Great Satrap dynasty at Ujjain.
58-7	The Vikrama Era commences.
A.D. 20-48	Gondophernes, Indo-Parthian ruler of the Punjab, reigning at Taxila.
48	Kadphises I. Kushān, conquers the Punjab.
77-8	Death of Kadphises I: accession of Kadphises II.
78	Saka Era commences.
120	Accession of Kanishka.
162	Death of Kanishka: accession of Huvishka.
182	Death of Huvishka: accession of Vāsudeva.
220	Death of Vāsudeva: break-up of the Kushān Empire.

Chapter VII

History of Kushāṇa

General

The rule of Kushāṇa kings in India marks and important epoch in Indian history. For the first time, after the fall of the Mauryas, there was a vast empire which not only embraced the whole of North India, but alsoo considerable territories outside it, as far as Central Asia. It stretched from Bactria to Magadhah and from Kashmiri to Saurashtra, under Wema Kadphises and his successors. India was thus brought into close contact with the outside world. The Kushāṇa kings were great patrons of art and architecture. Two of the most important schools of Indian art—the Gandhāra School and Mathurā School—flourished and reached new heights of glory, in the domain of Indian art.

Historical background

About the fourth century B.C., north-west India and the Punjab was divided into a number of small states.[1] The kingdom of Magadha extended upto the Punjab. It was then ruled by the king Nanda.[2] In 326 B.C. Alexander, king of Macedonia, invaded India and advanced upto river Beas.[3] He had, however, to retreat due to strong resistance offered by the various states.[4] While returning, Alexander placed, under the command of Philip, one of his officers, the conquered territory from lower Kabul valley upto the Hindukush, with its capital at Pushkalāvatī.[5] Philip was later murdered. About 322 B.C., Chandragupta Maurya after defeating Dhana Nanda, the king of Magadh, established himself as a powerful monarch of India.[6] Seleucus, a general of Alexander, advanced towards India to claim the territory conquered by Alexander, but had to cede the region beyond Hindukush to Chandragupta.[7] The Maurya empire thus covered a vast territory and included Kābul, Herāt and Gandhāra. The Mauryan dynasty ended[8] about 185 B.C. and was succeeded by the Śuṅgas. The Śuṅga dynasty collapsed about 75 B.c.[9] Thereafter, the north western India came under the rule of the Yavanas (Greeks), the Śakas (Scythians) and the Pahlavas (Parthians). About the middle of the first century, the Parthian rule was supplanted by that of the Kushāṇas.[10]

The Kushāṇas[11] belonged to nomadic tribe called the Yueh-chi. It is learnt from the Chinese historians that about 165 B.C., they lived in the land between Tun-huang country and K'i-lien range in Chinese Turkistān. There they were defeated and ousted from the land by a neighbouring tribe called the Hiung-nu, who killed the chief of the Yueh-chi horde and made a drinking a cup out of his skull. The widow of the slain king then assumed all powers and guided the tribe in the course of its westward migration. While the Yueh-chi were passing through the land to the north of Taklamakan desert, they came into conflict with a horde known as the Wu-sun. After having defeated the We-sun and slain their chieftain, the Yueh-chi marched on westward in search of suitable home. A small section of the people, however, went to south to settle on the Tibetan frontier and became known as the Little Yueh-chi. The main branch of the tribe, the Ta-Yueh-chi or great Yueh-chi, in the course of their westward migration, attacked the Śakas who dwelt in the plains, on the northern bank of the Jaxartes or Syr-Darya. The Śakas abandoned their territory ot the Yueh-chi and migrated into Ki-pin. Meanwhile, the son of the slain Wu-sun king grew upto manhood and drove the Yueh-chi further west into Ta-hia territory washed by the Oxus. M. Levi points out that the growth of this Wu-sun chief from infancy to manhood required time and the defeat of the Yueh-chi by him must have occurred in or about 140 B.C.[12] The Ta-hia, who were devoted to commerce and unskilled in war were quickly and easily reduced to condition of royal encampment, to the north of the Oxus, in the territory now belongong to Bukhārā. Theh Chinese envoy Chang-kien visited the Yueh-chi capital in that locality about 125 B.C.[13] The adventures of Chang-Kien as related by si-Ke (which work was completed before 91 B.C.) are retold in the annals of the first Han dynasty by Panku. The annals were completed after Panku's death by his sister in 92 A.D., with three important additions : (i) that the kingdom of the Ta-Yueh-chi has for its capital, the town of Kien-chi and Ki-pin lay on its southern frontier, (ii) that the Yueh-chi were no longer nomads, (iii) that the Yueh-chi kingdom had become divided into five principalities, viz., Hieou-mi (possibly Wakhān), Chouang-mi (possibly Hi-tun (Parwan on the Panjshir) and Kao-feu (Kābul)[14]. A further glimpse of the Yueh-chi is obtained from Fan-ye's Hou Han-shu or annals of the later Han dynasty which cover the period between 25 A.D. to 220 A.d. *Fan-ye,* who based his account on the report of the Pan-young (125 A.D.) and others[15] gives the following account of Yueh-chi's conquest after more than one hundred years of the division of the Ta-hia kingdom in the five principalities, the Yabgou (Savuga) of Kouei-chouang (Kushāṇa) named Kieou-tstieou-kio attacked and vanquished the four other Yabgous and called himself king (Wang), he invaded Ngan-si (the Arsakid territory i.e. Parthia) and took possession of the territory of Kao-fou (Kābul), overcame Po-ta and Ki-pin and became completely master of these kingdoms. K'ieou-tehen succeeded him as king. In his turn, he conquered Tien-tchou (India), and appointed a chief for governing it. From this time, the Yueh-chi became extremely powerful. All the other countries designated them Kushāṇa after their king but the Han retained the old name and called them Ta-Yueh-chi. Kieou-tsieou-kio has been identified with *Kujula Kadphises* or Kozola Kadaphes[16], the first Kushāṇa king who struck coins to the south of the Hindukush.

Kujula Kadphises or Kadphises I

According to Fan Ye's account, the reign of *Kadphises* I cannot be placed earlier than the first century. A copper coin of *Kujula Kadphises* with the representation of king's head proves that already under this king, the stream of Roman gold began to flow in it. According to whitehead's description, this coin is 'an unmistakable imitation of one of the early Roman emperors'.[17] Further, the *panjtar* inscription of the year 122 (65 A.D.) refers to a Gaushāna or Kushāṇa king. It is not clear whether this inscription relates to the period of Kadphises I or his son and successor. On this basis, however, it may be surmised that Kadphises I reigned roughly during the period from 15 A.D. to 65 A.D.[18]

Numismatic evidence suggests that he was an ally and afterwards the successor of *Kermaeus*, the last Greek prince of the *Kābul* valley. Dr. Bhandarkar observes that some coins bear on the obverse the name of the Greek prince, Hermaeus and on the reverse of Kujūla-Kapsa or Kasa without high sounding titles, while on the other coins the name of Hermaeus does not occur and from this he concludes that Kadphises was first subordinate to Hermaeus and later on acquired independence.[19] Sten Konow[20] thinks that when *Kujūla Kadphises* invaded *Ansi,* Hermaeus entered into alliance with him and perhaps actually supported him but the Kushāṇa ruler soon after ousted him from his kingdom, and the Chinese annals state that he seized *Kao-fu,* i.e. *Kābul*. To begin with he retained the bust of Hermaeus, but later on he abandonedit.[21] Tarn, however, considers that "joint issue" of Hermaeus and Kujūla Kadphises is impossible, that Kujūla Kadphises only imitated the coins because he was a relative of Hermaeus and at the same time hoped to get the *Greeks* who lived in the country to side with him against the *Parthians.*[22]

The coins of Kujūla Kadphises[23] have been found in large numbers in *Sirkap* (more than 2500 in all, including 412 of the 'Kadaphes' series) and it might be inferred that he added *Gandhāra* and *Taxilā* to his other conquests. It appears more likely that it was not Kujūla himself, but his son *Wema Kadphises* who annexed Taxilā and the rest of the Punjāb, if not Gandhāra. This would also accord with the testimony of the Hou-Han-Shu.

Wema Kadhpises or Kadphises II

Kadphises died at the old age on more than eighty and was succeeded by his son *Yen-Kao-tchen*, the Vima, Wima or *Wema Kadphises* of the coins, who is usually designated as *Kadphises II.*

It is said that Wema Kadphises 'again' conquered *T'ien-tchu*[24] and appointed a general there to carry on the administration. The description of the country given in the Hou-Han-Shu, however, points to the *Indus* country. The text runs : The kingdom of T'ien-tchu[25] is also called Shen-tu and is situated on the banks of a great river. The inhabitants mount on elephants in war, they are weaker than the *Yueh-chi*, they practise the religion of the *Buddha*. It has become a habit with them not to kill and not to fight. Parting from *Kao-fu*, which belongs to the Yueh-chi, and turning towards the south-west, one comes to the 'western sea', in the east one comes to the kingdom of *Pan-ki*, all these countries form part of *Shen-tu.* Shen-tu has several hundred other towns (besides the capital). At that time (i.e. probably when Pan-Young wrote towards A.D. 125) they were all dependent on *Yueh-chi,* the Yueh-chi had killed the king and installed a general on the throne to govern the population. Sten Konow observes that though this description is somewhat obscure, because it also mentions countries to the west and east, it seems clear that the country of Yen-Kao-Ichen or *Wema Kadphises* was situated on the *Indus.*[26]

According to Smith,[27] The hIndian dominions of *Kadphises II* certainly extended to the Ganges and probably at least as far south as *Benaras*. His empire extended westward to the frontiers of *Parthia* and included the whole of the countries now known as *Afghanistan,* Afghan Turkistān, *Bukhārā* and parts of Russian *Turkistān*.

According to Smith and Sten Konow, it was *Kadphises II* who established the *Saka* era of 78 A.D. There is, however, no inscription or coin of this monarch containing any data which is referable to an ear of his institution. On the other hand, there is evidence to show that *Kanishka* did establish an era and his method of dating was continued by his successors and we have dated ranging probably from the year 1 to 99. Ghosh[28] draws attention to some passages from the twelve texts translated by Maspero which state how *Emperor Ming* saw the Buddha in dream, after which he sent an embassy to India in order to gain information about Buddhims. The Chinese mission must have taken place between the years 61 A.D. and 75 A.D. Referring to this, Ghosh says[29] : The Ta-Yueh-chi king during that epoch was certainly not *Kanishka*. The edifying Buddhist texts would never have missed the chance of associating the honoured name of the Great emperor with the formal introduction of Buddhims in *China*. From this it appears that Kadphises II reigned about that time'.

Wema Kadphises was first to issue gold coins. He had a bilingual gold and copper coinage. His coins show, on the obverse, the king's head or figure, tilting or standing and commonly Śiva on reverse.[30] The Kharoshthi legend on the coins reads *Mahārājasarājādhirājasa sarvaloga iśvarsa mahiśvara Wema Kathphises tratarasa.*[31] Accordingn to Dr. Dhandarkar, Wema Kadphises was either a devotee of *Śiva* or belonged to the sect of Māheśvaras as appears from the emblem of Nandin on the reverse of his coins accompanied by a human figure holding a trident in its right arm representing Śiva.[32]

Kanishka

According to Sten Konow,[33] after the death of Wema Kadphises, disintegration of the Kushāṇa empire began to set in. Kanishka who belonged to the little *Yueh-chi*[34] tribe, however, invaded north-west India and strengthened the power of Kushāṇa. Dr. Smith[35] is of the opinion that *Kanishka* belonged to the Kushāṇa section of *Yueh-chi* nation as did the *Kadphises*. The chronological position of Kanishka has been a puzzle and some of the theories advanced by the scholars are : (i) Dr. Fleet thinks that Kanishka reigned before the Kadphises group, and was the founder of that reckoning commencing 58 B.C. which afterward came to be known as *Vikrama Samvat*. This has been controverted by Dr. Thomas and cannot be maintained.[36] Inscriptions, coins as well as the account of Huien Tsang clearly prove that Kanishka's dominions included *Gnadhāra*. According to Chinese evidence, however, Yin-mo-fu and not the Kushāṇas ruled Kipin (Kāpiśa Gandhāra) in the second half of the first century B.C. Moreover, Allan thinks that on the basis of gold coinage of Kanishka he can hardly be placed before *Titus* (79-81 A.D.) and *Trajan* (98-117 A.D.[37]). (ii) According to Marshall, Sten Konow and Smith, Kanishka's rule began about 125 to 144 A.D. and ended in the second half of the second century A.D. The *Sui Vihār* inscription indicates Kanishka's hold over a portion of at least of the lower Indus valley. It is learnt from *Junāgarh* inscription of *Rudradāman* that the *Mahākshatapa* also ruled over *Sindhu* and Sauvīra and he did not owe his position to anyone. If Kanishka reigned in the middle of the second century A.D., his dominions would not have included the lower Indus valley. Inscriptions discovered in India also indicate the dates of the Kushāṇa sovereigns as Kanishka I (1-23),[38] Vāsishka (24-28), Huvishka (28-26), Kanishka II son of *Vā-jheshka* (41) and *Vāsudeva* (67-98). Kanishka may, therefore, have originated an era. No era is, however, known in north-west India which commenced in the second century A.D. (iii) Dr. Majumdar believes that the era founded by Kanishka was the Traikuta-Kalahuri-cheri era of 248 A.D.[39] Prof. Jouveau-Dubrevil points out that this is not possible.

According to Fergusson, Oldenberg, Thomas, Banerji, Rapson and J.E. Van Lohuizen-De-Leeuw, Kanishka was the founder of that reckoning commencing 78 A.D., which came to be known as the Śaka ear.[40] The argument advanced against the opinion that Kanishka was the founder Śaka era, is that this era was not a northern one. This is not correct. The Śaka era was only temporarily superseded by the Gupta era and soon after the fall of the dynasty, the Śaka era was used again. If *Kanishka* was the founder of the era commencing from 78 A.D., he reigned during the period from the years 1-23, viz. 78 A.D.[41] to 101 or 102 A.D. The chronological position of Kanishka, however, remains uncertain.

Kanishka calls himself a Kushāṇa and his coins represent him as a powerfully built barbarian king, clad in the loose coat the huge boots, the common dress of

Turkistān.[42] The extent of his kingdom is incidentally shown by the private inscriptions of his subjects. The epigraphic records[43] give us contemporaneous notices to him with dates not only from *Mathurā* and from *Sāranāth* towards the east but also from *Sui Vihār* near *Bahāwalpur* on the north of Sind, from *Mānikiala* near *Rāwalpiṇḍī* in the *Punjāb* and from Yeda in Yusufzai country, beyond the Indus. Kanishka is credited with having completed in his earlier years the subjugation and annexation of the secluded vale of *Kashmir.*[44] He showed a marked preference for the delightful country, where he erected numerous monuments and founded a town. He carried his arms across the formidable passes of the *Karakoram* (Tsung-ling) mountains the might have penetrated as far eastward as *Kashgar,* or even *Khotān.*

The Chinese traveller, Yuvan chwang,[45] gives the following account: when Kanishka reigned in *Gandhāra,* his power reached the neighbouring states and his influences extended to distant regions. As he kept order by military rule over a wide territory reaching the east of the *Tsung-ling,* a tributory states of *China* to the west of Yellow river sent him the royal princes as hostages.

It appears that Kanishka came to power in the U.P. region and later on conquered the *Punjāb* and the North-Western Frontier Province and established his capital at *Purusapurā* or *Peshāwar.* Evidently he was originally a governor of *Wema Kadphises* and declared his independence in 78 A.D.,[46] when another governor became independent about that time in *Taxilā.*

Tibetan sources state[47] that king Kanishka led an army into India and overthrew the king of Soked, i.e. Sāketa or *Ayodhyā.* The Chinese translation of Kumāralāta's *Kalpanā-mandilika,* which was composed shortly after the reign of Kanishka states that "in the family of *Kiu-sha,* there was a king called *Chen-ttan-kia-ni-toha* (devaputra Kanishka). He conquered *Tung-tien-tohou* (Eastern India) and pacified the country.[48]" Eastern India, in the Buddhist annals, signified the region to the east or *Ku-chu-wen-ki-lo* of *Kajangola* near the *Rājmahal* hills in the eastern *Bihar.*[49]

From the epigraphic records, it is found that the present U.P.,[50] *Punjāb,* North Western Frontier Province, Northern Sind were included within his empire. The Sānchī Museum inscription of the year 22 shows that in the South his sway extended as far as the *Mālwā* region where his son, *Vāsiska,* acted as one of his viceroys. From the *Si-yu-ki,* it appears that *Kashmir* was also a part of his kingdom, and, the scene of his religious activities. Levi thinks that the sway of Kanishka also extended over the north-western part of the Deccan. Kanishka's empire was a vast one. In the north, it extended as far as *Bokhara,* in the south to *Ujjain* and in the east as far as *Mathurā* (eastern U.P.)[51]

Numismatic evidence and the testimony of the Peshawar Casket inscriptions show that he actually became a convert to Buddhism possibly at the commencement of his reign. To discuss[52] the various aspects of Buddhism, Kanishka called the last great

Buddhist council which was held probably in Kashmir. Its deliberations were guided by *Vasumitra* and *Aśvaghosha*. The members, 500 in number, devoted themselves to a thorough examination of the theological literature, from the most remote antiquity and elaborated huge divisions of the canon, i.e. *Tripiṭaka*. The works so proposed and prepared included the *Mahāvibhāśa* which still exists in Chinese. When the labours of the council were completed, the commentaries were copied on the sheets of copper, which were deposited in a stūpa built for this purpose by order of King Kanisha.[53] This council gave a new impetus to the development of Buddhism. Sanskrit was adopted as the medium through which the initiated were instructed. The Council seems to have regularised and systematised many of the changes that were in progress long before Kanishka. The changes in the creed found concrete expession in the Buddhist art of his time. Inspite of his devotion to Buddhism, Kanishka honoured the numerous gods worshipped in the different parts of his vast empire. On his coins, the figures of Hindu, Greek, Mithraio, Zorastrian and Elamite gods[54] are found.

Kanishka was a great builder of stūpas and cities. He erected in the capital town a monastery and a huge wooden tower in which he placed some relics of the Buddha.[55]

One of the topes found at *Mānikiāla* contained an inscription and is dated in the eighteenth year of Kanishka.[56] On opening it, a square chamber was f ound at a height of 10 feet above the ground level. In this was a gold cylinder enclosed in one of silver and the again one is copper. The inner one contained four gold coins, ten precious stones and four pearls. These were, no doubt, relics which the tope was intended to preserve.

The court of Kanishka was adorned by the celebrated Buddhist teachers Pārśva and Vasumitra, the great Buddhist poet and philosopher, Aśvaghosa, the well-known philosopher Nāgārjuna, and the immortal authority on Āyurveda, Charaka.[57]

Kanishka ruled his vast empire through subordinate rulers enjoying the status of satraps and great satraps. The Sarnath Buddhist image inscription dated in third regnal year of Kanishka (A.d.81) records the installation of Friar Bala's image of the Bodhisattva at Benaras by Mahāshatrapa Kharapallana and Kshatrapa Vanaspara. The northern-most part of India was also administered by satraps, as indicated by several Kharoshthi inscriptions.

An extensive gallery of gods and goddesses with their Greek, Indian and Persian names adorn the coins of Kanishka. Among them mention may be made of Śiva, Buddha, the Wind god, the Fire god, the Moon god, the Sun god, the Elmite or Sumerian mother-goddess Nana, Nanaia, the war god, Orlagno, the Greek Sun god, Helios. On the obverse of some of the coins, Kanishka is shown as standing, wearing peaked helmet, long heavy coat and trousers. Some of the coins have also the legend Shāonānoshāo Kanīshki Koshāno of the king of kings, Kanishka, the Kushāṇa.[58]

A strange legend is related about his death. It is said that the people grew weary of his insatible ambition. 'The king;, they said, "is greedy, cruel and unreasonable. His campaigns and continued conquest have wearied the mass of his servants. He knows not how to be content, but wants to reign over the four quarters. The garrisons are stationed in distant frontiers, and our relatives are far from us. Such being the situation, we must agree amongst ourselves and get rid of him. After that we may be happy". As he was ill, they covered him with a quilt and smothered him, and he died. The reign of Kanishka appears to have terminated about A.D. 101 or 102.

Vāsishka

Kanishka was probably succeeded by Vāsishka. He may have been identical with Vājheshka, the father of Kanishka of the Ārā inscription, and Jushka of the *Rājatarangini*, the founer of *Jushkapur,* modern Zukur to the north of Śrīnagar. It appears from the inscriptions that he ruled over Mathurā and eastern Mālwā. A Brāhmī inscription of the year 28 engraved on the pedestal of a Bodhisattva image, now in the Sānchī Museum, refers to the erection of a shrine and the establishment of an image of Buddha in the Dharmadeva monastery by one Madurika, the daughter of Veera, during the reign of the *Mahārajā rājālirāja devaputra Shahi Vasashka.* This proves that he held sway in the Sānchī region also. His dates range between the years 24 and 27, i.e. between 102 A.D. and 106 A.D.

Huvishka

Next came Huvishka to the imperial throne. His known dates range between the years 28 to 69, i.e. between 106 A.D. and 138 A.D. A Mathurā inscription[59] represents him as the grandson of a king who has the Appellation *Sachadharmathita* i.e. steadfast in the true law which occurs on the coins of Kujūla Kaphsa.

According to *Rājatarangini,* Huvishka ruled simultaneously with Jushka and Kanishka, i.e. Va-jheshka and Kanishka of the *Ārā* inscription of the year 41. The Wardak Vase[60] inscription possibly proves the inclusion of Kābul within his dominions. He held sway over an extensive empire comprising Kābul, Kashmir, the Punjāb, Mathurā and perhaps Uttar Pradesh. He is described as *Māhārājārājatirāja* Huvishka. He was a patron of Buddhism. During his reign, Kashmīr was mostly a land of Buddhas, who by practising the law of religious medicancy had acquired great renown. It is said that a Bodhisattva lived then in this country as the sole lord (spiritual of the land, namely, the glorious Nāgārjuna) who resided at Shadarahadvana. His name is associated with a town in Kashmir known as Hushkapura and with a monastery at Mathurā. His coins bear figures of Greek, Persian and Indian deities and also on one of his coins, the remarkable figure of Roma.[61]

Kanishka II

Smith does not admit that the Kanishka of the *Ārā* inscription was different from the great Kanishka. Luders, Fleet, Kennedy and Sten Konow, on the other hand distinguish between the two Kanishkas.[62] According to Luders, Kanishka of the *Ārā* inscription was a son of Vasishka and probably a grandson of Kanishka I. Kanishka II had the titles *Mahārajārājatirāja devaputra* and possibly *kaisara.* It is probable that he and not Kanishka I, was the founder of the town of Kanishkapura in Kashmīr. Luders assumes that Vasishka succeeded the great Kanishka and that, on his death, the empire was divided—Kanishka II, the son of Vasishka, ruling in the north, while Huvishka held sway in India proper. Later on, Huvishka also became master of the north. It is possible that Kanishka II is identical with that Kanishka who, according to *Tārānātha*, was a prince of great wealth, who erected four great stūpas at the four points of the compass and provided for the maintenance of 30,000 bhikshus.[63]

The territory which was under control of Vasudeva I is not known. No Kharoshthi inscription bearing his name has been found in the North-West, and only his *Brāhmī* inscription have been discovered in Mathurā and its environs. This shows that the Kushāṇas at that time had lost their over the extreme north and north-west India.

Vāsudeva I

The next Kushāṇa king was Vāsudeva I. His dates range between they years 67 to 98, i.e. 145 A.D. to 176 A.D. He does not appear to have been a Buddhist. His name indicates that the Kushāṇas had taken to Hinduism.

His coins exhibit the figure of Śiva attended by his bull Nandi.[64] A fragmentary relief of the Kaushāṇa period in the collection of the Mathurā Museum depicts a royal personage with a companion reverently approaching a Śiva-linga. They were Kushāṇa dress and first of these may represent Vāsudeva himself. A king named Vāsudeva is mentioned in *Kāvya Mīmāṁsā* as a patron of poets and a Sabhāpati apparently President of a society of learned men.

Kanishka III and Vāsudeva II

Very little is known about the successors of Vāsudeva I. The most important of them appear to have been Kanishka III (180 A.D.-210 A.D.) and Vāsudeva II (210 A.D.-230 A.D.) who are known from their coins. Vāsudeva II is probably identical with the Yueh-chi king Potiao of the Chinese annals who sent an embassy to the Chinese in 230 A.D. Kanishka III and Vāsudeva II had control over the Panjāb, N.W.F.P. and Afghānistān. Yu-houan, author of the Wei-he, speaks of Ta-yuch-chi's sovereignty over Ki-pin, Ta-hia, Kao-fu and T'ien-tchou, about the middle of the third century. Shortly afterwards, the Kushāṇa empire broke into pieces and disappeared as an important power in fourth century A.D. The provincial governors in the North-West India and the Punjāb declared their independence. Moreover, the tribes known as the Yaudheyas, Kunindas and the Ārjunāyanas who had played an important role in the Punjāb during the pre-Mauryan period organised a revolt and expelled the Kushāṇas from their homeland.

REFERENCES

1. Pāṇini; IV. 1. 169; 2.131; 2.118, 2.45; 2.53; V.3.117; VII.3,2; VIII. 3. 97. Mc Crindle; *J.W.; I.I.A;* pp. 59,60, 111-112,114,121,224,232,274,347.
2. Mc Crindle, J.W.; *I.I.A.* p. 221-222.
3. *Ibid.*, p. 121.
4. Mc Crindle, J.W.; *I.I.A.* p. 227.
5. *Ibid.*, p. 72.
6. *Ibid.*, p. 310.
7. *Ibid.*
8. Cowell, E.W. Thomas, F.W.; *Harṣa-carita* of Bāṇa Tr. p. 183-194.
9. Nilakantha Sastri, *A comprehensive History of India,* Vol. 2, p. 102.
10. *Ibid.*, p. 229.
11. Sten Konow; *C.I.I.*, Vol. II, Part I, p. lxiii.
12. *J.R.A.S.;* 1903, p. 22.
13. *Ibid.*, p. 20.
14. *Ibid.*, p. 21.
15. Sten Konow, Vol. II, Part I, p. Liv.
16. *J.R.A.S.;* 1913, p. 632.
17. Catalogue of Coins in the Punjāb Museum, Vol. I, p. 173.
18. Sten Konow; *C.I.I.*, Vol. II, Part I, p. 70.
19. Bhandarkar, R.G. : *A peep into the Early History of India,* pp. 39-40.
20. Sten Konow, *C.I.I.*, Vol. II, Part I, p. Lxiv.
21. *Ibid.*
22. Taran, W.W.; *The Greeks in Bactria and India,* p. 570.
23. Marshall, J.; *Taxilā,* p. 67.
24. *C.H.I.*, p. 584.
25. Sten Konow; *C.I.I.*, Vol. II, Part I, p. Lxvii.
26. *Ibid.*
27. Smith, V.A., *J.R.A.S.*, 1903, p. 31.
28. Ghosh, H.C.; *The Date of Kanishka,* I.H.Q. Vol. V, 1929, p. 71.
29. *Ibid.*
30. Sten Konow, *C.I.I.*, Vol. II, Part I, p. Lxviii.
31. Whitehead, R.B., *Catalogue of Coins in the Punjab Museum,* Vol. I, p. 183.
32. Bhandarkar, R.G. : *A Peep into the Early History of India,* p. 40.
33. Sten Konow, *C.I.I.*, Vol. II, Part I, p. Lxxvi.
34. *Ibid;* p. xvii.
35. Smith, V.A., *Early History of India, 4th Edn.*, pp. 272-73.
36. *J.R.A.S.;* 1913, pp. 637, 994 ff.
37. *Cambridge Short History,* p. 77.
38. *J.R.A.S.;* 1913, p. 980, 1924, p. 400.

39. *J.R.A.S.;* 1905, pp. 566-68.
40. Van Lohuizen-De-Leeuw, J.E., *The Scythian Period,* pp. 382-383.
41. Nilkantha Sastri, K.A., *A Comprehensive History of India,* Vol. II, p. 234.
42. Kennedy, J., *The Secret of Kanishka,* p. 671.
43. *Ibid.*
44. *J.R.A.S.;* 1903, p. 31.
45. Walters, T., *On Yuan Chwang,* Vol. I., pp. 124-5.
46. *J.R.A.S.;* 1912, p. 674.
47. *Ep. Ind.,* XIV, p. 142; *I.A.,* 1903, p. 382.
48. *I.A.,* 1903, p. 385.
49. Cunninghams, *Ancient Geography of India,* ed. S.N. Majumdar Sastri, p. xliii.
50. *I.H.Q.,* xxvii, p. 294.
51. *Ibid.*
52. Sten Konow, *C.I.I.,* Vol. II, Pt. I, p. lxxix.
53. Smith, V., *Early History of India,* 4th Edn., pp. 283-4.
54. *J.R.A.S.;* 1912, p. 1003-4.
55. Beal, S., *Life of Hiuen-Tsiang,* p. 63.
56. Fergusson James, *History of Indian and Eastern Architecture,* p. 94.
57. *Indian Antiquary,* 1903, p. 382 ff.
58. Whitehead, R.B., *Catalogue of Coins in the Punjab Museum,* Vol. 1, pp. 186-194.
59. *J.R.A.S.;* 1924, p. 402.
60. Sten Konow, *C.I.I.,* Vol. II, Pt. 1, p. 170.
61. *Camb. Short History,* p. 79.
62. Sten Konow, *C.I.I.,* Pt. II, Vol. I, p. Lxxx.
63. Nilkantha Sastri, K.A., *A Comprehensive History of India* (ed.), Vol. II, p. 247, Ind. Ant.. p. 348.
64. Ind. Ant., p. 348; Marshall, *Taxilā,* p. 71.

Chapter VIII

The Imperial Guptas : Harsha A.D. 320-647

With the gradual break-up of the Kushān Empire, there ensues another dark period in the history of Northern India, and we may assume that it was followed by a period of disorder of which no traces have survived. Early in the fourth century A.D. the curtain rises once again with the appearance on the scene of a Hindu Rājā who bears the historical name of Chandragupta. Chandragupta, who may have been an adventurer of lowly origin, seems to have owed his rise to greatness to his marriage with a princess of the name of Kumāra Devī, of the famous Licchavi clan of Vaisālī which had been so powerful at the time of the Buddha, but had been temporarily eclipsed by the rise of the Maurya dynasty. Chandragupta established himself as master of the Ganges valley as far as the junction of the Ganges and Jumna at Prayāga, the modern Allahābād: his capital was the ancient city of Pātaliputra, the modern Patna, and he celebrated his coronation on February 26th, A.D. 320, by the establishment of the Gupta Era and by striking coins in honour of himself and his Licchavi consort, with the title of King of Kings (Mahārājādhirājā). Chandragupta died in A.D. 330 and was succeeded by his son Samudragupta. For this great monarch, whose very existence had been forgotten, we are fortunate in possessing a detailed record in the shape of an inscription—a *prasasti* or panegyric, composed by his poet laureate, Harisena, and engraved on a pillar of the time of Asoka, originally erected at Kausāmbī. There is some irony in finding this courtly panegyric in polished Sanskrit describing a conquering campaign, partly obliterating the simple Pālī record of him who strove to teach mankind that "the chiefest conquest is the Law of Piety." The Allahābād inscription describes Chandragupta's choice of his successor:

> ' "Here is a noble man!" With these words the father embraced him with shivers of joy that spoke of his affection, and looked at him with eyes heavy with tears and overcome with love—the courtiers breathing freely with joy and the kinsmen of equal grade looking up with sad faces—and said to him, "Protect then this whole earth." '*

* J. F. Fleet, Gupta Inscriptions, in *Corpus Insc. Ind.* vol. III, Kausāmbī is Kosam in the Allahābād district.

Acting on his father's dying behest, the young king on his succession set forth on a *digvijaya* or Conquest of the Four Quarters, which was the first duty of the Kshatriya ruler. The panegyrist divides Samudragupta's conquered opponents into four classes—kings who were slain and their dominions annexed; kings who were defeated and taken prisoners, but reinstated as tributaries; "frontier kings," who escaped by paying homage, and "distant kings," who sent embassies acknowledging his power. Among the first were the various rulers who had sprung up in Hindustan with the decay of the Kushān power; these were 'violently uprooted' and their kingdoms taken. Thus the whole of northern India as far south as the Narbadā and as far east as the Jumna and Chambal rivers was permanently incorporated in Samudragupta's dominions. To the second category belonged the 'kings of the forest country,' whom he made his servants, and those of the south, who were captured but spared. These were rājās whose territories lay in Orissa, between the Mahānadi and Godāveri rivers. Beyond this, Samudragupta's progress was checked by the allied armies of a confederacy headed by Vishnugopa, the Pallava monarch of Kānchi, and Samudragupta returned home, laden with spoil, to his capital. Among the 'frontier' and 'distant' kings who paid him homage and sent embassies were the rulers of Assam (Kāmarūpa), of Samatata, at the confluence of the Ganges and Brahmaputra rivers, and of various Saka, Kushān and other tribes in Rājputāna, Mālwā, Gujarāt and the Punjab. His fame even spread as far as distant Ceylon. Maghavarman, King of Ceylon (A.D. 350-380) was anxious to found a hostel for Sinhalese monks who went on pilgrimage to the Bodhi tree at Bodh Gayā, which was in Samudragupta's territory. He therefore sent an embassy with rich presents. Samudragupta gave the necessary permission, and a splendid monastery sprang up, with six halls and three lofty towers, surrounded by a wall thirty or forty feet high. It was decorated in brilliant colours, and contained an image of the Buddha cast in gold and silver and adorned with gems and precious stones. It accommodated more than one thousand monks, including, of course, a number from Ceylon.

Soon after his victorious march through south-eastern India, Samudragupta offered in state the Horse Sacrifice, the traditional Brahmanical symbol of his overlordship over India. His favourite epithet is Sarvarājāccheta, 'exterminator of all other kings.' He issued a series of fine gold coins, one of which shows him playing the lyre. Samudragupta was an accomplished and versatile ruler. Though an orthodox Brahmin, he employed as his councillor the learned Buddhist author Vasubhandu. In the intervals between his conquests and the cares of administration, he solaced himself with the study of music and literature. He was himself a musician and poet, and delighted in taking part in religious discussions. He was a liberal patron of the drama, and his reign was marked by the erection of many splendid buildings, adorned with painting and sculpture. He fully deserved the title of "Poet King" (Kavirājā), and the inscription speaks of him as "full of compassion and tenderness of heart, a veritable incarnation of goodness."

His son Chandragupta II, who took the title of Vikramāditya, "Sun of Valour," had doubtless acted as Yuvarājā or Regent in the closing years of his father's long reign. He succeeded to the throne in A.D. 380. He transferred his capital from Pātaliputra to Ayodhya, the chief town of Kosala or Oudh, associated with legends of the hero-god Rāma. Here he proceeded to make war upon the Saka satrap of Ujjain, a very powerful ruler, whose ancestors, on the break-up of the Āndhra empire of the Deccan, had overrun Kacch, Kāthiāwār, part of Sind, a large portion of Gujarāt, and the Konkan.* Ujjain is an ancient city, the Indian Greenwich,† and the meeting place of trade routes from the ports of the west coast, and others running to Sind and the great marts of the Gangetic plain. No doubt the acquisition of the western ports added immensely to the resources of the Gupta Empire. Probably Chandragupta made his residence at Ujjain for a part of his reign, and this is the origin of the popular legends about the semi-mythical Rājā Bikram of Ujjain, at whose court flourished the "Nine Gems" of literature. In particular, it was the traditional place where, at the spring festival, the dramatist Kālidāsa presented his dramas before the king.

The Gupta dynasty reached the height of its glory and prosperity under Chandragupta II, and we are fortunate in possessing a detailed account of it from the pen of Fa Hian (Fa Hsien), one of the band of heroic Chinese pilgrims who made their way to India between the fifth and seventh centuries, in order to visit the holy places of Buddhism and study in the monasteries, and collect manuscripts and images to take back to their own country. In order to reach India, it was necessary to join one of the numerous caravans skirting the formidable Taklamakan desert, dreaded by travellers of every age, and to traverse the lofty mountain ranges of the Hindu Kush and the Pamirs, over snow-clad passes 16,000 feet above sea-level. One of the earliest to undertake the journey was Fa Hian, who was in India from A.D. 401 to 411. Fa Hian gives a striking picture of a peaceful, prosperous and well-governed country.‡ Speaking of Pātaliputra he tells us of the splendid car-processions held every month, when images of the Buddha were carried round, and the occasion was marked with games and music and the offering of incense and flowers, and of the excellent charitable arrangements. "The nobles and house-holders have founded hospitals within the city, to which the poor of all countries, the destitute, crippled and diseased, may repair. They receive every kind of requisite help gratuitously.

* *Ante,* Chapter VI, p. 93.

† Ancient Indian astronomers reckoned the first degree of longitude from Ujjain.

‡ Fa Hian's Travels are translated by S. Beal, in *Buddhist Records of the Western World,* I. xxiii-lxxxiii, from which the following quotations are taken.

Physicians inspect their diseases and, according to their cases, order them food and drink, medicine or decoctions, everything in fact which may contribute to their ease. When cured they depart at their convenience."

He speaks in glowing terms of the justice, clemency and efficiency of the government. The inhabitants, he says, are prosperous and happy. Only those who farm the royal estates pay any portion of the produce as rent; and they are not bound to remain in possession longer than they like. The king inflicts no capital punishment, but merely fines offenders, and even those convicted of incitement of rebellion after repeated attempts are only punished with the loss of the right hand. The Chief Ministers have fixed salaries allotted to them. The people of the country drink no intoxicants and kill no animals for food, except the Chandālas or Pariahs, and these alone eat garlic or onions. The Pariahs live outside the walls; if they enter the town they have to strike a gong with a piece of wood to warn passers-by not to touch them.

"In this country they do not keep swine or fowls, and do not deal in cattle; they have no shambles or wine-shops in their market-places. In commerce they use cowrie-shells. The Pariahs alone hunt and sell flesh. Down from the time of the Lord Buddha's Nirvāna, the kings, chief men and householders have raised vihāras for the monks, and have provided for their support by endowing them with fields, houses, gardens, servants, and cattle. These church-lands are guaranteed to them by copperplate grants, which are handed down from reign to reign, and no one has had the temerity to cancel them. All the resident priests, who are allotted cells in the vihāras, have beds, mats, food, and drink supplied to them; they pass their time in performing acts of mercy, in reciting the scriptures, or in meditation. When a stranger arrives at the monastery, the senior priests escort him to the guest-house, carrying his robes and his alms-bowl for him. They offer him water to wash his feet, and oil for anointing, and prepare a special meal for him. After he has rested a while they ask him his rank in the priesthood, and according to his rank they assign him a chamber and bedding. During the month after the rain-rest, the pious collect a united offering for the priesthood; and the priests in their turn hold a great assembly and preach the Law... When the priests have received their dues, the householders and Brahmins present them with all sorts of robes and other necessaries; and the priests also make one another offerings. And so, ever since the Lord Buddha passed away from the earth, the rules of conduct of the priesthood have been handed down without intermission.*

Fa Hian traversed India from West to East. On arriving at Tāmaralipti, at the mouth of the Gauges, he took ship to Ceylon. The voyage, of about 1,200 miles,

* Beal, *op. cit.*, Chap. XVI.

occupied only fourteen days. Here, in the heart of Hīnayāna Buddhism, he stayed for some time, until the sight of a Chinese taffeta fan, offered at a Buddhist shrine, so affected him that he burst into tears. He decided to return, and took a passage in a merchantman carrying 200 passengers, mostly Hindu traders, to Java. From Java, another vessel took him to Kwan Chow, on the south-eastern coast of China, where he arrived after an adventurous and perilous journey; he was twice nearly drowned, but he managed to save his precious manuscripts. He had been away fifteen years. Three years had been spent on the outward journey, nine years in India, and three years on the homeward voyage. "In all the countries of India, the dignified carriage of the priesthood and the surprising influence of religion cannot be described. But because our learned doctors had not heard these things, he was induced, regardless of personal risk, to cross the seas and encounter every kind of danger in returning home"*

Chandragupta II died in A.D. 415. He was succeeded by Kumāragupta (415-455) and Skandagupta (455-467). The Central Asian nomads were now once more on the move. The Ephthalite or White Huns, called Hūna by Indian writers, who had settled on the banks of the Oxus in the old kingdom of Bactria, commenced to spread southwards. For a time they were held up by Skandagupta. The inscription on the pillar of victory which he set up at Bhitāri describes how he galloped into the courtyard of the palace at Ayodhya to inform his mother of his victory over the barbarians, "just as Krishna, having slain his enemies, betook himself to his mother Devakī." He commemorated his success by building a magnificent temple to Vishnu. India was saved, but only for a time; his brother Puragupta was powerless to check further incursions, and the Gupta Empire began to break up. In A.D. 484 the Ephthalite Huns invaded Persia, defeated and slew the Sassanian king Fīroz, and carried off his daughter. After this, they entered the Punjab, under a chieftain named Toramāna, overthrowing the Kushān and other local rulers, and setting up a kingdom with its capital at Sākala or Siālkot. Toramāna was succeeded in A.D. 510 by his son Mihiragula; he is described by Buddhist writers as a monster of iniquity, who destroyed stūpas and monasteries, and put the peaceful inhabitants of Gandhāra to the sword. North-Western India was now part of the vast Hūna empire which stretched from Persia to Khotan, and the Guptas were its tributaries. Mihiragula, however, was prevented from advancing further eastwards by a confederacy of Hindu princes headed by Yasodharman, who defeated him in A.D. 528 and compelled him to retire to Kashmir, where he died. The Hūna, Gurjara and other tribes which had entered the Punjab and had penetrated to what are now Rājputāna and Gujarāt settled down in the country, inter-married with the inhabitants, and were admitted into the Hindu fold. Further Hūna inroads were prevented by the fact that their empire in Central

* Beal, *op. cit.*, p. lxxxiii.

Asia was being broken up by the Turks. The barbarian invasions form a turning point in the history of northern India, introducing as they did, new elements destined to revolutionise Hindu society.

The curtain now rings down upon the scene for nearly a century. When it rises, we find three prominent states in the Ganges Valley, the Guptas of eastern Mālwā, no doubt a branch of the imperial family, the Maukharis of Kanauj, and the Vardhanas of Thānesar, a city north of Delhi.* They were constantly at war with one another, and with the Hūna and Gurjara tribes. In A.D. 605 Prabhākara Vardhana, the rājā of Thānesar, died, leaving two sons, Rājya and Harsha, and a daughter Rājyasrī, who was married to the rājā of Kanauj. The young prince Rājya had hardly succeeded when he heard that his brother-in-law had been assassinated, and his sister thrown into prison and cruelly treated by his neighbour the rājā of Mālwā. When he went to her rescue, he, too, was treacherously killed by Sasānka, the rājā of Gauda (Bengal). Harsha was a lad of sixteen, of a deeply religious character, and he had entertained the idea of retiring to a Buddhist monastery. But on hearing of his brother's murder, he took the field, and decisively defeated the Mālavas and their allies. After some difficulty he succeeded in tracing his sister, whom he rescued just as, in despair, she was about to ascend the funeral pyre. He was now asked by the ministers to ascend the vacant throne of Kanauj. After some hesitation he accepted; he made Kanauj his capital, and the two kingdoms were united. Kanauj is described as a handsome city, with temples, museums and monasteries.

After his accession. Harsha "went from east to west, sub-duing all who were not obedient. During this time the elephants were not unharnessed, nor the soldiers unhelmeted." After six years of incessant campaigning he was able to reign in peace for thirty years, without striking a blow. His empire stretched from the mouth of the Ganges to the Sutlej, and included Mālwā, Gujarāt and Kāthiāwār. But his sphere of influence stretched much farther, and a number of neighbouring rulers were glad to submit and become his allies. Harsha now took the title of Emperor of the "Five Indies," the Punjab, Kanauj, Bengal, Mithila or Darbhanga, and Orissa. His Empire, however, stopped short at the Vindhyas. When he tried to invade the Deccan, the Chalukya monarch Pulikesi held the passes in force and Harsha's army could make no impression on the sturdy hillmen. Chariots, elephants and heavy cavalry were useless in this wild and rugged country.

Harsha was a just and able ruler. He was profuse in his charities. "In all the highways of the towns and villages throughout India he erected hospices, provided food and drink and stationed there physicians with medicines for travellers and poor persons round about, to be given without stint." He and his family had strong leanings

* See R. Mookerji, *Harsha* (Oxford 1926), and authorities there quoted.

towards Buddhism, and Buddhist establishments were generously endowed; at one time the slaughter of animals was forbidden under pain of the most drastic penalties. But for reasons of state, the Emperor was eclectic in his religion, and paid equal reverence to Siva, the Sun (Sūrya), and Buddha. The inscriptions show that Harsha's empire was divided into a number of provinces, each with its governor and minor officials. But he did not depend upon his officers for reports; he travelled incessantly over his vast domains, hearing petitions and redressing grievances. "He was an indefatigable worker, and the day was too short for him. He devoted one period of it to affairs of state, and the remainder to religious works and exercises."

The year A.D. 630 of the reign of Harsha was signalised by the arrival of the learned Hiuen Tsang (Yüan Chuang), "the Master of the Law," the most celebrated of the Chinese pilgrims who visited India in order to study Buddhism and to travel in the footsteps of the Blessed One. He had started, at the age of twenty-nine, in the previous year. Travelling by the northern route (lake Issik-Kul, Tashkhend, Samarkand), he reached Gandhāra after encountering great perils by desert, robbers, flooded rivers and precipitous mountain passes. He stayted in India until 645, spending eight of the fifteen years in Harsha's dominions. Hiuen Tsang's account, being that of an eye witness of unusual breadth of view and reliability, is one of the most important documents on medieval India which we possess, and is worth quoting in some detail:*

> "The towns and villages have inner gates; the walls are wide and high; the streets and lanes are tortuous, and the roads winding. The thoroughfares are dirty and the stalls arranged on both sides of the road with appropriate signs. Butchers, fishers, dancers, executioners, scavengers, and so on, have their abodes without the city. In coming and going these persons are bound to keep on the left side of the road till they arrive at their homes. Their houses are surrounded by low walls, and form the suburbs. The earth being soft and muddy, the walls of the towns are mostly built of brick or tiles. The towers on the walls are constructed of wood or bamboo; the houses have balconies and belvederes, which are made of wood, with a coating of lime or mortar, and covered with tiles. The different buildings have the same form as those in China; rushes, or dry branches, or tiles, or boards are used for covering them. The walls are covered with lime or mud, mixed with cow's dung for purity. At different seasons they scatter flowers about. Such are some of their different customs. The *sanghārāmas* (monasteries) are constructed with extra-ordinary skill. A three-storied tower is erected at each of the four angles. The beams and the projecting heads are carved with great skill in different shapes. The doors, windows, and the low walls are painted profusely;

* For Hiuen Tsang's travels, see Beal, *Buddhist Records of the Western World*, and *Life of Hiuen Tsang;* and T. Watters, On *Yuang Chang* (R.A.S. 1904-5).

the monks' cells are ornamental on the inside the plain on the outside. In the very middle of the building is the hall, high and wide. There are various storeyed chambers and turrets of different height and shape, without any fixed rule. The doors open towards the east; the royal throne also faces the east. Their clothing is not cut or fashioned; they mostly affect fresh white garments; they esteem little those of mixed colour or ornamented. The men wind their garments round their middle, then gather them under the armpits, and let them fall across the body, hanging to the right."*

Hiuen Tsang found the caste system in full operation. The Brahmins were engaged in religious duties. The Kshatriyas were the hereditary governing class, and the king was always, except in the case of usurpers, a Kshatriya. The Vaisyas were the tradesmen and merchants, and agricultural and menial work was left to the Sūdras to perform.

"The Kshatriyas and Brahmins are cleanly and wholesome in their dress, and they live in a homely and frugal way. There are rich merchants who deal in gold trinkets and so on. They mostly go barefooted; few wear sandals. They stain their teeth red or black; they bind up their hair and pierce their ears. They are very particular in their personal cleanliness. All wash before eating; they never use food left over from a former meal. Wooden and stone vessels must be destroyed after use: metal ones must be well polished and rubbed. After eating they cleanse their mouth with a willow stick, and wash their hands and mouths."†

The dead were cremated, thrown into a river, or exposed in a forest. Old people often committed suicide in the Ganges.

Of the morals of the people and the administration of government the picture is pleasing :

"With respect to the ordinary people, although they are naturally light-minded, yet they are upright and honourable. In money matters they are without craft, and in administering justice they are considerate. They dread the retribution of another state of existence, and make light of the things of the present world. They are not deceitful or treacherous in their conduct and are faithful to their oaths and promises, and in their rules of government there is remarkable rectitude, while in their behaviour there is much gentleness and sweetness. With respect to criminals and rebels, these are few in number, and only occasionally troublesome. When the laws are broken or the power of the ruler violated, then the matter is clearly sifted and the offenders punsihed. There is no infliction of corporal punishment; they are simply left to live and die, and are not counted among men.

* *Beal, Buddhist Records,* pp. 73-5.

† *Op. cit.*, p. 76.

When the rules of morality or justice have been violated, or a man is dishonest or wanting in filial love, his nose or ears are cut off and he is expelled from the city to wander in the jungle till he dies. For other faults besides these, a small fine is exacted in lieu of punishment. In investigating crimes, the rod is not used to extort proofs of guilt. In questioning the accused, if he answers frankly, his punishment is proportioned accordingly, but if he obstinately denies his fault, in order to probe the truth to the bottom, trial by ordeal is resorted to.

"As the administration of the government is founded on benign principles, the executive is simple. The families are not entered on registers, and the people are not subjected to forced labour. The crown-lands are divided into four parts. The first is for carrying out the affairs of state; the second, for paying the ministers and officers of the crown; the third, for rewarding men of genius; the fourth, for giving alms to religious communities. In this way, the taxes on the people are light, and the services required of them are moderate. Every one keeps his worldly goods in peace, and all till the soil for their subsistence. Those who cultivate the royal estates pay a sixth part of their produce as tribute. The merchants who engage in commerce travel to and fro in pursuit of their calling. Rivers and toll-bars are opened for travellers on payment of a small sum. When the public works require it, labour is exacted but paid for. The payment is in strict proportion to the work done."*

Of the army we learn interesting details. "The military guard the frontiers and put down disturbances. They mount guard at night round the palace. The soldiers are levied according to the requirements of the service; they are promised certain salaries and publicly enrolled." The army was divided into infantry, cavalry, chariots and elephants. The commanding officer role in a chariot drawn by four horses abreast, his bodyguard around him and a charioteer at either hand. The elephants wore armour plate; the infantry depended chiefly on their long spears and large shields. The army advanced protected by a cavalry screen.

Hieun Tsang was struck by the prosperity of the country. The standard of living was high. Payment was sometimes made in kind, but gold and silver coins were in circulation, and cowrie shells and pearls were also used for the purpose. The soil was fertile and highly cultivated, and large numbers of different kinds of fruit and vegetables were grown. Wheaten cakes, parched grain, sugar, *ghī* and preparations of milk were the staple diet, but fish, venison and mutton were consumed as occasional dainties. Beef, and the flesh of certain wild animals, together with onions and garlic, were taboo, and to eat them entailed loss of caste.

Learning, as in medieval Europe, was religious in character, and was imparted in the monasteries. Religious works were written down, except in the case of the Vedas,

* *Op. cit.*, pp. 83-4.

which were handed down orally and not transmitted to paper or to leaves. The script in use was Brāhmī, said to have been revealed by the god Brahmā. It was the parent script of India and other scripts were derived from it. Sanskrit was the language of the learned, and Sanskrit grammar had been reduced to regular rules. The purest Sanskrit was that of Middle India.

Hiuen Tsang pays a high tribute to the patience and perseverance of the Brahmin preceptors. A man's education often lasted from nine to thirty years of age. "When the disciples are thirty years old, their minds being settled and their education finished, they go into office, and the first thing they do is to reward the kindness of their teachers." He speaks with admiration of the esteem with which learning was held in India; a number of disinterested men of wealth and position gave themselves up to lifelong study, refusing all invitations to court and honours and rewards of every kind. Most interesting of all, however, is the pilgrim's account of his visits to the famous college of Nālandā in Bihār, where he spent five years.* Students flocked thither from all parts of the East. The disciple on arrival was at first treated as a guest and, after examination, he was assigned his place in the routine of the monastery. Exemption from menial work was granted after he had proved his worth. Discipline was strictly in accordance with the rules of the Buddhist scriptures and breaches were severely punished.

> "The pursuit of pleasure belongs to the worldly life, the pursuit of knowledge to the religious life. To return to a secular career after taking up religion is considered disgraceful. For breaking the rules of the community the transgressor is publicly rebuked; for a slight fault he is condemned to enforced silence; for a graver fault he is expelled. Those who are thus expelled for life wander about the roads finding no place of refuge; sometimes they resume their former occupation."

The regular curriculum consisted of grammar, mechanics, medicine, logic and metaphysics. There was keen rivalry between the adherents of the Greater and Lesser Vehicles, and Hiuen Tsang gives a lively account of the discussions which took place. "Learning and discussing, they found the day too short, day and night they admonished each other, juniors and seniors mutually helping to perfection."

> "When a man's renown has reached a high distinction, he convokes an assembly for discussion. He judges of the talent or otherwise of those who take part in it, and if one of the assembly distinguishes himself by refined language, subtle investigation, deep penetration, and severe logic, he is mounted on an elephant covered with precious ornaments and conducted by a retinue of admirers to the gate of the monaste y. If, on the contrary, one of the members breaks down in his argument, or uses inelegant phrases, or violates a rule in logic, they daub him with mud and cast him into a ditch."†

* The site of Nālandā was throughly explored by Dr. Spooner in 1915, and the accuracy of Hiuen Tsang's description confirmed. See *Revealing India's Past* (India Society 1939), pp. 130-1.

† *Op. cit.*, p. 81.

On one occasion a professor of the Lokātya sect, who were extreme materialists, wrote out forty theses and hung them on the gate of the Nālandā college with the notice: "If anyone can refute these principles, I will give him my head as a proof of his victory." Hiuen Tsang accepted the challenge and defeated his rival in a public disputation. He spared his head and made him his disciple.

Hiuen Tsang's introduction to the court of Harsha took place under unusual circumstances.* At the urgent request of Kumāra, king of Assam, he paid a visit to that country. Harsha, who was on tour at the time, and encamped at Rājagriha (Rājgīr in the Patna district), heard of this, and sending a messenger to his vassal he peremptorily demanded the presence of the Doctor of the Law at his camp. Kumāra sent back a message to say that he could have his head but not his guest. "I will trouble you for your head," was Harsha's reply. Kumāra dared not displease his powrful suzerain and he accompanied Hiuen Tsang with the best grace he could muster. On arriving at the royal encampment, the pilgrim was questioned by Harsha about his native country. He then delivered a homily on the Mahāyāna doctrine. An interesting sidelight on the position of women in India at that time is thrown by the fact that the king's widowed sister set beside him and took a leading part in these discussions. Harsha, who had hitherto been attracted to the Hīnayāna school of Buddhism, was greatly impressed and at once conceived the plan of calling a great public assembly at his capital in order to hear an exposition of the doctrine. He despatched a proclamation to the four quarters of his empire summoning to Kanauj "all disciples of the various religious sects or schools, the Srāmanas (Buddhist monks), Brahmins and heretics of the Five Indies, to investigate the treatise of the Master of the Law from China". He then proceeded to the capital, with his guest and the Rājā of Assam. The two kings marched in state down the Ganges, on opposite sides of the river, accompanied by a vast retinue, on foot and in boats, and preceded by elephants and musicians beating drums, playing on horns, flutes and harps, and sounding trumpets. On their arrival they found an enormous assembly of princes, nobles, officials and monks of various sects awaiting them. Harsha and Kumāra entered Kanauj arrayed in the likeness of the gods Indra and Brahma, holding a canopy over a golden figure of the Buddha carried on a gorgeously caparisoned elephant. They were escorted by a body of war-elephants in full armour, bearing musicians who sounded their drums and raised their music, while the king scattered pearls, gold and gems in honour of the "Three Jewels" of the Buddhist faith. On arrival they found that a vast debating hall, with a tower and a life-sized Buddha, had been erected, and a huge assembly had gathered there. The smaller Buddha image was solemnly installed, the King bearing it on his shoulder and making offerings to it. A feast was held and at its conclusion Hiuen Tsang delivered his discourse. Proceedings went on in this fashion for five days, varied by processions, feasts and other ceremonies. Hiuen Tsang triumphed so successfully over his opponents that it was rumoured that his life was in danger, whereupon the Emperor issued a proclamation that "if anyone should hurt or touch the pilgrim he should at once be beheaded, and

---

* *Op. cit.*, I, pp. 206-224.

whoever spoke against him should have his tongue cut out." After this, it is not altogether surprising to learn that "the followers of error withdrew and disappeared, so that when eighteen days had passed, there was none to enter the discussion."

Conspiracies did not end there. A fire suddenly broke out in the thatched pavilion over the gateway, to the consternation of everyone, and when the king went to see what had happened, a man rushed uot, knife in hand. The officers were paralysed with fright, but Harsha, with great presence of mind, seized him and handed him over to the magistrates, strictly forbidding them to harm him. "What have I done," said the king, "that you have attempted such a deed?" The man confessed that he had been hired by the Brahmins, who were furious at the favour shown to the Buddhists. They had plotted to set fire to the assembly hall by means of burning arrows, and hoped to assassinate Harsha during the stampede which they thought would ensue. Having failed in this, they hired this man to lie in wait for him in a narrow passage. About five hundred Brahmins were arrested, and it speaks volumes for the humanity of Harsha that he merely punished the ringleaders. The rest were pardoned and banished to the frontiers.

Hiuen Tsang had the good fortune to witness another remarkable assembly, which was held at Prayāga, on the sandy plain between the Ganges and the Jumna where millions of Hindus now assemble annually to celebrate the Khumba Mela. This was the quinquennial Salvation Festival, at which the King distributed in charity all the wealth in his treasury.* The proceedings lasted for seventy-five days, the King and his retinue staying in thatched buildings. Invitations were issued "throughout the Five Indies to Srāmanas, heretics, Nirgranthas (Jain ascetics), the poor, the orphans and the bereaved to come to the arena of charity and receive the royal gifts," and elaborate arrangements were made to accommodate the half-million people of the various sects who assembled from all quarters. Ten thousand Buddhists each received one hundred gold pieces, a pearl, a cotton garment, food, drink and perfumes. At the end of a month the accumulation of the preceding five years was exhausted. The royal treasury was empty; "except for the horses, elephants and military accoutrements, which were necessary for maintaining order and protecting the royal estate, nothing remained." The King gave away his jewels, ornaments, and even his clothes and had to beg from his sister Rājyasrī and old second-hand garment, and having put it on, he paid worship to the Buddhas of the ten regions.

At the end of this remarkable assembly, Hiuen Tsang felt that the time had come to depart to his own country. He had been sixteen years away and was terribly homesick. Harsha tried to load him with gifts, but he refused everything save a fur-lined coat and some money for his personal expenses. He took with him 657 manuscripts and numerous relics and images of the Buddha and Buddhist saints in gold, silver, crystal and sandalwood. He was escorted to the frontier, and eventually reached China. His home-coming was celebrated by a welcome in which all classes of the population, from the

---

* No doubt Harsha was inspired by the legend of the Benevolent Prince in the *Vessantara Jataka*. See Max Müller's essay on *Buddhist Charity,* in *Chips from a German Workshop,* I. 446.

Emperor and his court to the peasants, took part. He arrived in the year A.D. 646. The rest of his life he spent in translating and editing his treasures, and in 664 he passed joyfully to his rest in Maitreya's Paradise, there to await the return of the Lord of Pity to this world, when, he was confident, he would revisit the scene of his earthly labours.

Harsha is Hiuen Tsang's hero. He describes him as a man of eminent wisdom and great learning. "His skill in literature was profound. He cherished and protected the four kinds of creatures and deeply respected the Three Treasures. From the time of his birth to his last hour, his face never crimsoned with anger, nor did his hands ever injure a living thing. During the fifty years and more of his reign, the wild beasts became familiar with men and the people did not injure or slay them. Such were his love and humanity." Making due allowances for the pilgrim's natural enthusiasm for his patron, we may endorse this eulogy. Harsha was a remarkable man, and stands beside Asoka and Akbar among the greatest rulers that India has produced. Soldier and administrator, unwearied in his efforts for the good of his subjects, pious and merciful, a patron of literature and himself a poet and dramatist of distinction, he stands forth on the page of history, a bright and fascinating figure. It is a matter of minor interest that Harsha, who composed his own inscriptions, is the only medieval Hindu monarch whose autograph has come down to us, engraved on a copper-plate.

According to Kalhana, the historian of Kashmir, Harsha'a reign ended disastrously. "Endowed with rare talents and famous for his good government and piety, he fell under the influence of evil counsellors, and became cruel and suspicious. Abandoned by all, and an outlaw in his own country, he was assassinated by his troops."

Thanks no doubt to the visit of Hiuen Tsang, Harsha was on excellent terms with T'ai Tsung, the illustrious Emperor of the Thang dynasty, and sent a Brahmin envoy to the Chinese court. The Emperor in return despatched a distinguished mandarin to Kanauj. He was about to return, loaded with presents, when Harsha was murdered, and his minister Arjuna, who had started the revolution against his master, attacked the Chinese envoy, who only just succeeded in escaping to Nepal. He complained to Srong-tsan-Gampo, the Tibetan ruler, who was the Emperor's son-in-law, and a Tibetan army invaded northern India and put Arjuna to death. After this, Harsha's dynasty came to an end, as he left no descendants. It was the last of the great paramount kingdoms of the north; when we next get a clear view, the country is parcelled out among a number of Rājput clans, each claiming equality with the other.

LEADING DATES

A.D. 320	Accession of Chandragupta I. Commencement of the Gupta Era.
330	Accession of Samudragupta.
360	Embassy from Meghavarman, King of Ceylon.
380	Accession of Chandragupta II.
395	Conquest of Western India.
401-410	Fa Hian visits India.

415	Accession of Kumāragupta.
455	Accession of Skandagupta. The Huns invade India.
480-90	Break up of the Gupta Empire.
528	Defeat of the Huns by a Hindu Confederacy.
606	Accession of Harsha Vardhana.
606-612	Conquest of Northern India by Harsha.
620	Defeat of Harsha by Pulikesi, the Chalukya King of the Deccan.
630-645	Hiuen Tsang in India.
647	Death of Harsha.

Chapter IX

Religion, Art and Letters in the Gupta Period

The Development of Hinduism

The most striking feature of the period between the downfall of the Maurya dynasty (*c.* 185 B.C.) and the eighty century A.D. is the gradual emergence of Hinduism in the form in which we now know it. The Brahmin priests once more re-asserted their power; animal sacrifices were revived, and Brahmanical philosophers began to evolve a practical way of life in answer to that propounded by Jainism and Buddhism. These sects, though they temporarily prospered in various parts of India, when they were patronised by powerful sovereigns, were never the religion of the masses; as time went on, Buddhism approximated more and more to Hinduism. The older gods have now receded into the background, and even Indra, the popular deity of the heroic age, has taken an inferior position. Gradually all these were superseded or absorbed by the Hindu Trimurti or Triad, Brahmā, Vishnu and Siva, representing God in his threefold aspect of creation, preservation and destruction. Brahmā, the demiurge, quickly fell into desuetude, and orthodox Hindus to-day are either Vaishnavas or Saivas. Vishnu and Siva represent opposite aspects of religion. Vishnu is mild and benevolent, ready to assist his followers; Siva, the god of destruction, is severe and terrible and worshipped from motives of fear rather than love. The popular religious myths about Siva and Vishnu were collected in eighteen long Sanskrit poems known as Purānas or "old stories," which consist of legendary accounts of the creation of the world and of the gods, saints and heroes of ancient times, together with genealogies of kings, and rules about prayers, pilgrimages and festivals and forms of worship. The Purānas are the Bible of popular Hinduism; the nearest parallel to a Purāna in modern Western literature is Milton's Paradise Lost, with its legends of the Creation and of heroic combats between the Powers of Good and Evil.

Vishnu is the subject of the majority of the Purānas. His favourite epithet is Bhagavān, the Adorable, and his worshippers are known as Bhāgavatas. He offers salvation to all, irrespective of caste, which may be won by devotion rather than by the performance of ritual or penance. This accounts for the popularity of Vaishnavism among the masses. One of the features of the religion of the age was the emergence of the doctrine of Avatars or Incarnations; Vishnu was incarnate from time to time in various forms to save the world from the assaults of the demons or powers of evil. "Whensoever the Law (*dharma*) fails, and lawlessness uprises, I bring myself to birth. To protect the good, to destroy evil-doers, to establish righteousness, I am born from age to age."* Ten incarnations of Vishnu are described in the Purānas. As the Fish, he saved Manu, the father of the human race, from the Cosmic Flood; as the Tortoise he supported on his back Mount Mandara, which the gods used as a churning-stick in order to churn from the Sea of Milk the fourteen precious objects for the benefit of mankind; as the Boar, the Man-Lion and the Dwarf he slew various demons determined to destroy the world; as Parasu Rāma, "Rāma with the Axe," the champion of Brahmanism, he exterminated the Kshatriyas—a reference, no doubt, to the long struggle between Brahmin and Kshatriya for spiritual supremacy, which ended in the victory of the former. The first six incarnations are purely mythical; the next three are historic or semi-historic personages. Rāma and Krishna are deified heroes of the Epic period, while Buddha was regarded by the Vaishnavas as an incarnation of Vishnu sent to mislead demons and sinners. To these must be added Kalki, the Avatar who, like the Buddhist Maitreya, is yet to come. In the Puranic age, each deity had his female counterpart or "energy" (Saktī). That of Vishnu is Lakshmi, the goddess of prosperity and beauty, who rose from the ocean when it was churned by the Gods and Demons (Fig. 16). Vishnu is represented in art as sleeping upon the World-Serpent, Shesha or Ananta, or riding upon his *vāhan* or vehicle, the bird Garūda (Fig. 19). The practice of depicting the gods as many-armed and many-headed now became more and more popular. This has been criticised as unaesthetic by European writers, but is in reality no more so than the winged cherubs or angels of Christian mytholody, the Greek centaurs or Egyptian sphinxes. The god holds in his hands the emblems of his power, the thunder-bolt, the discus, the conch shell, the lotus and the trident. The sālagrāma, a fossil ammonite found in the Gandak river, is supposed, on account of its resemblance to the discus, to be sacred to Vishnu, and his sacred plant is the tulsi or basil plant (*Ocymum sanctum*).

The most popular of the Avatars under which Vishnu is worshipped in modern India is Krishna. Krishna first appears in the Mahābhārata as the charioteer of Arjuna, and in his mouth is put that remarkable poem, the *Bhagavad Gītā*, or "Song of the Adorable." Arjuna is aghast as the prospect of a conflict in which so many heroes are doomed to perish at the hands of their kins-folk. Krishna consoles him by propounding the theory of Karma Yoga or union with the World-Soul by means of action. Action without attachment is the ideal. Each caste has its *dharma* or divinely appointed duty. The *dharma* of the Brahmin is religion; of the Warrior it is war; of

* *Bhagavad Gītā,* IV. 8.

Fig. 16 : The Churning of the Ocean.

the Sūdra it is menial service. But all service is of equal merit if it is performed in honour of Him Who is the Author of all. The warrior's duty is to slay his opponent—it is no sin if he does so as a duty, uninspired by any personal feelings and regardless of the result or fruit of his action. In the concluding portion of this great philosophical poem, Krishna reveals himself to the wondering Arjuna as the All God :

> Nor source nor midst nor end : infinite force,
> Unnumbered arms, the Sun and Moon thine eyes;
> I see Thy face as sacrificial fire,
> Blazing, its splendour burneth up the worlds.

The Bhagavad *Gītā* has been to generations of pious Hindus what *The Imitation of Christ* has been to Christians, and some authorities have detected Christian influences in its teaching.

Krishna, the "dark" God, is probably non-Aryan, and this hypothesis is strengthened by reference in Puranic literature to conflicts between Indra and Krishna which appear to be symbolic of the gradual replacement of the older Vedic god by a newer indigenous cult. Krishna was said to have been the son of Vasudeva, a Yādava chieftain of the Lunar Race; he was born at Mathurā, the chief centre of his worship; legends, which have many analogies with the Christian Gospel, tell of his early escape from a massacre of the Innocents by Kamsa, the Indian Herod. He grew up as a herdsman, and medieval Indian art and literature are full of stories of his youthful amours with the Gopis or milk-maids and especially his beloved Rādhā. Rādhā's love for Krishna mystically typifies the yearning of the soul for union with God. the story of Krishna, as narrated in the tenth chapter of the *Bhāgavatā Purāna* and the *Gītā Govinda* of Jayadeva, is intensely popular, and has been reproduced in every Indian varnacular. In art, Krishna is represented as a beautiful youth playing on a flute, or as an infant lying on a lotus (Fig. 17). Rāma, the hero of the *Rāmāyana*, was not yet more than a demi-god.

Fig. 17 : Krishna Playing on the Flute.

Fig. 18 : The Lingam, Phallic Emblem of Siva.

Siva, or Mahādeva, "the Great God," is the antithesis of Vishnu. He has been identified with the Vedic storm-god, Rudra, but in some of his aspects may perhaps even be traced back to the early civilisation of the Indus valley. He is the Lord of Yogis, who seek union with the World Soul by intense concentration, and he sits for endless ages in meditation among the snowy peaks of the Himālayas, smeared with ashes and wearing a necklace of skulls; the river Ganges flows from his hair. In another aspect he is the god of fertility and procreation. He is worshipped under the symbol of the *lingam* or phallus, and his vehicle is Nandi, the bull (Fig. 18). A stone bull, often of gigantic size, always faces the doorways of his shrines. He is the embodiment of cosmic energy, and as such is sometimes represented as the Lord of the Dance (Nātarājā). His consort is Parvatī or Umā, a goddess of sublime beauty and sweetness; in her terrible form of Kālī or Durgā, she is worshipped with bloody and obscene rites. At her temple at the Kālī Ghāt in Calcutta, goats are sacrificed to her in the Durgā Pūjā festival, and she is associated with the Tantric or "Left Hand" worship known as the Saktī Pūjā.*

What chiefly distinguishes later Hinduism from the religion of the Vedas is that it now becomes definitely anthropomorphic. The god is represented by an idol dwelling in a temple, which is treated as a royal personage. He has a wife and children: every morning he is awakened by hymns sung by attendant Brahmins and dancing girls. He is bathed, anointed, dressed in costly robes and taken out in a palanquin or chariot. Offerings of flowers, fruit, coconuts and betel are laid at his feet, and incense is burnt and lights waved before him.

But the worship of the greater gods is mostly confined to the higher castes. The fundamental religion of the majority is mainly animistic, and when trouble comes in the shape of disease, drought or famine, it is to the older deities that the peasant turns. These godlings are usually represented by sacred stones or rude images, and are to be propitiated rather than adored. Animals such as fowls, goats or buffaloes are offered to them. Among the Khonds, one of the primitive tribes, a human victim known as the *meriah* was until recently sacrificed in order to secure fertility for the fields. Certain animals, such as monkeys, peacocks and snakes, and certain trees such as the Pipal (*Ficus religiosa*) are regarded as sacred. No account of Hinduism can be considered complete without a reference to the worship of the cow. In Vedic times, the cow was sacrificed and eaten at weddings and other feasts; the fatted calf was specially reserved for the visit of a seer or other distinguished guest. Later, however, it came to be regarded as a sacred animal, and in the *Mahābhārata* we are told that the cow-killer will suffer in hell for as many years as there are hairs on her body. In some Hindu states the slaughter of a cow is still a penal offence, and from

* Dubois. *Hindu Manners, Customs and Ceremonies,* trans. H. K. Beauchamp (1906). Chapter IX For Parvatī, see Fig. 21, p. 141.

time to time it is made the occasion for blood-thirsty riots between Mussulmans and Hindus. As an expiation for offences against caste, the delinquent is required to partake of a mixture of the five products of the cow. The pious Hindu, when he feels himself to be dying, grasps the tail of a cow, as this will ensure a safe passage to heaven.

Hinduism is hard to define. It is not a creed, like Christianity or Islam, but a way of life—a collection of rites, traditions and mythologies, sanctioned by the sacred books and propagated by Brahmanical teaching. All Hindus, however, believe in caste and pantheism; they regard all their countless deities as merely manifestations of the all-pervading divine energy. With these they associate the doctrines of rebirth and Karma. Every act has its consequences in a future existence. The keystone of the system is the Brahmin: he is the ascetic who by penance can attain to supernatural powers; the priestly ministrant of indispensable rites; and the learned man who alone is able to expound the sacred lore, and in secular life help the king to govern the state according to the rules laid down in the scriptures. A caste-Hindu's life, from birth to death, is a long succession of ceremonies, for the due performance of which the Brahmin is indispensable.*

Fig. 19 : Vishnu, with Brahmā and Lakshmi, reclining on Ananta, the World-Serpent.

Literature and Science

Literature in India has always depended upon court patronage, and the rise of the Guptas was accompanied by great activity in many fields. This was facilitated by the introduction of written books, which were in common use all over India by the fourth century A.D. In the north they were written on birch-bark, while in the south

* See L. S. S. O'Malley, *Popular Hinduism,* Cambridge 1935, Chapter V.

leaves prepared from the talipot and palmyra palms, *Corypha talifera* and *Borassus flabelliformis,* were used. Few early specimens have survived. The earliest is a medical treatise found by Lieutenant Bower in Turkestan in 1890: its date is A.D. 350. As Hinduism regained its ascendancy, there was a great revival of Sanskrit. Two outstanding features of the period were the systematisation of existing knowledge and the appearance of secular literature. Older works, such as the Epics and Purānas, were re-arranged in their present form : the *Mahābhārata*, which was originally a secular poem describing the fate of the Kurus at the hands of the treacherous Pāndavas, was recast by Vaishnava Brahmins as a religious and didactic work with the Pāndavas as its heroes, and the epic utilised to inculcate Brahmanical views about *dharma*. About the same time, the Dharmasāstras, or text-books embodying the teaching of the Brahmanical Schools on the rules of caste, were compiled from the earliest Sūtras; the law books of Yajnavalkya, Nārada, and, most famous of all, the Mānava-dharmasāstra, or laws of Manu, probably belong to the Gupta period. In this work, the rules of *dharma* or conduct for each caste are rigidly laid down. The first book deals with cosmogony; the next five with the four *āsrama* or storages of the Brahmin's life as student, house-holder, anchorite and mendicant; the seventh and eighth with the Kshatriya's duties the rules of government; the ninth with domestic law—women, husband and wife, parents and children, and inheritance; the tenth with the origin, development and rules of caste; and the eleventh and twelfth with laws of morality, the nature of good and evil, and penances and expiation for sin. Elaborate precautions are taken for preserving the purity of the Brahmins: for them, travel to foreign countries, and even into certain parts of India, is prohibited. Strict injunctions about diet, education and marriage are given; girls are to be married at puberty, and the remarriage of widows is forbidden. "Until death let the widow live a life of endurance, self-restraint and chastity, yearning to fulfil the law of wives to one thousand, that most excellent law."*

The very touch of Sūdra or outcast brings defilement. Fantastic penalties are prescribed for the Sūdra who dares to study the sacred texts: if he listens to a recital of the Vedas his ears are to be filled with molten wax; if he repeats them his tongue is to be torn out; if he remembers them his body is to be cut asunder. Needless to say these penalties were never enforced in practice.

Universities for secular and religious studies flourished at Nālandā and other centres of learning. Medical science was widely studied, and Sanskrit medical treatises were the base of much of the later Arabian learning which reached Europe in the Middle Ages. Dissection was practised, and students were trained in "holding the lancet, in cutting, marking and piercing with it, in extracting darts, in cleansing wounds, in causing them to dry up, the application of ointments and in the

* *Mānava-dharma-sāstra* V. 158. (Sacred Books of the East, vol. vii.)

administration of emetics, purges and oily enemas." In astronomy, much was due to the Alexandrian Greeks, to whom the Indians freely acknowledged their indebtedness. "The Greeks are barbarians," says the Hindu astronomer, Varāhamihira, "but the science of astronomy originated with them, and for this they must be reverenced like gods." Hindu astronomers had discovered that the heavenly bodies were spherical, and shone by reflected light; they were aware of the diurnal motion of the eaerth on its axis and had calculated its diameter. Brahmagupta (A.D. 628) anticipated Newton by declaring that "all things fall to the earth by a law of nature, for it is the nature of the earth to attract and keep things." The Vaisesika school of physicists propounded and atomic theory. In mathematics the theorem of Pythagoras was understdood, a value was calculated for π, a table of sines given, and a rule laid down for the solution of simple equations.*

In imaginative literature, the chief developments were the Kāvya or Court Epic, which might be in prose as well as verse, drama, lyric poetry, and prose romances or fables. The galaxy of writers, popularly known as the Nine Gems, who graced the court of the Gupta Kings, was, however dwarfed by the towering genius of Kālīdāsa, who was equally eminent as a lyric poet and dramatist. Kālīdāsa's chief poems are the *Raghuvamsa,* or "Story of the Race of Raghu," the *Kumāra Sambhāva* or 'Birth of the War-god,' the *Ritu Samhāra* or 'Cycle of Seasons,' and the *Meghadhuta* or 'Cloud Messenger,' a lyrical gem which won the admiration of Goethe. The date of Kālīdāsa is a matter of considerable uncertainty, but it is supposed that he lived at Ujjain about A.D. 400. The 'Cloud Messenger' consists of a lyrical monologue put into the mouth of Yaksha or spirit in the court of the god Kubera, who has been banished from his home in the Himalayas to Central India Sitting in exile, he watches the dark rain-cloud hurrying northwards, and gives it a message to bear to his beloved wife. In fancy he pursues the cloud in its journey over the Indian scene:

> On Nāga Nadi's banks thy waters shed,
> And raise the feeble jasmin's languid head.
> Grant for a while thy interposing shroud,
> To where those damsels woo the friendly cloud;
> As while the garlands' flowery stores they seek,
> The scorching sunbeams tinge their tender cheek,
> The ear-hung lotus fades, and vain they chase,
> Fatigued and faint, the drops that dew thy face.

Only less famous than Kālīdāsa as a lyrical and erotic writer was Bhartihari, the Indian Horace, whose *Sringāra Sataka* or 'Century of Love' is full of charming but cynical epigrams.

---

* Alberuni's *India,* trans. Sachau, I. 23. *Legacy of India* (Oxford 1937), p. 335 ff.

The following translations give some idea of Bhartihari's muse in its varying moods:

"You are a lord of acres,
But we are lords of song;
And we subdue the subtle
If you subdue the strong;
The rich of you are speaking
The wise in me believe;
And if you find me irksome
Why then I take my leave!"

What profit are the Vedas,
Or books of legal lore?
Or those long-winded stanzas
Repeated o'er and o'er?
What gain we by our merits?
A dwelling in the skies—
A miserable mansion
That men of sense despise!
All these are huckstering methods,
Give me that perfect way
Of self-contained fruition
Where pain is done away!

The witty, elegant and versatile Bhartrihari, recluse, courtier, philosopher, grammarian and poet in turn, was typical of the many-sided culture of the period. According to one story, he took monastic vows more than once, but found the attractions of the world too much for him. In the end, however, he retired to a Buddhist monastery and assumed the yellow robe, and died in the odour of sanctity in A.D. 651.

Among the prose romances the most remarkable are the *Dasa Kumāra Charita* or 'Adventures of the Ten Princes' of Dandin and the *Kādambari* and *Harsha Charita* of Bāna. These are classed by Sanskrit writers on style as prose kāvyas or epics. Bāna's prose is the extreme example of highly polished and ornate Sanskrit; his endless compounded words and his fantastic similes are triumphs of ingenuity, but make little appeal to western taste. Here, for example, is a typical description of a grief-stricken princess:

"Lost in the forest and in thought, bent upon death on the root of the tree, fallen upon calamity and her nurse's bosom, parted from her husband and happiness, burnt with the fierce sunshine and the woes of womanhood, her mouth closed by silence as well as by her hand, she was held fast by her companions as well as by grief."

Mention must also be made of the famous collections of beast-stories, the

Panchatantra and the *Hitopadesa* or 'Book of Wise Counsels.' These stories, the successors of the Buddhist Jātakas, were carried to the courts of Bagdad, Byzantium and Cairo, and ultimately found their way to the West, where they had an immense influence upon the literature of medieval Europe. Chaucer, Shakespeare and, in modern times, Rudyard Kipling have borrowed indirectly from this source.

The Drama

The word *nātaka* or drama comes from the Sanskrit *nrit*, to dance, and this derivation throws a flood of light on the origin of the Indian theatre. From Vedic times Indians were fond of dancing and recitations, and dramatic representations at religious festivals are referred to in Asoka's inscriptions. No doubt the first plays resembled the *yātra* still popular in Bengal, and on occasions such as the spring festival, episodes such as the death of Ravana, the abduction of Sītā, the binding of Bali, the slaying of Kamsa, or Krishna's adventures with the Gopis were crudely enacted. Pānini (*c.* 400 B.C.) speaks of actors as singing, and specifically mentions dramas as represented both by action and declamation, the theme being recited off stage and accompanied in mimic pantomime. Jayadeva's celebrated *Gīta Govinda*, or 'Song of the Cowherd,' is a later example of the lyrical dialogue from which the drama proper arose. The earliest dramas must have been not unlike European miracle and mystery plays. In the time of Kanishka (A.D. 120) the drama was used by religious teachers like Asvaghosha for purposes of edification. Later, a regular court-drama arose, with elaborate rules, which are embodied in a work on dramatic criticism known as the Nātya Sāstra, or 'Treatise on the Drama.'

The Indian and Elizabethan theatres have many common characteristics. Plays were not acted, as in Greece,* on a public stage in an amphitheatre, but in the courtyard of a palace or a private house. The stage itself was a plain wooden floor, at the back of which was a curtain, which served as a tiring house for the actors. Female parts were taken by boys, and the scenery was of the simplest, much being left to the imagination of the audience. A stock character is Vidhūsaka, the fool or parasite. As in the Greek theatre, there was little action, and violent or indecorous scenes were not acted. The plots were usually romantic like those of the New Attic Comedy, and commonly turned upon a love affair; after mutual misunderstandings the lovers are united, for tragedy is contrary to the Sanskrit canons of art, which prescribe a happy ending. The dialogue is a mixture of verse and prose; kings, Brahmins and noblemen speak Sanskrit, while women and the lower orders employ one or other of the Prākrits according to their status. The play starts with a prayer,

* Weber's theory of the indebtedness of the Indian drama to Greece rests on insufficient evidence. It has been shown that in most respects the so-called resemblances are the result of mere coincidence.

and this is followed by a prologue, in which the manager (*sutradhāra*) discusses the drama with some of the cast, incidentally commending the author and elucidating the plot for the benefit of the audience.

To write a history of the Indian drama would require a volume to itself, and mention can only be made here of one or two outstanding masterpieces. One of the earliest of the classical dramas is 'The Toy Cart' (*Mricchakatika*), ascribed to an otherwise unknown King named Sūdraka, which gives us a vivid glimpse into the social life of an Indian city in the 5th century A.D. The play opens with a busy scene in the streets of old Ujjain. A festival is taking place; the streets are being decorated; girls are grinding paint to adorn the house-fronts; garlands of flowers are being hung over the doors, and the smell of cooking is in the air. Ujjain has all the vices of a great city. In the evening the anrrow, cobbled streets are crowded with loose persons, cut-throats, courtiers and courtesans, and are not particularly safe for the ordinary citizen. Gaming-houses are provided by the state, and Act II opens with a gambler who has 'welshed,' and escapes pursuit by crouching in a ruined chapel and pretending to be an image of the god! The central figure of the play is the courtesan Vasantasena, for, in ancient India, as in Greece, the *hetaira* held a dignified and honoured position and enjoyed the friendship of men of wit and learning. Vasantasena is strangled by a villain named Samstanaka, a hanger-on of the court, whose advances she has rejected; and he uses his corrupt influence to fasten the crime upon a noble but simple-minded Brahmin named Charudatta. The scene in the court, where Charudatta is on trial for his life, is vividly described:

The court looks like a sea; its councillors
Are deep engulfed in thought; its tossing waves
Are wrangling advocates: its brood of monsters
Are these wild animals, Death's ministers.
Attorneys skim like wily snakes the surface;
Spies are the shell-fish cowering midst its weeds,
And vile informers, like the hovering curlew,
Hang fluttering o'er and pounce upon their prey.

Charudatta is condemned and actually led away to the execution-ground, amid the sorrowing farewells of the citizens, But all's well that ends well: Vasantasena is not dead, but only rendered unconscious. A Buddhist priest, who had witnessed the crime, intervenes, and Charudatta magnanimously rescues the villainous Samstanaka from a well-deserved lynching at the hands of the enraged mob. This excellent play, which combines the elements of the New Attic Comedy with the thrills of a modern melodrama, has been performed with success in Germany. It takes its name from an incident in the sub-plot, in which the lost jewels of Vasantasena are found in a boy's toy cart.

Visakhadatta's *Mudrā Rākshasa* or 'Seal of the Minister;, on the other hand, is an historical play, dealing with the plots by which the wily minister Chanakya overthrew the last of the Nanda Kings of Pātaliputra, and raised his master Chandragupta Maurya to the throne. The contrast between the two rivals, Chandragupta and Rākshasa, is strongly drawn. When the plots against the usurper fail, the defeated ex-minister exclaims:

Fortune in all befriends
The cruel Chandragupta. When I send
A messenger of certain death to slay him,
She wields the instrument against his rival,
Who should have spoiled him of one-half his kingdom,
And arms and drugs and strategies are turned
In his behalf against my friends and servants.

But all the dramas of the period pale before those of Kālidāsa, the Indian Shakespeare. "It is impossible to conceive language so beautifully musical and magnificently grand as many of the verses of Kālidāsa." Of Kālidāsa's three plays, *Mālavikāgnimitra* or "The Friendship of Malavika and Agni," *Vikramorvasī* or 'Urvasī won by Valour,' and *Sakuntalā*, the last is recognised on all hands to be the greatest of all the classical Sanskrit dramas. "Of the arts the best is the drama; of dramas, *Sakuntalā; of Sakuntalā*, the fourth act; of that act, the verses in which Kanva bids farewell to his adopted daughter." The plot is taken from a theme in the *Mahābhārata*. King Dusyanta, when hunting in the forest, comes to the hermitage of the sage Kanva, where he is greeted by the hermit's foster-daughter, the beautiful Sakuntalā. The king falls in love with her, and they are wedded in the simple Gandharva fashion, which requires nothing else save the mutual plighting of troth. Presently the King is recalled to his capital by affairs of State. He leaves his signet ring with Sakuntalā, promising to return in due time and take his bride to his capital. Sakuntalā, alas, is so wrapped up in her love that she neglects the summons of the sage Durvasas, who puts a curse on her for neglecting to serve a Brahmin. The curse is that, as Sakuntalā forgot her duty to the Rishi, so the man she loves shall forget her. A curse, once uttered, cannot be recalled, but at the earnest request of Sakuntalā's companions, the irascible old man so far modifies it by saying that when her lover sees his ring, his memory will return. Sakuntalā, of course, knows nothing of this.

Sakuntalā waits in vain for her royal lover and, finding that she is to bear a child, she determines to go to court to seek him. The fourth act, in which the heroine says farewell to her home, her parents, and the flowers she has tended is the climax of the drama, of unsurpassed tenderness and beauty. Her pet gazelle follows her in a vain attempt to bring her home; the very trees bow their heads in sorrow. Kanva speaks to her solemnly and movingly of her duties as a wife and sends her on her way. Voices in the air waft her a sad farewell:

The journey be auspicious; may the breeze,
Gentle and soothing, fan thy cheek: may lakes,
All bright with lily-cups, delight thine eyes;
The sunbeam's heat be cooled by shady trees;
The dust beneath thy feet the pollen be
Of lotuses.

Sakuntalā, alas, drops her ring in a river on her way, and when she reaches the court her husband fails to recognise her. Years pass, and a fisherman is arrested for being in possession of a royal signet ring, which he has found in the belly of a fish. As soon as he sees the ring, the King's memory returns, and stricken with remorse he seeks in vain for Sakuntalā. At last, when engaged in a campaign against the demons, he sees a boy playing, quite unafraid, with a lion-cub. The King, little knowing that the child is hiw own, takes his hand. Just then, Sakuntalā appears and is recognised, and the lovers are reunited.

After Kālidāsa, the drama continued to flourish for some centuries at the courts of local rulers. The learned Harsha, among his multifarious activities, managed to find time to compose a number of heroic plays, not distinguished by originality. The last of the great dramatists of the Augustan age of Indian literature is Bhavabhūti, whose *Mālatī and Mādhava* has been compared to Macbeth. It contains a famous act, in which the heroine, entrapped in the temple of the demon-goddess Chamanda, is about to be sacrificed, when Mādhava breaks in, slays the priestess and rescues her. For weird horror, the scene in the burning-ground where Mādhava invokes the help of the obscene spirits of the place, is unsurpassed :

Now wake the terrors of the place, beset
With crowding and malignant fiends; the flames
From funeral pyres scarce lend their sullen light,
Clogges with their fleshy prey, to dissipate
The fearful gloom that hems them in. Pale ghosts
Sport with foul goblins, and their dissonant mirth,
In shrill respondent shrieks is echoed round.

This is Bhavabhūti in his severer mood, but he can write equally well in a lighter vein. Here is his incomparable description of the heroine of The Last Story of Rāma (*Uttara Rāma Charita*):

'Tis Sītā: mark
How lovely, through her tresses dark
And floating loose, her face appears,
Though pale and wan and wet with tears.
She moves along, like Tenderness
Invested with a mortal dress.

Not without reason, Indian critics look upon Bhavabhūti as only a little lower in rank than Kālidāsa himself.

Gupta Art

Gupta art and architecture have suffered severely from time and the ravages of Hun and Muslim raiders, and comparatively few specimens have survived. Those, however, which have been recoverd, show that the glowing descriptions of Hiuen Tsang and Bāna are not exaggerated. One reason, doubtless, why so much has perished is because the houses were mostly of painted and lacquered wood and this has not withstood the ravages of time. Temples containing the images of gods and of the Buddha begin to make their appearance: the earliest of these are the little Hindu shrines at Sānchi, Erān and Tigowa (Fig. 20). The characteristics of Gupta temples are flat roofs without spires, short pillars with massive square capitals, and statues of the river goddesses Gangā and Yamunā guarding the entrance. At Bhitargāon in the Cawnpore district is a brick temple of the period, with a high tower and brilliantly executed terra-cotta ornamentation. The famous shrine at Bodh Gayā, marking the site of the Buddha's Enlightenment, and so admired by the Chinese travellers, has been altered and restored beyond recognition. Many of these temples are decorated with stone panels in low relief, of a very high quality. Some of the most striking of these are found in a ruined shrine at Deogarh in the Jhānsi district.* One of the panels depicts Siva as the Mahāyogi. The god is represented as four-armed, and is in converse with a yogi. He is surrounded by flying figures hovering in the air over

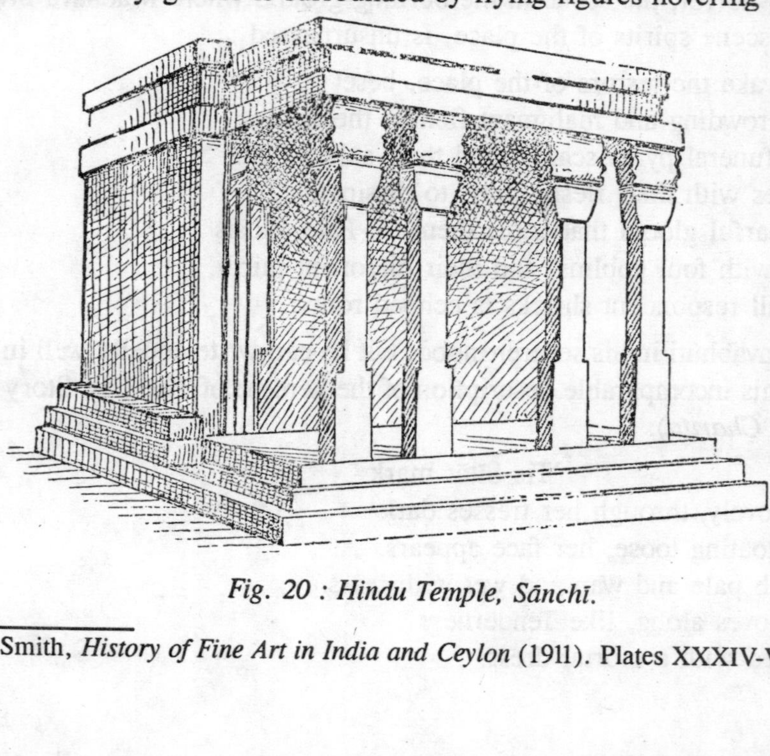

Fig. 20 : Hindu Temple, Sānchī.

* V. A. Smith, *History of Fine Art in India and Ceylon* (1911). Plates XXXIV-V.

his head. Another panel represents Vishnu sleeping in the folds of Ananta, the serpent of Eternity. Above are Indra, Siva and Parvati, together with Brahmā, seated on a lotus. The extraordinary vigour, and at the same time, the calm and majestic repose and dignity of these figures is extremely impressive. The same majestic serenity characterises the Buddhist art of the period. The Buddha figure which originated in Mathurā in the Kushān period now reaches its highest pitch of development. One of the most striking examples is the seated Buddha in white sandstone discovered at Sārnāth. There are other fine specimens in the Mathurā Museum. Metal work reached a high degree of proficiency, and the colossal 4th century Buddha from Sultānganj, now at Birmingham, weighing over a ton, is a noble figure, cast in pure copper by the *cire perdue* process (Plate VIa). Indian rulers were fond of setting up 'pillars of victory' to commemmorate their conquests. Usually these were of stone, but the most celebrated of all is the iron pillar at Delhi, erected by Kumāragupta I in A.. 415 in honour of his father. It is a solid shaft of pure, rustless wrought iron, 16 inches in diameter and 23½ feet high, and weighs about six tons. Even to-day there are comparatively few foundries where a similar mass of metal could be turned out. Another colossal iron pillar, broken into three pieces, belonging to the same period, has been found at Dhār in Central India.*

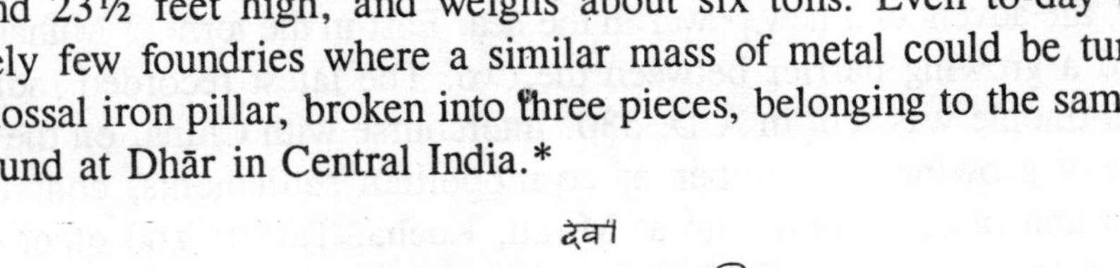

Fig. 21 : Parvati, the Consort of Siva.

* See an article entitled *Iron in Ancient India*, by S. C. Britton, in *Nature*, August, 18th, 1934, p. 238.

Chapter X

Intercourse with China, Tibet, and the Far East

China, Tibet, Nepal and Kashmir

During the Gupta period, intercourse with the West gradually dwindled. The capture of Rome by the Goths (in A.D. 410), the rise of the Neo-Sassanian Empire and, later, the advent of a new power in the near East in the form of Muhammadanism, interposed a growing barrier between the two. The latest recorded Indian embassy to Constantinople was sent in A.D. 530. Intercourse with China, on the other hand, was steadily growing. A number of cosmopolitan settlements, containing Indian merchants and priests, sprang up at Miran, Kucha, Turfan, and other sites on the silk-route which skirted the Taklamakan desert.* These have yielded a rich store of frescoes, statuettes and other remains, which reveal a mixed culture, containing Hellenistic, Iranian, Indian and Chinese elements. At Miran is a Buddhist shrine decorated with frescoes, and bearing an inscription in Kharoshthī characters to the effect that they are "the work of Titus, who has received 3,000 *bhamakas* for them." Titus was, no doubt, a 'Yavana' artist from Gandhāra. At Tun-Huang is the famous Cave of the Thousand Buddhas, with its hybrid frescoes and stucco images, showing clearly the blending of Graeco-Indian and Chinese art. Large numbers of manuscripts and other documents have also been discovered. A well-known story relates how the Emperor Ming-ti (A.D. 64) dreamt that he saw a 'golden man' enter his palace, and being told that this was the Buddha, sent to India for Buddhist scriptures and was converted. The Kushān king Kadphises II, after an unsuccessful war, sent ambassadors to China in the reign of the Emperor Ho-ti (A.D. 89-105). Kanishka conquered Kashgar and Khotan, and carried off hostages who dwelt for some years in a Buddhist monastery at his capital. One of these was a Han prince. In A.D. 148 a Parthian prince was employed in translating Buddhist Sūtras into Chinese, and in A.D. 401 Fa Hian reached India. From that time onwards, a steady stream of pilgrims and scholars crossed the desert in search of knowledge, and brought back manuscripts, relics and statues which had a profound effect on Chinese culture. A Buddhist colony

* Aurel Stein, *On Ancient Central Asian Tracks* (1933).

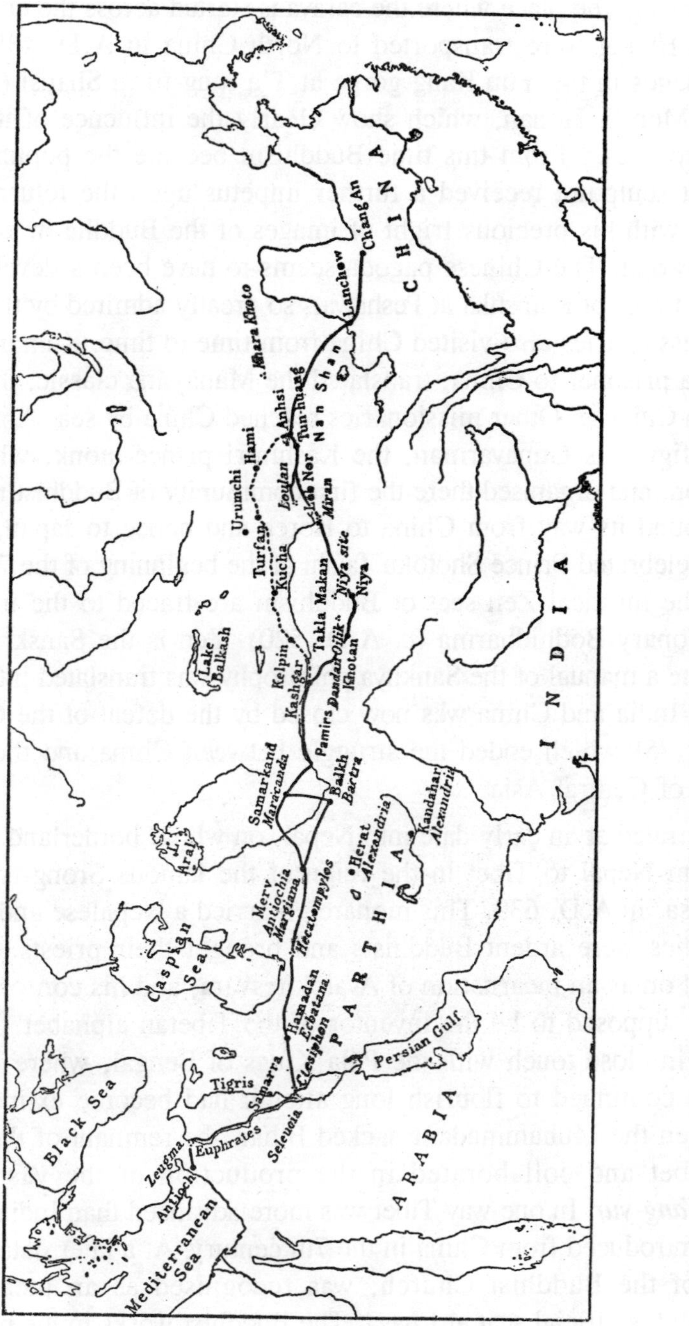

Map 6 : Indo-Chinese Trade Routes.

sprang up at Tun Huang, the place where the caravans started across the desert. Some families from Tun Huang were transported to North China in A.D. 439 and they carved rock-cut images in the Yün Kang gorge at T'a tung-fu in Shansi (A.D. 460-495) and at Lung Men in Honan, which show clearly the influence of their Gupta and Gandhāra prototypes.* From this time Buddhism became the popular religion of China. Buddhist sculpture received a further impetus upon the return of Hiuen Tsang in 645 B.C. with his precious fright of images of the Buddha in gold, silver, crystal and sandal-wood. The Chinese pagoda seems to have been a development of the celebrated relic tower of Kanishka at Peshawar, so greatly admired by the Buddhist pilgrims. Indian missionaries also visited China from time to time. Kumārajīva, who had been taken as a prisoner to China, translated the Mahāyāna classic, the Lotus of the Good Law, into Chinese. Other missionaries reached China by sea. Among these, the most striking figure is Gunavarman, the Kashmiri prince-monk, who reached Nankin from Ceylon, and organised there the first community of Buddhist nuns (A.D. 424). Buddhism found its way from China to Korea and hence to Japan, where its promoter was the celebrated Prince Shotoku Taishi at the beginning of the 7th century. The doctrines of the mystical Zen sect of Buddhism are traced to the influence of the Buddhist missionary Bodhidharma (*c.* A.D. 520). Zen is the Sanskrit Dhyāna. About the same time a manual of the Sānkhya philosophy was translated into Chinese. The route between India and China was now closed by the defeat of the Chinese by the Arabs in A.D. 751 which ended the struggle between China and the Moslems for the supremacy of Central Asia.

Buddhism penetrated at an early date into Nepāl, on whose borderland the Master was born, and from Nepāl to Tibet in the reign of the famous Srong-tsan-gampo, the founder of Lhasa, in A.D. 639. This monarch married a Nepalese and a Chinese princess; these ladies were ardent Buddhists and brought their priests with them. This king is looked on as an incarnation of Avalokitesvara, and his consorts of Tārā. He is traditionally supposed to be the inventor of the Tibetan alphabet. In the 11th century Tibet was in close touch with the Pāla Kings of Bengal, where Buddhism, in a corrupt form, continued to flourish long after it had become extinct in other parts of India. When the Muhammadans sacked Bihār, the remnant of the Buddhist monks fled to Tibet and collaborated in the production of the vast Buddhist encyclopedia, the *Tang-yur.* In one way Tibet was more advanced than India, as block-printing had been introduced from China in the 7th century. At a later date, the Dalai Lama, the head of the Buddhist Church, was recognised as an incarnation of Avalokitesvara, with his official seat at Lhasa. The Buddhist works in the monasteries in Tibet have not yet been thoroughly explored, and its best known artistic products are its bronzes and temple banners. Tibetan Buddhism to-day is a strange mixture of

* J. H. Lindsay, *Indian Influences on Chinese Sculpture,* Indian Art and Letters, 1936, p. 125.

Mahāyāna doctrine and Mongolian demon-worship and exhibits interesting features. The Abbé Huc, who visited Lhasa in 1845, was greatly struck by the resemblances between Lamaistic and Catholic ritual. "The crosier, the mitre, the dalmatic, the cope or pluvial which the grand llamas wear on a journey, or when they perform some ceremony outside the temple: the service with a double choir, psalmody, exorcisms: the censer swinging on five chains and contrived to be open or shut at will: benediction by the llamas with the right hand extended over the heads of the faithful: the chaplet, sacerdotal celibacy, lenten retirements from the world, the worship of saints, fasts, processions, litanies, holy water, these are the points of contact between the Buddhists and ourselves."* This was perhaps due to the close association betwen Tibetan and Nestorian monks in China at monasteries like Hsian-fu, between A.D. 635 and 841. The secluded valley of Nepāl was for a time a feudatory of the Gupta Empire, and afterwards came under Tibet. The art of Tibet and Nepal have much in common. Both excelled in the production of copper-gilt statues of the numerous Mahāyāna gods the goddesses inlaid with turquoise and other precious stones. The Frontispiece is a Tibetan representation of Tārā, the consort of Avalokitesvara, of the 16th century A.D. The State of Kashmir was also culturally important, because it lay on the route between India and China. It formed part of the Mauryan and Kushān empires, and was afterwards for a time subject to China. In the 8th century A.D. it became independent and was a flourishing kingdom until the Muhammadan conquest. The Mogul emperors regularly visited Kashmir to escape the heat of the Indian plains, and beautified it with ornamental gardens. The wooden architecture once common all over India still survives in Kashmir as in Burma.

Burma, Java, Sumatra and Cambodia

Mention has been made already of early voyages of Hindu merchant-adventurers from the ports of Western India to the head of the Persian Gulf and the Red Sea. At the same time, similar activities were taking place in the Bay of Bengal. In one of the early Buddhist stories, the *Mahājanaka Jātaka*, we hear of the son of a banished prince who determines to go to sea. He proceeds to the inland port of Champā, now Bhāgalpur on the Ganges. "Having got together his stock-in-trade (pearls, jewels and diamonds), he put it on board a ship with some merchants bound for Suvarnabhūmi (the Golden Chersonese), and bade his mother farewell, saying that he was sailing for that country... There were seven caravans with their beasts embarked on board. In seven days the ship made 700 leagues, but having run too violently in its course, it could not hold out." Other Jātaka tories tell of merchants from Broach, and of a Brahmin from Benares, all of whom were bound for Suvarnabhūmi or the Golden Chersonese, *i.e.,* Pegu and Moulmein. The port at which they landed was Thatun at

* Max Müler, *Last Essays,* First Series (1901), p. 251.

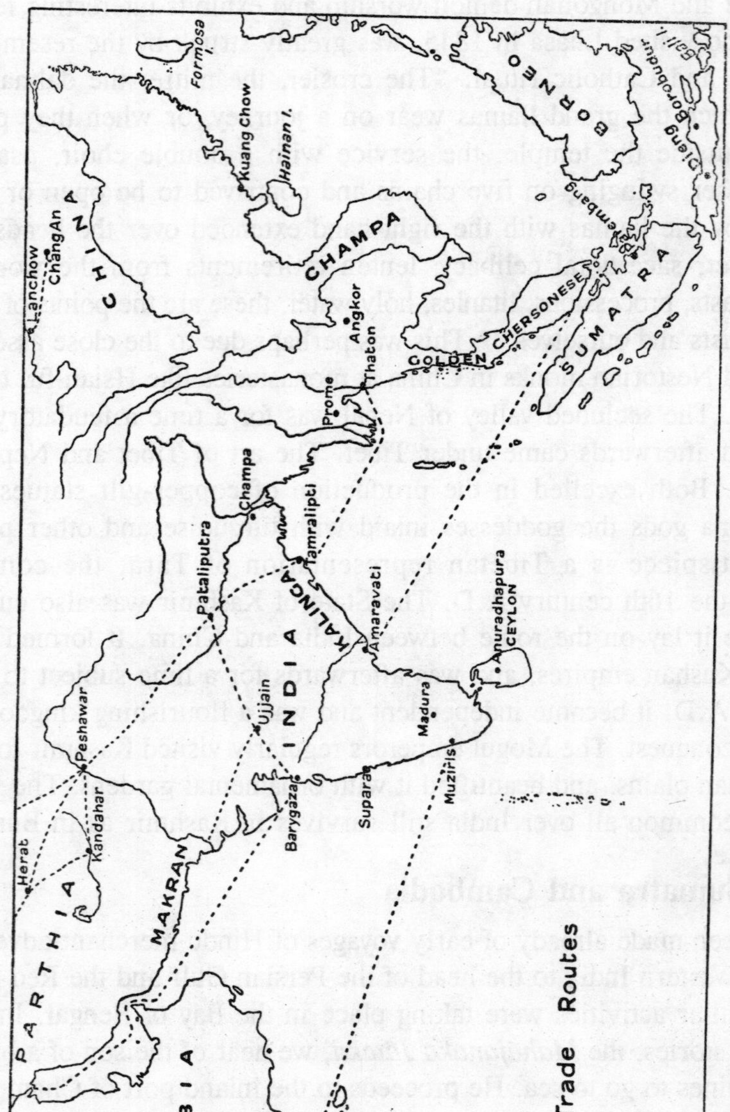

Map 7 : Indian Trade Routes.

the head of the Gulf of Martaban. There was also a brisk trade between Thatun and Amarāvatī on the Kistna river. According to the Ceylon chronicles, Burma was converted to Buddhism by two of Asoka's missionaries, but actually the apostle was probably Buddhagosha, the famous Sinhalese scholar of the 5th century A.D. Buddhist and Hindu remains of the Gupta period are found at Thatun, Pegu and Prome. Thatun was destroyed by Anawrata, the great king of Pegu, in A.D. 1080. He took back with him Buddhist monks, relics and manuscripts, and Burma became a stronghold of Hīnayāna Buddhism. The kingdom of Pegu was overthrown by the Tartars under Kublai Khān in A.D. 1284. Magnificent remains, covering many miles, are found at the old capital of Pagan on the Irrawady. Burma took her religion from India, but her ethnic affinities are with the north, and the Indian influence was quickly assimilated.

From an early period there was a flourishing trade between Gujarāt and the Malay Archipelago. The Gujarāt merchants exported printed cotton goods and took in exchange various spices. An old Gujarāti proverb says that of those who went to Java, few returned, but those who did, had made their fortunes. Fa Hian tells us that large ships, carrying over 200 passengers, frequently made the voyage from Ceylon to Java. Soon after this Javanese court was said to have been converted to Buddhism by Prince Gunavarman of Kashmir. The Chinese pilgrim, I-tsing, twice visitd Srīvijaya (Palembang in S.E. Sumatra) in 671 and 698; he found there over 1,000 monks, and was enabled to study Sanskrit, in spite of the distance from India. Another learned visitor was Dharmapāla, a Mahāyāna scholar from Nālandā. Ships plied regularly between Tāmralipti, the celebrated port at the mouth of the Ganges, and Palembang. In consequence of Buddhist missionary activity, I-tsing tells us, "many kings and chieftains of the Southern Ocean admired and believed in Buddhism." Sumatra was ruled from the seventh to the fourteenth century by the powrful Sailendra dynasty, which seems originally to have come from Malacca, and was in close touch with Ceylon and the Chola Kings of Southern India.

Java was colonised by Hindu settlers, both from Gujarāt on the West coast of India, and from Kalinga or Orissa on the East. These emigrations have been attributed to foreign inroads, which forced the inhabitants to seek fresh homes overseas. According to local tradition, the first colony from Western India set out in A.D. 75 under a prince called Aji Saka, but was compelled to withdraw owing to a pestilence. A second attempt followed in A.D. 603. "It having been foretold," say the Javanese chronicles, "to a king of Gujarāt that his kingdom would decay and go to ruin altogether, the prince resolved to send his son to Java, and, possessing the written record of Aji Saka, which had been preserved in his family, he gave it to his son, and embarked him with about 5,000 followers for that island. Among these followers were people skilled in agriculture, artificers, men learned in medicine, able writers and military men. They sailed in six large ships and upwards of a hundred small, and after a voyage of four

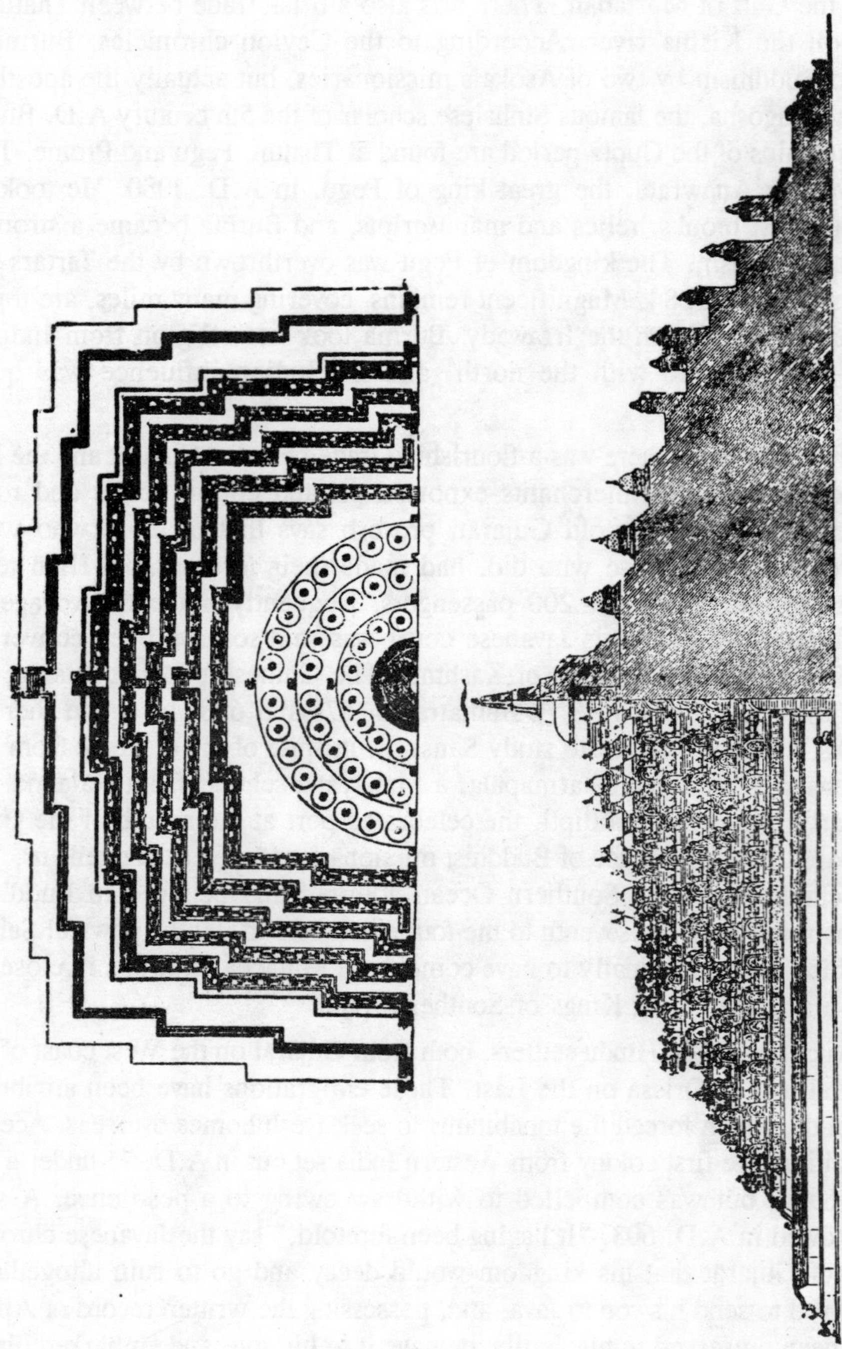

Fig. 22 : Plan and Elevation of the Buddhist Temple at Borobudur, Java.

months, reached what they thought to be the island of Java; but it did not accord with the account given by Aji Saka, so they re-embarked. In a few months they came in sight of an island with a long range of mountains, and some of them, with the prince at their head, effected a landing at the western extremity, while a part were driven southward. They soon met with the grain *jawa-urit*, as described by Aji Saka, and ascertained that they had at last reached their destination."

The earliest remains are the Hindu shrines on the Dieng plateau, which show clear traces of Pallava and Chalukya influence. From A.D. 732 to 1250, Middle Java came under the rule of the Sailendra dynasty of Srīvijaya in Sumatra. These kings were Mahāyāna Buddhists, and maintained a close touch with the motherland. One of them built a monastery at the great university of Nālandā. To them we owe the wonderful shrine of Borobudur, the grandset of all the monuments of the Buddhist faith (Fig. 22). It stands in an almost ideal setting overlooking the Vedu valley, a paradise of green rice-fields, bamboos and palm trees, with a background of distant volcanoes. The architects erected it round a conical hill, which they crowned with a central stūpa, surrounded by a number of smaller ones. The sides of the hill have been enclosed in a series of seven stone terraces leading up to the central shrine at the apex, and forming a procession path. The walls of these terraces are ornamented with exquisite reliefs illustrating episodes in the lives of the Buddha and various legends, as told in the *Lalita Vistara*, and *Jātaka Mālā* and other Buddhist books, and are crowned with niches containing Buddha figures, gazing down upon the scene with serene and majestic dignity.* In the upper panel of Plate VII, the Bodhisattva is seen setting out on his first chariot-ride, when the sight of the sick man brought home to him the miseries of human life; in the lower, the pious prince Sibi is offering his 'pound of flesh' in order to ransom the dove (being weighed on the scales) from the hawk which is perched in the neighbouring tree.

In the middle of the thirteenth century the power of the Sailendra rulers in Java seems to have come to an end, and the succeeding Javanese dynasty made their residence at Prambanan. To this period belongs the famous group of Hindu shrines known as the Loro Jongrang, containing temples to Brahma, Siva and Vishnu, ornamented with reliefs, taken from the Rāmāyana and other Hindu sources, which rival those of Borobudur. This period was abruptly brought to an end by some great calamity, probably an earthquake, and from the middle of the tenth century East Java became the seat of the ruling power. Javanese culture reached its zenith under the kings of Majāpahit (1294-1478). During this period Java was the undisputed queen of the Eastern Archipelago and Indian, Arab and Chinese merchants flocked to her

---

* For Java and Cambodia, see H. W. Ponder, *Java pageant, and Cambodian Glory* (1935), and H. C. Candee, *Angkor the Magnificent* (New York, 1924). The history is summarised in the Journal of the Greater India Society, 1934-5.

ports. Classical Javanese literature flourished, and versions of episodes from the Sanskrit epics, the Marriage of Arjuna and the Battle of the Bhāratas, were composed. The drama, still popular in Java, developed original forms in the puppet and shadow plays, in which scenes from the Javanese national history were celebrated. Much of the ancient Hidnu culture of Java has been preserved in the little island of Bali, which was untouched by the wave of Islamic invasion.

Cambodia was visited by Hindu traders who made their way up the Mekong river before the Christian era; the settlers traced their origin to a marriage between an exiled Indian prince and a Nāga princess. The offspring were Kambujas or Cambodians. At first the Cambodians appear to have been tributaries of China. Cambodian ambassadors went to the Chinese court with tribute in the form of gold, silver and spices. On one occasion they took an elephant, which the Emperor refused "because it might do harm to his subjects." In the 6th century A.D. a line of Brahmanical Hindu rulers appear on the scene. They took the affix of *varman* (Protector) which seems to show that they were Pallavas. The first king appears to have been Srutavarman (*c.* A.D. 400), but Cambodian culture reached its climax under Jayavarman II (*c.* A.D. 802-869). Cambodia was now connected with Java, and was evidently influenced by the artistic movement which produced Borobudur. Yasovarman, a powerful monarch, built for himself a new capital, named Yasodarapura or Angkor, which was completed in A.D. 900. This stupendous city is square in shape, enclosed in four walls each 3,000 yards long, and surrounded by a moat 110 yards wide. The moat is crossed by five bridges, elaborately ornamented and leading to triple tower-crowned gateways. The roads running through the gateways converge on the square in the centre of the city, where stand the Royal Palace and the Bayon temple. The temple is surmoutned with towers bearing gigantic masks of human faces and decorated inside with bas-reliefs representing endless scenes from the daily life of the city—kings, soldiers, elephants, horses and chariots, and the thousands of dancing-girls who performed the ritual dances for which Angkor was celebrated. A fitting commentary on these reliefs is a description by a contemporary Chinese traveller, Chu Ta Kuan, who went to Angkor as an interpreter or secretary to the ambassador of Kublai Khan in 1225.*

> "When the king goes forth there is cavalry at the head of his escort... musicians and banners... women of the palace to the number of several hundred, dressed in gorgeous brocades, with head-dresses of flowers, bearing great candles, even in daylight... glided chariots drawn by goats and horses, princes and high officials mounted on elephants, then the king himself, bearing the sacred sword, standing on a royal elephant, whose tusks are ringed with gold; bearers in uniform hold over him white parasols with golden handles; around him are troops of

* *Memories of the Customs of Cambodia*. Trans. P. Pelliot, Bulletin de l'Ecole Francaise, 1902.

elephants forming a guard. Each day when the king holds audience in the council chamber, for he gives judgment twice a day, his coming is heralded by music, the king is borne in a golden litter; when the conch shells are blown, the golden curtains are drawn aside by two girls; holding the Sacred Sword he shows himself to his people behind a golden window; his skirt is of jewelled cloth, embroidered in a floral design reserved especially for the royal garments; on his head is a golden fillet entwined with jasmine flowers; great ropes of pearls encircle his neck, while on his wrists and ankles he wears gold bracelets; on his fingers are rings set with cat's-eyes; the soles of his feet and the palms of his hands are tinted red."

The Khmer kings of Cambodia waged fierce and unending wars with their neighbours, and no doubt employed the captives taken in battle to erect their sumptuous buildings; trade prospered, and cargoes from all parts of the east found their way to the mouth of the Mekong. The golden age of the Khmers was the reign of Sūryavarman II (A.D. 1112) during which was erected the most magnificent of all the temples at Angkor Vat.

"Covering an area of three and a half square miles, this vast monument, overpowering in size and exquisite in design, is surrounded by a moat 700 feet wide. Three concentric squares form decreasing terraces, elevated one above another, with long galleries of repeated columns crowned by the final towers, which soar up to the sky in one splendid sweep of graceful symmetry. The long causeway, some 40 feet in width, passes through the western entrance, straight down to the gateway of the second terrace, bordered with the most dramatic architectural motifs of the Khmers—the Nāgā. The body of the serpent forms the rail and the upreared sevenfold head guards the temple entrance.

"Along the walls of the galleries are the bas-reliefs—kings and soldiers are priestly processions, interspersed with representations of legendary incidents from the Hindu epics. Hundreds of Tevadas and Apsaras smile gaily from the walls and each stone of the mighty towers carries its burden of carved beauty. The gateways and accompanying stairways are placed at the four cardinal points, finally converging under the central tower in a tiny cell-like chapel, where it is supposed that the king rendered his accounts to heaven. Had the Khmers left but this single monument it would have placed them among the great artists of the world, so perfect is its architecture and so rare its art."*

The Cambodian capital was first plundered by the King of Champa in A.D. 1177 but recovered its former prosperity. In the fourteenth century fierce wars were waged with the Siamese kings, which ended in the decline of the Khmer dynasty. In 1385

* *Angkor : A Royal Romance.* By Lucille Douglas. Indian Art and Letters (1932), p. 109.

Angkor was sacked and its inhabitants carried off captive. It was again taken in 1417, and this was the end. Nowhere in the world does the jungle obliterate the work of men's hands with such devastating rapidity as in Cambodia, and all the great temples were soon swallowed up and forgotten, to be discovered again in 1861, when they were by a mere chance revealed to the astonished eyes of a French naturalist, who stumbled upon this vast pile of ruins rising like a fairy palace on the banks of the Tonla Sap lake.

Chapter XI

The History of the Deccan

The Deccan (Dakshināpatha or South Land), lying between the Vindhya Mountains and the Tungabhadra River, was the latest part of India to be overrun by the Indo-Aryan from the North. It is spoken of in the epics as covered by dense forests, haunted by 'demons' and aboriginal tribes, Rākshasas and Dasyus. Into this forest, the Dandakaranya or Mahākāntāra, the Indid settlers penetrated with difficulty. To them the Vindhyas seemed so lofty that they shut out the sun. There are, however, legends of an early colony led to the south by the Sage Agastya, who was reputed to have been the first to introduce Aryan customs into Southern India. The *Aitareya Brāhmana* speaks of the Deccan as being inhabited by the Āndhras, and says they were the descendants of the Vedic seer Visvāmitra. In the *Rāmāyana* we are told that Rāma, when he was banished from Ayodhya, went to the Dandaka forest, where he spent his time in fighting demons. He settled at the town of Panchāvati, which is popularly identified with the holy city of Nāsik at the source of the Godāvari, a great place of pilgrimage. We may reasonably suppose that the penetration of the Deccan began about the seventh century B.C. The invaders drove the aboriginal tribes who resisted them into the mountain fastnesses; with the rest they intermarried and incorporated them into their own society. The aborigines learnt the language of their conquerors, but at the same time preserved some of their original words and phonetic peculiarities. This led to the formation of the Mahārāshtri Prakrit, the parent of the modern Marāthī language. The principal settlements were probably in the tableland of Vidharba or Berār, but the remoter parts of the country remained in a wild state for a long time. The author of the *Periplus Maris Erythraei*, in the first century after Christ, speaks of the Deccan as still consisting of desert regions and vast mountains, swarming with wild beasts of every description, leopards, tigers and elephants, huge snakes, hyenas, and monkeys of various kinds. Three centuries later than this, the Chinese pilgrim Fa Hian found it precipitious and dangerous; the traveller was unable to make his way without guides, who passed him on from one to another. The earliest historical event in the annals of the Deccan was the despatch by Asoka, in the year 256 B.C., of a Buddhist mission to the Rāshtrikas, Āndhras and others on the borders of his kingdom. The Rāshtrikas, later called the Mahārāshtrikas or Mahārathas, the ancestors of the Marāthās, were the people inhabiting the country round Poona; the Pitenikas were the inhabitants of the district of Paithan, and the Bhojas were the people of Berār. The Pulindas appear to have been the wild tribes such as the Bhils. According to the Ceylon chronicles, at the head of the mission to the Deccan was a monk named Rakhita, at the head of the mission to the Deccan was a monk named Rakhita, and he penetrated as far as Banavāsi in the Dharwar district, later the capital of the Kadamba dynasty. He is said to have made 60,000 converts.*

The rise of the Āndhras dates from the decline of the Maurya Empire after the death of Asoka in 232 B.C., when various subject nations began to throw off the yoke and established their independence. Who exactly the Āndhras were is obscure, but it is generally believed that they were Dravidian-speaking Telugus, who originally lived between the deltas of the Godāveri and Kistna rivers. The Āndhras quickly extended their sway over the whole of the Deccan; their principal towns were Srī Kakulam, not far from Masulipatnam, Dharanikota or Amarāvati, near the mouth of the Kistna in the Guntur district, Paithan in the north-west of what is now Hyderabad, and Nāsik in the north-western Deccan. Pliny speak of the Āndhras as having thirty walled towns, numerous villages, and an army of 100,000 infantry, 2,000 cavalry and 1,000 elephants. The Āndhra or Satakarni dynasty ruled for four and a half centuries, from 225 B.C. to A.D. 225. The Āndhra kings made frequent wars upon their eastern and western neighbours, the Kalingas of Orissa, and the powerful Saka Satraps of Ujjain and Orissa. It is in reference to his conquest of the latter that the Āndhra King Gautamīputra Srī Satakarni (*c.* A.D. 120) boasts in an inscription that he "restored the glory of the Āndhra race" by rooting out Sakas, Pahlavas (Parthians) and other foreigners from the land. This boast, however, was not entirely accurate: though the Āndhra King took Nāsik from the Sakas, his son married a daughter of Rudradāman, the Saka Satrap of Ujjain.

At the height of their power, the Āndhra kings governed the Deccan from sea to sea, and being in possession of the ports of the western coast, they were extremely prosperous. Paithan and Tāgara (the modern Ter in the Hyderabad state) were the great emporia for the distribution of trade both from the Arabian Sea and the Bay of Bengal. Paithan is described by a contemporary Jain writer as a prosperous town, with splendid temples and palaces and wide streets, surrounded by high walls and a moat. Roads must have been good and communications easy, for the Nāsik cave inscriptions record donations from inhabitants of Sind and Northern India; while, on the other hand, Nāsik merchants were among the donors to the Bharhut stūpa near Allahābād. It is interesting to note that the Buddhist cave-monasteries were principally excavated at the side of the trade-routes running over the three great passes leading into Deccan—the Bhor Ghaut, the Nānā Ghaut, and the Thāl Ghaut. Although

* Hiuen Tsang found 100 monasteries at Banavāsi, with 100,000 monks.

the Āndhra kings were orthodox Hindus they were liberal patrons of Buddhism, and made grants of land for the maintenance of monastic communities. There seems to have been no antagonism between the Buddhists and Hindus; the yellow-robed Bhikkhus or mendicants from the monasteries in the hill-side wandered at will among the Hindu villages as its foot, preaching and collecting alms from the peasantry without let or hindrance.

The inscriptions throw a flood of light upon social conditions under the Āndhras. The Āndhra Kingdom was divided into three provinces, each governed by its hereditary chieftains. These feudatory nobles enjoyed a large measure of independence. Below them were district officers, secretaries and clerks. The rural districts were divided into villages and homesteads, each with its headman. Trade was in the hands of gilds, which were very powerful organisations; we hear of gilds of oil-pressers, mechanics, potters, weavers, corn-dealers, bamboo-workers, and braziers. The gilds, as in medieval Europe, decided their affairs in an assembly, at which each member had a vote. The gild regulated hours of work, wages, and competition among its members. Recusants were fined, and the money thus collected was for feeding beggars and other charitable purposes. The head of the gild was the Seth or chief merchant. Great fortunes must have been made in trade, for an inscription tells us of a merchant-prince, the Seth Bhūtpala of Vaijayanti, who paid for the excavation of the great hall at Kārla. The gilds acted as banks, and money was deposited with them at fixed rates of interest, which varied from five to seven and a half per cent. Funds for religious endowments were invested in these banks. Other classes mentioned in the inscriptions are traders, heads of caravans, physicians, goldsmiths, druggists, cultivators, carpenters, gardeners, and blacksmiths. Village self-government has always been a feature of Indian life, and we learn from a Nāsik inscription that municipal affairs were managed by the *naigama sabhā* or corporation. There was a regular coinage of gold, silver, copper and lead. It is significant that some of the coins bear the figure of a ship. One of the most generous benefactors of the day was the Saka prince Ushavadatta of Nāsik, who according to his inscriptions, spent vast sums in rest-houses, wells, tanks, ferry-boats and schools, excavating caves for the monks, feeding Brahmins and other charities. Prākrit rather than Sanskrit was the language of the Āndhra court. A considerable literature in the Mahārāshtri Prākrit sprang up, and one famous work, written in that dialect, is the *Sapta Sataka* or seven centuries of verse, which contains some of the most charming lyrics written in any Indian language.

The later history of the Deccan has been laboriously pieced together from inscriptions. It is largely a stroy of the battles of kites and crows: the martial rulers of the Deccan, like their descendants the Marāthās, appear to have spent most of their time in making war on their neighbours. The story of these campaigns is of little interest in itself to the general reader, but a brief outline is necessary in order to understand the contributions of the Deccan to Indian culture. It is probable that these campaigns were, except on rare occasions, waged between the kings and their retainers, and had little effect in the people at large.

The causes which led to the downfall of the Āndhra Empire in the third century A.D. are obscure, but as usual it gave the signal for the rise of a number of local dynasties, which continued to flourish with varying fortunes until they they were absorbed into the empire of the all-conquering Chalukyas. Special mention must be made of the Vākātakas of Berār, who came into prominence about A.D. 300. A little less than a century later, a Vākātaka monarch married a daughter of the great Gupta emperor Chandragupta II. This alliance was of the utmost importance, for it made the Vākātakas the channel through which the art and culture of Northern India found its way to the Deccan, whence it was ultimately transmitted, through the Pallavas of Kānchī, to Southern India. Another local dynasty which sprang up about the same time in what is now known as Kanara, the country between the southern portion of the Western Ghāts and the sea, was that of the Kadambas. The founder of the Kadamba line was a young Brahmin named Mayuravarman, and the story of how he revolted against his overlords, the Pallavas of Kānchī, is graphically told in an inscription, written in the ornate *Kāvya* style, by the court poet:

> "In the Kadamba family there was an illustrious chief of the twice-born named Mayuravarman, adorned with sacred knowledge, good disposition, purity and the rest. With his preceptor Virasarman he went to the city of the Pallava lords and, eager to study the whole sacred law, entered the college as a mendicant student. There, enraged by a fierce quarrel with a Pallava horseman, he reflected, 'Alas, that in this Kali-age the Brahmins should be so much feebler than the Kshatriyas! For if to one who has duly served his preceptor's family and earnestly studied his branch of the Veda, the perfection of holiness depends on a king, what can be more painful than this? And so, with a hand more dexterous in grasping the *Kusa* grass,* the fuel, the stones, the ladle, the melted butter and the oblation vessel, he unsheathed a flaming sword, eager to conquer the earth. Having swiftly defeated in battle the frontier guards of the Pallava lords, he occupied the inaccessible forest stretching to the gates of Srīparvata... When the enemy, the kings of Kānchi, came in strength to fight him, he, in the nights when they were marching or resting in rough country, in places fit for assault, lighted upon the ocean of their army and struck it like a hawk, full of strength. So he bore that trouble, relying solely on the sword of his arm. The Pallava lords, having found out this strength of his, as well as his valour and lineage, said that to ruin him would be of no advantage, so they quickly chose him for a friend. Then, entering the king's service, he pleased them by his acts of bravery in battle, and obtained the honour of being crowned with a fillet offered by the Pallavas... He also received

* Kusa grass (*Saccharum spontaneum*) was used in various Brahmanical ceremonies.

a territory bordered by the water of the western sea and bounded by the Prehara, secured to him under the compact that others should not eneter it."*

The Kadamba capital was at the ancient city of Vanavāsi in the forest which covered the Dharwar district. The numerous inscriptions, temples and other remains point to a well-governed and prosperous state. The Kadambas ruled until the middle of the sixth century A.D., when they were conquered by the Chalukyas. Another dynasty which for some centuries played an important part in the history of the Deccan was the Gangas, of what is now the state of Mysore. The Gangas and their offshoots had a long and prosperous reign, lasting from the second to the eleventh century A.D. They were zealous patrons of the Jains, and the colossal statue of the Jain saint Gomatesvara at Sravana Belgola was erected by the minister of a Ganga king in A.D. 984 (Fig.23). About a century later, a monarch of an eastern branch of the dynasty built the famous temple of Jagannath at Puri in Orissa.

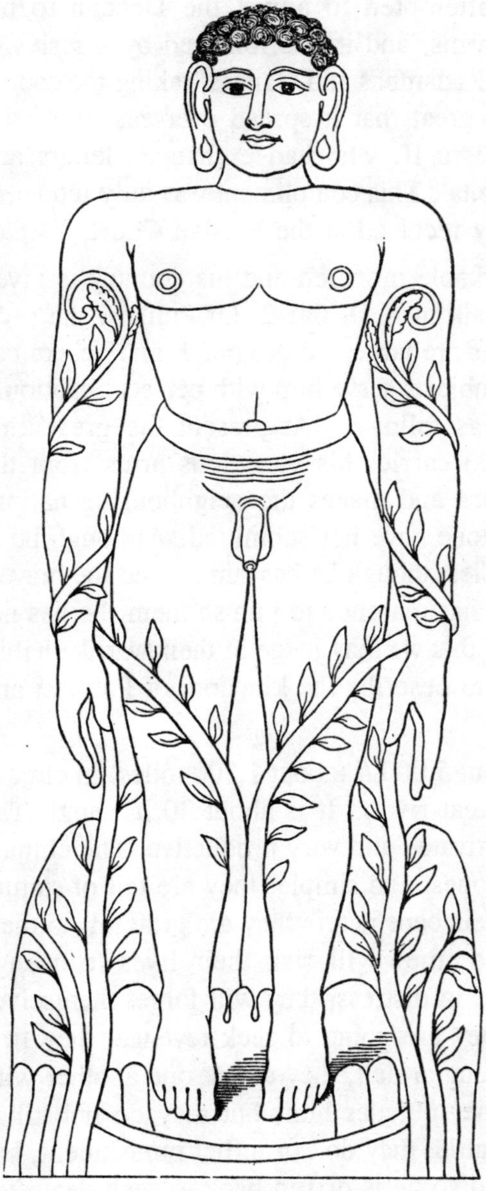

Fig. 23 : Colossal Statue of the Jain Saint Gomatesvara, Sravana Belgola, Mysore.

About A.D. 550 the great Chalukya dynasty appears on the scene. The Chalukyas were almost certainly of foreign origin, being part of a horde of Gurjara invaders from Central Asia which split into two streams; the first found its way into Rājputāna and the Deccan, and the second, some four centuries later, into Gujarāt. The name will survives in the Chalke or Salunke family among the Marāthās. Their crest was the Boar, the symbol of Vishnu, and obsequious bards provided them with a pedigree going back to the city of Ayodhya in the heroic age.

The first capital of the Chalukya kings was at Vātāpi, the modern Badāmi in the

* *Epigraphia Indica,* vol. viii, p. 24.

Bijāpur district. Badāmi is in a picturesque spot nestling in the lap of red sandstone hills with a pretty lake, surrounded by jungle: its caves and temples bear testimony to its former eminence. The greatest of the earlier monarchs of the Chalukya dynasty was Pulikesi II (A.D. 608-642). Some twelve years after his accession, he repulsed an attack of the Emperor Harsha, who attempted to annex the Deccan to his dominions. This was a remarkable feat of arms, and it was followed by a series of campaigns, in which Pulikesi conquered the Kadambas and Gangas, taking the capital of the former. Pulikesi's reputation was so great that it spread overseas to Persia, and in A.D. 625 the the Persian king Khusru II, who had exchanged letters and presents with him, sent an embassy to his capital. This compliment was duly returned, and the Indian ambassadors were hospitably received at the Persian Court.

An interesting description of this remarkable monarch and his country is given by Hiuen Tsang, who visited Pulikesi at Nāsik in A.D. 641-2. Of Pulikesi, he says, "He is of the race of the Kshatriyas; his ideas are large and profound, and he extends widely his sympathy and benefactions. His subjects serve him with perfect devotion." Of Harsha's Deccan campaign he speaks as follows: "At present the great king Sīlāditya ('Sun of Virtue,' a title of Harsha) carries his victorious arms from the East to the West; he subdues distant peoples and makes the neighbouring nations fear him: but the people of this kingdom alone have not submitted. Although he is often at the head of the troops of the Five Indies, though he has summoned the bravest generals of all the kingdoms, and though he has marched to punish them, he has not been able to vanquish their opposition. From this we may judge of their warlike habits and manners." The traveller then proceeds to describe the kingdom of Pulikesi and its habitants:

> "Mo-ho-la-ch'o (Mahārāshtra) is about 5,000 *li* (about 1,700 miles) in circuit. The capital borders on the west on a great river.* It is about 30 *li* round. The soil is rich and fertile; it is regularly cultivated and very productive. The climate is hot; the disposition of the people is honest and simple; they are tall of stature and of a stern vindictive character. To their benefactors they are grateful; to their enemies relentless. If they are insulted, they will risk their lives to avenge themselves. If they are asked to help one in distress, they will forget themselves in their haste to render assistance. If they are going to seek revenge, they first give their enemy warning; then, each being armed, they attack one another with lances. When one turns to flee, the other pursues him; but they do not kill a man who submits. If a general loses a battle, they do not inflict punishment, but present him with a woman's clothes, and so he is driven back to seek death for himself. The country provides for a band of champions to the number of several

* Nāsik on the Godāvari, the northern capital and Pulikesi's headquarters during the war with Harsha.

> hundred. Each time they are about to engage in conflict they intoxicate themselves with wine, and then one man with lance in hand will meet ten thousand and challenge them to fight. If one of these champions meets a man and kills him, the laws of the country do not punish him. Every time they go forth, they beat drums before them. Moreover they inebriate many hundred heads of elephants, and taking them out to fight, they themselves first drink their wine, and then, rushing forward in mass, they trample everything down, so that no enemy can stand before them. The king, in consequence of his possessing these men and elephants, treats his neighbours with contempt. He is one of the Kshatriya caste and his name is Pu-lo-ki-she (Pulikesi). His plans and undertakings are widespread, and his beneficent actions are felt over a great distance. His subjects obey him with perfect submission."*

Soon after Hiuen Tsang's visit, Pulikesi's reign was tragically terminated. The Pallavas of Kānchi were the 'family foes' of the Chalukyas, with whom they carried on an almost unending struggle. These dynastic wars were usually waged in obedience to the percepts of the laws of Manu; Brahmins, temples and non-combatants were spared.† But on this occasion the Pallava king Narasimhavarman behaved like a barbarian. He sacked Vātāpi, sparing neither age nor sex, and destroying temples. Pulikesi either fell in battle or was put to death. The fortunes of his house were subsequently restored by his son Vikrāmaditya, and Kānchi, the enemy's capital, was captured, but spared the horrors of pillage.

About A.D. 750 the Chalukyas were overthrown by the Rāshtrakūtas, apparently an indigenous line of rulers, descended from the Mahārāshtrikas of Āndhra times. It is probable that they originally held a subordinate position as petty chieftains, but seized the opportunity, when the Chalukyas were exhausted by wars with their neighbours, to overthrow them. The greatest of Rāshtrakūta kings was Krishnan I (A.D. 757-800), who excavated that magnificent rock-cut shrine, the Kailāsa temple at Ellora. A copper-plate grant thus describes the achievement:

> "Krishnarājā caused to be constructed a temple of a wonderful form on the mountain of Elapura. When the gods, moving in the aerial cars, saw it, they were struck with wonder and constantly thought much over the matter, saying to themselves: 'This temple of Siva is self-existent, for such beauty is not to be found in a work of art.' Even the architect who constructed it was struck with wonder, saying, when his heart misgave him as regards making another similar attempt, 'Wonderful! I did not know how it was that I could construct it!' "

---

* Beal, *Buddhist Records of the Western World,* II. 225. *Cf. Life of Hiuen Tsang,* p. 146.

† "When a rājā has conquered a country," says Manu, "he should respect the deities which are worshipped, distribute largesse, and reassure the people by proclamations."

The empire of the Rāshtrakūtas stretched at one time from Mālwā in the north to Kānchī in the south, and a royal viceroy ruled in Gujarāt. The Rāshtrakūtas kept on good terms with the Arabs of Sind, and a Muhammadan traveller describes the ruling king as one of the four great monarchs of the world, the others being the Caliph, the Emperor of China and the Emperor of Byzantium. During this period, Buddhism finally disappeared from the Deccan. In A.D. 973 the Rāshtrakūtas, worn out by incessant wars, came to an end. "As a light extinguished by a fierce flame, of the once flourishing Ratta rule there remained only the memory."

Of the remaining Hindu dynasties, mentioned need only be made of the Hoysalas of Halebid in Mysore (A.D. 1047-1327) and the Yādavas of Deogiri in Hyderabad. The Hoysalas were originally Jains, but in the eleventh century, a great reaction in favour of orthodox Hinduism arose all over Southern India, and Jainism was practically exterminated, except in a few local centres. The Hoysala kings marked their return to the Hindu fold by the erection of a number of remarkable temples at their capital, which will be described in due course. Deogiri, the modern Daulatābād, was very prosperous, and the wealth of the Deccan attracted the attention of the ambitious Alā-ud-dīn, the nephew of the Sultan Jalāl-ud-dīn Khilji of Delhi. In 1294, Alā-ud-dīn, on the pretence of an expedition of Mālwā, suddenly crossed the Vindhyas with a picked force of 8,000 troopers. Deogiri was invested, and the reigning monarch, Rāmchandra, was forced to pay the almost incredible ransom of 600 maunds of pearls, two maunds of jewels, and 4,000 pieces of silk, besides an annual tribute to Delhi. In 1307, the Muhammadan invasions were renewed by a general named Malik Kāfūr. Halebid was taken the Hoysala ruler was made prisoner. In 1318, Harpāla, the son-in-law of Rāmchandra, was captured, and on the pretext that he had rebelled was barbarously flayed alive. Hindu rule in the Deccan was at an end.

Deccan Architecture

Few remains of the numerous Buddhist stūpas, which must at one time have existed all over the Deccan in the time of the Āndhras, have survived. The most celebrated was the great stūpa at the ancient capital of Amarāvatī at the mouth of the Kistna river, fragments of which at present adorn the main staircase of the British Museum. It is of a similar type to the contemporary stūpas at Bharhut and Sānchī, which it closely resembles. It was probably begun in the second century B.C., but the marble slabs enclosing the drum and the stone railings were added about four centuries later. Both are covered with innumerable carvings in low relief, chiefly depicting scenes from the life of the Buddha. In the earlier of these, the Master is represented by symbols; in the later work, the Buddha figure appears. These sculptures give a vivid picture of the happy, care-free life of the time—the palaces and walled towns, the houses and the temples. "It would hardly be possible to exaggerate the luxurious beauty or the technical proficiency of the Amarāvati reliefs," says a recent authority. "This is the most voluptuous and the most delicate flower of India's sculpture." (Fig. 24.) One of the marble slabs gives a vivid representation of the great stūpa as it was in the days of its glory.

Fig. 24 : Translation of the Buddha's begging-bowl, Amarāvati.

The most characteristic feature of the Deccan was, however, the rock-hewn vihāras or monasteries carved out of the hill-side for Buddhist communities. According to the Master's percept, the monks were enjoined to retire for meditation and study during the monsoon-season for the "rain-rest." Permanent quarters were soon needed as the communities expanded, and the practice of excavating them from the solid rock became more and more general. The custom of cutting rock-hewn chambers apparently originated in Egypt; from Egypt it spread to Persia, whence it may have reached India in Mauryan days at the time of the general turnover from wood to stone. The designers of the Indian rock temples chose the solid rock face, and not an existing cave, for their work. The trap was hewn away piece by piece through the opening intended for door and window by pick and chisel, leaving the stone required for pillars and stūpa in its place. The usual form which the vihāra took was that of a central hall or chapel, with cells, refectories, and other chambers grouped round it. The monks' cells were small, flat-roofed cubicles with stone couches; in some of the refectories long stone tables were provided for dining. The monks sat on the

Fig. 25 : Horseshoe Arch, Buddhist Vihāra.

floor in front of the tables to eat their food. A stone cistern supplied with fresh water from a spring was a necessary adjunct. The chapel resembled the interior of a Christian church; usually it was in the form of a basilica with a central nave and rows of pillars forming aisles and supporting a barrel-shaped roof. At the further end was an apse containing a stūpa surmounted by an umbrella. The stūpa is now no longer of brick, but of solid stone. In the earlier examples the stūpa is plain, but later ones often bear a figure of the Buddha carved in high relief. The chapel was lighted by a ribbed and latticed horseshoe-shaped window over the entrance-door which illuminated the stūpa facing it. The structure clearly betrays the fact that it is a translation into stone of an earlier wooden model. Wooden ribs, though no longer necessary, span the roof; the umbrella over the stūpa is of wood; the horseshoe window is of wooden design (Fig. 25). Even the original wooden joists and beams are reproduced in stone. The pillars are copies of wooden originals, and their bases are modelled on the earthenware pots which were formerly used to protect them from the ravages of white ants. The principal groups of caves are at Bhājā, Bedsa, Kārla, Junnar and Nāsik (end of second century B.C. to second century A.D.), Kanheri and Ajantā (second century B.C. to seventh century A.D.), Aurangabad (fourth century A.D.), and Ellora (sixth to eighth century A.D.). Some of the edifices at Ellora are Jain, and at this place and at Bādāmi, as well as at Elephanta in Bombay harbour, are Hindu cave-temples.

The most perfect example of the earlier type is at Kārla, overlooking the old road from the Deccan to the cost by way of the Bhor Ghaut. The original porch has been much damaged by a fall of rock from above, but in front of it stands a massive stone column surmounted by a lion capital. Then comes the facade with its three doorways surmounted by an arched window and a musicians' gallery. At the two sides of the door are groups of figures in relief, representing, no doubt, the donors. Entering, we find ourselves in a lofty cathedral-like nave, 124 feet long, 45 feet high and 45 feet wide. Massive pillars with bell-capitals, running alone the aisles, are surmounted by groups of figures seated upon elephants. These support arches of teak, which still withstand the ravages of time. At the further end is the apse, with its solid stone stūpa, crowned with a wooden umbrella. In the top of the stūpa is a receptacle for a relic. (Fig. 26.)

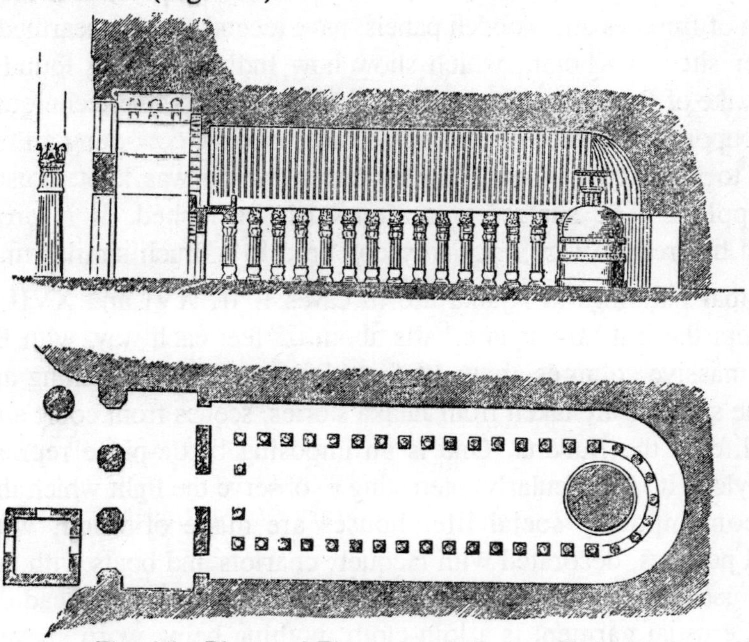

Fig. 26 : Plan and Elevation of Chaitya Hall, Kārla.

The Buddhist caves at Ajantā, not far from Jalgaon in Khāndesh, were excavated in a wild and lonely glen amid the most romantic surroundings, and their inhabitants could scarcely have chosen a more ideal spot for a monastic retreat. They are chiefly remarkable for the famous paintings which adorn their walls, and were probably executed in the time of the Vākātaka and earlier Chalukyan dynasties (A.D. 550-642). The former, as we have seen, were the successors of the Āndhras in Berār, and were the main channel through which Gupta culture reached the Deccan. With the overthrow of Pulikesi II by the Pallavas in A.D. 642 the work came to an end.

Painting was already a well-known and widely practised art in India. It is frequently referred to in early Buddhist and epic literature, and in the dramas a portrait of the heroine is almost a stock device. Hiuen Tsang frequently mentions monasteries and halls adorned with paintings, and similar references abound in the romances of Bāna. Kādambari's palace at Ujjaịn had "painted halls filled with gods and demons, Siddhas, Gandharvas, genii and snakes." The connection between the Ajantā frescoes and classical Sanskrit literature is very intimate; some of the scenes represented might have been taken straight froṃ the stage. At first there was a puritanical prejudice against the employment of painting to adorn Buddhist monasteries, but as time went on this was relaxed, and frescoes were used to represent scenes from the Jātakas, just as bas-reliefs were employed in the case of the earlier stūpas. The extant examples of early Indian painting are few and far between; this delicate work has only survived the ravages of time and vandals, ancient and modern, at Ajantā, Ellora, Bāgh in Mālwā, Sigiriya in Ceylon, and a few other secluded spots; some remarkable examples, both of frescoes and wooden panels, have recently been unearthed at Dandan Ulig and other sites in Khotan, which show how Indian painting found its way to China in the wake of Buddhism. In the case of wall-paintings, the technique employed was to spread upon the surface of the rock a layer of clay, cow-dung and rice husks, and over this to lay a coat of white lime-plaster, which was kept moist while the colour was applied. The surface was afterwards burnished. It is probable that sculptures and bas-reliefs were originally coloured in a much similar manner.

The principal paintings at Ajantā are in caves I, II, XVI and XVII, and XIX. All these, except the last, are square halls about 65 feet each way, with flat ceilings supported on massive columns about 14 feet high, and thus presenting an immense wall space. The subjects are taken from Jātaka stories, scenes from court and domestic life, and the life of the Buddha. One is an imposing battle-piece representing the invasion of Ceylon. It is particularly interesting to observe the light which the paintings throw upon contemporary social life: houses are made of wood, with pillared verandahs and porches, decorated with lacquer; chariots and boats with awnings and platforms are used for conveyance; princes wear richly jewelled head-dresses and waist-belts. The usual garment is a loin-cloth, nothing being worn above the waist;

the fineness of the material often gives the impression of nudity. The same *joie de vivre,* and the same tenderness towards and understanding of animal life, pervade the Ajantā paintings as the Amarāvati reliefs. "On the hundred walls and pillars of these rock-carved temples, a vast drama moves before our eyes: a drama played by princes and sages and heroes, by men and women of every condition, against a marvellously varied scene, among forests and gardens, in courts and cities, on wide plains, and in deep junlges, while above the messengers of heaven move swiftly across the sky. From all these emanates a great joy in the surpassing radiance of the face of the world, in the physical nobility of men and women, in the strength and grace of animals and the loveliness and purify of birds and flowers."* Plate VIII reproduces a typical fresco from Cave I; above is a palace scene, while below we have a portion of a Jātaka story about a demon who served up human heads on a platter.

Besides the painted halls, the Ajantā caves include a number of *chaitya* halls or chapels, ranging from the second century B.C. (Nos. IX and X) to the seventh century A.D. (No. XXVI). Nos. XIX and XXVI, with their elaborate facades, their carved pillars and their stūpas, adorned with colossal images of the Buddha (standing in No. XIX and seated in the European attitude in No. XXVI), are striking examples of the later or Mahāyāna type. Her we see the transition from the chapel (*chaitya*) to the cave temple proper (Plate IX).

The transition is also emphasised in the group of Jain and Buddhist cave-temples at Ellora, about sixteen miles from the old Yādava Capital of Deogiri, of about the 6th to 8th centuries A.D. Caves I-XII are Buddhist. The Visvakarma cave (No. X) with its two-storied facade and colossal seated Buddha, resembles Ajantā cave XXVI. Next come fifteen or sixteen shrines, of which the most remarkable is No. XV, the Das Avatāra, or cave of the Ten Avatars. This is a two-storied structure, consisting of a courtyard surrounded by small chapels. The reliefs decorating the walls illustrate in striking manner the world of difference which separates Buddhism from Brahminism. Instead of the Master in one of his many incarnations for the salvation of the human race, we behold Siva in his terrific form, a chaplet of skulls round his neck, gripping his victim, while his consort Kālī holds a bowl to catch his blood. Cave XXIX, with its dignified wedding of Siva and Parvati, strikes a softer note. Cave XXXI, the Indra Sabhā and Jagannātha Sabhā, consists of a group of Jain shrines, with nude figures of Parsvanāth and Mahāvīra.

The most remarkable feature of Ellora is, however, the Kailāsa temple dedicated to Siva, which takes its name from the Indian Olympus. This amazing structure is, in fact, not a cave at all. The masons who constructed it hewed out of the living rock of the sloping hillside a pit 276 feet long and 154 feet wide, to the depth of 107 feet, leaving in the middle a solid monolith from which the temple was carved. In

* W. Rothenstein, *Ajanta Frescoes* (Oxford 1915), p. 28.

the centre of the court is the shrine of the lingam, surrounded by five chapels, and preceded by a square hall. In front of this again is a porch, containing the Nandi or Bull, which invariably faces the entrance to Saiva temples, flanked by two lofty stone columns. The three buildings and the outer gateway are connected by a flying bridge. The shrine is supposed on the backs of elephants, which are carved in a life-like manner. On one wall is a frieze representing scenes from the Rāmāyana. In another relief, the demon Rāvana is seen trying in vain to overthrow Kailāsa, the mountain home of Siva: above the god remains majestic and unmoved, while Parvati clings in terror to his side. The Kailāsa temple has always been looked on as one of the architectural marvels of the world. As one of the earliest European visitors remarks, "it is a wonder to see so great a mass in the air, which seems to slenderly under-propped that one could hardly farbear to shudder on first entering it." This temple was constructed, as has been already mentioned, by the Rāshtrakūta King Krishna I. He probably took as his model the Papanāth temple at Pattakadal. Contemporary with this is the Siva cave-temple carved from the hill-side on the picturesque island of Elephanta or Ghārpuri in Bombay Harbour. It contains many fine sculptures, the most striking being the gigantic three-headed Siva (Plate X).

The excavation of cave-temples, which appears to be so remarkable a feat to western eyes, was, as Fergusson points out, really more economical than quarrying the stone and carrying it for many miles over bad roads. As time went on, however, the cave-temples were gradually replaced by structural buildings in stone, though the Hindu architects, with their usual conservatism, at first modelled them upon the earlier forms. Thus the little temples at Ter and Chezarla (Fig. 27), and the Lad Khān temple at Aihole in the Bijāpur District, are strict copies of a Buddhist cave chapel and a Hindu cave temple respectively. The later Brahmanical structural temple is modelled on the Buddhist chapel. The apse becomes the cells or shrine, the stūpa being replaced by the image of the God. Above the shrine a steeple (*sikara*) was erected; in buildings of the Chalukyan type, this was of a low pyramidal form. In the neighbourhood of Bādāmi are numerous small but beautifully designed Saiva temples. The Chalukyan style reaches its climax under the Hoysala dynasty. Of the many noble temples of the period, the most notable are those erected at Somnāthpur, Belur and Halebid. These temples are polygonal in plan and stand upon a richly carved plinth. Inner and outer wals are elaborately decorated with a mass of sculptured bas-reliefs and ornaments; they are usually the work of a school of artists. The Somnāthpur temple, erected by King Vināditya Balāla in about A.D. 1043, is the earliest and in many respects the best; the triple cells, each crowned by a pyramidal roof, are attached to a square pillared hall, which is entered through a portico, and the whole is enclosed in a cloistered court (Plate XI). The latest and most elaborate is the temple at Halebid, an imposing shrine, which was still unfinished at the time of Muhammadan invasion in A.D. 1310.

Fig. 27 : Early structural temple, Chezarla, Deccan.

"The great double temple at Halebid," says Fergusson, "stands on a terrace ranging from five to six feet in height and paved with large slabs. On this stands a frieze of elephants, following all the sinuosities of the plan, and extending to some 710 feet in length, and containing not less than 2,000 elephants, most of them with riders and trappings sculptured as only an oriental can represent the wisest of brutes. Above these is a frieze of 'Shardulas' or conventional lions, the emblems of the Hoysala Balālas who built the temple. Then comes a scroll of infinite beauty and variety of design; over these a frize of horsemen and another scroll, over which is a bas-relief of scenes from the Rāmāyana, representing the conquest of Ceylon and all the varied incidents of the Epic. This, like the other, is 700 feet long... Then come celestial beasts and celestial birds, and all along the east front a frieze of groups from human life, and then a cornice with a rail divided into panels, each containing two figures. Over these are windows with pierced slabs, like those of Belur, only not so rich or varied... In the centre, in the place of windows, is first a scroll, and then a frieze of gods and heavenly Apsaras, dancing-girls and other objects of Hindu mythology... Every god of the Hindu Pantheon finds his place... Some of these are carved with a minute elaboration of detail which can only be reproduced by photography, and may probably be considered as one of the most marvellous exhibitions of human labour to be found even in the patient East."*

* Fergusson, *History of Indian and Eastern Architecture* (1891), p. 401.

LEADING DATES

c. B.C. 309	Jain migration to the Deccan.
225 B.C.-A.D. 225	The Āndhra dynasty.
A.D. 225	Fall of the Āndhras. Rise of Kadamba and other dynaties.
550-642	The Chalukyas of Bādāmi.
608-642	Pulikesi II, Chalukya.
A.D. 642	Pulikesi II killed by the Pallavas.
674	Chalukya line restored.
757	Chalukyas overthrown by the Rāshtrakūtas.
760	Krishna I, Rāshtrakūta, builds the Kailāsa temple at Ellora.
820	Sankara Āchārya, Vedānta philosopher.
973-1190	Second Chalukya dynasty (Chalukyas of Kalyāni).
1047-1327	Hoysalas of Mysore.
1190-1318	Yādavas of Deogiri.
1175-1250	Rāmānuja, Vaishnava philosopher.
1294	First Muhammadan invasion of the Deccan by Alā-ud-din. Capture of Deogiri.
1318	Harpāla, last King of Deogiri, put to death by the Muhammadans.
1326	Overthrow of the Hoysala dynasty.

Chapter XII

Southern India : The Tamils, The Pallavas, and Ceylon

Southern India, the land of the Dravidian-speaking Tamils* and the Damirike of Ptolemy, corresponds roughly to the Madras Presidency, and comprises that part of the Indian peninsula which lies to the south of the Tungabhadra river.

Dravidian India was early divided into three kingdoms, the Pāndyas in the extreme south, the present Madura and Tinnivelly district, the Cheras or Keralas who were settled along the Malabar coast, and in what are now the States of Travancore and Cochin, and the Cholas, located to the north of the Pāndyas as far as the Pennār river and along the East Coast, which from this circumstance was known as the Chola mandalam or Coromandel coast.

Southern India seems to have been only vaguely known to the Indid tribes settled on the north of the Vindhyas. There are dim traditions of the mission of the Vedic sage Agastya, who is said to have established a Brahmanical monastery on the Podiyur hill, and doubtless Brahmins from the north were invited from time to time to the courts of the Tamil Kings. But they must have found the Dravidian language already too well developed for them to do more than introduce Sanskrit forms and enrich the vocabulary with Sanskrit words. The varius Dravidian alphabets are probably derived from a northern source. But northern influence remained a mere veneer, and was confined to the higher classes. The common people continued to practise their ancestral cults of gods and goddesses or 'Mothers,' and to propitiate demons of smallpox and other plagues. Many customs, such as polyandry and matriarchy, unknown in Northern India, survive in the South. The case-system was adopted, but only in a modified form. The Brahmin early asserted his spiritual ascendancy, but the Kshatriya and Vaisya castes are practically non-existent. Society consists of Brahmins, Sūdras and Parayans or Pariahs, the latter representing the old South Indian stock. The number of 'occupational' castes is very large.† The Tamils were a hardy

* Tamil is the oldest and principal Dravidian tongue; others are Telugu, the Āndhra language, and Kanarese, the language of Mysore. Malayālam is a later development of Tamil. "Dravida" and Tamil are two forms of the same word.

† E. Thurston, *Castes and Tribes of Southern India* (1909).

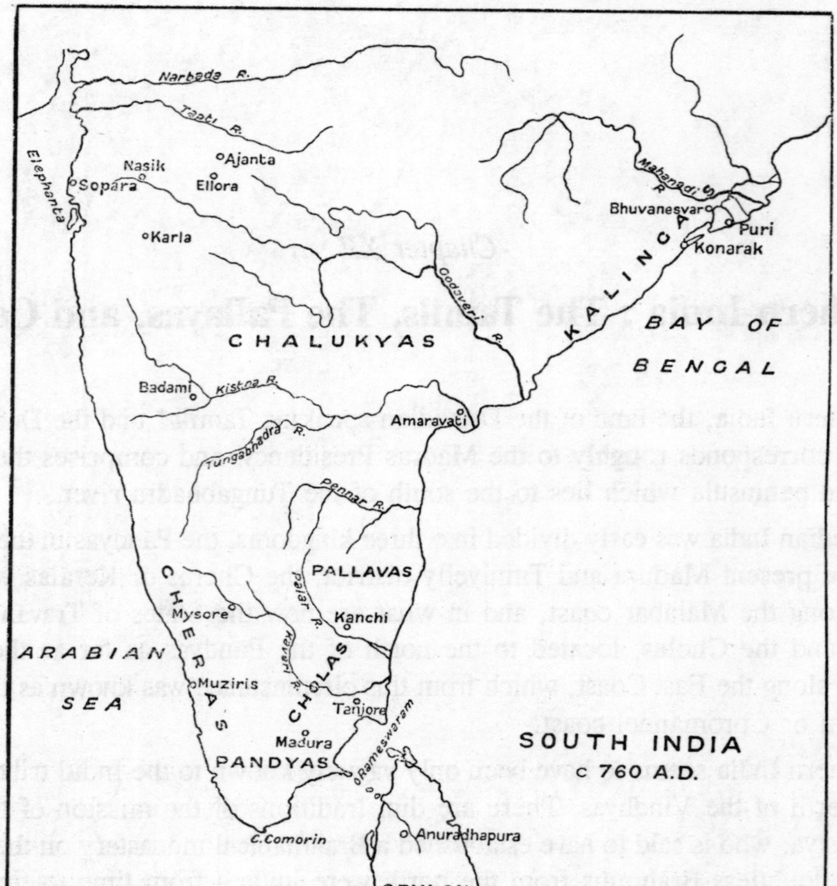

Map 8 : South India.

peasant folk and made good soldiers; monuments to warriors who had fallen in battle are common objects. They were bold sailors and skilled agriculturists. The pearl and conch fisheries go back to prehistoric times, and the land was well tilled and irrigated. Pottery, weaving and metal-work were the usual village occupations. The villagers enjoyed a certain degree of local self-governments; the head of the group was the Kiravan or Pāndiyan, the hereditary Chief or Elder. The northerners, when they first began to penetrate the country south of the Kistna, found an advanced civilisation already established. The *Rāmāyana* speaks of Madura as adorned with gold and jewels. But the first reference to Dravidian India which can be dated with any degree of accuracy occurs in the grammarian Katyāyana (fourth century B.C.) who mentions the Pāndyas and Cholas. Megasthenes, the Greek envoy at the Court of Chandragupta Maurya, knew that the Pandyan Kingdom comprised that portion of India which extends southward to the sea, and possessed a powerful army and great wealth derived from its pearl-fisheries. About the same time, Jain missionaries began to find their way to the south; in 258 B.C. they were followed by Asoka's Buddhist mission to the Pāndyas and Cholas, as far as the Tamrapārni river in the Tinnivelly district.

Southern India owed her prosperity to the possession of a number of commodities for which western nations had an urgent need—spices and precious stones. Trade with the Yemen and the Red Sea must have gone on from very early times; we hear in the Bible how Hiram, King of Tyre, ent his "Ships of Tarshish" from Ezion Geber (Akaba on the eastern arm of the Gulf of Suez) on a triennial voyage to Ophir, probably Sopāra on the Bombay coast, to fetch "ivory, apes and peacocks" and "a great plenty of almug trees and precious stones" for the temple then being built by his powerful ally King Solomon. The Hebrew names for these commodities clearly reveal their Indian origin.*

Other articles of commerce were pepper, ginger, cinnamon, rice, coral, pearls, beryls, silk, muslin and tortoise-shell.† Peacocks and rice had reached Greece, probably by way of the Persian Gulf, as early as 450 B.C.

A landmark in the history of the foreign trade of Southern India was the discovery about A.D. 45, by an Alexandrian merchant named Hippalus, probably from Arab sailors, of the existence of the seasonal winds or monsoons. This enabled mariners to run across the Arabian Sea instead of hugging the coast. The journey to the Indian coast from Aden now only occupied forty days and could be accomplished even quicker. Alexandria was brought within three months' journey of India, which was thus nearer to the west than at any subsequent time until A.D. 1843 when the Red Sea route was opened. This had an important influence upon cultural relations. With the establishment of the *Pax Romana* after the battle of Actium in 31 B.C., the demand for Oriental luxuries all over the Roman Empire was very great. Pliny estimates the drain upon the Imperial Treasury at over a million sterling, and his estimate is confirmed by the extraordinarily numerous finds of Roman coin at various spots in Southern India and Ceylon.‡ Among these, curiously enough, is a coin of Claudius struck to commemorate the conquest of Britain. The principal exports were now pepper and beryls, and the value which the ancient world placed upon the former is attested by the fact that among the ransom levied by Alaric upon Rome in A.D. 410 was 3,000 lbs. of pepper. The beryl was used for the cameos so greatly prized by

* I Kings x. 22. II Chron. x. 21. Ivory, Hebrew *Shen habbin;* 'elephants' teeth,' Skt. *ibha danta;* 'apes' Herbrew *koph,* Skt. *kapi;* 'peacocks,' Hebrew *tuki-im,* Tamil *tokei,* Greek *ταϖς*.

† 'Rice,' *οευζα*, Tamil *arisi*; 'pepper,' *πέπεει*, Tamil *pippali;* 'giner,' *ζιγγιβεεις*, Tamil *inchiver;* 'cinnamon,' *χαοπιος*, Tamil *karppu;* beryl, *βheυλλος* Skt. *vaidūrya.*

‡ R. Sewell, *Roman Coins found in India.* J.R.A.S., 1904, p. 591

the Greeks and Romans. The Alexandrian pamphlet, the *Periplus Maris Erythraei* of about A.D. 81, gives a lively account of the trade with Southern India. The chief port was Muziris or Mushiri, the modern Cranganore, where there appears to have been a Roman colony and a temple of Augustus.* The vast numbers of Roman copper coins found at Madura point to the fact that there was another Roman colony at the ancient Pāndiyan capital. Tamil poets speak of the Yavana ships which came to the Tamil ports with gold and wine which they exchanged for spices. It was the practice of the Tamil rājās to employ Roman mercenaries of bodyguards, and frequent mention is made of these "dumb Mlecchas," with their long coats and armour and their murderous swords, who might be seen acting as sentries at the palace gates. Western artisans were also patronised at the local courts. Starbo tells us that in 25 B.C., on the accession of the Emperor Augustus, a Pāndiyan King sent an embassy to congratulate him. The ambassadors, who set sail from Barygaza (Broach) and went overland from the Persian Gulf, took with them various Indian beasts, birds and snakes as presents, and a letter written in Greek offering an alliance and a free passage through his dominions to Roman citizens. The embassy took four years to reach Samos. With it went a Jain or Buddhist monk named Sarmanochegas (Srāmanāchārya), who, imitating the famous Kalanos in the time of Alexander the Great, immolated himself on a pyre at Athens.†

Hiuen Tsang, writing in A.D. 640, says that the climate of the Pāndiyan Kingdom was hot, and the inhabitants dark-complexioned and firm and impetuous in disposition. They were immersed in commerce and took little interest in learning. Here, as everywhere in the South, Buddhism was in decay. There were hundreds of Jain and Hindu Temples, but Buddhist monasteries were everywhere in a state of disrepair with only a handful of monks, and in some places only the walls were standing. Shortly after Hiuen Tsang's visit, a Pāndiyan King, named Nedumaran, who had been a Jain but was converted to the Saiva faith on his marriage to the daughter of a Chola monarch, instituted a ferocious persecution of the followers of the Jain sect at Madura, in which 8,000 Jains were said to have perished. The Pāndiyan Kings were constantly at war with their neighbours, the Cholas and Pallavas, and with the Kings of Ceylon. The armies of the great Sinhalese monarch, Parākrama Bāhu (A.D. 1164-1197) at one time penetrated as far as Madura, but were forced to retreat. The Pāndiyan kingdom reached its zenith under Jatavarman Sundara (A.D. 1215-1271). It is interesting to note that the Venetian traveller, Marco Polo, on his way back from China in 1293, paid a visit to the Coromandel and Malabar coasts. He tell sus that foreign merchants were welcomed and that the country was prosperous and well

* This is shown on the ancient Roman map known as the Peutinger Tables. V. A. Smith, *Early History of India,* p. 463.

† Priaulx, *Indian Embassies to Rome,* Journal of the Royal Asiatic Society, xix. 294.

governed. He was particularly struck by the pearl-fisheries; the King wore a nacklace of huge pearls round his neck. There was a flourishing trade between Southern India and Arabia on the one hand and China on the other. Marco Polo was the first modern European traveller to visit Southern India, if we except the Saxon Sighelm, who was supposed to have been sent by King Alfred in A.D. 800 to the famous shrine of Saint Thomas at Mylapore near Madras.

The Pāndyas were succeeded by the Cholas, who quickly absorbed the Cheras or Keralas. Hiuen Tsang describes the Chola country in A.D. 640, before it had arisen to its subsequent greatness, in disparaging terms : "It is deserted and wild, a succession of marshes and jungle. The population is very small, and the troops of brigands go through the country openly. The climate is hot, the manners of the people dissolute and cruel. The disposition of the men is naturally fierce: they are attached to heretical teaching. The *Sanghārāmas* (monasteries) are ruined and dirty as well as the priests. There ae some tens of Deva (Hindu) temples, and many Nirgrantha (Jain) heritics."

The history of the Chola monarchs begins with Parāntaka I in A.D. 907, and reaches its climax with Rājārājā the Great (A.D. 985-1018) and his immediate successors. By A.D. 1005 Rājārājā, in a succession of campaigns, made himself ruler of the whole of the present Madras Presidency. He encouraged foreign trade, and a Tamil scholar has drawn a vivid picture of the great port of Puhar at the mouth of the Cauvery as it was under the Cholas:

> "The town was divided into two parts, one of which was called Maruvūr-Pakkam and adjoined the sea coast, and the other, which was situated to the west of it, was called Pattinappākkam. Between these two portions of the city was a large area of open ground, planted with trees at regular intervals, where the great market was held. The principal streets at Pattinappākkam were the Royal Street, the Car Street and the Bazaar Street. The merchants, Brahmins, farmers, doctors and astrologers resided in separate streets. Surrounding the palace were the houses of the charioteers, horse and elephant riders and soldiers who formed the bodyguard of the king. Bards, minstrels and panegyrists, actors, musicians and buffoons, chank-cutters and those skilled in making flower garlands and strings of pearls, timekeeprs whose duty it was to cry out the number of each *nalikai,* or division of time, as it passed, and other servants of the palace, also resided within the limits of Pattinappākkam. Near the beach in Maruvūr-Pakkam were the raised platforms and godowns and warehouses with windows shaped like the eyes of the deer, where the goods landed from ships were stored. Here the goods were stamped with the tiger-stamp (the emblem of the Chola kings) after payment of customs duty, and passed on to the merchants' warehouses. Close by were the settlements of the Yavana (Greek) merchants, where many attractive articles were

always exposed for sale. Here were also the quarters of foreign traders who had come from beyond the seas, and who spoke various tongues. Vendors of fragrant pastes and powders, of flowers and incense, tailors who worked on silk, wool or cotton, traders in sandal, *aghil*, coral, pearls, gold and precious stones, grain merchants, washermen, dealers in fish and salt, butchers, blacksmiths, braziers, carpenters, coppersmiths, painters, sculptors, goldsmiths, cobblers and toymakers, had their habitation in Maruvūr-Pakkam."*

Rājārājā built a navy, and despatched an overseas expedition which conquered Ceylon. The Cholas were now the undisputed masters of Souther India. The Chola kings belonged to the Saivite sect, and in A.D. 1011 Rājārājā commemorated his victories by building a magnificent temple to the god Siva at Tanjore, on the walls of which he inscribed the story of his victorious career. His son Rājendra Chola Deva I (A.D. 1018-1035) greatly augmented his father's navy, by means of which he made the Cholas the predominant power in the Bay of Bengal. The Chola armies marched as far as the Ganges, where they inflicted a defeat on Mahipāla, the king of Bengal. A Tamil poem picturesquely recounts how "the war-elephants of the Chola drank the water of the Ganges at Mannai, and Kādaram (perhaps Kedah in the Malay peninsula), where the roaring crystal waves washed the sand mixed with red good, was annexed." He built the Gangaikonda Cholapuram temple in celebration of his invasion of Bengal.

The Cholas waged almost incessant wars with their martial neighbours, the Chalukyas, on the opposite side of the Tungabhadra river, in which first one and then the other obtained the mastery. The dynastic rivalry between the two powers was at last ended by a marriage alliance between the daughter of a Chola princess and a prince of the Eastern branch of the Chalukya line. The Chola power had already begun to decline when the invasion of Malik Kafūr in 1310 broke the power of all the Hindu states in the south.

We are fortunate in being able to gather a great deal of information from the inscriptions, probably belonging to the tenth century A.D., in the Vaikuntanath Perumal temple at Uttaramallur, about the Chola kingdom. Local self-government had reached an advanced stage of development. The unit was the village. Groups of villages formed a *kurram,* which had its assembly or council, composed of representatives chosen by lot, and its treasury, and appointed officers to administer justice and to supervise roads and tanks. The State claimed one-sixth of the produce, and payment was made in kind or in cash. A regular survey or Domesday Book was prepared. The currency was in gold; silver does not appear to have been used.

The Chola Kings were great builders and all their work was on a stupendous

* V. Kanakasabhai, *The Tamils Eighteen Hundred Years Ago* (1904), p. 25. See also V.A.N. Sastri, *The Colas* (Madras, 1935), p. 96.

Fig. 28 : Vimāna or Tower of a Dravidian Temple.

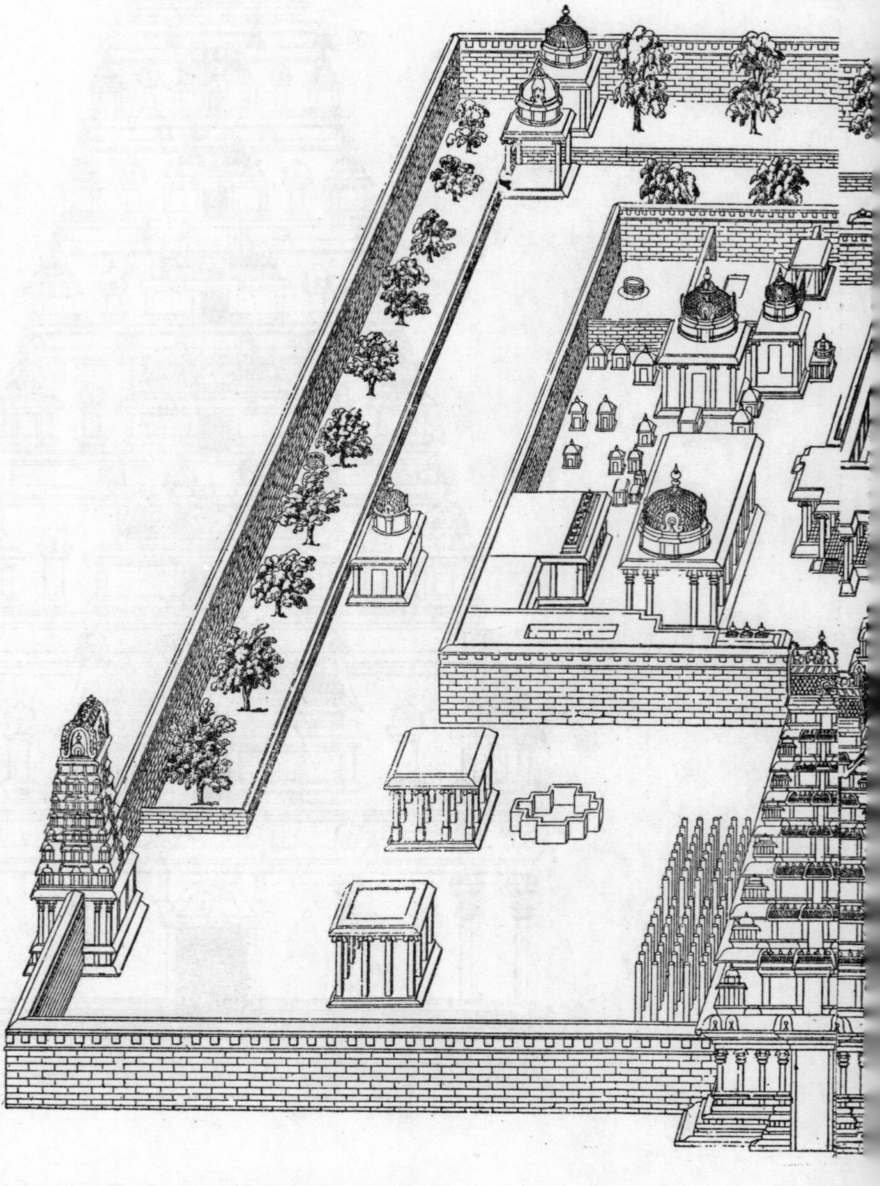

Fig. 29 : Temple of Tiruvalur.

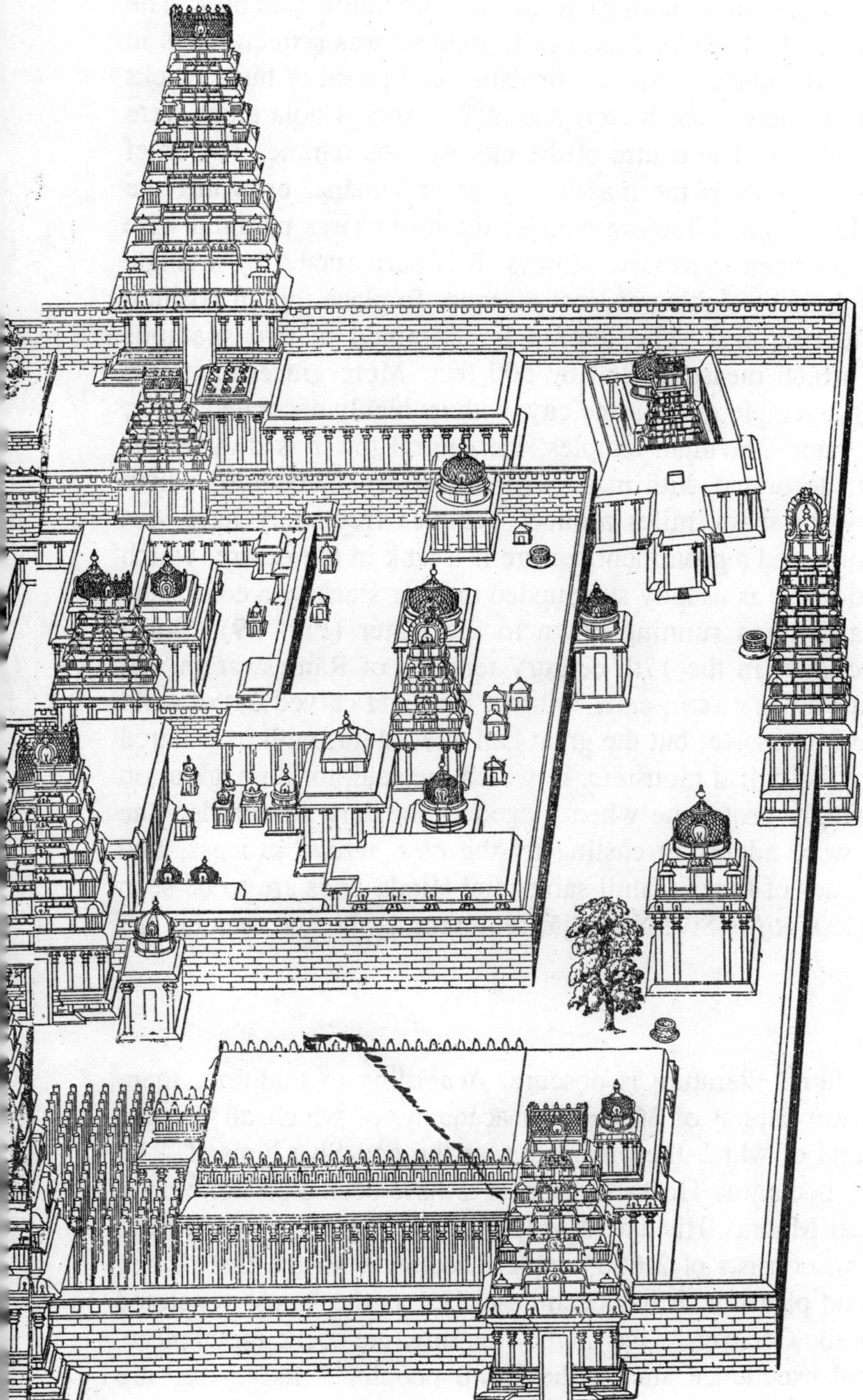

Fig. 29 : Temple of Tiruvalur.

scale. Their most characteristic undertakings were vast irrigation schemes. The embankment of the artificial lake built by Rajendra Choladeva was sixteen miles in length, with stone sluices and channels. Anicuts or dams, composed of huge blocks of dressed stone, were thrown across the Kāveri and other rivers. Chola cities were elaborately planned and laid out. The centre of the city was the temple. The chief feature of the early Tamil temples is the massive tower or vimāna, crowning the central shrine (Fig. 28). In the great Tanjore temple, the tower rises pyramid-wise to a height of 190 feet in thirteen successive storeys. It is surmounted by a single block of stone, 25 feet high and weighing at least 80 tons. To place this in position was a remarkable engineering feat. The temple is contained in two spacious courtyards, the larger of which measures 250 by 500 feet. More graceful, if less imposing, is the Subramānya temple in the same city, with its highly decorated tower, less severe in outline. In later Dravidian temples, the central tower is dwarfed by lofty gopura or gateways, decorated with masses of stucco ornamentation, which dominate the flat country for many miles around. Temples frequently have vast enclosures within their walls, and a prominent feature is a tank in the centre, which is used for religious ablutions. It is usually surrounded on four sides by a colonnade with pillared cloisters and steps running down to the water (Fig. 29). Tamil architecture reaches its climax in the 17th century temples of Rāmeswaram and Madura. The corridors at Rāmeswaram, each 700 feet long and carved out of solid granite, and dignified and impressive; but the great hall at Madura, with its pillared hippogryphs and other mythological monsters, in which the sculptor's imagination has run riot, is bewilderingly grotesque when judged by western standards. The South Indian craftsmen were adepts in casting by the *cire perdue* process, and numerous fine copper statues of kings, Tamil saints and Hindu gods are to be seen in the museums. A notable *motif* is Siva Nātārājā, representing the god dancing the cosmic dance (Fig. 30).

Tamil Literature

The early history of Tamil literature is obscure. According to tradition, there was at the ancient Pāndiyan capital of Madura an academy, of which all learned scholars were members and of which the president was the god Siva himself. The greatest of the early Tamil poets was Tiruvalluvar, said to have been a pariah weaver who lived at Mylapore near Madras. His date is very doubtful, but he probably lived about A.D. 100. His *Kural* consists of 2,660 couplets dealing with the three stock subjects, virtue, wealth and pleasure. It has been described as the "most venerated and popular book south of the Godāveri... the literary treasure, the poetic mouthpiece, the highest type of verbal excellence among the Tamil people."* Its sayings are enshrined in the hearts of the common folk.

* G. U. Pope, *The Sacred Kurral of Tiruvalluvar-Nayanar* (London, 1866), pp. ii-x.

A few typical verses from the Kural will explain Tiruvalluvar's philosophy of life, though they give but a faint idea of the terseness and vigour of the original:

Fig. 30 : Siva Nātārājā

Forgiving trespasses is good always,
Forgetting them is even higher praise.

If each his own as neighbour's faults would scan
Could any evil hap to living man?

Though men should injure you, their pain
Should lead but to compassion,

Do naught but good to them again
Else look to thy transgression.*

Another collection of moral epigrams is the *Nāladiyār*; its contents have become household words in Tamil-speaking homes. Dr. G. U. Pope, the great authority on the subject, says that they are pervaded by a strong sense of moral obligation, an earnest aspiration after righteousness, a fervent and unselfish charity, and generally a loftiness of aim which are almost Christian.† In the indigenous schools the children are still taught to read by means of moral maxims alphabetically arranged.

Early Tamil poetry is non-sectarian in character. Much of it shows traces of Jain influence, and Jainism, which reached the south in the 4th century B.C., was very popular, especially among the mercantile community.‡ In the 9th century A.D., however, a counter-reformation in favour of orthodox Hinduism set in, and the Jain sect was almost exterminated. The leader of the movement was the famous Sankara Āchārya, who went about the country, preaching and converting the masses, and setting up many monasteries for the study of the Sanskrit scriptures. Sankara was born in A.D. 788, became an ascetic in 820, and died at Kedarnāth in the Himālayas, after preaching all over India. Sankara taught the unqualified monism of the Vedānta. The Hindu triad, Siva, Vishnu, Brahmā, is a manifestation of Brahman, the sole, impersonal reality. All objects of sense are Māyā, Illusion, for which the human soul in its ignorance thirsts as the deer thirsts for the mirage water of the desert. When this ignorance is dispelled, and the identity of the individual with the World Soul is realised, Liberation is attained. Sankara wrote a number of commentaries on the Vedas and Upanishads, and for his work in systematising Hindu philosophy he has been compared to Saint Thomas Aquinas.

But Sankara's austere philosophy amade little appeal to the heart. This came from his later opponent Rāmānuja (A.D. 1175-1250) who taught a "qualified monism"; the World Soul, individual souls and matter are all equally real. To Sankara's intellectualism he opposed salvation by faith in Vishnu in his various incarnations. "It was the school of Rāmānuja," says Doctor L. D. Barnett, "that first blended in full harmony the voices of reason and devotion, by worshipping a Supreme Being of infinitely blessed qualities, both in His heaven and as revealed to the soul of man in incarnate experience... There is first the belief in a Primal Being who is indeed infinite, but infinite in qualities of goodness; secondly, the doctrine that in his love for His creatures the Supreme becomes incarnate in divers blessed forms to save

* See *The Sacred Kural*, by H. A. Popley; *Hymns of Alvars*, by J.S.M. Hooper; and *Hymns of the Tamil Saints*, by Kingsbury and Phillips (Heritage of India Series) from whom the above quotations are taken.

† *The Nāladiyār* (Oxford 1893), p. xi.

‡ The principal centre of Jainism is Sravana Belgola in Mysore. It is the seat of the Jain Pontiff of Southern India.

men from sin and sorrow, and lead them to union with Him; and thirdly, the teaching that the Supreme may be reached by any suppliant, who worships him in perfect, self-forgetting love."* This is the doctrine of Bhakti or devotion to a personal deity, which had already been foreshadowed in the Bhagavad Gītā. Rāmānuja taught at Kānchi, the great centre of Hindu learning in Southern India, and the influence of his teaching in the later devotional poetry of the Tamils was very marked.

The greatest of the later sectarian poets in Manikka Vāsagar of the tenth century A.D., the author of the *Tiruvāsakam* or Sacred Utterance. It is said that he came from Tanjore, and lived at the end of the ninth century A.D., and that he was a minister at the Pāndiyan Court. He was converted by his Brahmin Guru, and, giving up the world, devoted himself to the composition of hymns in honour of Siva:

The Ruddy One, Who wears the ashes white, Whose home
None reach or know, Who dwells in every place, to loving ones
The True, the Sage whom hearts untrue still deem untrue.

To him Siva is the object of intence personal devotion:

Thou madest me Thine,
Didst fiery poison eat, that I
Might thine ambrosia taste—I, meanest one.

A beautiful example of Manikka Vāsagar's poetic genius is the following:

Now anigh Indra's East
Draws the sun; dark flies apace
At the dawn; and the sun
Of the kindness in Thy face
Riseth high'r, even high'r,
As like fair flowers opening,
Eyes unclose from their sleep,
Eyes of Thee our beauteous King.

Hear how now clouds of bees
Humming bright fill all the air.
Siva, Lord, dweller in
Holy Perundurai fair,
Thou wilt come to bestow
Favours rich. Oh show Thy face!
Mountain-joy, ocean-bliss,
From Thy couch rise in Thy grace!

The hymns of the Adiyārs or Saivite poets from the Devarām or Divine Garland, which is to them what the Vedas and Purānas are to the people of Northern India.

* *The Heart of Hinduism* (1913), p. 42.

At the same time the Alvārs or wandering teachers of the rival sect of the Vaishnavas were celebrating, in equally heartfelt verse, the praises of Vishnu. A Prayer for Release from Transmigration will serve to illustrate the poetry of Nammalvār, the greatest of the Tamil Vaishnava poets:

> Eternal Lord of Angels, Who dost deign to veil Thy form
> In all Creation's varied state, to save poor souls:
> Vouchsafe in all Thy grace to stay and hear Thy servants' cry
> That we be saved the dire return to former wretchedness,
> When we mistook the body for the soul and sinned all sins,
> Which clung to us and fixed us evermore to mortal frames.

Many of the Vaishnava hymns, particularly those relating to Krishna, are of an erotic character; in them, by a symbolism familiar to mystics of all ages, the longing of the soul for God is typified in the yearning of the mistress for her absent lover. The hymns of the twelve Alvārs have been collected into a volume known as the *Vaishnava Prabhandam,* a collection of 4,000 verses. This is the Prayer Book of the Vaishnava sect, and many of its followers know them by heart. Hymns from the *Prabhandam* are recited in the daily temple service at the great Vaishnava shrine of Srīrangam in Trichinopoly, and no other occasions such as marriages and funerals. It is impossible to do more than refer to Tamil secular poetry, which is of a voluminous and varied character, and to the literature of the Kanarese or the Telugu languages: the latter mostly belongs to a later date, when the glories of Hindu India blazed once more into a brief but dazzling sunset brilliance at Vijayanagar.

An interesting question which may be here considered is the extent to which Tamil poetry was affected by Christian influence. A flourishing Christian community existed in Southern India from very early times. As we have already seen, the Indian Church in Malabar was probably founded by Saint Thomas, and was reinforced by refugees from Persia during the persecutions started by the Sassanian King Sapor II between A.D. 339 and 379. The Malabar Church appears to have been widely diffused, and ancient stone crosses with Pehlevi inscriptions have been unearthed at St. Thomas's Mount near Madras, Kottayam in Travencore, and other places in the Madras Presidency. At late as the 15th century an Italian traveller, Nicolo Conti, says that St. Thomas was buried in a beautiful cathedral at Mylapore, and worshipped by Nestorian heretics, who were thickly scattered about the country, "in like manner as the Jews among us." But the Malabar church never had a separate existence. It was essentially foreign and dependent on the Catholics of the East: the language of its liturgy was Syriac. Christianity appears never to have taken root in India, and there is no reference to it in either Sanskrit or any vernacular language. We are driven, therefore, to the conclusion that the resemblances in Tamil devotional poetry to the teaching of the Gospel, like those between the stories of the birth and childhood of

Krishna and Christ, the doctrine of the Avatars of Vishnu and the Incarnation, and the parallels between the Gītā and the New Testament, are probably due to coincidence. The Malabar church suffered heavily at the hands of the Portuguese. After the Synod of Diamper in 1599, heretical books were ruthlessly destroyed; the Nestorian breviaries were brought into conformity with the Roman rite, and the Bishops were compelled to make their submission to the Pope.*

The Syrian Christians were by no means the only foreign settlers along the west coast. It became a favourite refuge from religious persecution in other lands. A Jewish colony which claimed to date from the Dispersion was granted a charter to settle in Cranganore by a Tamil king in A.D. 918. The Zoroastrians, who had driven out the Christians, were themselves compelled to leave their homes and to seek shelter in Gujarāt, bringing with them their Sacred Fire, by the Muhammadan invasion of Persia in the eighth century. To a different category belong the Moplahs, the descendants of Arab merchants who married Indian women. None of these intruders exercised any cultural influence, as far as can be ascertained, upon the country of their adoption.

The Pallavas

The origin of the gifted and important Pallava dynasty is obscure, and little or nothing was known of it until recent years. It arose into prominence about A.D. 325 on the east coast in the country between the mouths of the Kistna and Godāvari rivers. The Pallavas appear to have been intruders and to have formed no part of the original Tamil kingdoms. The supposition that they were a branch of the palhavas or Parthians of North-Western India is now generally abandoned,† and it is believed that they were an indigenous dynasty, who rose to power at the time of the dissolution of the Āndhra Empire. Their leaders, not unlike the founders of the kingdom of Vijayanagar some seven centuries later, collected round them numbers of Kurumbas, Maravas, Kallas and other predatory tribes, and formed them into a strong and aggressive power. It is significant that the world Pallava is synonymous in Tamil with rascal or robber. About A.D. 350 the Pallavas established themselves on the east coast, in the Chola territory, and occupied the famous city of Kānchi or Conjeeveram, which, like Madura, was one of the great seats of learning of Southern India. Mahendravarnam (A.D. 600-625) began the fierce wars against the Chalukyas for the possession of the province of Vengi, which went on intermittently for the next two centuries. He was at first a Jain by religion, but was converted to orthodox Hinduism; he is said to have turned a great Jain temple into a shrine dedicated to Siva, and this, no doubt,

* *The Early Spread of Christianity,* by A. Mingana. John Rylands Library Bulletin, 1926, p. 435.

† It has, however, been recently revived by the Rev. R. Heras, S.J. *Journal of the University of Bombay,* Jan. 1936.

was the fate of many early buildings, both Jain and Buddhist, when the reaction against these heresies set in. Hiuen Tsang, who spent the 'rain-rest' of A.D. 640 at Kānchī, tells us that the climate was hot, but the country was fertile and produced fruit and flowers. Precious stones were abundant. The people were honest, truthful and courageous, and loved learning. Their writing and language differed only slightly from that of Northern India. The various sects, Hindus, Jains and Mahāyāna Buddhists, flourished side by side. The perennial conflict between the Pallavas and the Chalukyas continued with varying fortunes, until the Chalukya King Vikramāditya II captured Kānchī in A.D. 740. From this date the fortunes of the Pallavas steadily declined, until they were finally incorporated, about A.D. 900, in the Empire of the all-conquering Cholas.

The cave and structural temples and other architectural remains of the Pallavas form an important chapter in Hindu art, which can only be briefly touched upon here.

The town of Mahāvallipuram or Māmallapuram was named after King Nārasimhavarnam (A.D. 625-645), who enjoyed the title of Māmalla or Great Champion on account of his victories over the Chalukyas. He excavated many cave-temples, decorated with fine reliefs. The side of a wall of rock contains a still more striking series of sculptures in relief, usually known as Arjuna's Penance. It is now held, however, that it represents the Descent of the Ganges. Most remarkable of all, however, is the group of monolithic Rathas or temples known as the Seven Pagodas, each carved from a single granite boulder standing upon the sea-shore, somewhat in the manner of the Kailāsa temple of Ellora. Apart from their grace and beauty of workmanship, these buildings form an interesting link between the Buddhist cave temple and the structural Dravidian temple. The finest is the Dharma Rājā Ratha. The work appears to have been interrupted by the Chalukyan invasion of A.D. 670 and remained unfinished. To the later period, A.D. 674-800, belong the structural temples, including the Shore temple at Māmallapuram and the famous Kailāsanātha temple at Kānchī, where the transition to the Chola style is clearly seen. One of the many features of interest is to be found in the life-like portrait images of the Pallava kings and their queens with which these buildings are adorned.

Ceylon

The history of Ceylon, the Lanka Dvīpa of the Sanskrit poets, is bound up closely with that of India. The original inhabitants of the island are apparently represented by the Veddas, a primitive tribe still surviving in Uva and the Eastern Province. Indian immigrants found their way from both Orissa and Gujarāt at an early date, and the island was already in an advanced state of civilisation at the time of the arrival in 246 B.C. of the Buddhist mission headed by Mahinda and Sang-hamitta, the son and daughter of Asoka, with a branch of the Bodhi Tree, which they planted at Anurādhapura in the heart of the island. In the reign of Devānāmpiya Tissa monasteries and dāgobas began to be built. Soon after this, the Tamil invasions started, and a Tamil King named Elāra reigned over Central and Northern Ceylon from 189 to 145 B.C. The struggle between the Tamils and Sinhalese went on with fluctuating fortunes, until the invaders were driven back and Anurādhapura was re-occupied by the great national hero Duttugemvnu (101-77 B.C.), who, in fulfilment of a vow, erected the gigantic Ruanveli and Mirisvetiya dāgobas. These immense domes, as large as the Egyptian pyramids, must have presented an imposing sight when they stood, in their original coats of dazzling while plaster, against their background of a vivid green jungle.

In the 5th century A.D. Fa Hian visited Ceylon on his homeward voyage, and he gives a vivid description of Anurādhapura as he saw it in the days of its glory—the Brazen Palace, nine storeys high, with its 1,600 pillars and its bronze roofs, and the many other wonders, including a Buddha of jasper holding in his hand a pearl of great price. The Tooth Relic, which had been smuggled into Ceylon from Northern India in a princess' hair, was carried in procession at public festivals, and dramatic representations of episodes in the life of the Buddha were enacted. The isolated fortress known as Sigiri or Lion's Rock, with its remarkable frescoes, was constructed at this period as a refuge by a usurper named Kassapa (A.D. 479-497). In A.D. 846 Anurādhapura was abandoned in favour of Polonaruwa, which was less exposed to invasion, but in 1003 the Chola armies overran the northern half of the island and held it for half a century. Then once more the Sinhalese reconquered the middle country, and in A.D. 1153 Parākrama Bāhu was crowned king of Lanka. This was the Golden Age of Sinhalese culture. Parākrama Bāhu adorned his capital with gigantic statues of the Buddha, temples, schools, debating-halls and hospitals. The streets of Polonaruwa were straight and board, and the city was surrounded by a fortified wall. The slaughter of animals was forbidden. So good was the government, even in remote districts, that "a woman might traverse the island with a jewel in her hand and not be asked what It was." Vast irrigation schemes were undertaken. Merchants from West and East met in Ceylon, which lay on the high-road of sea-borne commerce, and pilgrims from China were frequent visitors.

In the 14th century, the power of the Sinhalese kings began once more to decline, and renewed Tamil invasions caused Polonaruwa to be abandoned like Anurādhapura before it. Buddhism suffered severely, and in the words of the chronicler, "the whole island resembled a dwelling in flames, or a house darkened by funeral rites." One of the reasons for the rapid decay was the immense amount of money lavished on religious establishments, and the enervating effect of the monastic life on large numbers of the population. Another may have been malaria. In A.D. 1266, the reigning monarch moved his capital to the hill-fastness of Kandy, whither the Sacred Tooth and other precious relics were transported; the low country was mostly in Tamil hands. In A.D. 1522 the Portuguese appeared on the west coast; they are described as white and beautiful, wearing boots and hats of iron, eating a sort of white stone and drinking blood, and using cannon with a noise louder than thunder, the balls shot from which, after traversing a league, would break a castle of marble. In 1658 they were expelled by the Dutch. Ceylon became a British Crown Colony in 1798; the last King of Kandy was deposed in 1815.

Fig. 31 : Ornament from the Summit of a Tamil Temple, shewing the Makara, a mythological monster.

LEADING DATES

The Pallavas

c. A.D. 325	Rie of the Pallavas.
600-625	Mahendravarnam.
610	Defeat of the Pallavas by the Chalukyas.
625-645	Nārasimhavarnam. The Seven Pagodas.

640 Hiuen Tsang at Kānchi.
642 The Pallavas take Badāmi and defeat the Chalukyas.
740 Overthrow of the Pallavas by the Chalukyas.

The Cholas

c. A.D. 900 Rise of the Cholas.
985 Rājārājā The Great.
1003 Ceylon overrun by the Cholas.
1035 Rajendra Choladeva. Expeditions to Bengal and Pegu.
1052 Defeat of the Cholas by the Chalukyas at the battle of Koppam. Decline of Chola Empire.

Chapter XIII

Medieval India : The Rājpūts and the Muhammadan Conquest

With the death of Harsha in 648, the curtain once more descends upon Northern India: when it again rises two centuries later, the scene is radically changed. A new order of society has arisen, the central figures of which are the numerous clans of a race calling themselves Rājpūts or 'Sons of Kings'. To-day there are thirty-six Rājpūt clans, who trace their descent from the Sun, Moon, and Sacred Fire; their titular head is the Sisodia Rānā of Mewar, who exercises religious as well as royal functions, as 'priest-king' of the god Siva. The Rājpūts claim to be the ancient Kshatriyas and found their ideals of conduct upon the heroes of the Hindu epics; but modern research seems to show that they are mainly the descendants of the Gurjara, Hūna and other Central Asian tribes who found their way across the north-west frontier in the fifth

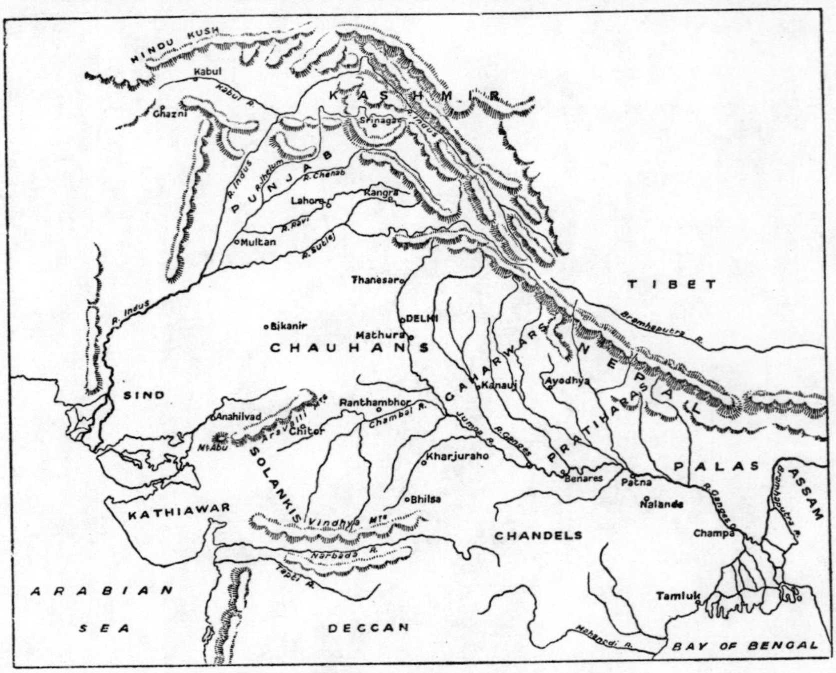

Map 9 : Northern India, c. A.D. 1000.

and sixth centuries.* These invaders carved out kingdoms for themselves and eventually settled down in the country, taking Hindu wives; the ruling classes had no difficulty in persuading obsequious Brahmins to admit them into the Hindu fold, and to provide them with genealogies going back to heroic times, very much as Virgil and Livy traced the ancestry of the founders of the Roman Empire back to the heroes of the Trojan War. Confirmation for the theory of the foreign origin of many of these clans is found in the Puranic legend about the creation of the Agnikula or Fire-born Rājpūts. When Parasurāma, 'Rama with the axe,' had, at the behest of the Brahmins, destroyed the ancient Kshatriyas, the land was left masterless, whereupon the gods repaired to Mount Ābu in Southern Rājputāna, and there from the sacred firepit proudced the four 'fire-born' clans, the Powar, the Parihār, the Chauhān and the Solanki. There is little doubt that here we have an allegorical account of the rite by which the foreign chieftains were initiated into Hinduism. It is interesting to note that the destruction of the original Kshatriya caste is admitted. Other Rājpūt clans, such as the Chandel, appear to have originated in indigenous tribes like the Gonds, who rose to power and were similarly ennobled and admitted into the Hindu fold.

But of their foreign origin the Rājpūts quickly lost all recollections. They regarded themselves as coming of the bluest blood in the country, and quickly developed into a haughty and exclusive aristocracy, intensely jealous of its privileges. Kings assumed a semi-divine status, and were surrounded by hosts of retainers. They patronised learning, and their courts were filled with Brahmin scholars, poets and dramatists. Commerce flourished, and the land waxed rich. Magnificent temples, fortified cities and palaces were erected and their treasuries filled with untold wealth. A feature of court life was the bard, the Bhāt or Chāran, who recited the heroic deeds of the Rājpūt noble's ancestors. The bard was an important and favoured person, for not only was he the repository of the unwritten history of the clan, but he was the undisputed authority on all genealogical matters. He was the registrar of the family's births, death and marriages, and his verdict was final in settling disputes about the division of ancestral property or of caste and consanguinity in the case of wedlock. The bard's person was sacrosanct—he acted as a herald in war, and as a pledge for the fulfilment of contracts. If these were broken, the bard would commit *trāgā* (religious suicide) and bring the most terrible of curses upon the head of the offender. The Rājpūt's ruling passion, and indeed his only congenial occupation, was war. The boy, on reaching puberty, was initiated into knighthood, as in medieval Europe, by the ceremony of *karg bandai,* or binding of the sword. He was brought up on stories of the epics of old. His pattern was Rāma, the prince of Hindu heroes. He was taught to respect women, spare the fallen and those who asked for quarter, and never strike a foul blow. A suppliant who had taken sanctuary by his hearth was

* V. A. Smith, *Early History of India,* 4th edn., p. 427 ff, and authorities there quoted.

sacred. The old ballads abound in stories illustrating the almost quixotic chivalry of the Rājpūt. When not fighting, he spent his time in hunting and hawking, or in feats of arms; during his leisure hours he was entertained by his bards and dancing girls, or sat drinking opium-water (*kusumba*) with his retainers. Many centuries later, the French traveller Bernier says, "if the Rājpūt is a brave man, he need never entertain an apprehension of being deserted by his followers; they only require to be well led, for their minds are made up to die in his presence rather than abandon him to his enemies. It is an interesting sight to see them on the eve of battle, with the fumes of opium in their heads, embrace and bid adieu to one another, as if certain of death." The Rājpūt has been compared to the Scottish Highlander. His loyalty to his chieftain and clan was intense, and being too proud and indolent to undertake menial work, he spent his time in quarrelling with his neighbour and raiding his territory. Haughty and punctilious, he seized upon the most trivial slight as an offence to be wiped out in blood: on one occasion, a sanguinary campaign was fought because a rājā, when out hawking, had picked up a partridge which had fallen over his neighbour's boundary. The ballads give a vivid picture of the warriors passing the night before the battle, listening to recitations from the *Mahābhārata*, longing for the morning as a lonely wife longs for her husband, and asking. "When will the night pass away: when will the morning come: the time of battle?"* The younger sons of the family frequently wandered to foreign courts in search of adventure, offering their swords and often carving out fresh principalities for themselves. Women enjoyed great freedom. The Rājpūtinī exercised the ancient Kshatriya right of Maiden's Choice; she accompanied her husband in the hunting field and even to war, and at his death in battle, proudly mounted the pyre by his side. The bardic literature resounds with the praises of these heroines. When the Muhammadans invaded the land, the women is a besieged town committed the horrie rite of *jauhār* or mass suicide in order to escape defilement, wrose than death, at the hands of the unclean barbarian. That treasury of old Rājpūt legend, Tod's *Rājasthān*, gives many examples. After the first siege of Chitor, the widow addresses the page who has seen her husband fall:

" 'Boy, tell me, ere I go, how bore himself my lord?'

'As a reaper of the harvest of battle! I followed his steps as the humble gleaner of his sword. On the bed of honour he spread a carpet of the slain, whereon, a barbarian his pillow, he sleeps ringed by his foes.'

'Yet once again, oh boy, tell me how my lord bore himself?'

'Oh mother, who can tell his deeds? He left no foe to dread or to admire him.' She smiled farewell to the boy, and adding, 'My lord will chide my delay,' sprang into the flames."†

---

* A. K. Forbes, *Rās Māla* (1924 edn.), I. 31.

† Tod, *Annals and Antiquities of Rājasthān* (1914 edn.), I. 246.

The historic centre of the Rājpūt tribes was Bhinmāl in Southern Rājputāna, about 50 miles from Mount Ābu, where a powerful Gurjara kingdom had sprung up. About A.D. 800 a Gurjara chief occupied Kanauj, which was still considered to be the chief city of Northern India, and built up a kingdom which stretched from Bihār to the Sutlej, including Kāthiāwār. The most powerful ruler of this dynasty, who called themselves Parihār or Pratihāra Rājpūts, was Bhoja (A.D. 840-899). In the tenth century, the Parihār dynasty, weakened by wars, began to decline, and their tributaries, the Chandel rājās of Bundelkhand, to the south of the Jumna, asserted their independence. It is supposed that the founders of this dynasty were originally Gond chieftains. The principal ruler of the Chandel line was Dhanga (1000-1050), who, we shall see, was a member of the confederacy which opposed the Muhammadan invaders. The Chandel rājās were great builders. At Khajuraho, one of their chief towns, they erected a group of temples which are some of the most striking examples of the Northern style of architecture, and a number of beautiful lakes were constructed among the Bundelkhand hills by damming up valleys with huge blocks of masonry.

In Gujarāt, 'the country of the Gurjaras,' a kingdom was founded by a ruler of the Solanki or Chalukya clan named Mularājā in A.D. 961. The father of Mularājā was a young prince who, in accordance with the common practice of the younger brothers of a Rājpūt royal house, set out to seek his fortunes in foreign lands. His capital was at Anhilvād, about 50 miles north of Ahmadabad. It is now a mass of ruins, but a Jain chronicler was left us a vivid description of the city in the height of it power :

> "Anhilvād was twelve *coss* (leagues) in circuit, within which were many temples and colleges, eighty-four squares and eighty-four market-places, with mints for gold and silver coin. Each class had its separate quarter, as had each description of merchandise—elephants' teeth, silks, purples, diamonds, pearls, etc., etc.; each had its separate square. There was one market place for money-changers; one for perfumes and unguents; one for physicians; one for artisans; one for goldsmiths and another for silversmiths; there were distinct quarters for navigators, for bards, and for genealogists. The eighteen castes inhabited the city; all were happy together. The palace groaned with a multitude of separate buildings—for the armoury, for elephants, for horses and chariots, for the public accountants and officers of state. Each kind of goods had its separate custom-house, where the duties of export, import and sale were collected—as for spices, fruits, drugs, camphors, metals, and everything costly of home or foreign growth. It is a place of universal commerce. The daily amount of duties is one lakh of *tankhas* (£7,000). If you ask for water they give you milk. There are many Jain temples, and on the banks of a lake is a shrine to Sahaslinga Mahādeva. The population delights to a saunter amidst the groves of *champa* (magnolias), palms, rose-apples, sandal-trees and mangoes, with every variety of creeper, and fountains

whose waters are *amrit* (ambrosia). Here discussions take place on the Vedas, carrying instruction to the listener. There is no want of Jain priests, or of merchants true to their word, and skilled in commerce; and there are many schools for teaching grammar. Anhilvād is a sea of human beings. If you can measure the waters of the ocean, they you may attempt to count the number of souls. The army is numerous, nor is there any lack of bell-bearing elephants."*

The most powerful ruler of the line was Siddharājā (1094-1143). Siddharājā, whose name means 'lord of the magicians,' is still the popular hero of Gujarāt legend. One of his many exploits was the capture of the famous fortress of Junāgarh in Kāthiāwār, in order that he might obtain possession of the beautiful Ranik Devī, wife of the local ruler. The fort was betrayed, but Ranik Devī burnt herself on the funeral pyre rather than submit to the conqueror's embraces. Siddharājā was a great builder, and a patron of the Jain sect. At his court lived the famous Jain scholar Hemachandra, who was the royal pandit and annalist. Jainism flourished until the numerous puritanical restrictions which were placed on eating meat, taking life, gambling, betting, drinking, dancing and other amusements caused a revulsion in favour of Saivism. Jainism is still, however, very popular among the mercantile classes in Gujarāt. The dynasty of Anhilvād survived until 1297, when the generals of Alā-ud-dīn annexed Gujarāt to the Delhi Sultanate.

Other contemporary dynasties were the Powārs of Mālwā, and the Pālās of Bengal. Of the Powārs or Parmāras, the most powerful king was Bhoja (1018-1060), not to be confounded with his namesake of Kanauj. Bhoja was a scholar and a patron of learning, and has become proverbial as the ideal Hindu monarch. He was the author of numerous works on astronomy, architecture and poetry, and he adorned his capital at Dhār with many fine buildings, among which was a Sanskrit college, now a mosque. His great lake, 250 square miles in area, was a remarkable feat of engineering. Another important dynasty was that of the Pālas of Bengal and Bihār. The word *pāla* means protector, and the first ruler, Gopāla, restored the country to order after a long period of anarchy. Dharmapāla (790-815) and Devapāla (815-854) raised Bengal to the foremost place in Northern India. For a time they ruled as far west as Kanauj, and their successors repelled invasions by the Gurjaras, Rāshtrakūtas, and Cholas. Buddhism continued to flourish in Bengal long after it had become extinct in other parts of India, and the Pāla kings were in close touch with the Buddhist rulers of Tibet on the one hand and Java and Sumatra on the other. In the middle of the eleventh century, the Pālas were succeeded by the Senas, who ruled until they were overthrown by the Muhammadans in 1197. Bengal was still populated to a great extent by non-Hindus; the Senas sought to remedy this state of affairs by inducing high-caste immigrants from Hindustan to settle in the country.

* Forbes, *op. cit.* I, 239.

Fig. 32 : Triumphal Arch, Gujarāt.

In the Punjab, a Rājpūt kingdom had grown up render a rājā of the name of Jaipāl, whose capital was at Bhatinda in what is now Patiāla State. The Punjab was then, as always, the bulwark of Ḥindustan against invasions from the North-West. Sabuktigin, originally a Turki slave of the governor of Khorasān, had carved out for himself a kingdom at Ghazni in Afghanistan. To the horsemen of Central Asia, the untapped riches of India were a lure like the gold of Mexico and Peru to the hungry adventures who accompanied Cortez and Pizarro, and in 986 Sabuktigin made his first raid into the plains. In 991 Jaipāl summoned a confederacy of Rājpūt princes to resist the invader, but in vain. The Hindu army was disastrously defeated and Peshawar was taken. In 997 Sabuktigin was succeeded by his son Mahmūd, who, it is said, vowed to invade India every year. Each October he set out for the plains, retiring to his fastnesses, laden with plunder, as soon as the hot weather set in. In 1001 he inflicted another disastrous defeat upon his opponents. "The enemy of God, Jaipāl, and his children and grand-children and nephews and the chief men of his tribe and his relations were taken prisoners, and being strongly bound with ropes were carried before the Sultan, like as evildoers, on whose faces the fumes of infidelity are evident, who are covered with the vapours of misfortune, will be bound and carried to hell. Some had their arms forcibly tied behind their backs, some were seized by the cheek, some were driven by blows on the neck. A necklace was taken off the neck of Jaipāl, composed of large pearls and shining gems and rubies set in gold, of which the value was two hundred thousand dīnārs; and twice that value was obtained from the necks of those of his relations who were taken prisoners or slain, and had become the food of the mouths of hyenas and vultures. God also bestowed upon his friends such an amount of booty as was beyond all bounds and calculations, including five hundred thousand slaves, beautiful men and women. The Sultan returned with his followers to his camp, having plundered immensely, by God's aid, having obtained the victory, and thankful to God, the lord of the Universe. For the Almighty had given them victory over a province of the country of Hind, broader and longer and more fertile than Khurāsān."*

Jaipāl was released, but unable to survive the disgrace, burnt himself to death on a funeral-pyre. His son Ānandpāl sent ambassadors to the Kings of Ujjain, Gwalior, Kalinga, Kanauj, Delhi and Ājmīr, and collected a mighty host on the plains of Peshawar to resist the invader. Rich women sold their jewels to supply munitions of war; the poor spun cotton to clothe the troops. In the fierce battle which ensued, the Hindus were getting the upper hand, when the elephant on which Ānandpāl was mounted took fright and fled. This was the signal for a panic, and the army fled, pursued by the Muslim cavalry, leaving immense booty in the hands of the victors. Mahmūd then proceeded to capture the fortified temple of Kāngra, where among the treasures captured was "a house of white silver, like to the houses of rich men, the length of which was thirty yards and the breadth fifteen." The plunder which Mahmūd carried back to Ghazni contained "jewels and unbored pearls and rubies, shining like sparks or like wine congealed with ice, emeralds like fresh sprigs of myrtle, and diamonds in size and weight like pomegranates."

In the expedition of 1018, Bulandshahr surrendered, and the inhabitants accepted Islam. The invading hordes penetrated into the heart of Hindustan. The holy city of Mathurā was taken and its splendid shrine levelled to the ground. Five idols of red gold, five yards high, with jewelled eyes, were carried off. Kanauj was next attacked. Rājā Rājyapāl tamely surrendered. This so enraged his fellow-princes that an army under Ganda the Chandel deposed and slew him; but Ganda himself behaved no better

* Elliot & Dowson, *The History of India as told by its own Historians* (1867-77), II. 26.

when his turn came. He fled on the eve of the battle, having 580 elephants and much booty in the hands of the Muslims.

But the most famous of all Mahmūd's exploits was his audacious raid on the temple of Somnāth, dedicated to Siva, the Lord of the Moon, and standing on the edge of the sea, on the southern coast of Kāthiāwār in the realm of the Solanki ruler of Gujarāt. It enshrined a massive stone lingam, five cubits in height, which was regarded as being of special sanctity and attracted thousands of pilgrims. It was bathed every day in water brought all the way from the Ganges, and garlanded with flowers from Kashmir. The revenue of ten thousand villages was assigned for its support, and a thousand Brahmins performed the daily ritual of the temple. The original shrine, like so many in ancient India, was built of wood: it was supported by fifty-six teakwood pillars, coated with lead and inlaid with jewels.* A chain of massive golden bells hung over the idol: jewelled chandeliers, images of pure gold and veils embroidered with precious stones were stored in the treasury. The temple, together with the buildings to accommodate the ministrants, formed a regular town, surrounded by a wall and strongly fortified.

Mahmūd left Ghazni in December 1023 with 30,000 picked horsemen. He appeared suddenly before Multan, which surrendered. Here he obtained the necessary camels for the desert-crossing, and both Bikanīr and Ājmīr opened their gates to him. Six weeks' arduous marching brought him to Anhilvād, and the rājā, Bhīma by name, fled at his approach. Mahmūd probably marched against Somnāth by the route running along the southern coast of Kāthiāwār. On Thursday, January 30th, he broke through the *enceinte* of fortresses surrounding the town and approached the walls of the sacred city. The inhabitants, confident in the power of the god, jeered at the invaders from the battlements. Next day the assault began. The Muslims, after a severe struggle, succeeded in gaining a footing on the ramparts, but were too exhausted to do more. And now the Hindus began to realise their peril. All night long the temple was thronged with wailing crowds, beating their breasts and calling upon the deity to come to the help of his own. But there was neither voice nor answer. At dawn the attack was renewed, and step by step the defenders were forced back through the narrow winding streets to the walls of the shrine itself. Here a last despairing stand was made until at length the Muslims, planting their scaling ladders against the walls, stormed them with loud cries of *Dīn! Dīn!* Fifty thousand Hindus were put to the sword; others tried to escape by sea and were drowned. The treasure taken exceeded two million dīnārs in value. According to one story, the Brahmins who had submitted begged to be allowed to ransom the lingam, but Mahmūd would not listen. He refused, he said, to appear before the Judgement Seat as one who had taken money to spare an idol. The stone was broken in pieces and a portion of it buried in

* The present ruined stone temple at Somnāth was built later on the same site.

the threshold of the mosque at Ghazni, to be trodden under foot by true believers. The army returned home across the Slind desert, where it suffered terrible privations, being misled, it is said, by Hindu guides.*

Mahmūd 'the image-breaker' died in 1030, at the age of sixty-two. Iconoclast though he was, he was no barbarian. He enriched his capital with a great mosque, aqueducts and libraries, built from the spoils of India. He enjoyed the society of the learned, and among the poets and men of letters at his court were Firdausi, the author of the great Persian epic, the Shāh Nāma or Book of Kings, and the learned Abu Rīhān Muhammad, familiarly known as al-Bīrūnī, 'the foreigner.' al-Bīrūbī was an extraordinary man. His *Chronology of Ancient Nations* is an encyclopedic work on Indian religion, philosophy, mathematics and astronomy. It has been translated by Dr. E.C. Sachau (Trübner's Oriental Series, 1888). He is equally at home in Greek and Sanskrit, and quotes with assurance from Plato, the *Bhagavad Gītā* and the New Testament.

India now enjoyed half a century's respite from invasion. A number of fresh Rājpūt clans arose in Hindustan, which replaced those exterminated in the wars against Mahmūd of Ghazni. The chief of these were the Gaharwārs of Kanauj, the Tomāras of Delhi and the Chauhāns of Ājmīr. Rājā Jaichand Gaharwār (*c.* 1040) restored Kanauj to its ancient position as the premier city of Northern India, and a romantic legend tells how he celebrated the horse sacrifice to denote the fact of his overlordship, and summoned the Rājpūt princes to attend. Prithvi Rājā Chauhan of Ājmīr alone refused to do so, and Jaichand set up a golden statue of him and placed it at his threshold as his door-keeper. Presently Jaichand held a "Maiden's Choice" for the hand of his daughter, the princess Padmāvatī. But Padmāvatī, disregarding the assembled suitors, threw the garland round the neck of the statue, and Prithvi Rājā, riding in with his chosen companions, threw his bride across his saddle-bow and galloped off at full speed.

Meanwhile, the sultans of Ghazni had been drive out of their capital by their rivals, the Afghans of Ghor, who destroyed Ghazni and drove them to take refuge in Lahore. Muhammad Ghori continued the policy of raiding India, but on his first attempt to do so, he found himself confronted by a huge army commanded by Prithvi Rājā. In the ensuing battle, Muhammad was wounded in single combat and carried off the field, and his army fled in panic. Next year he returned, burning for revenge. The armies met once more at Tarāin, on the historic battle-ground of Kurukshetra. The Muhammadans spent the night telling their beads, the Hindus in listening to heroic stories recited by their bards. The next morning, Padmāvatī buckled on her husband's sword for the last time. "O Sun of the Chauhans," she said, "none has drunk so deeply both of glory and of pleasure as thou. Life is like an old garment;

* Elliot and Dowson, iv. 181.

what matters if we throw it off? To die well is life immortal." The battle which followed was the fiercest fought on that blood-drenched field, but no valour could prevail against the mounted archers of the Muslims. "Like a great building, the Hindu host tottered and collapsed in its own ruins." Prithvi Rāja was captured and put to death, and his queen, accompanied by her handmaids, mounted the funeral pyre. "For miles the stricken field was bestrewn with castaway flags and spears and shields, and heaped bows, jewelled swords and plumed casques, exquisitely chiselled and damascened gauntlets, breast-plates and gaily-dyed scarves, intermingled with the countless dead." Ājmīr, the fortress of Gwalior, and Delhi, founded recently by the Tomāras, fell. Kanauj was stormed and Jaichand was slain. The remnant of the Gaharwārs fled to the inaccessible desert, where they became known as the Rāhtors and founded the state of Jodhpur. One of the last places to surrender was Kalanjār, the Chandel stronghold, which opened its gates in 1203. "The temples were converted into mosques and abodes of goodness, the ejaculations of the bead-counters and the voices of the summoners to prayer ascended to the highest heaven and the very name of idolatry was annihilated."

In 1194 the Muhammadans began to move eastwards. The sacred city of Benares was taken by Muhammad Ghori's general, Kutb-ud-din Ibak. In 1199 Bihār was surprised by Muhammad ibn Bhaktiyār. "It was discovered that the whole of the fortress and city was a college, and in the Hindu tongue they call a college Bihār (Vihāra)". The 'shaven-headed Brahmins' (in reality, Buddhist monks) were almost exterminated, and with them expired the last pale flicker of Buddhism in India. The great university of Nālandā, with its precious library, was destroyed, and shrines and images were broken to pieces. The few survivors fled to Tibet, where they were kindly received. The Muslims soon after invaded Bengal, which was ruled over by the revered Lakshamana Sena. The capital of Bengal was Nuddea, and, by a clever trick, Muhammad ibn Bhaktiyār surprised the aged ruler while he was at dinner. Soon after A.D. 1200 the whole of Northern India except Rājputāna, Mālwā and part of Gujarāt, had been conquered, and Hindu supremacy was at an end.

The overthrow of the rich and martial kingdoms of Hindustān with such surprising ease is at first sight an astonishing fact. It was certainly not due to lack of valour on the part of the Rājpūt race. Its causes are to be found in the defects of the social organisation of the Hindus. Owing to this, fighting was left to a single caste, the Kshatriyas; the vast majority of the population was untrained in arms and indifferent to the fate of their country. National feeling did not exist, and even the martial clans had little sense of patriotism. In the face of common danger, it is true, they combined for a time, but otherwise they frittered away their strength in endless internecine quarrels. The Hindus, as al-Bīrūnī says, were too proud and self-centred to recognise the existence of outside nations, much less to learn from them, and their military tactics were old-fashioned. The infantry were an undisciplined rabble, and their chief reliance was placed on their war-elephants, which, even at the time of the invasion of Alexander, had proved to be worse than useless in the face of well-trained cavalry. The hardy Muslim invaders from the north were, man for man, bigger, stronger and better mounted than their opponents, who, for all their valour, were handicapped by a hot and enervating climate, and by a diet which was mainly vegetarian. The Muhammadan religion was a fighting creed; the extermination of the infidel and the destruction of idols were sacred duties; he who died in performing them was a Ghāzi and went straight to the joys of Paradise. The essence of Islam is brotherhood. All Muslims, of whatever race or social position, are equal in the sight of God. Merit was the only test of ability and a slave could rise to the throne of Delhi. In this it contrasted strongly with the endless divisions of caste-ridden Hinduism; and, lastly, the invaders were desperate men. They were carried forward by the lure of booty, by their own sense of superiority, and by their knowledge that if they were beaten there was no retreat; their only salvation lay in their swords.*

Culture and Social Conditions

The Rājpūt courts were great centres of literature and art. The drama, in particular, flourished, and found liberal patrons in many of the rājās, some of whom were themselves authors of plays. Of the later dramatists, the foremost was Rājasekhara, who lived at the courts of Mahandrapāla and Mahīpāla of Kanauj about A.D. 900. His drama, the *Karpurmanjari,* is written entirely in Prākrit. Much more important, however, is the famous *Gīta Govinda,* or 'Sons of the Cowherd,' written by Jayadeva, the Kavirāj or poet laureate of Lakshamana Sena of Bengal, on the eve of the Muhammadan conquest (A.D. 1200). This poem—half drama, half lyric—describes the loves of Krishna and the milkmaids, and, in particular, his beloved Rādhā. Two verses of Sir Edwin Arnold's translation will serve to illustrate its characteristics:

> One, with star-blossomed *champak* wreathed, woos him to rest, his head
> On the dark pillow of her breast so tenderly outspread,
> And o'er her brow with roses blown she fans a fragrance rare,
> That falls on the enchanted sense like rain in thirsty air;
> While the company of damsels wave many an odorous spray,
> And Krishna, laughing, toying, sighs the soft spring away.
> Sweetest of all that temptress who dancers for him now,
> With subtle feet which part and meet in the Rās measure slow,
> To the chime of silver bangles and the beat of roseleaf hands,
> And pipe and lute and viol, played by the woodlands bands,

* Lane-Poole, *Medieval India under Muhammadan Rule* (1903), pp. 62-4.

So, that wholly passion-laden—eye, ear, sense, soul o'ercome,
Krishna is theirs in the forest; his heart forgets his home.
Fig. 33.)

Fig. 33 : Krishna and Gopīs dancing the Rāsa Mandala.

At the same time, a flourishing school of literature arose in Kashmir, where, at the court of Srīnagar, Kalhana wrote the Rājatarangini, or 'River of Kings,' a metrical chronicle which is Hindu India's almost role contribution of history, and Somadeva produced his famous *Kathā Sarit Sāgara,* or 'Ocean of Tales,' the Hindu Arabian Nights.

A new departure was the rise of the vernaculars. The Rājpūt bards begin to sing in Hindu the deeds of their patrons: the most famous of these was Chand Bardai, who, in the *Prithirāj Raso*, celebrates the exploits of Prithirāj (Prithvi Rājā). A typical passage describes how Prithirāj carried off his bride, the fair princess Padmāvatī :

Then, on seeing King Prithirāj,
She smiled bashfully, hiding her face through shame.
Seizing her hand, putting her on horseback,
The King, the Lord of Delhi, took her away.
The rumour spread that, outside the city
They were carrying off Padmāvatī by force.
Drums are beat, there is saddling of horse and elephant,

They ran, armed, in all directions.
Seize! Seize! shouted each warrior.
Rage possessed the heroes and their King.

On the field fell heads and headless trunks of the foe.
The foe fell on the field of battle;
Turning his face towards Delhi,
Having won the battle, were Prithirāj,
All the chiefs were glad.*

Of social conditions, we obtain a clear picture from contemporary literature and also from the great work of al-Bīrūnī, the learned Muslim scholar referred to above. Women were well educated and took an active part in public life. Girls could read and write and understand Sanskrit; they learned to play, dance and paint portraits. The age of marriage, was, however, growing earlier, and the custom of Suttee was becoming more and more usual. Remarriage was forbidden, and the unfortunate women often preferred this dreadful alternative to the life-long misery of Indian widowhood. al-Bīrūnī was struck by the power of the Brahmin priesthood. The Vaisya caste was disappearing; Vaisyas were more and more regarded as Sūdras, and religious rites were confined to the higher castes. Turning to religion, al-Bīrūnī comments on the habit of making pilgrimages to sacred places, and particularly to rivers for bathing festivals. Benares was now the most sacred place in India. Many of the modern Hindu feasts—Holi at the commencement of spring, Divāli in the autumn and others—had already become fashionable. Famous shrines had sprung up in various spots. Of these, al-Bīrūnī mentions the great Lingam at Somnāth, destroyed by Mahmūd of Ghazni, the Idol of the Sun at Multān, and one of Vishnu at Thanesar. The three principal gods in the multitude of deities formed a Trinity. "There is an analogy between the Hindus and Christians, as the latter distinguish between the three persons, and give them separate names, the Father, Son and Holy Ghost, but unite them in one substance." But, he is careful to add, this is the religion of the vulgar. Educated Hindus abhor anthropomorphism: they believe God to be "One, Eternal, without beginning or end, acting by free-will, Almighty, All-wise, living, giving life, ruling and preserving." God is real existence, because "everything that exists, exists through Him." al-Bīrūnī gives a good account of classical Sanskrit literature, but it is significant that he says little or nothing of Jainism or of Buddhism. He describes in detail the Hindu belief in Karma. Emancipation is the result of true knowledge; "the soul turns away from matter, the connecting links are broken, the union is dissolved."

Turning to law, al -Bīrūnī was struck by the mildness of the Hindu criminal code. "In this regard," he acutely remarks, "the manners and customs of the Hindus

---

* Trans. Beames, *Journal of the Asiatic Society of Bengal,* vol. xxxviii, p. 152.

resemble those of the Christians, for they are like those of the latter, based on the principles of virtue and absence from wickedness... Upon my word, this is a noble philosophy, but the people of this world are not all philosophers! Most of them are ignorant and erring, who cannot be kept on the straight road, save by sword and whip." (II. 161.) In civil cases, written plaints were filed, oaths were taken and witnesses heard. Children inherited from the father, the daughter getting a fourth of the son's share. The widow did not inherit, but was entitled to maintenance by her late husband's family. At marriage the husband settled a sum upon his wife (*strīdāna*). Taxes were light: the land-tax was calculated on one-sixth of the value of the crop, and the trading community paid income tax.

But with all their splendid achievements in art, literature and science, says al-Bīrūnī, the Hindus had one fatal defect. "They are by nature niggardly in communicating that which they know, and they take the greatest possible care to withhold it from men of another caste among their own people; still much more, of course, from any foreigner. According to their belief, there is no country on earth but theirs, and no created being beside them has any knowledge of science whatever. Their haughtiness is such that if you tell them of any science or knowledge in Khorasan or Persia, they will think you to be both an ignoramus and a liar. If they travelled and mixed with other nations, they would soon change their minds, for their ancestors were not so narrow-minded as the present generation is." (I. 22.)

The Rājpūts were great builders, and their irrigation works, bathing-places, reservoirs and fortresses attest to their skill in engineering and architecture. The noble strongholds of Chitor, Ranthambhor, Māndu and Gwalior have played a conspicuous part in national history. The finest examples of domestic architecture are the Palace of Mān Singh at Gwalior, the Palace of the Winds at Udaipur, and the buildings at Amber, that 'rose-red city half as old as time'. Many of them stand by the side of beautiful artificial lakes, but the castle at Jodhpur, like those of medieval Europe, is perched upon a lofty and inaccessible rock overlooking the town, with frowning bastions and battlements. These edifices won the admiration of the Emperor Bābur, usually a severe critic of Indian things: "they are singularly beautiful... the domes are coverd with plates of copper-gilt. The outside of the wall is inlaid with green painted tiles. All around they have inlaid the walls with figures of plantain trees made of painted tiles." In Rājputāna where so much of the spirit of ancient India survives, architecture is still a living art.

The most striking feature of the medieval Hindu temples of the Northern or Indo-Aryan type is the loftily ribbed curvilinear or bulging spire (Figs. 34, 35). It is surmounted by a large cushion-shaped block of stone (*amalaka*) and above this is a vase-shaped cap or pinnacle. A characteristic group of temples built in this style, dating from A.D. 750 to 1200, is at Bhuvaneswara in Orissa. The majestic Linga

Rājā temple has a spire 180 feet high, rising imposingly above the surrounding buildings. At Konārak, on the neighbouring coast, is the famous Black Pagoda, now in ruins. Near it stand colossal monolithic horses and an elephant. The stone wheels

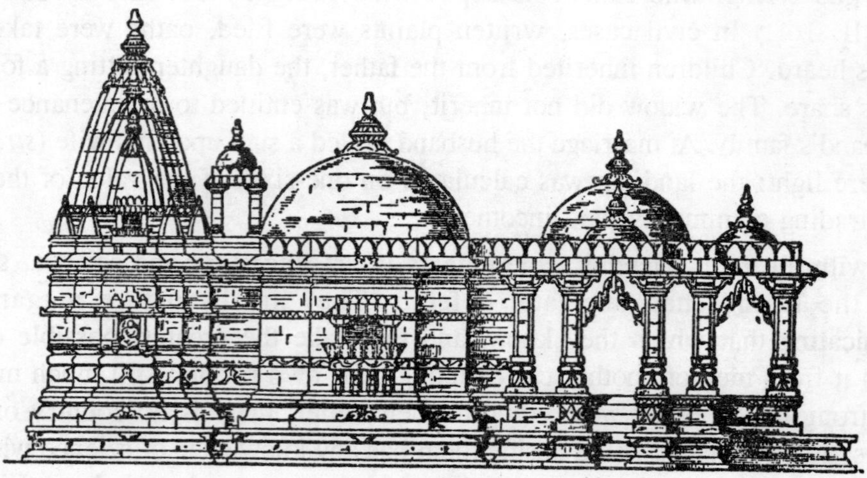

Fig. 34 : Hindu Temple with double Mandapa or Porch, Indo-Aryan type.

on the pediment reveal the fact that these temples were built in imitation of the processional cars, such as are taken out in honour of the god Jāgānāth (Vishnu) at Puri to-day; the curved spire is a copy of the bamboo scaffolding erected over them. The word *ratha* or car is actually used to denote this type of temple.* The White Pagoda at Puri is the scene of a famous pilgrimage but is architecturally inferior. Another notable group exists at Khajuraho in Bundelkhand: in these the lofty spire is made up of a number of smaller ones, and the sides are richly decorated with sculptures (Plate XII). In Gujarāt, a particularly ornate the florid school of architecture sprang up under the patronage of the Solanki kings of Anhilvād (Fig. 32). A characteristic example of this style is the temple of the Sun at Mundera, but medieval Hindu architecture finds its highest expression in the Jain temples which crown the summits of Mount Ābu in Southern Rājputāna, and of Girnār and Satrunjaya in Kāthiāwār. Of the temples at Dilwāra or Devalvāda at the former palce, the two most important are those of Vimala Shāh and Tej Pāl, whose halls of pure white marble, now beautifully mellowed by time, date from A.D. 1032 and 1232 (Plate XIII). They have often been described, and only a passing reference is necessary to what Fergusson calls "the lace-like delicacy of the fairy forms into white the patient chisel of the Hindu has carved the white marble." The principal feature is the octagonal dome of the vestibule, around which is a columned peristyle. The pendant from the centre of the dome of Tej Pāl's temple almost defies description. "It appears

* In the South, the word *Vimāna* or vehicle, the car in which the gods cross the heavens, is commonly applied to a temple (Fig. 40, p. 267).

like a cluster of the half-disclosed lotos, whose cups are so thin, so transparent and so accurately wrought, that it fixes the eye in admiration." The sacred mountain of Satrunjaya is less generally known; it is vividly described by the historian of Gujarāt:

> "There is hardly a city in India, through its length and breadth, from the river of Sind to the sacred Ganges, from Himāla's diadem of ice peaks, to the throne of his virgin daughter, Rūdra's destined bride, that has not supplied, at one time or other, contributions of wealth to the edifices which crown the hill of Palitāna; street after street, and square after square, extend these shrines of the Jain faith, with their stately enclosures, half palace, half fortress, raised, in marble magnificence, upon the lonely and majestic mountain, and like the mansions of another world, far removed in upper air from the ordinary tread of mortals. In the dark recesses of each temple one image or more of Adināth, of Ajit, or of some other of the Tīrthankars, is seated, whose alabaster features, wearing an expression of listless repose, are rendered dimly visible by the faint light shed from silver lamps; incense perfumes the air and barefooted, with noiseless tread, upon the polished floors, the female votaries, glittering in scarlet and gold, move round and round in circles, chanting forth their monotonous, but not unmelodious, hymns. Satrunjaya indeed might fitly represent one of the fancied hills of eastern romance, the inhabitants of which have been instantaneously changed into marble, but which fay hands are ever employed upon, burning perfumes, and keeping all clean and brilliant, while fay voices haunt the air in these voluptuous praises of the Devs."*

Little medieval sculpture has escaped the fury of Muhammadan iconoclasts. Mention has been made of the noble monolithic figures at Konārak. The reliefs on

Fig. 35 : Hindu Temple, Gujarāt

* Forbes, *Rās Māla,* I, 7.

the walls of the temples at Konārak and Bhuvaneswara are frankly erotic, and are based on the *Kāmasāstra*, the Indian *Ars Amatoria*. They illustrate the vein of sex-mysticism which runs through the Hindu religion and is especially prominent in the worship of Krishna; sexual congress is symbolic of the union of the individual and the World Soul. In Bengal and Bihār under the Pāla régime a flourishing school arose, which produced stately hieratic figures of Mahāyāna and Hindu gods and goddesses in black carboniferous shale. A magnificent figure of Sūrya, the Sun God, in the India Museum, South Kensington, is typical of the art of the period. Tārānāth, the 17th century Buddhist writer, speaks of two famous craftsmen, Dhīmān and his son Bitpālo, who flourished under the Pālas and were equally proficient in casting, painting and working in stone.

LEADING DATES

A.D. 725	Foundation of the Parihār Kingdom of Kanauj.
840-90	Bhoja, King of Kanauj.
750	Foundation of the Pāla dynasty of Bengal.
997	Accession of Mahmūd of Ghazni.
1001	Mahmūd of Ghazni defeats Rājā Jaipāl.
1008-19	Mahmūd of Ghazni's annual raids. Rājā Ānandpāl defeated and Kāngra and Kanauj taken.
1026	Sack of Somnāth by Mahmūd of Ghazni.
1030	Death of Mahmūd of Ghazni.
973-1048	al-Bīrūnī, the author of *The Chronology of Ancient Nations.*
1175-6	Muhammad Ghori commences to invade India.
1191-2	Battles of the Tarāin. Prithvi Rājā slain.
1193-7	Capture of Delhi and Benares.
1199-1200	Conquest of Bengal.
1206	Death of Muhammad Ghori.

Chapter XIV

The Early Muhammadan Dynasties of Delhi

Nothing in history is more remarkable than the rise of Muhammadanism. Muhammad was born at Mecca, on the border of the Red Sea, of the Arab tribe of the Koreish, in the year A.D. 570. For years he worked as a merchant, until in 620 he received, through the angel Gabriel, a new revelation, which was to supersede both Christianity and Judaism. His teaching at first only aroused derision and hostility, and this compelled him to flee from his birthplace at Mecca to the neighbouring town of Medina with a handful of followers. A.D. 622, the year of the Hijra or Flight, is reckoned as the beginning of the Muhammadan Era. From this time the tide gradually turned. A long was ensued, which ended in the capture of Mecca, and at the time of his death in 632, Muhammad was master of Arabia. The essence of Muhammadanism is its austere simplicity, and in that, doubtless, lay its appeal to peoples perplexed by corrupt and complicated religious beliefs.

The Muhammadan religion is summed up in the simple creed "There is no God but God, and Muhammad is the Prophet of God." The essence of its teaching is a belief in God and His Angels; in the Koran or Scripture revealed to mankind through His Prophet, Muhammad; in a final Resurrection and Judgment of man according to his works on earth; and in Predestination. Equally simple and direct are the obligations laid upon believers. They consist of almsgiving; prayer five times a day; the observance of the fast during the month of Ramazan, the ninth month of the Muhammadan year; and the Hāj, or pilgrimage to Mecca. Muhammadans abstain from eating pork and drinking wine; they bury their dead, and regard marriage as a civil ceremony. The great strength of Islam lies in its unity; Muslims all over the world are brothers, regardless of wealth, rank or nationality. Orthodox Muhammadanism is fiercely puritanical and monotheistic. It tolerates neither graven image nor likeness of anything in heaven above or earth beneath; the mosque, where the faithful assembled for public devotions every Friday, was an open courtyard surrounded by colonnades, and unadorned save for Koranic texts, a *mihrāb* or niche showing the direction of Mecca, a pulpit, and a minaret where the muezzin utters the call to prayer. No priest stands between God and the individual soul. Thus Muhammadanism is the very antithesis of Hinduism; the one has been called the religion of the desert and the other that of the jungle.

After the Prophet's death, the leadership passed to the Caliphs or Successors. The first of these, Abu Bakr, the Prophet's earliest friend, was the real founder of the Islamic Empire. In 658 a split occurred between the Arabs, who believed in the principle of free and democratic election, and the Perisans, who upheld the apostolic succession through Ali, Muhammad's son-in-law. The two sects arose in this manner are the Sunnis and the Shiahs. The Shiahs admit a number of beliefs and practices which the Sunnis book on as unorthodox and even idolatrous; they celebrate annually, at the feast of Muharram, the martyrdom of Hasan and Husain, the grandsons of the Prophet, and carry in procession Tazias or representations of their tombs. Under the Caliphs, the new religion spread like a forest-fire. East and west the Arabs carried their victorious arms. Northern Africa, Sicily and Spain were overrun. At one time the fate of Christendom hung in the balance, but the flood was at length stemmed at the battle of Tours (A.D. 732). In the east, the Byzantines were driven out of Syria, Damascus was taken in 635, and Alexandria was sacked in 642. In 641, at Nahavend, the army of the Caliph Omar overthrew Yezdegerd, the Sassanian monarch, and Persia, Mesopotamia and Central Asia passed into Muslim hands. In 757 the Caliph Al-Mansur founded a new capital at Bagdad on the Tigris, near the seat of the ancient Babylon. Here there grew up a mighty city which reached its zenith under the famous Harun al Rashid, the contemporary of Charlemagne. Bagdad took the place of Alexandria as the clearing-house of international culture. Here Jews, Manicheans, Christians, Zoroastrians, Buddhists and Hindus met and exchanged ideas. Greek books on the one hand and Sanskrit on the other were translated into Arabic. Arabic figures replaced the clusmy Roman numerals. Learned men in Bagdad corresponded with colleagues in distant Cordova. Through Bagdad Indian mathematical, astronomical and medical theories, and Indian folk-lore tales, found their way to medieval Europe. The great collection known as the Arabian Nights originated in Bagdad, and contains fables which are of Greek, Indian and Persian origin. The story of Sinbad the Sailor is of Indian origin, and it was from an Indian original, through the same medium, that the famus legend of the Horse of Brass found its way into Chaucer's *Squire's Tale*. Many collections of stories, such as the *Gesta Romanorum* and the *Fables of Pilpay,* so popular in medieval Europe, may be traced to this source.

The Arabas came into conflict with Indians for the first time early in the 8th century, when some Arab ships from Basra were attacked by Indian pirates from Sind. This led in 711 to the despatch of an expedition under Muhammad bin Kāsim to Debul, a seaport about twenty-four miles from Tatta on the Indus. Two years later, Multan fell and Sind became a Muhammadan province. Eastward of Sind the Muslim conquerors did not attempt to advance. The Arabs on the whole remained on friendly terms with their Hindu neighbours, with whom they frequently entered into trade relations. Very different were the attacks which presently began to descend upon India from the north-west, where the Turki praetorians, originally enlisted as a body-guard by their Arab rulers, had asserted their independence. One of the states which sprang up in this manner was that of Ghazni in Eastern Afghanistan, of which a Turki slave of the name of Sabuktigīn became ruler in 998. His son was the famous Mahmūd, the story of whose raids on India has been narrated in chapter XII. These Turki invaders have sometimes been described as fierce, plundering savages. This, however, is not the case. Mahmūd, as we have seen, was a man of culture and a patron of the arts; but Islām is a proselytising religion, and Mussalmans are enjoined to offer to idolators the choice between conversion and the sword. "People of the book," Christians, Jews, and perhaps Zoroastrians, might, it is true, be spared, provided that they submitted to their conquerors and paid the *jizya* or poll-tax, but no such concession was shown to the idol-worshipping Hindus. For them, Mahmūd and his followers felt a bitter hatred which may be compared to that of the Puritans under Cromwell for the Irish. To grind images to powder, to raze temples to the ground, and to send idolators, without distinction of age or sex, "to that fire which God has lighted for infields, and those who deny a resur-rection, say no prayers, hold no fasts, and tell no beads," was a religious duty. India was a *dār-ul-harb,* a land of warfare, handed over by God to true believers to plunder. "The whole country of India is full of gold and jewels, and of the plants which grow there are those fit for making wearing apparel, and aromatic plants and the sugar-cane, and the whole aspect of the country is pleasant and delightful. Now since the inhabitants are chiefly infidels and idolators, by the order of God and His Prophet, it is right for us to conquer them." Mahmūd died in 1030, and India enjoyed a respite until the rise of Muhammad Ghori, who overthrew his rivals the rulers of Ghazni, and in 1182 overran and conquered Sind and the Punjab. His invasions of India, and his overthrow of the heroic Prithvi Rājā at the battle of Taraori or Tarāin in 1192 have already been described.

Muhammad Ghori was assassinated in 1206, and on his death, his general and viceroy Kutb-ud-dīn Ibak, who had taken a foremost part in the conquest of Hindustan and Bengal, became the first Muhammadan Sultan of Delhi. He established the line of the so-called "Slave Kings," who occupied an uneasy and troubled throne until 1290. The most prominent of the Slave Kings was Sultan Iltutmish or Altamsh (1211-1236), and during his reign came the first threat of invasion by the dread Mongolian hosts under Chingiz Khān, who struck terror into the heart of India just as their predecessors the Huns had done. "Their eyes," says the poet, Amīr Khusru, "were so narrow and piercing that they might have bored a hole in a brazen vessel. Their stink was more horrible than their colour. Their faces were set on their bodies as if they had no neck. Their cheeks resembled soft leathern bottles, full of wrinkles and knots. Their noses extended from cheek to cheek, and their mouths from cheek-bone to cheek-bone. Their nostrills resembled rotten graves, and from them the hair descended as far as the lips." The court-annalist, Minhāj-i-Siraj, says that Chingiz Khān, though sixty-five years of age, was "a man of tall stature, of vigorous build, robust in body, the hair of his face scanty and turned white, with cat's eyes, possessed of great energy, discernment, genius and understanding; awe-striking, a butcher, just, resolute, an overthrower of enemies, intrepid, sanguinary, cruel." Fortunately this horror was averted, and the Mongolian hordes turned back at Peshawar, to sweep, plundering and murdering, through western Asia and on to the banks of the Dnieper. Iltutmish had himself formally recognised as Sultan of India by the Caliph in 1226. Ten years later he took the bold and unusual step of nominating as his successor his daughter Raziya, or Razziyat, who maintained an unavailing resistance against almost insuperable odds until her death at the hands of the nobles, who hated to be ruled by a woman, and above all a woman who had the bad taste to prefer an Abyssinian husband. "Sultant Raziya—may she rest in peace!—was a great sovereign, sagacious, just and beneficent, a patron of the learned, a dispenser of justice, the cherisher of her subjects, and of war-like talent, and was endowed with all the admirable attributes and qualifications necessary for kings; but as she did not attain the destiny in her creation of being computed among men, of what advantage were all these excellent qualifications to her?"* It was, inded, impossible for a woman, however brave and gifted, to struggle against the turbulent and disorderly factions of Delhi, and especially the band of intriguers known as "the Forty," who held the reins of power in their hands, and this gallant queen and her husband were assassinated in 1240.

After the usual interlude of disorder and misgovernment by incapable pretenders, order was restored by an aged general named Balban (1266-1286), who succeeded, by ferocious measures such as flaying his opponents alive, trampling them to death with elephants and lining the roads with gibbets, in stamping out rebellion. Balban's closing years were darkened by the death in battle against the Mongol hordes of his beloved son Muhammad. After his decease in 1286, all security of life and property was lost, and on one had any influence in the stability of the kingdom. His successor had not reigned a year before the chiefs and nobles quarrelled with each other; many people were killed upon suspicion and doubt, and people, seeing the trouble and hardship which had befallen the country, sighed for the renewal of the reign of Balban.

In the end, the nobles elevated to the throne in 1292 a mild and benevolent ruler of the Khilji tribe of the name Jalāl-ud-dīn. But Jalāl-ud-dīn, a man of 70, was ill-fitted to cope with the wild and turbulent spirits of his day. In 1294, his nephew, Alā-ud-dīn Khilji, undertook an expedition into the Deccan against Rāmchandra, the Yādava king of Deogiri. Returning laden with spoils, he cruelly murdered his unsuspecting old uncle, who had marched out to welcome him, and seized his throne

* Elliot & Dowson, II, 332.

(1296). The reign of Alā-ud-dīn was distinguished by the stamping out of the last embers of Hindu rule. In 1297, his armies, led by Malik Kāfūr, a eunuch who had been a Hindu slave, entered Gujarāt and annexed it. Rājputāna was next attacked, on the pretext that Hamir Deo Chauhān had harboured political refugees, and the strong fortress of Ranthambhor, which had defied all previous conquerors, was taken by storm. A similar fate overtook the great fortress of Chitor, where, it is said, Alā-ud-dīn's chief object was the hand of the beautiful princess Padminī. When capture was inevitable, the garrison of Chitor performed, for the first of many times, the horrible rite of *Jauhār*.* The women marched in long procession to the subterranean caverns, where they were burnt, and then their husbands sallied forth to meet death by the sword. In 1310-11 Malik Kāfūr undertook his famous raid into Southern India. The Muslim army marched through the fertile Tamil kingdoms, never before violated by the passage of a foreign invader, as far as the southernmost point of Rāmeswaram, where a mosque was erected. The great temple of Madura and other sacred shrines were despoiled of their treasures, and the plunder is said to have included 2,750 pounds of gold and over three hundred elephants. In the Deccan, Harpāla, the nephew of the Yādava king Rāmchandra who had submitted to Malik Kāfūr in 1309, rebelled. He was seized and flayed alive, and Deogiri, one of the strongest natural fortresses in Central India, passed into the hands of the conqueror. Hindu rule in the south was finally extinguished in 1327. During the early part of the reign of Alā-ud-dīn, there was a continual threat of invasion on the part of the dreaded Mongols, and in 1297 a number of Mongols who had settled in India were ruthlessly butchered, on the pretext that they were preparing to rebel in conjunction with their compatriots.

An interesting account of the administration of this ruler is given by the historian Barani:

> "The Sultan next directed his attention to the means of preventing rebellion, and first he took steps for seizing upon property. Whenever a village was held by proprietary right, in free gift, or as a religious endowment, it was to be brought back into the exchequer by a stroke of the pen. The people were pressed and amerced and money was exacted from them on every kind of pretext. All pensions, grants of land, and endowments were appropriated. The people become so absorbed in trying to keep themselves alive that rebellion was never mentioned. Next, he set up so minute a system of espionage that nothing done, good or bad, was hidden from him. No one could stir without his knowledge, and whatever happened in the houses of nobles, grandees and officials was brought by his spies

*"Jauhār is this: when they are certain that escape is impossible, they gather together their wives and children and goods, heap firewood round them and set it alight; then when all these are burnt, they rush into the fire and meet their death. It is with them a great act of devotion."—Maulana Ahmad: *Tarikh-i-Alfi*.

for his information, and their reports were acted on. To such a length did this prying go that nobles dared not speak aloud even in thousand-columned palaces, but had to communicate by signs. In their own houses, night and day, dread of the spies made them tremble. What went on in the bazaars was all reported and controlled.

"Thirdly, he forbade wine, beer, and intoxicating drugs to be used or sold; dicing, too, was prohibited. Vintners and beer-sellers were turned out of the city, and the heavy taxes which had been levied from them were abolished. All the china and glass vessels of the Sultan's banqueting room were broken and thrown outside the gate of Badāun, where they formed a mound. Jars and casks of wine were emptied out there till they made mire as if it were the season of the rains. The Sutan himself entirely gave up wine parties. Self-respectng people at once followed his example; but the ne'er-do-wells went on making wine and spirits and hid the leather bottles in loads of hay or firewood and by various such tricks smuggled it into the city. Inspectors and gatekeepers and spies diligently sought to seize the contraband and the smugglers; and when seized the wine was given to the elephants, and the importers and sellers and drinkers flogged and given short terms of imprisonment. So many were they, however, that holes had to be dug for their incarceration outside the great thorough-fare of the Badāun gate, and many of the wine-bibbers died from the rigours of their confinement and others were taken out half-dead and were long in recovering their health. The terror of these holes deterred many from drinking. Those who could not give it up had to journey ten or twelve leagues to get a drink, for at half that distance, four or five leagues from Delhi, wine could not be publicly sold or drunk. The prevention of drinking proving every difficult, the Sultan enacted that people might distil and drink privately in their own homes, if drinking parties were not held and the liquor not sold. After the prohibition of drinking, conspiracies diminished.

"Also, the Sultan commanded noblemen and great folk not to visit each other's houses, or give feasts, or hold assemblies; not to marry without royal consent, and to admit no strangers to their hospitality. Through fear of the spies, the nobles kept quiet, gave no parties, and held little intercommunication. If they went to the caravanserais, they could not lay their heads together or sit down cosily and tell their troubles. So no disturbance or conspiracy arose.

"The Hindu was to be so reduced as to be unable to keep a horse, wear fine clothes, or enjoy any of life's luxuries. No Hindu could hold up his head, and in their houses no sign of gold or silver or any superfluity was to be seen. These things, which nourish insubordination, were not to be found. Men looked upon revenue officers as worse than fever; to be a clerk was a crime; no man would give his daughter to such. Alā-ud-dīn was a king who had no acquaintance with learning and never associated with the learned. He considered that polity and government were one thing, and law another. 'I am an unlettered man,' he said, 'but I have seen a great deal. Be assured that the Hindus will never become submissive and obedient till they are reduced to poverty. I have therefore given orders that just enough shall be left them of corn, milk, and curbs, from year to year, but that they must not accumulate hoards and property.' Next day he said, 'Although I have not studied the science or the Book, I am a Muslim of the Muslims. To prevent rebellion, in which many perish, I issue such ordinances as I consider to be for the good of the state and the benefit of the people. Men are heedless, disregarding, and disobedient to my connands, so I have to be severe to bring them to obedience. I do not know whether this is lawful or unlawful; but whatever I think is for the good of the State or fits the emergency, that I decree.'

"The Sultan consulted with his most experienced ministers as to the means of reducing the prices of provisions without resorting to severe and tyrannical punishments. They replied that necessaries would never be cheap until the price of grain was fixed by tariff. Cheapness of grain is a universal benefit. So regulations were issued which kept down its price for some years. All the wise men of the age were astonished at the evenness of the price in the markets. The extraordinary part of the matter was that during the reign of Alā-ud-dīn there were years of deficient rain, but, instead of the usual scarcity ensuing, there was no lack of corn in Delhi and no rise in the price either in the royal granaries or in the dealers' importations. This was indeed the wonder of the age, and no other monarch was able to work it."*

The Sultan's later years were marked by a kind of megalomania, which caued him to look upon himself as a second Alexander, or even a new Muhammad. Alā-ud-dīn was not without ability, but his chief characteristic was his fiendish cruelty; he did not even spare the relatives or children of his victims, and neither age nor sex aroused in him the smallest feeling of pity.

In January, 1316, Alā-ud-dīn died or was murdered, and was succeeded, after the usual interval of disorder and murder which followed the death of a strong ruler, by Muhammad ibn Tughlak (1325-1347). This eccentric monarch was an fanatical and unscrupulous as his predecessor. He has been well described as a "mixture of opposites." He was a learned scholar, and well versed in Arabic and Persian literature, which he wrote with elegance and skill. He had a taste for philosophy and science, and was devoutly religious. In his private life he was abstemious to an unusual degree, and took no wine. But good qualities were counter balanced by a love of bloodshed amounting to sadism, and a passion for indulging in wild and fantastic schemes, which

* Elliot and Dowson, II, 179 ff.

brought ruin upon himself and his kingdom. Our knowledge of the reign of Muhammad ibn Tughlak is largely due to the visit paid to him by the famous Ibn Batuta, 'the traveller of Islam,' who stayed at his court from 1342 to 1347, and has left a detailed account of his experiences.* On his arrival, he was accorded a state-entry into Delhi.

"The day after our reception by the Sultan, each of us was given a horse from the royal stables, with saddle and bridle covered with ornament. The Sultan rode on a horse on entering his capital, and we did the like, riding with the advanced guard. Elephants were caparisoned in front of the king, carrying standards and sixteen parasols spangled with gold and precious stones, whilst another parasol was held over his head and the state housing, incrusted with diamonds set in gold, was borne before him. Small catapults were moutned on some of the elephants, from which, when the Sultan drew near the city, gold and silver pieces were discharged for the crowd to scramble for. This went on till we entered the palace. Thousands walked in the procession. Kiosks of wood covered with silk for women singers were set up."

Ibn Batuta gives a vivid character-sketch of this eccentric despot :

"Muhammad above all men delights most in giving presents and shedding blood. At his door is seen always some pauper on the way to wealth or some corpse that has been executed. Stories are rife among the people of his generosity and courage, and of his cruelty and severity. Yet he is the most humble of men and one who shows the greatest equity; the rites of religion are observed at his court; he is most strict about prayer and the punishment of those who neglect it. But his characteristic is generosity. Countries at some distance from India, such as the Yemen, Khorāsān, Persia, are full of anecdotes of this prince, and their inhabitants know him very well; and they are not ignorant, especially, of his beneficence towards foreigners, whom he prefers to Indians and favours and honours them greatly. He will not have them called 'foreigners', for he thinks that the name must wound the heart and trouble the mind of such.

"One of the grandees of India alleged that the Sultan had executed his brother without just cause, and cited him before the Kāzi. The Sultan went on foot to the court, without arms, saluted, made obeisance, and stood before the Kāzi, whom he had notified beforehand not to rise at his entry or budge from his seat of audience. The judge gave his decision that the sovereign was bound to satisfy the plantiff for the blood of the brother, and the decision was duly obeyed.

"The Sultan was severe upon such as omitted the congregational prayers, and chastised from heavily. For this sin he executed in one day nine people, one of

---

* Trans. Defrémery and Sanguinetti (1858), vol. iii.

> whom was a singer. He sent spies into the markets to punish those who were found there during prayer times, and even the men who held the horses of the servants at the gate of the hall of audience if they missed prayers. He compelled the people to master the ordinances for ablutions, prayers, and the principles of Islam. They were examined on these matters, and if ignorant they were punished. The folk studied these things at court and in the markets, and wrote them out. The Sultan was rigorous in the observance of the canonical law. He abolished in 1340-1 the dues which weighted heavily on commerce, and limited taxation to the legal alms and the tenth. Every Monday and Thursday he would sit in person, with assessors, to investigate acts of oppression. No one was hindred from bringing his plea before the king. When there was such a famine in India that a maund (80 lbs.) of corn cost six dīnārs,* he ordered six months' food to be distributed to all the inhabitants of Delhi from the Crown stores. Each person, great or small, free or slave, was to have a pound and a half Morocco weight (about 2 lbs.) a day."

One of the Muhammad ibn Tughlak's strange freaks was his evacuation of Delhi, the inhabitants of which had annoyed him writing scurrilous verses ridiculing his government, and throwing them into the council-hall by night. Delhi was by now a great city rivalling Cairo and Bagdad in size and prosperity. Suddenly an order was issued that the people were to leave the city in three days and migrate to a new capital which the Sultan proposed to found at Deogiri, over 600 miles distant, with the name of Daulatābād or City of Riches.

> "When they resisted," says the historian Barani, "a crier went round and proclaimed that after three days not a soul must be found remaining in Delhi. Most of them went, but some hid in the houses. They were rigorously hunted out. His slaves found a cripple and a blind man in the streets and brought them before the Sultan, who had the cripple fired from a catapult and the blind man dragged to Daulatābād, a forty days' journey; he fell in pieces by the way, and only a leg arrived. All the inhabitants left, abandoning their goods and merchandise, and the city became totally deserted. A man whom I believe assured me that one evening the Sultan went up to the flat roof of his palace and gazed upon Delhi, where no fire nor smoke nor light, was, and said, 'Now my soul is content and my mind is at rest.' Later on, he sent letters to the people of different provinces to come and repopulate the city. They ruined their own parts but did not fill Delhi, so vast, so immense is it, one of the largest cities, truly, in the world. When we arrived there we found it empty, abandoned, with only a very sparse population."†

---

* The reference is probably to the gold dīnār, equivalent to a gold mohur of the value of 15 rupees. For the maund, see p. 234, note.

† Elliot and Dowson, III, 239.

Another experiment of the Sultan was his debasement of the coinage. He issued a token copper currency to be used in the place of gold and silver. The result was what might have been expected.

> "This edict turned the house of every Hindu into a mint, and the Indians of the provinces coined crores and lakhs of copper coins, with which they paid their tribute and bought horses and arms and fine things of all sorts. The nobles, the village headmen, and landowners grew rich on these copper coins but the state was impoverished. In no long time distant countries would only accept the copper tanka as metal, and in places where reverence for the edict prevailed the gold tanka rose to be worth a hundred copper tankas.* Every goldsmith struck copper coins in his workshop, and the treasury was crammed with them. They fell so low, that they were counted no more valuable than pebbles or potsherds. Trade being disrupted, the Sultan repealed his edict, and in great wrath proclaimed that all copper coins would be redeemed in gold or silver at the treasury. Thousands brought them for exchange and their heaps rose up in Tughlakābād like mountains."†

Among Muhammad bin Tughlak's other mad and purposeless projects was an expedition for the conquest of China. The whole force despatched for the purpose was annihilated in the passes of the Himālayas in 1337-8. The Sultan in the end succeeded in reducing his entire kingdom to a state of bankruptcy. The people were ruined and had no money with which to pay their taxes, and the treasury was empty. A terrible famine broke out, and the peasants were reduced to eating human flesh. The soldiers were without pay and mutinous. As fast as one rebellion was stamped out in an orgy of bloodshed, another sprang up. Local rulers in Bengal and the Deccan and other provinces declared their independence, and set up kingdoms of their own. Death at length found the Sultan when he was on an expedition into the heart of Sind. The army, leaderless and in despair, persuaded his cousin, Firoz Shāh, reluctantly to accept the throne.

Firoz Shāh (1351-1388), a striking contrast to his predecessors, was the best of the Muslim rulers of Delhi previous to Akbar. He was a benevolent and enlightened man, and in many of his schemes of social reform, he was centuries in advance of his age. Instead of wasting the resources of the country upon military campaigns, he devoted all his energies to developing its wealth, and particularly to making good the drain upon the revenues caused by the hare-brained schemes of Muhammad ibn Tughlak.

---

* The word *tanka* is used in a variety of senses. The copper tanka was worth 60 reis or about *2d.* The silver tanka was equivalent to the rupee, and the gold tanka was equivalent to ten silver tankas. The lakh is 100,000 and the crore 100 lakhs.

† Elliot and Dowson, III, 240.

"By the blessing of God favourable seasons and abundance of the necessaries of life prevailed in the reign of Fīroz Shāh, not only in the capital, but throughout his dominions. During the whole forty years of his reign there was no appearance of scarcity, and the times were so happy that the people of Delhi forgot the reign of Alā-ud-dīn, although no more prosperous times than his had ever fallen to the lot of any Muhammadan sovereign. Grain was so cheap that in the city of Delhi wheat was eight *jitals* a maund and grain and barley four *jitals*. A camp follower could give his horse a feed of ten seers (20 lbs.) of corn for one *jital*.* Fabrics of all kinds were cheap, and silk goods, both white and coloured, were of moderate price.

"Sultan Fīroz had a great taste for the laying out of gardens, which he took great plains to beautify. He made twelve hundred gardens round Delhi and restored thirty which had been begun by Alā-ud-dīn. Near Salaura he made eighty gardens, and forty-four in Chitor. In all of them were white and black grapes of seven varieties, and the government share of the garden produce came to 80,000 *tankas* (£8,000), after deducting what was paid to owners and gardeners. The revenues of the Doāb in this reign amounted to eighty lakhs of *tankas;* and under the fostering care of this religious sovereign, the revenues of the territories of Delhi were six crores and eighty-five lakhs of *tankas* (£6,850,000). The Sultan, throughout his reign, in his great sagacity and prudence, endeavoured to circumscribe the extent of his dominions, but still the revenues amounted to the sum stated. All this large revenue was duly appointed out; each Khān received a sum suitable to his exalted position; amīrs and maliks also obtained allowances according to their dignity, and the officials were paid enough to provide a comfortable living. The soldiers of the army received grants of land enough to support them in comfort, and the irregulars received payment from the government treasury."†

In order to assist agriculture, he undertook a number of extensive irrigation schemes, and dug five great canals which were intended to distribute the waters of the Sutlej and Jhelum over a large area. Among his other measures for the welfare of his Muslim subjects, which have a singularly modern ring, were the setting up of employment and marriage bureaus. All the young men who were without work in the city of Delhi were to be produced by the Kotwāl or chief of police, their qualifications and other particulars noted down, and occupations found for them. By this means, discontent and crime in the capital were greatly reduced. In the case of Muslim girls who were too poor to find husbands, dowries were provided and

* The *jital* is a small copper coin, corresponding to the *pice*. Sixty-four *jitals* went to the *tanka* or rupee. The maund differs greatly in various localities, but the standard maund consists of 40 seers or a little over 80 pounds avoirdupois. The seer is 80 tolas or rupee-weights.

† Elliot and Dowson, II, 344 ff.

suitable matches arranged. This was a great boon to the widows and orphans of military officers and servants. In all these schemes, he was greatly helped by his minister, Khān Jahān, a Hindu convert, and a well-organised bureaucracy, for he himself was averse from taking an interest in the petty details of administrations. The practical wisdom of some of his measures is perhaps open to question. For instance, the practice of paying civil and military officers by means of fiefs instead of by fixed revenues from the Imperial treasury relaxed the control of the central governments and led to insubordination and rebellion; but among his many humanitarian actions was the abolition of those fiendish and horrible tortures and mutilations in which his predecessor took such an inhuman delight. "The Great and Merciful God made me His servant, and I hope and seek for His mercy by devoting myself to prevent the unlawful killing of Mussalmans and the infliction of any kind of torture upon them or upon any man." He even sent for the unhappy wretches who had been maimed and blinded in the preceding reign, and tried to recompense them for their sufferings as far as possible.

In one respect Fīroz Shāh fell short of the standard of humanity of the great Akbar. Religious tolerance was unknown to him, and he considered it to be a religious duty to employ every means in order to induce his Hindu subjects to embrace Islam. "I forbade the infliction of any severe punishment on the Hindus in general, but I destroyed their idol temples and instead thereof raised mosques... I encouraged my infidel subjects to embrace the religion of the prophet, and I proclaimed that everyone who repeated the creed and became a Mussalman should be exempt from the poll-tax. Information of this came to the ears of the people at large, and great numbers of Hindus presented themselves and were admitted to the honour of Islam. Thus they came forward day by day from every quarter and, adopting the Faith, were exonerated from the *jizya* (poll-tax) and favoured with presents and honours." The Brahmins, who had hitherto been exempted, were now ordered to pay like the rest. Furious at what they considered to be an insult to their order, they assembled outside the royal palace and threatened as a protest to starve themselves to death. Ultimately this tragedy was averted by a compromise, under which Brahmins were to pay a commuted sum of ten rupees a head. Attempts to spread the Hindu religion were sternly repressed, and it is said that a Brahmin was burnt alive for this offence. Hearing that certain new Hindu temples had been erected in defiance of orders, "Under Divine guidance I destroyed those edifices, and killed those leaders of infidelity who seduced other into error: the lower orders I subjected to stripes and chastisement, until this abuse was entirely abolished." Heretical Muslim sects were treated with equal severity.

Fīroz Shāh was a great builder, and he is credited with the erection of two hundred towns, forty mosques, thirty colleges, thirty reservoirs, fifty dams, one hundred hospitals, one hundred public baths, and one hundred and fifty bridges. He built a splendid new capital which he called Fīrozābād, and the two important towns of Jaunpur and Hissār. Not only did he put up new buildings but, unlike other rulers, he was careful about restoring 'the structures of former kings and ancient nobles.' In these far-reaching schemes, he was aided by his architects Malik Ghāzī Shāhna, and his deputy, Jāhir Sundhār, and a regular department of public works was set up. Labour was fortunately cheap, and the Sultan probably made extensive use of the 180,000 Hindu slaves captured for him by his provincial officers, and sent to work in various capacities in the capital. These slaves were, of course, forcibly converted to Islam, but were otherwise well cared for and kindly treated. Hindu temples were freely used to supply building material. One of his most remarkable feats of engineering was the removal as trophies to Delhi of the two gigantic monolithic pillars of the Emperor Asoka, one from Topra in the Ambālā district and the other from Meerut. A reference has already been made to the account given by a contemporary historian of the means employed in order to transport one of these columns in safety. Wrapped in coatings of wild cotton and skins, it was carefully lowered upon a specially constructed sled of 42 wheels, and drawn to the river by 8,400 men (probably the slaves mentioned above) pulling on the ropes. The column was then floated down the Jumna on a number of huge grain boats and erected on its new site by an ingenious and complicated system of pulleys.*

Fīroz Shāh died in 1388, at the age of 79, full of years and honours. In spite of his religious bigotry, his reign was long remembered as a brief respite from oppression by his subjects. "The peasants grew rich and were satisfied. Their houses were replete with grain, property, horses and furniture; everyone had plenty of gold and silver; no woman was without her ornaments and no house was wanting in excellent beds and couches. Wealth abounded and comforts were general." The demise of the monarch was the signal for an outbreak of civil war. Two orival claimants contended for the throne, and day by day battles were fought between them, "like the two kings in the game of chess." This deplorable state of affairs invited the attention of the invader from the North-West, ever ready to swoop down when the gateway of India is left unguarded. Timūr the Lame, the Tamberlane of English literature, a Barlās Turk whose hordes had already overrun the greater part of Central Asia, marched into the Punjab from Samarkand. "My principal object in coming to Hindustan," said Timūr in his autobiography, "was to accomplish two things. The first thing was to war with infidels, the enemies of the Muhammadan religion, and by this religious warfare to acquire some claim to reward in the life to come. The other was a worldly object: that the army of Islam might gain something by plundering the wealth of infields; plunder in war is as lawful as their mother's milk to Mussalmans who fight for their faith, and the consuming of that which is lawful is a means of grace."†

---

* V. A. Smith, *Asoka*, p. 121.

† For Timūr's autobiography, see Elliot and Dowson, III, 389.

In the autumn of 1398 he crossed the Indus with 90,000 cavalry, slaying and looting without mercy until he came face to face with the Indian army under the walls of Delhi. Now for the first time his Central Asian horsemen found themselves confronted with 120 gigantic war-elephants, plated with armour and carrying on their backs sharpshooters in howdahs. Between them were rocket-men and grenade-throwers. The prospect of attacking these formidable beasts daunted even the stoutest hearts. "When Timūr appointed posts for the various officers of the court," says the historian Yazdi, "and courteously desired the learned doctors of the law who accompanied the invasion where they would like to be placed, they answered, terrified by tales about the elephants, 'along with the ladies.' "* But the old warrior rose to the occasion. He followed the traditional Mongol tactics. Protecting his front by a line of entrenchments and palisades and tethered buffaloes, and sprinkling the ground with caltrops, he proceeded to attack the enemy in flank and rear. The result which invariably followed this manaeuvre ensued. The unwieldy beats stampeded, and started trampling down their own ranks. "The soldiers of India fought bravely for their lives, but the frail insect cannot contend against the raging wind, nor the feeble deer against the fierce lion." The invaders entered Delhi, and a chance dispute led to the sack of the unhappy capital.

> "A number of soldiers collected at the gate of Delhi and derided the inhabitants. When Timūr heard of it he directed some of the Amīrs to put a stop to it; but it was the divine pleasure to ruin the city and punish the inhabitants. It was brought about thus: Some ladies went into the city to see the Palace of a thousand columns which Malik Jauna had built in Jahanpanah; officers of the treasury had also entered to collect the indemnity; and several thousand soldiers, with requisitions for grain and sugar, had gone too. Their officers had orders to arrest every nobleman who had fought against Timūr and taken refuge in Delhi. When parties of soldiers were thus going about the city, numbers of Hindus and infidels in the cities of Delhi, Siri, Jahanpanah, and Old Delhi, seeing their violence, took up arms and attacked them. Many others set fire to their goods and threw their wives and children and themselves on the flames. The soldiers waxed the more eager for plunder and destruction. Bold as the striving Hindus were, the officers in charge kept the gates shut and allowed no more troops to enter; but there were some 15,000 men already in, busy all that Friday night in pillaging and burning the houses, and in the morning the soldiers outside broke in and added to the tumult. The whole place was sacked, and several palaces in Jahanpanah and Siri destroyed. This plundering went on through the 18th. Every soldier get more than twenty slaves, and some brought fifty or a hundred men, women, and children as slaves out of the city, besdies spoils of money, jewellery,

* Elliot and Dowson, III, 499.

and gold and silver plate beyond computation. On the 19th Old Delhi was remembered, where many Hindus had taken refuge in the great mosque, prepared to defend their lives. Two Amīrs with 500 trusty men were sent against them, and falling on them with the sword despatched them to hell. Towers were built high with their heads and their bodies were left to the beasts and birds of prey. On that day all Old Delhi was sacked. Such inhabitants as escaped death were made prisoners. Several thousand craftsmen were brought out and distributed by Timūr among the princes and officers; the stonemasons were reserved to build for the conqueror a great mosque at his capital, Samarkand."*

Timūr retreated in the spring of 1399, before the hot weather descended upon the Indian plains: on the way he sacked Meerut, and at Hardwār, that most sacred place of pilgrimage where the Ganges rises from the mountain, he slew the Brahmins and defiled the temple. Everywhere the slightest attempt at resistance met with instant retribution. His path through Northern India was marked with rapine and slaughter; none of her previous invaders, not even Mahmūd of Ghazni, had left such terrible traces of his incursion behind him. Delhi was so utterly ruined that the few surviving inhabitants died from famine or pestilence. "For two whole months, not a bird moved a wing in the city." Khizr Khān, whom Timūr left in charge of the country, was succeeded by three members of his family. The last of these abdicated in 1451, and was succeeded by an Afghan or Pathan nobleman named Bahlol of the Lodi dynasty. He is described as "a man of simple habits, pious, brave and generous," and on his death in 1489 the throne passed by his son Sikandar. The reign of Sikandar Lodi was often regarded by Muhammadan historians, in the troubled times that followed, as a kind of Golden Age:

> "Every business had its appointed time, and an established custom was never changed. He always behaved to the nobles and great men of his time in the way he did on the first day of the interview... The Sultan daily received on account of the prices of all things, and an account of what had happened in districts of the Empire. If he perceived the slightest appearance of anything wrong, he caused instant enquiries to be made about it. In his reign, business was carried on in an honest, straightforward way. A new sort of life obtained, for people high and low were polite, and self-respect, integrity and devotion to religion prevailed, like as had never been the case in former reigns. The study of *belles lettres* was not neglected... Factory establishments were so encouraged that all young nobles and soldiers were engaged in useful work... All the nobles and soldiers of Sikandar were satisfied: each of his chiefs was appointed to the government of a district, and it was his especial desire to gain the good-will and affections of the body of the people. For the sake of his officers and troops he put an end to wars and

* Elliot and Dowson, III, 502.

disputes with the other monarchs and nobles of the period, and closed the road to contention and strife. He contented himself with the territory bequeathed him by his father, and passed the whole of his life in the greatest safety and enjoyment, and gained the hearts of high and low."*

Sikandar was the first of the Muhammadan kings to take up his residence at Agra, and Sikandra, the burial place of the Emperor Akbar, is named after him. He died in 1517, after a peaceful and prosperous reign of twenty-eight years. Unfortunately his son, Ibrāhīm Lodi, was an arrogant and intolerant ruler, with none of his father's good qualities. His conduct led to continual revolts, and at length Daulat Khān Lodi, the governor of the Punjab, applied for help to Bābur, King of Kābul, with the result that Ibrāhīm Lodi lost his life on the field of Pānipat, as will be narrated in the following chapter.

Art and Literature

The early Muslim conquerors of Hindustan were bigots, but they were at the same time men of considerable taste and patrons of art and literature. Reference has been made to the short-lived splendours of the court of Ghazni during its brief period of prosperity. The Arabs had no arts of their own, and Islamic art is largely an adaptation to the requirements of the Muhammadan religion of indigenous elements borrowed from the various nations which they overcame. This was the case in India. The Turki invaders from the north brought with them important new ideas, the arch, the dome, and the minaret, and combined them with the art of the country. In this they were aided by the Hindu craftsmen whom they employed, and by the fact that in many cases they either re-fashioned existing Hindu temples, or used them as a quarry for new buildings. Indo-Islamic architecture then, is a fusion of Central Asian and Hindu concepts. This is clearly proved by the fact that widely different styles, modified to suit local requirements, arose in different parts of the country. The earliest and most characteristic building of the period is the Kuwwat-ul-Islam or Mosque of the 'Might of Islam,' built by Kutb-ud-din Ibak to commemorate the capture of Delhi in 1193. The cloisters enclosing the central courtyard are supported by richly carved pillars looted from Hindu and Jain temples. The whole is enclosed by a colonnade consisting of a lofty central arch, 53 feet high, flanked by lower ones and profusely decorated with Koranic texts.

The best of the later additions of the mosque is the southern gateway, built in 1311 by Alā-ud-dīn, and known as the Alāi Darawāzā, of red sandstone and white marble. This building is one of the most beautiful of all the monuments of Early Delhi. All, however, are dwarfed by the stupendous Kutb Minār, which towers above them and forms a conspicuous landmark for miles around. It is 238 feet high and

* Elliot and Dowson, III, 448.

Fig. 36 : Kutb Minār.

tapers gradually from base to summit. It consists of five storeys, the lower three being of red sandstone, and the remainder of white marble. The sides are fluted, and each storey has a richly decorated balcony. The surface of the stone is covered with beautifully incised inscriptions commemorating the sultans who built, added to, or restored the monument. This noble tower is rightly considered by Fergusson to be unsurpassed by any building of its type in the world. (Fig. 36.) Of the other monuments of the early Delhi sultans, the most impressive is the tomb of Tughlak Shāh, standing in stark and solitary grandeur in a strongly fortified citadel, rising out of what was once an artificial lake. "The sloping walls and almost Egyptian solidity of this mausoleum" says Fergusson, "combined with the bold and massive towers of the fortifications that surround it, form a model of a warrior's tomb hardly to be rivalled anywehre, and are in singular contrast with the elegant and luxuriant garden-tombs of the more settled and peaceful dynaties that succeeded." Another characteristic monument is the austere and stately tomb of Altamsh, A.D. 1235. (Plate XIV.)

One of the chief features of Hinduism has been its power of assimilation. Other invaders, Greek, Saka, Kushān and Hūna, were gradually absorbed into Hindu society. But the Muhammadans, with their strongly marked religious characteristics, remained apart. They lived as a garrison in a hostile country, holding little or no intercourse with their subjects. But it was inevitable that as time went on, these barriers should be gradually relaxed, though they were never entirely broken down. Hindus were largely employed as officials for administrative purposes, and in many districts Hindu chiefs were left undisturbed on condition that they submitted to their conquerors. Marriages between Muhammadans and the women of the country became more and more frequent, and the children adopted many of the customs of their mothers. Conversion of Islam was common among the lower orders on account of the tyranny of the caste-system, the prospects of escape from the poll-tax and other social advantages, but the converts retained their Hindu mode of life to a great extent. They avoided the eating of beef and widow re-marriage, and the Muhammadan villager to-day consults the Hindu astrologer and propitiates the local god in times of trouble. The veneration of the tombs of *pīr* or saints is very popular, and Hindu peasants join the Muslims in the rites performed at these shrines, whose occupants are believed to have the power of averting disease or other disasters.

Nor, on the other hand, was Hindu society unaffected by the social customs of its new rulers. The system of secluding women, unknown in early days, was adopted by the higher classes. Muhammadan dress and ceremonial came into fashion. One of the results of this intercourse was the rise of *lingua franca* known as Urdu or the camp language, which is a form of Western Hindi with a large admixture of Persian and Arabic words. It may be compared to Middle English, which arose in a similar way from a fusion of Norman-French and Anglo-Saxon, the languages of the conquerors and the conquered. Urdu is said to date from the end of the 13th century A.D., but the court language was Persian. Of the Indo-Persian poets at Delhi, the most famous was the poet Amīr Khusru, 'the parrot of Hind', who lived at the Court of Alā-ud-dīn.* Unlike the Hindu rājās, the Delhi Sultans encouraged history, and court chroniclers such as Minhāj-i-Sirā and Barani have left valuable records, which, unfortunately, are spoilt by their fulsome flattery and religious bias.

A point of contact between Hinduism and Islam destined later on to produce far-reaching results was established through the influence of the Persian Sūfis, a school of mystics which included famous poets such as Sādi, Jalāl-ud-din Rumi and Hafiz, who held, under the forms of orthodoxy, views which approximated more or less closely to Hindu pantheism. Some time in the fourteenth century, a teacher of the name of Rāmānanda, a disciple of the famous Hindu saint Rāmānuja, disgusted, it is said, by the narrow orthodoxy of Southern India, with its multiplicity of caste-rules and ceremonial observances, migrated to Benares. Here he founded a new sect for the propagation of *bhakti* or devotional religion. He taught in the vernacular and admitted all without distinction of creed or caste; among his twelve disciples were a Rājpūt, a currier, a barber and a Mussalman weaver named Kabīr. Kabīr quickly struck out a line of his own. To him all institutional religions were a hollow sham. "The beads are wood: the gods are stone: Ganges and Jumna are water: Rāma and Krishna are dead and gone, and the Vedas are empty words." Ceremonies, penances and asceticism are useless things; he pours ridicule on the ascetic, "with his great beard and matted locks, looking like a goat," who shaves his head, reads the Gītā and becomes a mighty talker. The barber, the washerwomen and the carpenter are nearer to God than the priest, "who leaves Brahma to worship a stone." "God is One, whether we worship Him as Allah or as Rāma. The Hindu worships Him on the eleventh day; the Muhammadan fasts at Ramazan; but God made all the days and all the months. The Hindu god lives at Benares; the Muhammadan god at Mecca; but He who made the world lives not in a city made by hands. There is One Father of Hindu and Mussalman, One God in all matter: He is the Lord of all the earth, my Guardian, and my Priest."

> Oh Servant, where dost thou seek Me? Lo, I am beside thee.
> I am neither in temple or in mosque: I am neither in Kaaba or Kailāsh.
> Neither am I in rites and ceremonies, nor in Yoga or renunciation.
> If thou art a true seeker, thou shalt at once seek Me:
> Thou shalt meet Me in a moment of time.
> Kabīr says: "O Sādhu! god is the breath of all breath."

* For Amīr Khusru, see Elliot and Dowson, III, 523.

In some of his songs, Kabīr touches the highest note of spiritual ecstasy:

I here the melody of His flute, and I cannot contain myself:

The flower blooms, though it is not spring: and already the bee has received his invitation.

The sky roars and the lightning flashes; the waves arise in my heart.

The rain falls, and my heart longs for my Lord,

Where the rhythm of the world rises and falls, thither my heart has reached:

There the hidden banners are fluttering in the air.

Kabīr says: "My heart is dying, though it lives."*

It is said that Kabīr's teaching gave so much offence that a complaint against him was lodged before the Sultan Sikandar Lodi, but the Sultan refused to interfere. Kabīr was, however, banished from Benares, and for the rest of his life he wandered about Northern India, accompanied by a band of disciples. He died in 1518, at Maghar near Gorakhpur. A beautiful legend is narrated of his death. His Hindu and Muhammadan disciples were disputing among themselves over the disposal of his body, when the spirit of the Master appeared and told them to lift the shroud. They did so, and lo! there was no corpse, but only a heap of rose-petals. Half of these were buried in Mussalman fashion at Maghar, and the remainder were taken to Benares and burnt, and the ashes scattered upon the broad bosom of Mother Ganges.

The followers of Kabīr, the Kabīrpanthis, number millions to-day, and his songs are sung all over Northern Hindustan. A weaver named Dādū founded a sect in Gujarāt which is an off-shoot of Kabīr's teaching. Its followers abjure temples and idols, do not believe in reincarnation and declare that salvation is only to be found in the Divine Name. A more important development was the rise of the reformed Hindu sect of the Sikhs, which will be described in due course.

LEADING DATES : THE SULTANS OF DELHI

(i) The Slave Kings (1206-1290)

A.D. 1206	Kutb-ud-dīn Ibak.
1210-11	Ārām Shah; Iltutmish.
1221-2	Period of Mongol invasions.
1236	Raziya.
1240	Bahrām.
1246	Nasīr-ud-dīn Mahmūd.
1266	Balban.
1286	Kaikobād.

* *One Hundred Poems of Kabīr,* trans. Rabindranath Tagore (1914).

(ii) The Khilji Dynasty (1290-1320)

A.D. 1290	Jalāl-ud-dīn (Firoz Shāh).
1296	Alā-ud-dīn (Muhammad Shāh).
1297-8	Conquest of Gujarāt. Mongol Raids.
1302-11	Malik Kāfūr's campaign in the South.
1303	Conquest of Chitor.
1315	Kutb-ud-dīn Mubārak.
1318	Overthrow of the Hindu Kingdom of Deogiri in the Deccan.
1320	Usurpation of Khusru Khān.

(iii) Tughlak Dynasty (1320-1388)

A.D. 1321	Ghyās-ud-dīn.
1325	Muhammad Ādil.
1351	Firoz Shāh.
1388-1450	Disputed successions.
1398	Sack of Delhi by Timūr.
1414-1450	The Sayyids.

(iv) The Lodi Dynasty (1450-1526)

A.D. 1450	Bahlol.
1489	Sikandar (Nizām Shāh).
1517	Ibrāhīm.
1526	First battle of Pānipat.

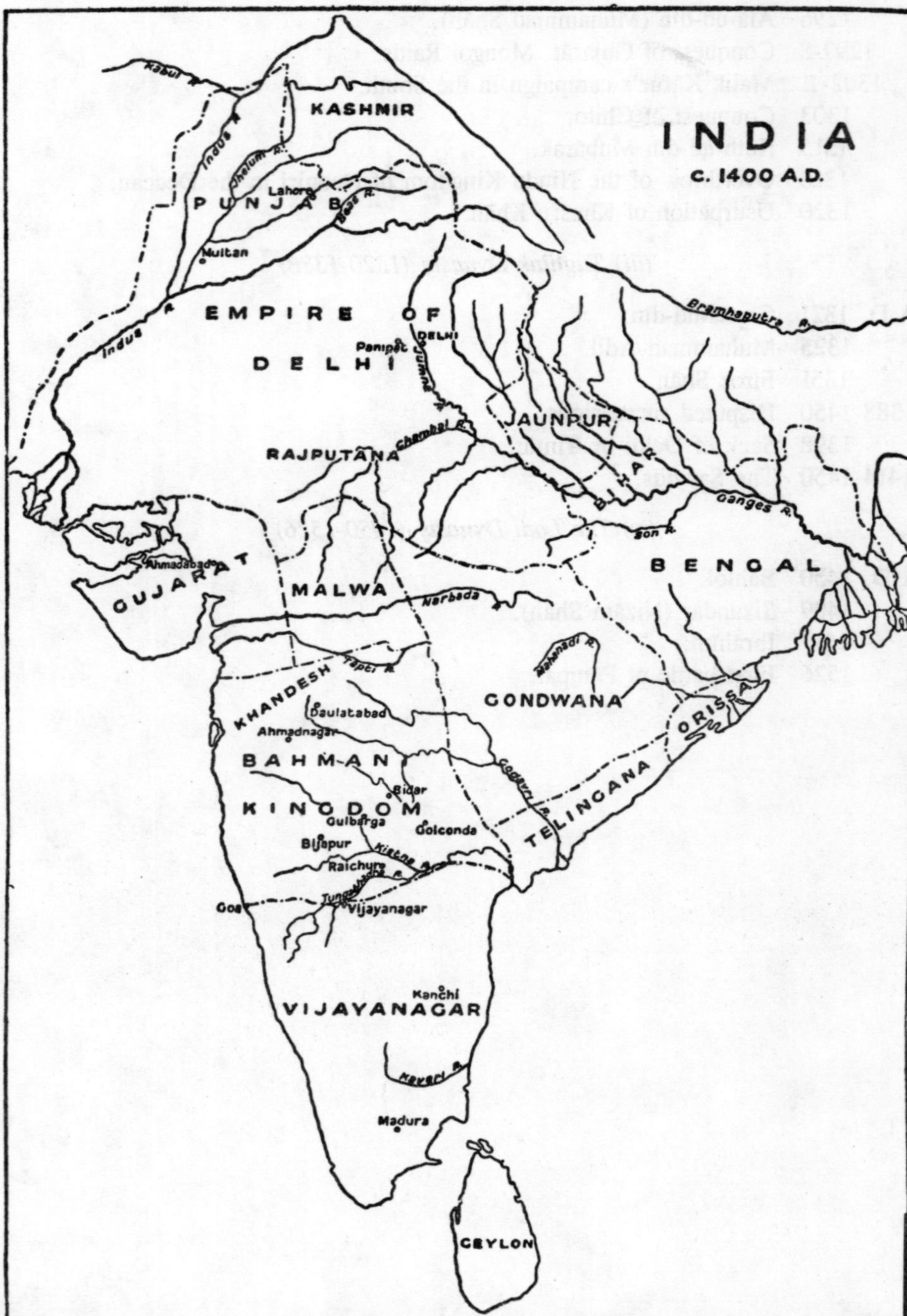

Map 10 : India, A.D. 1400.

Chapter XV

The Independent Kingdoms of Northern India and the Deccan

The Sultan of Delhi were at the best only able to maintain a precarious hold over their provincial governors in distant parts of India and, from time to time, as control of the central government was relaxed, these officers declared their independence. In this way independent Muhammadan kingdoms sprang up in various parts of India, which endured, with varying fortunes, until they were absorbed in the Mogul Empire. The states of Jaunpur, Māndu, Kashmir and Lakhnauti or Bengal can only be referred to in passing, but something must be said of the important kingdom of Gujarāt, which threw off the yoke about A.D. 1400. Ahmad Shāh (1411-1441) built as his capital the city of Ahmadābād. Standing as she does in the midst of the fertile plains of Gujarāt, Ahmadābād, with her looms for the weaving of fine silks and cottons and gold thread, and her easy access to the sea, quickly became the Venice of Western India. Contemporary visitors averred that "no city on earth was so beautiful, so charming and so splendid.... There is scarcely any commodity in Asia but may be seen there."

The best known of the Sultans of Gujarāt was the famous Mahmūd Bīgarhā (1459-1511), who made a great impression on foreign visitors such as the Italian traveller, Ludovico di Varthema. Tall and striking in appearance, he had enormous moustaches, like the horns of a bullock, and a beard which descended to his girdle. He consumed between twenty and thirty pounds of food a day. He was said to have dosed himself with antidotes against poison to such a degree that a fly which settled on him dropped down dead, and that he could kill a man by the simple process of breathing on him! He is the Prince of Cambay of Butler's *Hudibras,* whose

"daily food
Is asp and basilisk and toad."

Mahmūd came to the throne at the age of thirteen and, though a mere boy, quickly overcame his rivals. He overran Kāthiāwār and Cutch, and conquered the Hindu state of Champānīr. His successors carried on an incessant war against the Rājpūts of

Central India. In 1534 Chitor was taken by the Sultan Bahādur Shāh (1526-1537), who was Mahmūd Bīgarhā's grandson. The infant their, Udai Singh, was smuggled to a place of safety, and then thirteen thousand women, headed by the Rānī Karnāvatī, the young prince's mother, committed themselves to the flames, while the men rushed out to find death on the Muslim swords. Next year, Bahādur Shāh was severely defeated by the Emperor Humāyūn of Delhi, and in 1537 his chequered career was brought to an end in a brawl which broke out on a Portuguese man-of-war in the harbour of Diu, which he had been induced to visit in order to conclude a treaty. The history of the decline and fall of the Kingdom of Gujarāt, from the death of the Bahādur Shāh to its annexation by the Emperor Akbar in 1572, is little more than a confused tangle of intrigue and civil war.

Ahmadābād was famous for its handsome buildings. The Muhammadan conquerors had at their disposal the skilled Hindu craftsmen whose ancestors had constructed the temples of Anhilvād and Mount Ābu, and they used their opportunities to the full. The numerous mosques which adorn the city are of sandstone, quarried locally, and are distinguished by their tall, graceful minarets. These are seen at their greatest advantage in the tomb and mosque of Shāh Ālam (Plate XVa). The palm, however, must be given to the exquisite little tomb of the Rānī Sipri (1574) which has been described as a building which "only a Hindu queen could order, and only Hindu artists could carve." The Sidi Sayyidd mosque is noted for its magnificent perforated windows which are regarded as the climax of the stone-cutter's art. In the one there is a single tree whose branches endlessly intertwine; in the other are three trees and four palms. Mahmūd Bīgarhā erected a splendid palace for himself on the banks of an artificial lake at Sarkhej, a few miles outside the town. His greatest achievement, however, is the Jāmi Masjid or Public Mosque at the city of Champānīr, whic he captured in 1484. The mosque at Champānīr, with its dome supported on triple tiers of columns, its gateway flanked by towering minarets, and its richly decorated interior, is probably the most imposing of the Muhammadan buildings in Western India, but striking structures are to be seen at Cambay, Dholka, and other local centres. The step-wells, sluices and reservoirs of Gujarāt are almost as beautiful as the mosques and tombs.

In 1347, during the reign of Muhammad Tughlak, an Afghan general of the name of Hsaan Gangu Bahmani seized the opportunity to set up an independent state with its capital at Gulbarga in the south-west of the modern Hyderabad state. The Bahmani kingdom lasted from 1347 to 1482; at the height of its power it stretched from sea to sea, and included Hyderabad, the Northern Circars of Madras and part of the Bombay Presidency. The Bahmani kings spent most of their time in campaigns against their hereditary foes, the rulers of the Hindu empire of Vijayanagar, which sprang up on the banks of the Tungabhadra river in 1336. The power of the Bahmani kings

Fig. 37 : The Great Mosque, Gulbarga.

was greatly impaired by the perennial dissensions in the court, which was divided into two factions, the Deccanis and the Foreigners. In order to impose a check upon the pretensions of the local nobles, the rulers adopted the policy of inviting a number of adventurers from Arabia, Persia, Afghanistan and other countries, and gave them important posts. This caused a great deal of jealousy, and the friction was accentuated by the fact that, whereas the new-comers were mostly of the Shiah sect, the Deccanis were strictly orthodox .Sunnis. In addition, there were the Siddis or Africans and their half-caste progeny, who were despised by the Foreigners on account of their colour, and threw in their lot with the Deccanis.The Bahmani kingdom was divided into four provinces, each under its governor. These governors enjoyed a large measure of local independence: they raised armies, levied taxes, and appointed their own subordinate officers. In internal matters the Sultan was assisted by a council of eight ministers, who were in charge of such subjects as finance, foreign affairs, police and justice. The army was elaborately organised, and the person of the ruler was protected by a bodyguard divided into four reliefs, one of which was always on duty. The founder of the dynasty having died in 1358, his son Muhammad I succeeded him, and regularised his position by obtaining formal recognition of his title from the Caliph of Egypt. It is said that war between himself and his powerful Hindu neighbours was first started one night, when, flushed with wine, he rewarded a troupe of dancers by giving them a draft on the treasury of Vijayanagar. The rājā mounted the bearer of the missive on an ass, paraded him round the city, and drove him ignominiously out of the gates. The campaign that succeeded was remarkable for the employment, for the first time in Indian history, of artillery, which had been introduced by Turkish or European mercenaries. The Bahmani army advanced as far as the walls of Vijayanagar, but was unable to attack its fortifications: the slaughter of the peaceful cultivators which took place induced both sides to sign an agreement that in future non-combatants should be spared.

Muhammad II, who came to the throne in 1378, was a good ruler, who encouraged literature and invited the poet Hafiz from Shirāz to visit his court. He set up free schools for Muslim orphans, and did his best to alleviate the terrible famines, so common in Deccan history, which broke out between 1387 and 1395. Sultan Fīroz Shāh (1397-1422) was an accomplished and enlightened prince, and under him the Bahmani kingdom reached the zenith of its power. During his reign, the long peace with Vijayanagar was once more broken. For some time it seemed impossible to make any headway against the huge Hindu army, until one of the Sultan's officers formed the bold plan of entering the enemy's camp with a few confederates disguised as a troupe of jugglers. Here they made a sudden raid which threw the Hindu army into confusion, in the midst of which the Muhammadans attacked and completely defeated them. Peace was made, but another war, known as the War of the Goldsmith's Daughter, broke out soon after, over a beautiful girl whom the Vijayanagar troops had tried to abduct. It ended in the defeat of the Hindu rājā, who was forced to pay an enormous indemnity, surrender elephants and dancing girls, and give one of his daughters in marriage to the Sultan. The wedding was celebrated with great pomp, but failed to cement an alliance between the rival kingdoms. Fīroz Shāh spent his later years in the pursuit of pleasure. He was a great builder and a versatile scholar. He loved literature and music, and like Akbar, was interested in religion: it is said that he had read both the Old and New Testaments. He kept a vast harem of women of many nations, including Europeans and Hindus, and is reputed to have been able to converse with them all in their own tongues. He imported a number of European luxuries from Goa. In his later years he became an indolent voluptuary, and in 1422 he was murdered by his brother Ahmad. Ahmad Shāh carried on the dynastic war against Vijayanagar, and was responsible for the transfer of the capital of Bīdar, which stands in a commanding position, on a plateau 2,500 feet above sea. To the west extends a level plain covered with groves of mango and tamarind trees, out of which rise the noble mausoleums of the later Barīd dynasty, and the ruins of garden-houses, mosques and tombs in great profusion. The city adjoins the fort, space being left for an esplanade, and stretches southward along the crest of the eminence, being regularly laid out with broad streets. There was a plentiful supply of water. To-day Bīdar stands in solitary grandeur, towering above the green, level plain, and in the musician's gallery an old blind drummer still salutes the rising and the setting sun with his melancholy strains.

The last of the great rulers of the Bahmani dynasty was Muhammad Shāh III (1463-1482), who owed his success to a great extent to his devoted ancient minister Mahmūd Gāwān, a Persian belonging to an ancient family, who had migrated to the Deccan. "The character of Mahmūd Gāwān," says Meadows Taylor,* "stands out broadly and grandly, not only among his contemporaries, but amongst all the ancient Muhammadans of India, as one unapproachably perfect and consistent. His noble

* *Manual of India History* (1895), p. 176-7.

and judicious reforms, his skill and bravery in war, his justice and public and private benevolence have in the aggregate no equals." He lived on four shillings a day, slept on a mat, and used nothing but earthenware vessels. His vast wealth was devoted to endowing a Muslim College or Madrasah at Bīdar. The building, much damaged in

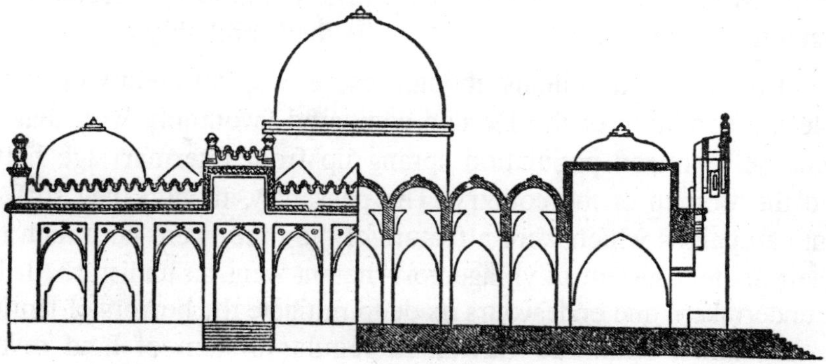

Fig. 38 : Section of Mosque, Bīdar.

later wars, still stands. It is 200 feet by 180, and it three storeys high, with airy and well-lighted lecture-rooms, a library which once contained 3,000 volumes, quarters for professors and students, and a mosque. The facade is inlaid with coloured tiles and decorated with Koranic texts, and at the corners are lofty minarets (Fig. 38).

Mahmūd's devotion to his master was ill-requited. He had served as regent during the prince's minority with examplary loyalty, spurning every temptation to usurp the throne or set himself up as an independent ruler. He had put down corruption with a strong hand, and had introduced reforms which drastically curtailed the powers of the local governors. This had made him unpopular; and, moreover, as he was a Persian, he was hated by the members of the Deccani faction, who determined to get rid of him. His rivals forged a treasonable letter to the Rājā of Orissa, which was placed before the Sultan when he was in his cups. Muhammad Shāh asked his minister what he considered to be the proper punishment for treason. "Death by the sword," was the reply. "You are condemned out of your own mouth," said the Sultan, showing him the letter. Mahmūd Gāwān in vain protested his innocence. "The death of an old man is of little moment," he warned the king, "but to Your Majesty it will mean the loss of your character and the ruin of your Empire." Then, kneeling down and repeating the creed, he submitted himself to the executioner. "Praise be to God for the blessings of martyrdom!" were his last words, uttered just before the sword fell. He was seventy-eight and had served the state faithfully for thirty-five years. Too late the Sultan discovered the plot. He was overwhelmed with remorse, and drank himself to death. In his delirium he constantly cried out that Mahmūd Gāwān was tearing him to pieces.

The minister's drying words proved to be prophetic. After his murder, the kingdom rapidly declined. Street-fighting between the Foreigners and the Deccanis was a matter of daily occurrence, and the later kings were mere puppets in the hands of their Turkish pretorians. A Turkish officer became *maire du palais*, and the last ruler appealed to the Mogul Emperor Bābur at Delhi to come to his rescue, after which he was obliged to flee to Ahmadnagar, where he died, probably of poison, in 1526.

The rule of the Bahmani Sultans, though severe, was not unduly oppressive, and on the whole the condition of the Deccan compared favourably with that of Delhi. As time went on, a mixed population sprang up from intermarriage between the invaders and the women of the country. The peasantry, though they suffered from the incessant campaigns which were a feature of the time, were not much interfered with, and their ancient system of village government went on undisturbed. Irrigation works were undertaken, and endeavours made to mitigate the horrors of famine. Trade flourished, and under Mahmūd Gāwān, a regular system of land revenue was introduced, by which payment was made in money instead of in kind. Athanasius Nikitin,* a Russian traveller who visited the Deccan between 1470 and 1474, says that there were villages at every two miles; the land was laid out in fields and well tilled; the roads were well policed and travelling was secure. His chief criticism was that the country was overstocked, and the poverty of the common folk constrasted too sharply with the luxury of the nobles. The latter, he says, went about in silver litters, with immense retinues of richly dressed retainers. He describes the reigning Sultan, Muhammad Shāh II, as a little man, about twenty years old; he had an enormous army, including armour-clad elephants with scythes attached to their trunks. In nearly every village was a mosque with a mullah who could instruct the children of the Koran, while the law was administered by a Kāzi or judge. In the towns were colleges for teaching Persian and Arabic, and endowed with lands for their maintenance. Hindus were not admitted to high office, and Hindu learning, though not interfered with, was not officially encouraged. Unfortunately, drink was the family failing of the Bahmani kings. Many of them, who during the early part of their reigns had proved to be enlightened and able rulers, became in their later years helpless debauchees, incapable of attending to affairs of state, and in consequence corruption, misgovernment and oppression, and fights between rival factions flourished unchecked.

Urdu literature was cultivated in the courts of the Deccan Sultans, who wished to emphasise their independence, cultural as well as political, of Delhi, and Hindu converts to Islam found it easier to acquire than Persian. Finally, Dakhni Urdu became the official language. After the fall of the Bahmani dynasty, Urdu was patronised by the rulers of Golkonda and Bijāpur, two of whom were themselves poets of

* Nikitin's travels have been edited by H. R. Major, *India in the Fifteenth Century* (Hakluyt Society, 1858).

considerable talent; indeed, Muhammad Kuli Kutb Shāh (1580-1611), is looked upon as one of the greatest and most versatile of all Urdu poets. Odes, elegies, love-songs, and the *ghazal,* stray couplets or rhymed aphorisms on love or morality, were the most popular literary forms.*

The Bahmani Sultans were great builders, and some of their most important edifices were the massive fortresses which they erected in various parts of their kingdom. The invention of artillery made it necessary greatly to strengthen these, and high walls with solid stone battlements and round bastions came into fashion. Perhaps the most remarkable of these fortresses is the famous stronghold of Daulatābād. This is an isolated hill 600 feet high, with absolutely sheer scarped sides, and a broad, deep moat running right round it. The only approach is by means of a tunnel which can at need be closed by an iron panel. A fire can be lighted against the panel, which then becomes red-hot and effectually bars further progress. The citadel has a triple girdle of walls, with bastions and loopholes, and on the summit is mounted a gigantic cannon, which sweeps the approaches to the fortress.

Five kingdoms, those of the Barīd Shāhs of Bīdar, the Kutb Shāhs of Golkonda, the Imād Shāhs of Berār, the Nizām Shāhs of Ahmadnagar and the Ādil Shāhs of Bijāpur, arose from the ruins of the Bahmani Sultanate, and prevailed with varying fortunes until they were absorbed by one another or by the Mogul Empire, but only the last two merit detailed mention. Ahmadnagar was founded by an officer named Ahmad Shāh, and is chiefly remembered on account of its 'noble queen,' Chānd Bībī, the regent who so gallantly defended it against the attacks of the Mogul army led by Prince Murād, son of the Emperor Akbar, in 1596. The assailants sprang a mine which blew up part of the walls, but Chānd Bībī fought in the breach at the head of her troops, clad in full armour and wearing a silver veil, and helping to repair the defences with wood, stones, and even corpses, so that all attacks were repulsed. It is said that, when the ammunition was expended, she used cannon balls of copper, silver and gold from the treasury, and even fired away her jewels. A temporary respite was secured by the cession of the province of Berar, but in 1599, the Imperial armies again attacked the city, and Chānd Bībī fell in a riot stirred up by some disaffected nobles who spread the report that "the Queen was betraying them to the Moguls." Soon after, the Mogul army took the city by storm and put the garrison to the sword. Ahmadnagar temporarily recovered its prosperity under an able minister of Abyssinian origin named Malik Ambar, who died in 1626. His son, Fath Khān, betrayed his master to the Emperor Shāh Jahān, and the state disappeared from the page of history in 1632.

Yusuf Ādil Shāh, the governor of Bijāpur, who declared himself independent in 1489, was a Georgian slave who had been purchased by Mahmūd Gāwān. According

* T. Grahama Bailey, *Udru Literature,* Heritage of India Series, Oxford, 1932, p. 14 ff.

to one story he was a younger son of the Sultan of Turkey, Murad II, who had been smuggled out of harm's way at the time of his brother's accession, and so escaped from the massacre which usually occurred on such occasions. Mahmūd Gāwān quickly recognised his ability, and promoted him to a responsible post. Yusuf Ādil Shāh was an enlightened monarch, and proved himself to be a worthy pupil of the great minister. He abandoned the Sunni sect and became a Shiah. He married a Marāthā lady, to whom he was devoted, and introduced the use of Marāthī as the official language of government; this was a great born to his Hindu subjects, who could now plead in their own mother-tongue. He admitted Hindus to offices of trust. The Muhammadan historian Firishta describes him as a wise and handsome prince, a good judge of human nature, eloquent, well-read and an accomplished musician. "Although he mingled pleasure with business, yet he never allowed the former to interfere with the latter. He always warned his ministers to act with justice and integrity, and in his own person showed them an example of attention to these virtues. He invited to his court many learned men and valiant officers from Persia, Turkestan and Rūm, also several eminent artists, who lived happily under the shadow of his bounty." The same enlightened and tolerant spirit inspired most of his successors, and forms a striking contrast to the cruelty and bigotry of many other Muhammadan rulers. Bijāpur must have been the best governed, happiest and most prosperous state in southern India during the two centuries of its existence. The fifth monarch, Ibrāhīm II (1580-1626), continued the practice of employing in responsible positions Brahmin officials, and invited Portuguese merchants and artists from Goa to his court. He was friendly towards Christianity, and endowed a number of Christian churches with lands for their upkeep. He was a patron of Urdu and Persian literature, and of music and painting, and founded a garden city at Nauraspur as a religious and literary centre. Bījāpur was almost constantly at war with its Muslim neighbours, but in 1564, the four Sultans of Bijāpur, Bīdar, Ahmadnagar and Golkonda combined against the Hindu Rājā of Vijayanagar, and disastrously defeated him at the battle of Tālikota, which will be described in the next chapter. The last great monarch of Bijāpur was Sultan Muhammad Ādil Shāh (1626-1656). He was compelled to make a formal submission to the Mogul Emperor in 1636, but afterwards he built up a mighty kingdom stretching from sea to sea. After his death a decline set in. Ravaged and weakened by the growing power of the Marāthās, Bijāpur at length succumbed to the implacable hatred of Aurangzeb in 1686, and its ruler was sent to die in the state prison at Gwālior.

The city of Bijāpur stands about 2,000 feet above sea-level, on a barren plateau in the south-west of the Bombay presidency midway between the Bhima and Kistna rivers. Its walls, with their handsome battlements and fine bastions, are over six miles in circumference. On them are mounted many cannon which are striking examples of the gun-founder's art, the largest being the famous piece known as the Mulk-ī-Maidān or Lord of the Plain, which weighs 40 tons and was cast in the foundries of

Fig. 39 : Section of Gol Gumbaz, Bijāpur.

Ahmadnagar. Of the multitude of buildings with which the city was once adorned, the most renowned in the Gol Gumbaz, the mausoleum of Muhammad Ādil Shāh, with its gigantic dome, the second largest in the world, which dominates the city. Its internal height in 178 feet. The austere dignity of this building with its plain massive walls, and its four corner-turrets, is in striking contrast to the Ibrāhīm Rauza, the tomb of his father, Ibrāhīm II, standing in what was once a walled garden, with its richly decorated walls and its perforated stone windows, filled with Koranic texts. (Plate XVb, Fig. 39). Many of the buildings—the Asaf Mahal, built to enshrine a relic of no less sanctity than a hair of the Prophet's beard, and the Sāt Manjali or Seven Storeyed Palace—were decorated with mural paintings, which have been sadly mutilated by that fanatical iconoclast, the Emperor Aurangzeb. Among the scholars who flourished at Bijāpur, the most famous was Muhammad Kāsim Firishta, who came from Astrābād on the Caspian Sea and originally settled at Ahmadnagar. He went to the court of Ibrāhīm Ādil Shāh II in 1589, serving under whom he was wounded in the field. His *History of the Muhammadan Power in India* is a classic of its kind, scrupulously fair and accurate, and free from the courtly subservience of other writers. It is our chief authority for the period up to the year 1612. It was translated into English by Colonel J. Briggs in 1829.*

Hitherto, all invaders of India had come by way of the north-western passes, but in 1498 a new factor appeared when, on May 20th, a momentous day in the history of the country, a Portuguese fleet of three tiny vessels and 160 men under Vasco da Gama, cast anchor in the harbour of Calicut. During the Middle Ages, the supplies of silk, calicoes, precious stones, cloves, pepper and medicinal drugs had continued to reach Europe, chiefly by the overland route through Kābul, Balkh, and Samarkand. Spices, and particularly pepper, played an important part in medieval economy, when variety of food and drink was hard to obtain, and the monotony was partly relieved by highly spiced and pungent dishes and beverages. Spices were also used for curing the meat upon which people chiefly lived during the winter months. The chief middlemen in this trade were the Venetians and Genoese, who had trading factories at Constantinople and at various commercial centres in the Levant. But with the capture of Constantinople of the Turks in 1453, these were cut off. Nor was it practicable to obtain supplies from Alexandria. The Sultan of Egypt took a toll of one-third of the profits on all goods, and in a single year Venice and Genoa paid him £300,000 in customs dues. In 1504, Venice could get no commodities at either Alexandria or Beyrout. The markets at Antwerp were crying out for spices, while the Italian ships were rotting at their anchorage and grass grew in the streets.

The honour of finding a way round Africa to India really belongs to that great geographer Henry the Navigator of Portugal, though, like Moses, he never entered the promised land. His chief motive was to lead a new crusade against the Muhammadans, by striking at the hidden sources of their wealth and power in the East. He died in 1463, but the school of sea-captains established by him continued their work. Year after year they explored the west coast of Africa, until at length, in 1487, Bartholemeo Diaz rounded the Cape of Good Hope. The way was now open, and ten years later, Vasco da Gama and his companions set out on their momentous voyage, and after picking up an Indian pilot on the African coast, eventually reached their destination. When asked by the astonished Zamorin his object in coming, da Gama replied characteristically, "Christians and spices." He eventually reached home after many adventures, bringing with him a priceless cargo of cloves, nutmeg, pepper and precious stones.

After the return of Vasco da Gama, the Portuguese sent out an expedition which established itself in Cochin. The Sultan of Egypt found himself outwitted; his monopoly of the Eastern trade was seriously threatened. He fitted out a fleet at Suez, which sailed to the Indian coast. Here it joined hands with the local powers, but the Portuguese disastrously defeated the combined Indian fleets. In 1510, the greatest of all the Portuguese viceroys, Affonso de Albuquerque, arrived on the scene. He saw

* The standard work on Bijāpur is *Bijāpur and its Architectural Remains,* by H. Cousens (Bombay, 1916).

that the Portuguese, being a small nation, could not hold extensive territories. His plan was to seize a series of key positions—Ormuz at the mouth of the Persian Gulf, and Malacca, the gateway of the eastern seas and the centre of the spice trade. By this means, he hoped to ruin the Muhammadans, whom he regarded with a fanatical hatred. "It is very certain," he said, "that if we take this trade of Malacca away out of their hands, Cairo and Mecca will be entirely ruined, and to Venice no spices will be conveyed, except what merchants go and buy in Portugal." His attempt to capture Aden, which would have closed the entrance to the Red Sea, failed. In order to have a base of operations, he seized the important harbour of Goa, the principal port of the Sultans of Bijāpur. He made Goa the Portuguese capital in the East, and adorned it with splendid churches and public buildings. Albuquerque encouraged intermarriage with the Indians, trained Indian troops to fight in European fashion and appointed Indian officials to administer his territory. The Hindus were on the whole regarded with toleration; the Portuguese at first allowed them to practise their religious customs, the only exception being made in the case of Suttee. The Muhammadans, on the other hand, were attacked without mercy, prisoners were treated with fiendish cruelty, and no quarter was shown to them. Gradually the Portuguese established a string of posts along the west of India, at Bombay, Diu, Daman and other places; during this process, they came into conflict with the Sultan of Gujarāt, and, as has been already narrated, the unfortunate Bahādur Shāh was murdered on board a Portugueses vessel in 1537.

'Golden Goa,' at the height of her glory, was a splendid and opulent city. A sixteenth century visitor says: "The traffic was so great that it is impossible to imagine it; the place was immensely large, and it was inhabited by people rich not with riches like ours, but with richness like that of the Crassi and others of those old days. And such merchandise! Diamond, rubies, pearls, and, besides all that, the hrose trade. That alone produces a revenue in the city of 120 to 150 thousand ducats."* But in 1540 the policy of toleration towards Hinduism was reversed; an order was issued that Hindus should not practise the rites of their religion, and Hindu places of worship were demolished. The Holy Office was set up, and dreaded dungeons of the Inquisition were filled with heretics and relapsed converts. This made Hindus in great numbers leave Portuguese territory. The turning-point was the destruction of Vijayanagar in 1565. "By the destruction of the Kingdom of Besnagar," says a contemporary historian, "our State was much shaken, for the bulk of the trade undertaken by all was for this kingdom, to which they carried horses, velvets, satins and other sorts of merchandise, by which they made great profits; and the Custom House at Goa suffered much in its revenue, so that from that day till now, the inhabitants of Goa began to live less well; for baizes and fine cloths were a trade of great importance for Persia

* Sewell, *A Forgotten Empire* (1900), p. 210.

and Portugal, and it then languished, and the gold Pagodas, of which every year more than 500,000 were laden in the ships of the kingdom, were then worth 7½ tangas, and to-day are worth 11½, and similarly every other coin."*

The climate of Goa was notoriously unhealthy, especially to Europeans who had not learnt how to adapt themselves to it, while intermarriage with Indians led to degeneracy. Society became rotten to the core and morals were extremely lax. "Profligacy had become the predominant and fashionable vice, and men gave themselves up the sensual pleasures peculiar to oriental life. Nor was the public administration less tainted. The civic virtues of Albuquerque and Castro were supplanted by corruption and venality; justice was bought; public offices were put up for sale; and the martial spirit degenerated into effeminacy, sloth and indolence, as in the last days of the Roman Empire."† The final blow was the loss of the command of the sea. In 1580, the Spanish and Portuguese crowns were united, and Portugal was involved in the defeat of the Armada. Cut off from their base, haughty, intolerant and poverty-stricken, the Portuguese were already on the down-grade when the English and Dutch appeared upon the scene. To-day, Old Goa stands as a melancholy monument of departed glory. Among the numerous churches which have survived the ravages of time, the most striking is that which enshrines the remains of the saintly Francis Xavier, 'the Apostle of the Indies,' and one of the earliest followers of Ignatius de Loyola, who came to the East in 1542, and died off the coast of China ten years later. The shrine of the saint is a place of pilgrimage for Hindus and Christians alike.

LEADING DATES

Independent Muhammadan Kingdoms of Northern and Central India

(i) Kingdom of Bengal (1199-1338).
(ii) Kingdom of Jaunpur (1398-1476).
(iii) Kingdom of Gujarāt (1398-1572).
(iv) Kingdom of Māndu (1297-1531, conquered by Gujarāt; 1564, becomes part of the Mogul Empire).
(v) Kingdom of Khāndesh (1398-1601).

The Bahmani Kingdom of Golkonda and Bīdar (1347-1482)

(i) The Barīd Shāhis of Bīdar (1490-1574) annexed by Ahmadnagar.
(ii) The Ādil Shāhis of Bijāpur (1490-1686) suppressed by Aurangzeb.
(iii) The Nizām Shāhis of Ahmadnagar (1490-1637) annexed by Shāh Jahān.
(iv) The Kutb Shāhis of Golkonda (1518-1687) suppressed by Aurangzeb.
(v) The Imād Shāhis of Berār (1490-1574) annexed by Ahmadnagar.

* Diego de Couto, *Decades* (1602), viii, 15. For Pagodas, see chap. XV, p. 269 *note;* and for the tanga *(tanka)* or dīnār, chap. XIII, p. 233 *note*.

† Fonseca, *Sketch of the City of Goa* (Bombay, 1878), p. 168.

Chapter XVI

The Empire of Vijaynagar

The history of the empire of Vijayanagar, the hereditary rival of the Bahmani kings and their successors, is of extraordinary interest. It was the Hindu reply to the challenge of the Muhammadan invasion of Southern India at the beginning of the fourteenth century; for almost who hundred and fifty years it stood as a bulwark against the torrent which threatened to sweep away South Indian culture together. Vijayanagar, with its rich markets, attracted a number of foreign visitors who have left accounts of what they saw, and from these we are able to reconstruct a fairly accurate picture of the great and opulent state at the height of its power.

The foundation of Vijayanagar is usually attributed to two brothers named Hakka and Bukka. It was said that they were officers in the service of the Hindu kingdom of Warangal, in what is now the eastern part of Hyderabad State, and when that state was overthrown by the Muhammadans in 1323, they fled to the wild and inaccessible country on the banks of the Tungabhadra, river, where, amidst dense jungle, rugged granite boulders and rocky defiles, they gradually rallied round them outlaws, refuges and fighting men of every caste who had fled from the invaders. In 1336, they commenced to build the city which they called Vijayanagar, the City of Victory, and completed it about seven years later. Quarrels quickly arose with the Bahmani kings, but, as had been mentioned already, the Muhammadans, though they ravaged the country up to the walls of the town, were unable to penetrate the fortifications, which had been built with great skill so as to take full advantage of the natural features of the ground. In 1406, it was hoped that an alliance between the two kingdoms might be brought about by the marriage of the daughter of the Vijayanagar king Deva Raya I to the Sultan Fīroz. The splendour with which the wedding was celebrated shows that, even at this early date, Vijayanagar was a flourishing city.

> "From the gate of the city to the palace, being a distance of six miles, the road was spread with cloth of gold, velvet, satin, and other rich stuffs. The two princes rode on horseback together, between ranks of beautiful boys and girls, who waved plates of gold and silver flowers over their heads as they advanced,

and then threw them to be gathered by the populace. After this the inhabitants of the city made offerings, both men and women, according to their rank. After passing through a square directly in the centre of the city, the relations of Dewul Roy (Deva Raya), who had lined the streets in crowds, made their obeisance and offerings, and joined the cavalcade on foot, marching before the princes. Upon their arrival at the palace gate, the Sultan and Roy dismounted from their horses, and ascended a splendid palanquin, set with valuable jewels, in which they were carried together to the apartments prepared for the receptions of the bride and bridegroom, when Dewul Roy took his leave and retired to his own palace."*

The marriage, however, did not effect the hoped-for results. The haughty Hindu monarch, who considered it an unheard-of condescension to give his daughter to a Muhammadan, only escorted his son-in-law a short way back to his camp. Fīroz Shāh was enraged, swore that one day he would wipe out the affront in blood. Deva Raya, hearing this, made an insulting reply.

During the reign of Deva Raya II (1421-1448), Vijayanagar was visited by two travellers who have left interesting accounts of their experiences.The first was an Italian named Nicolo Conti, who arrived soon after the monarch's accessin.† He tells us that the king had 1,200 concubines, who accompanied him in litters wherever he went. Nicolo Conti was greatly impressed by the religious festivals which he witnessed: the god was taken in procession in a car, beneath the wheels of which, as at the festival of Jagannāth at Puri, the devotees were often crushed to death; others practised the barbarous rite of hook-swinging, being suspended from a mast by a hook inserted in the mucles of the back. At the Dīvālī or Feast of Lamps the temples were illuminated with innumerable tiny lights, while at the Holi or Spring Festival, passers-by, as now, were treated with horse-play and jests, and sprinkled with saffron-water.

Twenty years later he was followed by Adbur Razzāk, an ambassador from the Sultan of Herāt. Abdur Razzāk had originally been sent to the Zamorin at Calicut, but that ruler had received a peremptory order from Deva Raya to present himself at the capital and he dared not disobey his powerful overlord. Abdur Razzāk accompanied him. The party reached the capital at the end of April 1443 and were met by a numerous cortège, which conducted them through the city to their lodgings. Abdur Razzāk thus describes his impressions:‡

"The city of Bijanagar is such that the pupil of the eye has never seen a place like it, and the ear of intelligence has never been informed that there existed anything to equal it in the world. It is built in such a manner that seven citadels and the same number of walls enclose each other. Around the first citadel are

* Firishta, *History of the Deccan,* trans.Briggs (1909 edn.), II. 386.

† *India in the XVth Century* (Hakluyt Society, 1857).

‡ Elliot and Dowson, IV, 89.

Fig. 40 : Stone Car-Temple, Vijayanagar.

stones the height of a man, one half of which is sunk in the ground while the other half rises above it. These are fixed one beside the other in such a manner that no horse or foot soldier could boldly or with ease approach the citadel.

"The seventh fortress is to the north and is the palace of the king. The distance between the opposite gates of the outer fortress north and south is two parasangs, and the same east to west.

"The space which separates the first fortress from the second, and up the third fortress, is filled with cultivated fields and with houses and gardens. In the space from the third to the seventh, one meets a numberless crowd of people, many shops, and a bazaar. By the king's palace are four bazaars, placed opposite each other. On the north is the portico of the palace of the *rai* (king). Above each bazaar is the lofty arcade with a magnificent gallery, but the audience-hall of the king's palace is elevated above all the rest. The bazaars are extremely long and broad.

"Roses are sold everywhere. These people could not live without roses, and they look upon them as quite as necessary as food.... Each class of men belonging to each profession has shops contiguous the one to the other; the jewellers sell publicly in the bazaars pearls, rubies, emeralds, and diamonds. In this agreeable locality, as well as in the king's palace, one sees numerous running streams and canals formed of chiselled stone, polished and smooth."

Soon after his arrival, Abdur Razzāk was granted an interview with the monarch.

"One day some messengers sent from the palace of the king came to see me, and at the close of the same day I presented myself at court.... The Prince was seated in a hall, surrounded by the most imposing attributes of state. Right and left of him stood a numerous crowd of men arranged in a circle. The king was dressed in a robe of green stain, around his neck he wore a colar, composed of pearls of beautiful water, and other splendid gems. He had an olive complexion, his frame was thin, and he was rather tall; on his cheeks might be seen a slight down, but there was no beard on his chin. The expression of his countenance was extremely pleasing.... If report speaks truly, the number of the princesses and concubines amounts to seven hundred."

During the second half of the fifteenth century, a number of important events occurred, which profoundly influenced the history of Southern India. The Bahmani Empire broke up, and as we have seen, it was replaced by the four Sultanates of Bijāpur, Ahmadnagar, Golkonda, and Bīdar. The Portuguese appeared upon the west coast, and eventually established themselves at Goa. The Portuguese looked upon the Muhammadans as their inveterate foes, and for this reason were inclined to be friendly with Vijayanagar, and presently the two states developed a flourishing trade which greatly enriched them both. The mines in the Vijayanagar territories were famous for their diamonds, many of which were of enormous size, and it is said that the famous Kohinoor came from one of them. The Italian traveller Caesar Frederici (1567),* says that "the merchandise which went every year from Goa to Beznagar were Arabian horses, velvets, damaska and satins, Portuguese taffeta, and pieces of china, saffron and scarlets; and from Beznagar they had in Turkey for their commodities, jewels and pagodas, which be ducats of gold;† the apparel they use in Beznagar is velvet, satin, damask, scarlet, or white bumbast cloth, according to the estate of the person, with long hats on their heads called *Colae.*"‡

The Vijayanagar kings kept a vast number of horses in their stables, and the horse-trade alone came to 150,000 ducats annually. The Emperor of Vijayanagar offered Albuquerque £20,000 in return for a monopoly in horses, as these imported animals were for superior to the local breeds, and he wished to keep them from his rival the Sultan of Bijāpur. The fact that the offer was refused speaks for itself.

---

* In Ramusio, *Navigationi e Viaggi* (1606), III, 389.

† The pagoda was a gold coin worth about 3½ rupees. On it was the boar, the emblem of the god Vishnu.

‡ *Kullayi,* the hall hats which may be seen on statues on the Vijayanagar rulers.

In 1509, a dynastic revolution brought to the throne Krishna Rāya, during the twenty years of whose reign the Empire of Vijayanagar reached the zenith of its power. We are fortunate in obtaining vivid glimpses of this ruler from the accounts written by two Portuguese merchants, Domingo Paes and Fernão Nuniz, who visited Vijayangar at different times during his reign. Paes went in the train of one Christoão de Figueriedo, who was trading in elephants and horses. The party made its way through densely populated and well-irrigated country. Paes was struck by the splendid temples he passed on his way. These temples were dedicated to different gods, whose images were representations of men and women, bulls, apea, a man with an elephant's trunk and tusks, and a plain round stone. The idol was fed every day, and girls attached to the temple danced before it. One shrine in particular moved his admiration on account of its carving.

> "You must know that it is a round temple made of a single stone, the gateway all in the manner of joiners' work, with every art of perspective. There are many figures of the said work, standing out as much as a cubit from the stone, so that you see on every side of them, so well carved that they could could not be better done, the faces as well as all the rest; and each one in its place stands as if embowered in leaves; and above it is in the Romanesque style, so well made that it could not be better. Besides this, it has a sort of lesser porch upon pillars, all of stone, and the pillars with their pedestals so well executed that they appear as if made in Italy; all the cross pieces and beams are of the same stone without any planks or timber being used in it, and in the same way all the ground is laid with the same stone, outside as well as in."*

Paes' account of Vijayanagar confirms in a striking manner that of Abdur Razzāk. On approaching the capital, the party began to pass through the gates which pierced the concentric lines of fortifications, linking up the hills in the midst of which the city stood. The land between the inner and outer walls was intensively cultivated and very fertile, and the pastures well stocked with flocks and herbs. It was irrigated by five stone aqueducts leading from the river. The city was, therefore, so well supplied that it could stand a siege for an almost indefinite period. On reaching the inner town, the travellers proceeded down a street 'as wide as a place of tourney,' lined throughout with rows of fine houses; the sides of the road were planted with shade-giving trees. Here and there were noble temples, standing in their own precincts, their lofty spires covered with carvings. The market stalls were loaded with provisions; vegetables and fruit were abundant; but the people, though Hindus, were no vegetarians, and mutton and pork were on sale in large quantities. Paes observes that meat of all kinds, except beef, was freely consumed, except by the Brahmins. In another street were the merchants' shops. "There you will find all sorts of rubies,

* Sewell, *A Forgotten Empire* (1904), pp. 240-1.

diamonds, emeralds, seed pearls and cloths, and every sort of thing on earth you may wish to buy." The craftsmen had their own quarter, with two small shrines for their private use. Paes notes the existence of confraternities or gilds, like those in contemporary Europe. What, however, most impressed him was the immense size and populousness of the city, far exceeding anything he had seen in the west.

> "The size of this city I do not write here, because it cannot all be seen from any one spot, but I climbed a hill whence I could see a great part of it; I could not see it all because it lies between several ranges of hills. What I saw from thence seemed to me as large as Rome, and very beautiful to the sight; there are many groves of trees within it, in the gardens of the houses, and many conduits of water which flow into the midst of it, and in places there are artificial lakes; and the king has close to his palace a palm-grove and other rich-bearing fruit-trees. Below the Moorish quarter is a little river, and on this side are many orchards and gardens with many fruit-trees, for the most part mangoes and areca-palms and jack-trees, also many lime and orange trees, growing so closely one to another that it appears like a thick forest; and there are also white grapes. All the water which is in the city comes from the two tanks of which I have spoken, outside the first enclosing wall.
>
> "The people in this city are countless in number, so much so that I do not wish to write it down for fear it should be thought fabulous; but I declare that no troops, horse or foot, could break their way through any street or lane, so great are the numbers of the people and elephants."*

Shortly after arrival, the Portuguese presented their credentials to the Emperor, and were graciously received. Krishna Raya profoundly impressed Paes, who speaks of him as "gallant and perfect in all things." He describes him as of medium height, fair and intelligent. His face was pitted with smallpox. He was a great athlete, and kept himself fit for war by constant gymnastic exercises and by riding. "He was the most feared and perfect king that could possibly be: cheerful of disposition and very merry: he is one that seeks to know foreigners and receives them very kindly, asking about all their affairs, whatever their condition may be. He is a great ruler and a man of much justice, but subject to sudden fits of rage." He received the visitors dressed in a white silk robe embroidered with golden roses: round his neck was a diamond necklace of great value, and on his head "a cap of brocade in fashion like a Galician helmet." The Royal Palace stood in an enclosure in the heart of the city. Here dwelt the sovereign with his bodyguard, his twelve wives and their numerous retinues, his dancing girls and retainers. The private apartments of the royal family were in a separate building, known as the House of Victory. The Portuguese were given the unusual privilege of visiting this. One room was panelled with ivory, from

* Sewell, *op. cit.*, p. 256-7.

top to bottom. "The pillars had roses and flowers of lotuses, all of ivory, and all well executed, so that there could not be better—it is so rich and beautiful that you could not discover another such. On this same side is designed in painting all the ways of life of the men who have been here, even down to the Portuguese, from which the king's wives can understand the manner in which each lives in his own country, even to the blind and the beggars."

Paes then goes on to describe the festival of Mahānavami or Nine Nights, in honour of the god Siva, which he witnessed. It began every afternoon at three o'clock, and was prolonged far into the night, the arena being illuminated with countless tiny lamps. The king was seated on a dais, surrounded by his nobles. Before him was the idol of the god in whose honour of the festival was held, with Brahmins on either side fanning it with horse-tail fans. Proceedings opened with a ritual dance by the nautch-girls. "Who can fitly describe the great riches these women carry on their persons? Collars of gold with so many diamonds and rubies and pearls, bracelets on their arms, girdles below and anklets on their feet." After this came wrestling, sham fights, car-processions and a parade of elephants and horses from the royal stables, followed by the king's horse of state, "caracoling and prancing, as do all horses here, being trained in that art." The scene closed with a procession of the maids of honour of the Queens; in tall caps and carrying lights in golden vessels. They were so loaded with jewels that they could barely walk. At the conclusion of the festival came a review, an even more dazzling spectacle. Soldiers were drawn up everywhere, lining the roads and the flat roofs of the houses and the slopes of the surrounding hills "in such a way that you see neither plain nor hill that was not covered with troops." The infantry consisted of archers, musketeers, and foreign mercenaries armed with bombs, spears and fire-missiles; the cavalry were clothed in quilted leather tunics, with metal head-pieces, and the elephants carried on their backs groups of armed men in howdahs. When all was ready, Krishna Raya and his staff came out and rode down the line to inspect it.

> "The king leaves his palace riding on the horse of which I have already told you, clothed in the many rich white cloths I have already mentioned, with two umbrellas of state all gilded and covered with crimson velvet, and with the jewels and ornaments which they keep for the purpose of wearing at such times: he who ever wears such jewels can understand the sort of things so great a lord would wear. Then to see the grandeur of the nobles and men of rank, I cannot possibly describe it all, nor should I be believed if I tried to do so; then to see the horses and the armour that they wear, you would see them so covered with metal plates that I have no words to express what I saw, and some hid from me the sight of others; and to try and tell of all I saw is hopeless, for I went along with my head so often turned from one side to the other that I was almost falling

backwards off my horse with my senses lost. The cost of it all is not so much to be wondered at, as there is so much money in the land, and the chiefs are so wealthy.

"There went in front of the king many elephants with ther coverings and ornaments, as I have said; the king had before him some twenty horses fully caparisoned and saddled, with embroideries of gold and precious stones, that showed off well the grandeur and state of their lord. Close to the king went a cage such as is seen at Lisbon on the day of the Corpo de Dios festival, and it was gilded and very large; it seemed to me to be made of copper silver; it was carried by sixteen men, eight on each side, besides others who took their turns, and in it was carried the idol of which I have already spoken. Thus accompanied the king passed along gazing at his soldiers, who gave great shouts and cries and struck their shields; the horses neighed, the elephants screamed, so that it seemed as if the city would be overturned, the hills and valleys and all the ground trembled with the discharges of arms and musquets; and to see the bombs and fire-missiles over the plains, this was indeed wonderful. Truly it seemed as if the whole world were collected there.

"In this way it went on till the king arrived at the palace, where the tent was that I have already mentioned, and he entered this and performed his usual ceremonies and prayers. You must not think that when the king passed the troops moved from their positions: on the contrary they stood motionless in their places till the king returned. As soon as the king had finished his ceremonies he again took horse and returned to the city in the same way as he had come, the troops never wearying of their shouting; as soon as he passed by them they began to march. Then to see those who were on the hills and slopes, and the descent of them with their shouts and beating of shields and shaking of arrows and bows that were without count. Truly, I was so carried out with myself that it seemed as if what I saw was a vision, and that I was in a dream. Then the troops began to march to their tents and pavilions in the plains, which were in great number; and all the captains accompanied the king as far as the palace, and thence departed to rest themselves from their labour."*

In 1520, Krishna Raya determined to attack his hereditary foe, the Sultan of Bijāpur. The bone of contention was the rich and fertile province of Raichur, which lay between the Kistna and Tungabhadra rivers. The Portuguese accompanied the army to the field, and a vivid account of the campaign has been left by Fernão Nuniz, one of Paes' companions. He says that the royal encampment resembled a moving city. It had a bazaar laid out in regular streets, with markets, where provisions,

* Sewell, *op. cit.*, p. 278.

clothing and even jewellery and other luxuries were for sale. On the morning of the battle, "the drums and trumpets and other music in the King's camp began to sound, and the men to shout, so that it seemed as if the sky would fall to the earth; then the neighing and excitement of the horses, and the trumpeting of the elephants, it was impossible to tell how it was." The battle was going against the Hindus, when Krishna Raya put himself at the head of his men. "Who ranges himself with me?" he cried. He gave one of his pages an iron ring, to show to his queens in the event of his death, "so that they might burn themselves according to custom" The result was that the Bijāpur army was completely defeated, and the fortress of Raichur was invested. At the siege the Portuguese did excellent work as sharpshooters, and Figueriedo brought down the commandant with a lucky shot. Raichur then capitulated, and Krishna Raya, as merciful as he was brave, assured the inhabitants that their lives and property should be spared. In 1529 this great king, warrior and scholar, a patron of art and literature and wise and bountiful in the distribution of his almost fabulous wealth, was gathered to his fathers. Among his many buildings, the temple of Vitthalswami, the gigantic granite monolith of Narasimha (Vishnu in his incarnation as the Man-Lion), and the exquisite bas-reliefs, illustrating scenes from the *Rāmāyana*, which decorate his private chapel, have survived the ravages of time and Mussalman iconoclasts, and give us a faint idea of the almost unimaginable splendours so vividly depicted in the pages of Paes.* (Plate XVI.)

After the death of Krishna Raya, the empire began slowly to decline. The succeeding monarch became a puppet in the hands of his minister, Rāmrājā. In 1558, Rāmrājā combined with his old enemy, the Sultan of Bijāpur, to attack the kingdom of Ahmadnagar. The Vijaynagar troops behaved outrageously. The country was laid waste, and the peasants put to the sword; horses were stabled in mosques, and Hindu rites were practised in Muslin holy places. "The infidels," says Firishta, "who for many years had been wishing for such an event, left no cruelty unpractised. They insulted the honour of the Mussalman women, destroyed the mosques, and did not even respect the sacred Koran." Husain Shāh of Ahmadnagar was forced to sue for peace. When he entered the victor's presense, Rāmrājā rose and took him by the hand. "Husain Nizam Shāh, who possessed great pride, called for a basin and ewer and washed his hands as if they had been polluted by the touch of Rāmrājā, who said in his own language, 'If he were not my guest, I would cut off his hands and tie them round his neck'. Then calling for water, he also washed, and such were the bad feelings that prevailed, that a tumult nearly occurred on the spot." After this incident, Rāmrajā treated ambassadors from the Muslim states with open discourtesy. "When he admitted them to his presence, he did not suffer them to sit, and treated them with the most contemptuous reserve and haughtiness. He made them attend

* A. H. Longhurst, *Hampi Ruins Described and Illustrated,* Calcutta, 1925.

when in public in his train on foot, not allowing them to mount till he gave orders." Rāmārājā's insolent conduct so enraged the sultans that they resolved to curtail his powers by a general league of the Faithful against him. Emissaries were secretly sent from court to court, and the united sultans, laying aside their differences, combined to crush the common enemy of Islam. The combined armies of the four states of Bijāpur, Ahmadnagar, Golkonda and Bīdar, assembled on the plain outside Bijāpur in December 1564. Meanwhile, Rāmrājā, who had heard what was happening, called up his forces. Levies poured in from all parts of the kingdom, and he took up a strong position on the banks of the Kistna river, about twenty-five miles from the town of Tālikot. All the fords were strongly held, but the Mussalmans, by a clever ruse, managed to outwit the Hindus, and crossed unopposed. A battle was now inevitable, and the two hosts were drawn up facing one another on the morning of January 23rd, 1565. Both sides realised that on the result depended the question whether the supremacy of Southern India should be in Hindu or Muslim hands. The Hindus had over-whelming superiority in numbers, but the allies had the advantage of the excellent park of artillery belonging to Ahmadnagar, commanded by a skilled Turkish officer. Rāmrājā was now an old man of ninety-six, and too infirm to mount a horse, but he was carried to be filed on a litter, and took his place in the centre of the line on a magnificent throne; by his side were heaps of gold and jewels, to be distributed as rewards for valour. The battle opened with furious charges by the hindu cavalry, which were repulsed by the Muhammadan artillery, who fired bags of small copper coins at close range. These had a terrible effect upon the closely packed Hindu forces. In the confusion the elephants belonging to the Nizām Shāh dashed forward, and the litter-bearers, taken with sudden panic, dropped their precious burden and fled. Rāmrājā was captured and taken to Hussain Nizām Shāh, who struck off the old man's head with his own hand, saying, "Now I am avenged of thee! Let God do what he will to me!" The head was mounted on a lance and carried to the front line. When they saw it, the Hindus, terror-stricken, broken and fled, pursued in every direction by their enemies, who slaughtered them till the Kistna ran red with blood. The plunder was so great that every private soldier was loaded with jewels, arms, horses and slaves. The Sultans kept only the elephants for their own use.

Meanwhile the utmost confidence prevailed in the city. The inhabitants had so often seen the tide of invasion rolled back from their impregnable walls, that they went on with their daily work undisturbed by what was happening outside. But now news of a great defeat began to trickle through, and the princes who had been left behind to guard the capital packed up the contents of the royal treasury on elephants and basely made off. It is said that over five hundred of these beasts were required to transport the treasures. On the tenth day the enemy arrived, and forced an entrance with little difficulty. They killed and plundered without mercy, and it is said that the work of destruction went on for three months. The magnificent stone-carving was smashed to pieces with crowbars and hammers, and where it defied human efforts, fires were lit to burst it open. Firishta says that the state never recovered from the blow. It lingered on for some time, but the petty chiefs became independent rulers, and the proud capital was a forlorn ruin, inhabited only by tigers and other wild beasts. The battle of Tālikot was the end of Hindu dominion in Southern India. A sadly diminished kingdom governed by Rāmrājā's descendants sprang up at Penukonda. In 1585 its capital was transferred to Chandragiri. In 1639 the Rājā of Chandragiri gave Francis Day, the English factor, the site of the city of Madras. The last independent Hindu State in Southern India was that of the Nāyaks of Madura, which flourished for a time in the 17th century.

So perished the mighty Hindu Empire at Vijayanagar, unequalled in Indian annals for its grandeur, luxury, and almost fabulous wealth. At the height of its power it stretched from sea to sea, and included the whole of India south of the Kistna river. It was divided into a large number of provinces, each under a ruler who was practically independent, provided that he paid his dues to the Treasury, furnished his contingent of troops when called upon, and attended the Court on fixed occasions. But the lot of the common people was far from happy. Taxation was heavy and the wealth was in the hands of a few. "The nobles," says Nuniz, "are like renters, who hold all the land from the king; they also pay him every year 60 lakhs as royal dues. The lands, they say, yield 120 lakhs, of which they must pay 60 to the king, and the rest they retain for the pay of the soldiers and the expenses of the elephants which they are obliged to maintain. For this reason the common people suffer much hardship, those who hold the lands being so tyrannical." The law was terribly severe.

> "The punishments that they inflict in this kingdom are these: for a thief, whatever theft he commits, howsoever little it be, they forthwith cut off a foot and a hand, and if his theft be a great one he is hanged with a hook under his chin. If a man outrages a respectable women or a virgin he has the same punishment, and if he does any other such violence his punishment is of a like kind. Nobles who become traitors are sent to be impaled alive on a wooden stake thrust through the belly, and people of the lower orders, for whatever crime they commit, he forthwith commands to cut off their heads in the market-place, and the same for a murder unless the death was the result of a duel. For great honour is done to those who fight in a duel, and they give the estate of the dead man to the survivor; but no one fights a duel without first asking leave of the minister, who forthwith grants it. These are the common kinds of punishments, but they have others more fanciful; for when the king so desires, he commands a man to be thrown to the elephants, and they tear him to pieces. To people are so subject to him that if you told a man on the part of the king that he must stand still in a street holding a stone on his back all day till you released him he would do it."*

* Sewell, *op. cit.*, p. 383.

Barbarous customs were practised; immense numbers of sheep, goats and buffaloes were sacrificed at religious festivals, and at the death of the king or a great noble the women of his harem were forced to submit to the rite of *suttee*. This must have led to terrible holocausts, for we know that the number of women in the royal palace was incredibly large. The traveller Nicolo Conti goes so far as to say that as many as 3,000 women perished in this way at the royal obsequies. Among the lower orders, the widow was often buried alive with her husband. Prostitution was encouraged; every temple had its crowds of *devadāsīs,* or 'handmaids of the god,' and the prostitutes' quarter was one of the sights of the capital. "The splendour of these houses, the beauty of the heart-ravishers, their blandishments and ogles are beyond description," says Abdur Razzāk, with puritanical horror. These girls were skilled dancers and singers, and many of them amassed enormous fortunes. The revenues derived from the brothels were used to pay the police, whose duty it was "to acquaint themselves with all the events and accidents that may happen within the seven walls, and to recover everything that may be lost or that may be abstracted by theft; otherwise they are fined." It is against this background that the splendours of Vijayanagar must be viewed.

LEADING DATES

A.D. 1336	Foundation of Vijayanagar.
1337-1478	The Sangama Dynasty.
1443	Visit of Abdur Razzāk.
1478-1496	The Sāluva Dynasty.
1496-1567	The Narsinga Dynasty.
1509-1529	Reign of Krishna Rāya.
1522	Visit of Domingo Paes.
1542	Rāmrājā usurps the power.
1543	Alliance with Bijāpur against Ahmadnagar.
1565	Battle of Tālikot.

Chapter XVII

The Foundation of the Mogul Empire

"In the month of Ramazan, in the year eight hundred and ninety-nine (June 1494), and in the twelfth year of my age, I became King of Ferghāna." With these words, Zahīr-ud-dīn Muhammad, surnamed Bābur, 'the Tiger', commences his famous Memoris.* A Jaghtai Turk by race, he was descended from Timūr the Lame on his father's side, and Chingiz Khān on his mother's. Thus there ran in his veins the blood of the two greatest conquerors that Asia has ever seen. Bābur's father was the ruler of the little principality of Ferghāna, now in Russian Turkestan, a picturesque and fertile valley in the heart of the mountains,watered by the mighty Syr Darya and abounding in fruit, flowers, and game of every kind. Bābur's father, Amar Shaikh Umar, died as the result of the collapse of his pigeon-house. His son gives a delightful pen-picture of him. "He was of low stature, brownish hair and very corpulent. He used to wear his tunic extremely tight; insomuch that as he was wont to contract his belly when he tied the strings when he let himself out again, the strings often burst.... He had a poetic nature, but no taste for composing verses.... He was a middling shot with the bow; he had an uncommon force with his fists, and never hit a man whom he did not knock down.... He was a pleasant companion, and in the course of conversation used often to cite, with great felicity, appropriate verses from the poets. He was a humane man. He played a great deal at backgammon, and sometimes at games of chance with the dice."

The boy king was soon called upon to show the mettle of his breed. He is described as "handsome in his person, his address engaging and unaffected, his countenance pleasing and his disposition affable." He was enormously strong, and an expert swordsman, rider and archer; there was no river which he could not swim, and he could run along the battlements, leaping over the embrasures, with a man under each arm. He defeated the attempts of his uncles to depose him, and three years later, at the age of fifteen, he set out for the conquest of Samarkand, the capital of his great ancestor, the Amir Timūr. Stripling though he was, he was already a strong disciplinarian. His troops had plundered some traders, but "an order to restore

* Translated by Leyden and Erskine and edited by King, 1921.

everything having been given, the first watch of the next day had not passed before nothing, not a tag of cotton, not a broken needle's point, remained in possession of any man of the force; all was back with its owners." At the end of 1497, the dream of his life was realised, and 'silken Samarkand' opened its gates to him. Bābur's pride and joy at his achievment knew no bounds. His memoirs are filled with enthusiastic descriptions of its magnificent buildings, its public baths, observatories, palaces, mosques and colleges, some of them the work of imported Indian craftsmen. Even more did he delight in its gardens and pleasure grounds; he mentions especially the Bāgh-i-dīlkūsha, the heart-delighting garden, with its kiosk decorated with paintings of Timūr's exploits in Hindustan. Bābur, however, did not remain long in Samarkand. He was dangerously ill; a rumour was spread abroad that he was dead, and the whole country broke into revolt. Deserted by his followers, he had to spend the winter a homeless wanderer in the hills with a handful of friends. It is impossible here to give a detailed account of his adventures during these early years, his second conquest of Samarkand, the siege during which he and his followers lived on the flesh of dogs and asses and fed their horses on mulberry leaves, and his escape once more to the mountains, where he was the guest of a doughty old lay of one hundred and eleven, who told him stories of the days of great Timūr and his invasion of India. In 1504, tired of wandering about 'like a king on a chessboard', Bābur determined to strike southwards and make an attempt to occupy the throne of Kābul, which was in danger of passing from his family. The little band which set out on this quest was a motley one. "The followers who still adhered to my fortunes, great and small, exceeded two hundred and fell short of three hundred. The greater part of them were on foot, with brogues on their feet, clubs in their hands, and long frocks over their shoulders. Such was their distress that among us all we had only two tents. My own tent was pitched for my mother." One evening, as the party mounted the high passes of the Hindu Kush mountains, a new star, low and bright on the southern horizon, burst upon their view. "I said, 'This cannot be Canopus!' They answered, 'It is indeed Canopus.' " One of Bābur's companions thereupon broke out into the following couplet:

> "O Canopus, how far dost thou shine, and where dost thou rise?
>
> Thine eye is an omen of good fortune to him on whom it falls."

Kābul was taken without much difficulty, and Bābur speaks with approval of his new capital, with its gardens, and fruit-trees, and its pleasant climate. What was more important, it was on the highway to India. Hither every year came the Indian caravans, bringing bales of cloth, slaves, sugar, drugs and spices.

> "From the year 910 (A.D. 1504), when I obtained the principality of Kābul, up to the date of the events I now record (i.e., the defeat of Sultan Ibrāhīm Lodi), I had never ceased to think of the conquest of Hindustan. But I had never found

a suitable opportunity for undertaking it, hindered as I was, sometimes by the apprehensions of my Begs, sometimes by disagreements between my brothers and myself. Finally all these obstacles were happily removed. Great and small, Begs and captains, no one dared to say a word against the project. So in 925 (A.D. 1519) I left at the head of my army, and made a start by taking Bajaur.... From this time to 932 (A.D. 1525-6) I was always actively concerned in the affairs of Hindustan. I went there in person at the head of an army, five times in the course of seven or eight years. The fifth time, by the munificence and liberality of God, there fell beneath my blows an enemy as formidable as Sultan Ibrāhim, and I gained the vast empire of Hind."

Bābur's determination was strengthened by the fact that he had now assumed the title of Pādshāh, or head of the house of Timūr, and he regarded the Punjab as part of his ancestral possessions. From 1519 he began to feel his way towards the Indian plains, and it is typical of the man that, unlike his predecessors, he refused to allow his troops to molest the common folk.

"As it was always in my heart to possess Hindustan, and as these several countries...had once been held by the Turks, I pictured them as my own, and was resolved to get them into my own hands, whether peacefully or by force. For these reasons, it being imperative to treat the hillmen well, this order was given: 'Do no hurt or harm to the flocks and herds of these people, nor even to their cotton-ends and broken needles!"

To the Indian people he sent a proclamation in advance. "Our eye is on this land and on this people; raid and rapine shall not be." Anxious to avoid war, he sent an envoy to the Sultan of Delhi, proposing a friendly settlement of his claims, but the envoy was detained at Lahore. Bābur made four preliminary reconnaissances into the Punjab, and in 1524 he received an invitation from Daulat Khān, the Viceroy of Lahore, to join him in deposing the reigning sovereign, Ibrāhīm Khān Lodi, whose haughty and arrogant behaviour had driven his nobles to open rebellion. His uncle, Alam Khān, was to be placed upon the throne of Delhi and, in return for his services, Bābur's claims to the Punjab were to be recognised. But it soon became evident that Daulat Khān was merely using his new ally as a catspaw in his own ambitious schemes, and Bābur determined to conquer India for himself.

"On Friday, the first of Safar 932 (November 17, 1525), when the sun was in Sagittarius,* I set out on my march to invade Hindustan."

His whole force, including camp-followers, amounted to only 12,000 men, but the longer the odds the better Bābur was pleased. He first encountered the faithless Daulat Khān, who had girded on two swords and come out to meet the intruder. But

* Actually the sun was in Scorpio. It enters Sagittarius on November 23rd.

Daulat Khān's army fled at the first attack, and the old man, his two swords derisively hung round his neck, was led into his conquerors' presence. According to the custom of the times he could look for nothing except death by torture. But Bābur was as merciful as he was brave. "I called you Father," he said. "I showed you more respect and reverence than you could have desired or expected. What evil have I ever done you, that you should come in this style against me, with these two swords by your side, and attended by an army, stir up tumult and confusion in my territories?" Daulat Khān could only stammer a few confused words in reply. He was dismissed and allowed to retire to his ancestral estates. After this, Bābur says, "I placed my foot in the stirrup of resolution and my hand on the reins of confidence in God, and marched against Sultan Ibrāhīm, the son of Sultan Iskander, the son of Sultan Bahlol Lodi Afghan, in whose possession the throne of Delhi and the dominions of Hindustan at that time were; whose army in the field was said to amount to a hundred thousand men and who, including those of his Amīrs, had nearly a thousand elephants." The two forces met on the field of Pānipat, in the corridor between the desert and the mountains where the fate of India has been so often decided. Bābur's army was few in number, but it consisted of tried warriors, under a commander who had been a soldier since boyhood. Moreover he had one priceless asset. Firearms were still a novelty in Indian warfare, and Bābur had in his employ a trained body of matchlockmen and a battery of artillery under an experienced Turki officer of the name of Ustād Ali. In order to make the best possible use of his tiny force, Bābur followed the traditional Turki tactics. Along his front he drew up a line of waggons, seven hundred in all, linked together with ropes of hide and strengthened with breastworks; behind these he disposed his artillery and musketeers, who were thus secured from being ridden town. Gaps were left along the line, through which bodies of cavalry could make a sortie. His left and rear were protected by a strong palisade of logs and trenches; his right rested upon the town of Pānipat. His idea was to tempt his opponent to attack on a narrow front, where his superiority of numbers would be of little assistance of him, and then to take him in flank with his Turki horsemen. His anticipations proved to be correct. Sultan Ibrāhīm was a rash and inexperienced youth and did not know how to handle his forces. A more cautious commander would have blockaded his enemy, as the Afghans did the Mārāthas on the same ground in 1761. But Bābur, by means of harassing tactics, succeeded in provoking his opponent into attacking him. On April 21st, at dawn, huge masses of infantry and elephants advanced to storm the waggons, and were met at close range with a withering fire. This threw them into confusion; the front ranks became mixed up with the rear, and meanwhile the mounted archers were galloped round them, pouring in volleys of arrows, so that they could neither advance nor flee. The battle was decided by a cavalry charge, and by noon the Afghan forces were in full retreat, leaving over 20,000 men dead on the field. Bābur's men had slain three times their own number, and among the fallen was Sultan Ibrāhim himself. "By the grace of God," writes Bābur, "this difficult affairs was made easy to me, and that mighty army in the space of half a day was laid in the dust."

Bābur at once occupied Agra and Delhi, and proclaimed himself Sultan. He fills many pages of his Memoirs with descriptions of his new realm, the customs and institutions of the people, and the flora and fauna of the country. Bābur was not favourabley impressed by Hindustan, with its triple curse of heat, dust and strong winds.

"Hindustan is a country that has few pleasures to recommend it. The people are not handsome. They have no idea of the charms of friendly society, of frankly mixing together, or familiar intercourse. They have no genius, no comprehension of mind, no politeness of manner, no kindness or fellow-feeling, no ingenuity or mechanical invention in planning or executing their handicraft works, no skill or knowledge in design or architecture; they have no horses, no good flesh, no grapes or musk-melons, no good fruits, no ice or cold water, no good food or bread in their bazaars, no baths or colleges, no candles, no torches, not a candlestick.... Beside their rivers and standing waters, they have some running water in their ravines and hollows; they have no aqueducts or canals in their gardens or palaces. In their buildings they study neither elegance nor climate, appearance nor regularity.... The chief excellency of Hindustan is, that it is a large country and has abundance of gold and silver. The climate during the rains is very pleasant. On some days it rains ten, fifteen and even twenty times. During the rainy season inundations come pouring down all at once, and form rivers, even in places where at other times there is no water. While the rains continue on the ground, the air is singularly delightful, insomuch that nothing can surpass its soft and agreeable temperature. Its defect is, that the air is rather moist and damp. During the rainy season you cannot shoot even with the bow of our country and it becomes quite useless. Nor is it the bow alone that become useless: the coats of mail, books, clothes, and furniture all feel the bad effects of the moisture. Their houses too, suffer from not being substantially built. There is pleasant enough weather in the winter and summer, as well as in the rainy season; but then the north wind always blows, and there is an excessive quantity of earth and dust flying about. When the rains are at hand, this wind blows five or six times with excessive violence, and such a quantity of dust flies about that you cannot see one another. They call this an *āndhi* (storm or tempest). It gets warm during Taurus and Gemini, but not so warm as to become intolerable. The heat cannot be compared to the heats of Balkh and Kandahar. It is not half so warm as in these places. Another convenience of Hindustan is that the workmen of every profession and trade are innumerable and without end. For any work, or any employment, there is always a set ready, to whom the same employment and trade have descended from father to son for ages."

Bābur's difficulties were by no means at an end. His troops, who were hillmen and hated the plains, especially as the invasion had corresponded with the hot weather, began to grumble. They wanted to take what plunder they could lay land upon and return to Kābul, Bābur, however, calmed them by a statesman like address:

> "I told them that empire and conquest could not be acquired without the materials and means of war: that royalty and nobility could not exist without subjects and dependent provinces: that by the labours of many years, after undergoing great hardships, measuring many a toilsome journey and raising various armies; after exposing myself and my troops to circumstances of great the danger, to battle and bloodshed, by divine favour, I had routed my formidable enemy, and achieved the conquest of the numerous provinces and kingdoms which we at present held: 'And now, what force compels, and what hardship obliges us, without any visible cause, after having worn out our life in accomplishing the desired achievement, to abandon and fly from our conquests, and to retreat back to Kābul with every symptom of disappointment and discomfiture? Let not any one who calls himself my friend ever henceforward make such a proposal. But if there is any among you who cannot bring himself to stay, or to give up his purpose of returning back, let him depart.' Having made them this fair and reasonable proposal, the discontented were of necessity compelled, however unwillingly, to renounce their seditious purposes."

Those who wished to return were allowed to do so; the others were richly rewarded with lands and money. Bābur also adopted a conciliatory attitude to the Afghan nobles, which won many of them over. Meanwhile, he tried to make conditions of life more supportable for himself. At Agra, which he found so ugly and detestable that it filled him with disgust, he busied himself in digging wells, laying out pavilions, baths, water-courses and gardens, and planting roses and narcissi and shade and fruit trees.

Bābur was now confronted with a more formidable danger. The Rājpūts, who had been so decisively crushed by Muhammad Ghori, had been steadily regaining their power during the period of the decline of the Delhi Sultanate, despite defeats at the hands of the Kings of Gujarāt. The leader of the Hindu confederacy was Rānā Sangram Singh, the ruler of Mewar, the premier state of Rājputāna, who claimed descent from the Sun. The Rānā was an opponent of a very different stamp from Ibrāhīm Khān Lodi: he was a seasoned veteran who had defeated the Afghans in eighteen pitched battles, a 'fragment of a warrior' scarred by eighty wounds, who had lost an arm and an eye in the field and had had his leg shattered by a cannon ball. Rānā Sanga, as he was called, had expected that Bābur was a mere raider who would quickly retire over the mountains; when he found that he had come to stay, he advanced to expel the intruder, and restore Hindu rule in Delhi. The Rājpūt army consisted of 80,000 horses and 500 elephants, commanded by 120 chieftains of note.

When Bābur heart of the advance of the Rājpūt host, he took the field against it on February 11th, 1527. We do not know the exact strength of his army, but it was considerably strengthened by local contingents; new cannon had been cast, and Bābur had devised some ingeniously constructed wheeled tripods for the support of the heavy matchlocks, which greatly increased their mobility. He took up a position at Kānua, about ten miles from Sīkrī, and here he waited the approach of his opponent. As before, his front was covered by a barricade of waggons linked by iron chains, so as to break up a cavalry charge, and along this line the artillery and matchlock-men with their tripods were disposed at intervals. The rear was protected by trenches, and on the two flanks were the *tulugma* or cavalry wings, who were to deliver the decisive blow. As the mighty host approached, the little force in its entrenchments began to lose heart, and men started to desert. Bābur thereupon took a characteristic step to restore their confidence. Of late years, in defiance of the laws of the Koran, he had been a heavy drinker. Now he poured out all the wine in the camp on the ground; his gold and silver goblets were broken up and given to the poor, and he took a solemn vow never to touch wine again, if God granted him victory. Then he addressed his men in stirring words:

> " 'Noblemen and soldiers! Every man that comes into the world is subject to dissolution. When we have passed away and gone, God only survives, unchangeable. Whoever comes to the feast of life must, before it is over, drink from the cup of death. He who arrives at the inn of mortality must one day inevitably take his departure from that house of sorrow—the world. How much better is it to die with honour than to live with infamy!
>
> " 'With fame, even if I die, I am contented;
> Let fame by mine, since my body is Death's.'*
>
> " 'The Most High God has been propitious to us, and has now placed us in such a crisis, that if we fall in the field, we die the death of martyrs; if we survive, we rise victorious, the avengers of the cause of God. Let us then, with one accord, swear on God's Holy Word that none of us will even think of turning his face from this warfare, nor desert from the battle and slaughter that ensues, till his soul is separated from his body' ".

Inspired by a sudden wave of loyalty, the whole host sworn upon the Koran "not to spare themselves in sacrifice and devotion so long as the breath of life was in their bodies."

* From Firdausi's *Shāh Nāma*.

On March 16th, "when the sun was spear-high," the Rājpūts advanced to the attack. From nine o'clock till noon the battle raged with the utmost fury, but in the end, Bābur's firearms decided the day. The matchlocks on their movable tripods were quickly shifted to threatened points, and the artillery of Ustad Ali inflicted terrible losses upon the closely packed ranks of the Hindus. In the end, when the enemy had spent themselves in fruitless assaults, Bābur was able to employ his favourite enveloping tactics. He sent word to his flanking parties to wheel and charge, while at the same time he ordered his guns forward, and sent out the household troops at the gallop on each side of his matchlock men, who also advanced firing. The Rājpūts broke and fled. "They were scattered abroad like teazed wool, and broken like bubbles on wine." As usual, the unwieldy Hindu hosts had proved to be no match for their more mobile opponents, and 'the mountain-formed, demon-looking elephants' were merely a source of danger of their own side. Bābur commemorated his victory, after the fashion of his ancestors, by erecting a tower of skulls upon the battle-field.

The battle of Kānua had momentous consequences. It destroyed the last hope of the Rājpūts to restore Hindu supremacy in Northern India, and it established the Mogul dynasty upon the throne of Delhi. Bābur followed up his success by capturing the Rājpūt stronghold of Chanderi, and by defeating the Afghan rulers of Bengal on the river Gogra near Patna. But he had little time to consolidate his conquests. Worn out by a life of almost ceaseless toil and adventure, he passed away in 1530, in his favourite garden at Agra, at the ealry age of forty-seven. He was laid to rest in the distant city of Kābul, amid the mountains and meadows which he loved so well. A pathetic story is told of his last illness. His favourite son, Humāyūn, was desperately sick, and Bābur, distraugth with anxiety, asked a holy man what he could do to save him. The holy man suggested that God might receive as a sacrifice the most precious of his possessions. Thereupon Bābur walked three times round his son's bed, crying out "O God! if a life may be exchanged for a life, I, Bābur, give my life for Humāyūn." Afterwards he was heard to exclaim: "I have prevailed! I have borne it away! I have saved him!" And from that day, Humāyūn began to recover, while Bābur, soon after, slowly sickened and died.

Bābur's character is thus summed up by an old writer. "He possessed eight fundamental qualities: lofty judgment, noble ambition, the art of victory, the art of government, the art of conferring prosperity on his people, the talent of ruling mildly the people of God, ability to win the hearts of his soldiers, love of justice." Poet, artist and warrior, he was a born leader of men, never so happy as in the midst of some wild adventure or carousing with a party of boon companions in a fair garden beside a flowing stream. It would be possible to quote from his Memoirs innumerable passages to illustrate the finer traits of his character, but one must suffice. On one occasion, he and his followers were lost in deep snow in the high passes between

Herāt and Kābul. A cave was discoverd, but Bābur refused to take shelter in it. "I felt that for me to be in a warm dwelling and in comfort, while my men were in the midst of the snow and drift—for me to be within, enjoying sleep and ease, while my followers were in trouble and distress, would be inconsistent with what I owed them, and a deviation from that society of suffering that was their due. So I remained sitting in the snow and wind in the hole that I had dug out, with snow four hands thick on my head, back and ears." Small wonder that such a leader could command the unswerving devotion of his followers!

Bābur's love of beauty was as keen as his sense of humour. It is these qualities which make his Memoirs a never-failing source of pleasure to the reader. Here are some typical extracts for the year 1519:

October 14th. "Next day I went to the Garden to Fulfilment. It was the season of its beauty. Its lawns were a sheet of trefoil; its pomegranate trees were yellowed to autumn splendour; it was their season, and the fruit hung red on the trees. The orange trees were green and bright with countless oranges, but the best were not ripe. I was never to delighted as now with the Garden of Fulfilment."

Ocrober 18th. "We halted at Jagdālik. Towards evening prayer there was a drinking party; most of the household were present. Near the end, Gedai Muhammad grew very noisy and troublesome, and when he got drunk, slid down on the cushion by my side, whereupon Gedai Taghai picked him up and carried him out. Marching thence before daybreak, I explored the valley of the Barik-āb; some *turak* trees were in great beauty. We halted there, and having dined seasonably, drank wine in honour of the rich crop. We made them kill a sheep picked up on the road, had some meat dressed, and amused ourselves by kindling oak-branches."

Again and again he dwells with enthusiasm upon the mountain scenery, the flowers and fruits and buildings of his native land, while in a few deft touches he pictures for us the characters of the various members of his family. In the year before his death, amidst the heat and dust of the Indian summer, he notes, "To-day they brought me a musk-melon. As I cut it up, I felt a deep home-sickness and sense of exile from my native land, and could not forbear from weeping." As his cousin says "he excelled in music and other arts. Indeed, no one of his family before him ever possessed such talents, nor did any of his race perform such amazing exploits or experience such strange adventures."

Bābur left four sons, Humāyūn, Kamrān, Hindal and Askari: with his dying breath he nominated Humāyūn, his favourite, as his successor. Humāyūn was duly seated on the throne of Delhi, while his brother Kamrān established himself in Kābul and the Punjab. Humāyūn's reign began well. He invadcd Gujarāt, which had never submitted to Bābur, and himself led the storming party which escaladed the walls of the strong fortress of Champānīr. But in the campaign against Sher Khān, the Afghan governor of Bihār, he was less fortunate. Sher Khān surprised his camp on the banks of the Ganges in 1539, and Humāyūn was obliged on flee for his life. A hunted fugitive, he crossed the Rājputāna desert with a handful of followers, and sought refuge with the Rājā of Mārwār. But suspecting treachery, he was forced once more to fly, and after terrible privations, in which several of the party died of thirst, he at length reached Amarkot in Sind. Here he left his wife Hamida, while he himself went on to Persia to enlist the sympathy of Shāh Tamāsp of Persia. A messenger caught him up a few days later, with the news that Hamida had borne him a son (October 15th, 1542). The child was named Akbar. Humāyūn was so poor that, in place of the costly robes and jewels usually presented on such an auspicious occasion, all he could do was to break up a piece of musk which he carried and distribute it.

Shāh Tamāsp received the fugitive kindly, but made it a condition of his help that Humāyūn should become a member of the Shiah sect. Humāyūn had no choice but to accept this humiliating proposal, and with the help of his Persian allies he defeated Kamrān and captured Kābul. Kamrān and his brother were blinded and banished to Mecca. Meanwhile, an Afghan nobleman, Sher Khān of the Sūr tribe, had seated himself on the throne of Delhi, with the title of Sher Shāh. He was a just and able ruler. On being told that his beard was growing white, he replied that "it was true that he obtained the throne in the evening of his life; a circumstance which he always regretted, as it left him so short a time to be of use to his country and his people."* Sher Shāh laid the foundations of the administrative reforms of Akbar's minister, Todar Mal. "He set up courts of justice in every place, and was ever busy in founding charities. For the easement of poor travellers, he made a rest-house on every road at an interval of two leagues, and one such road with rest-houses ran from the Punjab to Sunargaon in Bengal, and others from Agra to Burhānpur and to Chitor, and from Lahore to Multān. In each rest-house were separate lodgings for Hindus and Moslems, supplied with pots of water, beds and food, and grain for the horses. In each rest-house two horses were kept for quick despatch of news. 'If my life last long enough,' he said, 'I shall build a fort in every district, to be a refuge for the oppressed and a curb to the turbulent, and make all the earthen rest-houses of brick for the safety and protection of the highway.' If a robbery occurred and the perpetrators not discovered, the Āmils (district officers) and governors were instructed to arrest the headmen of the neighbouring villages, and compel them to make good; for it is generally established that highway robberies occur only by the connivance of these headmen." The historian Firishta records that so great was the security that travellers and merchants lay down to sleep without apprehension of robbery. Hindustan was divided into 47 districts, and the land revenue carefully assessed. To prevent extortion, governors of provinces were changed every two years. Sher Shāh punished

* Elliot and Dowson, IV, 409 ff.

oppression ruthlessly, not even sparing his own kith and kin. A new coinage was introduced, the rupee being fixed at 178 grains.

Unfortunately, this wise and able ruler was killed by an explosion of a powder magazine in 1545. He lies beneath a stately mausoleum at Sahasrām in Bihār. His successors, Istam Shāh (1545-1554) and Muhammad Ādil Shāh (1554-1555) were worthless rulers, and the real power was in the hands of a low-born Hindu minister named Hemu. In 1555, Humāyūn returned with his Persian allies. Humāyūn recovered Delhi, only to die, in the following year, as the result of a fall on the marble stairs of his palace. He was a man of great natural talents, a dignified, stately sovereign, brave in battle, gay in feast and very generous. As a youth he had shown great promise as a soldier, but he was addicted to the family failing of drug-taking. This, perhaps, accounts for the instability and weakness of character of his later years, and was the chief cause of the disasters which dogged the footsteps of this unlucky ruler.

Note on the Word Mogul

Bābur, was, as is stated above, a Barlas Turk. He cordially disliked the Moguls, who were responsible for his expulsion from his ancestral home. Mogul is, of course, the same word as Mongol, and is properly only used to denote the narrow-eyed, pagan hordes of Chingiz Khān. But the word Mogul (Portuguese Mogor) was applied loosely in India to all foreign Muhammadans from Central Asia, and so, by the irony of history, the Emperors of Delhi of the House of Timūr came to be known to Europeans by the little of 'The Great Mogul,' as the Sultan of Turkey was called 'The Greak Turk' and the Safavi Shāh of Persia 'The Sophy.'

LEADING DATES

A.D.	1524	Bābur's invasion of India.
	1526	First battle of Pānipat. Bābur Emperor of Delhi.
	1527	Defeat of the Rājpūts at Kānua.
	1530	Death of Bābur and accession of Humāyūn.
	1540	Defeat of Humāyūn at Kanauj.
	1542	Accession of Sher Shāh.
	1545	Death of Sher Shāh.
	1555	Restoration of Humāyūn.
	1556	Death of Humāyūn.

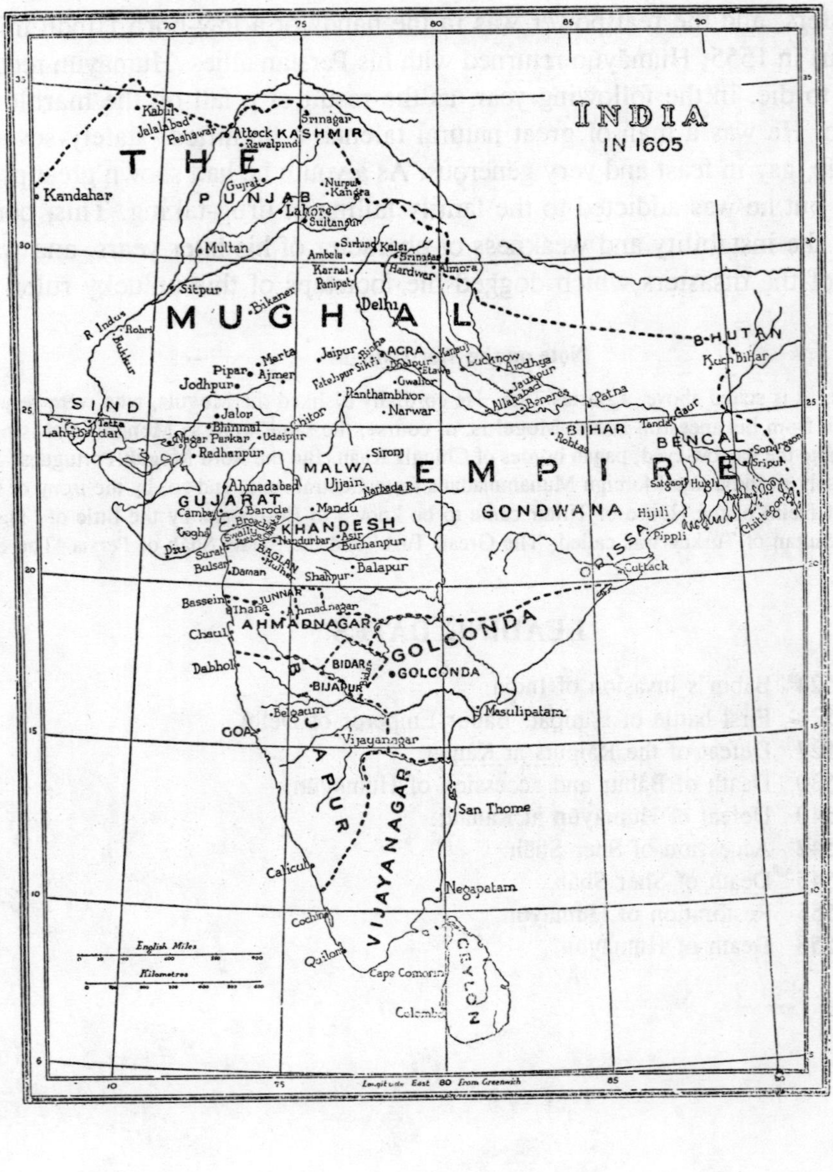

Map 11 : India in 1605.

Chapter XVIII

Akbar Pādshāh

At the time when the unlucky Humāyūn came by his death, Akbar, a boy of thirteen, was nominally Governor of the Punjab, though the real power lay in the hands of his guardian, Bairām Khān, a Persian of the Shiah sect, and one of his father's most devoted followers. When the news arrived, Akbar was hastily enthroned at a place called Kalānaur in the Gurdāspur district; the brick platform on which the simple ceremony took place is still preserved. Meanwhile, in the capital, Hemu, the minister of the Sur family, was making a bid for restoring Hindu supremacy. He proclaimed himself Emperor with the title of Rājā Vikramāditya, and by bribing the Afghan nobles managed to collect a formidable following. Bairām Khān and his young protégé advanced to expel the usurper, and the two armies met on the historic field of Pānipat. Hemu's troops attacked with much gallantry, and would probably have been successful had not their commander fallen from his elephant, pierced through the eyeball by an arrow. As was usual in eastern battles, the fall of the leader was the signal for a general panic, and the Delhi troops broke and fled. The dying Hindu was dragged into Akbar's presence and despatched. According to one story, Bairām Khān wished Akbar to flesh his sword upon his opponent, but the young Prince indignantly refused to do so. Following up his victory, Bairām Khān occupied Agra and Delhi, and the princes of Sher Shāh's family were allowed to retire to their estates. Gwalior and Ājmīr were taken, and Akbar was firmly established on his throne. The young prince, however, now found himself little more than a puppet in the hands of an intriguing Court. There were two factions, one led by the Regent, Bairām Khān, and the other by Akbar's foster-mother Māham Anaga, and her son Adham Khān. Akbar determined to rid himself of both. In 1560 he announced that he would take the reins of Government into his own hands, and the Regent received a polite hint to go upon a pilgrimage to Mecca. After an attempt at resistance, Bairām Khān bowed to the inevitable and started off. He never reached his destination; on the way he was assassinated by a man who owed him a private grudge.

For the time being Akbar seemed to have profited little by the change. The power was now entirely in the hands of Māham Anaga and Adham Khān. In 1560 Adham

Khān invaded the fertile kingdom of Mālwā, and laid siege to its capital, the fortress of Māndu. Māndu is a singularly lovely spot, and is adorned with buildings of rare beauty. Its ruler, Bāz Bahādur, was the son of one of Sher Shāh's generals, and his romantic love for his beautiful consort Rūpmatī has been often celebrated by painter and poet. Adham Khān advanced through Mālwā with fire and sword, leaving a trail of misery behind him. Bāz Bahādur fled at the approach of the Mogul forces, but when the conqueror entered the harem to take possession of the most coveted prize of all, he found Rūpmati lying dead with the maids around her; she had poisoned herself rather than submit to his embraces. Mālwā now became a Mogul province, but Adham Khān behaved with great insolence on his return: he attempted to annex the bulk of the spoils for his private use, and only surrendered them with very bad grace. The climax came two years later when Akbar appointed a trusted servant, Shams-ud-dīn, as Prime Minister. Adham Khān with a party of ruffianly followers forced his way into the palace and proceeded to stab Shams-ud-dīn to death. Akbar, hearing the noise, rushed out and felled Adham Khān to the earth with a blow from his fist. He then ordered the attendants to pick up the unconscious man and hurl him over the battlements. Māham Anaga was so shcoked at the news of her son's death that she turned her face to the wall and died. The rest of the petticoat faction were banished from the court, and Akbar was king at last, at the age of twenty.

Akbar as a boy had shown little inclination for study. He was the despair of his tutors. His could never be persuaded to learn to read and could barely sign his name. But neither writing nor reading were looked upon as indispensable to culture in the East; he had a prodigious memory, and would listen for hours while others read to him. He was endowed with the keen sense of beauty which distinguished all his family, and loved flowers and gardens, buildings, pictures and music. He had an intensely enquiring mind, and was deeply interested in religion and philosophy on the one hand and in science and mechanics on the other. He was immensely strong, tireless, and utterly fearless. He could ride or march all day in the hottest sun; he could stun a man with his fist, and kill a tiger with a blow of his sword; he revelled in the joy of battle, and would mount horses that no one else dared to ride. He played polo in the dark with an ignited ball of his own invention. He would tame elephants that had run wild and killed their keepers. On the other hand, his mind was filled with a ceaseless desire to find the Truth, which haunted him throughout his life. His favourite poets were the Sūfi mystics, and in 1557, at the age of fourteen, he had a singular spiritual crisis. He mounted his horse and rode away into the desert, where he remained for many hours in solitary meditation. It is possible that even at this early age he experienced the religious ecstasy which Sūfis induce by the constant repetition of the Divine Name. These incidents appear to have been recurrent. At the age of twenty, he tells us, "I experienced as internal bitterness, and from lack of spiritual provision for my last journey, my soul was seized with exceeding sorrow."

Such was the complex character of the young prince who, having rid himself of various evil influences, emerged from 'behind the veil' in 1562 to find himself in charge of the destinies of an Empire. Akbar's originality of character soon asserted itself. Former rulers, with few exceptions, had been solicitous of the interests of their Muhammadan subjects only. Akbar had a wider vision. He would unite all, Muslim and Hindu alike, without distinction under the aegis of the Crown. One of his first steps towards the consummation of this plan was his marriage, in the same year, to the daughter of the Rājpūt chief, Rājā Bihār Māl of Āmber, Rājā Bihār Māl, together with his son, Mān Singh, and his nephew, Bhagwān Dās, were enrolled as nobles in the Mogul court and given high commands; Akbar had begun his policy of winning over his most dangerous opponents of his side. At the same time the *jizya,* or poll-tax on non-Muslims, and the pilgrim-tax, both of which were deeply resented by Hindus as badges of servitude, were remitted at considerable loss to the Treasury.

A vivid picture of Akbar's daily life when in residence at the Court has been preserved for us. Aroused at dawn by the playing of musical instruments, he devoted the earliest hours of the day to religious meditation. He then showed himself to the assembled people at the audience-window while the multitude came and prostrated themselves; the women brought their sick infants for the royal benediction and offered presents on their recovery. Next he went to the Hall of Public Audience. Here was held a levée, which was attended by members of the Royal Family and great Officers of State, and petitioners with grievances had ready access to the Royal Person. The Emperor impressed everyone by his accessibility and his kindly and affable manner. Affairs of State occupied most of the forenoon, and then Akbar retired to his apartments for the heat of the day. Here he partook of the single meal which was all that he ate; the food was of the simplest, for the Emperor was frugal to the point of asceticism in his private life, and in his later years he was almost a vegetarian. It was not right, he said, to make one's stomach the grave of animals. The afternoon was spent in inspecting the household troops and the stables; immense numbers of horses and elephants were kept, and if any of the animals were in poor condition, their grooms were punished. Akbar would then superintend any building operations which were in progress, or would visit the Imperial Arms Factory, in which he took a special interest. The Emperor was of a mechanical turn of mind. He had invented several ingenious devices, and had made a number of improvements in casting gun barrels which greatly increased their range and accuracy. After the business of the day was finished, there were recreations, such as polo, fights between animals in the open space outside the walls, and games of backgammon (*pachīsi*) played with living pieces in the presence of the Court; the ladies at the harem looked on from behind their marble lattices. After dark, the Emperor listened to musicians, readers or story-tellers, or initiated religious or philosophical discussions which lasted far into the night. One of Akbar's characteristics was his power to dispense with sleep.

But in the earlier years of his reign, Akbar had little leisure. He tells us that he was compelled to abstain from philosophical discussions, "lest the necessary duties of the hour should be neglected." Until his Empire was reduced to a state of submission, no scheme of organised government could be introduced. The opposition came from two quarters, Muslim and Hindu. The earlier Mussalman aristocracy looked upon the Moguls as intruders, and many of them disliked Akbar's unorthodox "Persianised ways" and his liberal treatment of the Hindus. A rebellion of the disaffected Uzbeg nobles, headed by Ali Kuli Khān, the Governor of Jaunpur, was crushed with merciless severity after a battle which took place near Allahābād in 1567. Akbar now turned his attention to the Hindus; already in 1564, the fertile Hindu kingdom of Gondwāna had been annexed by his general Āsaf Khān. The beautiful and gallant Rānī Durgavātī, who led her troops to battle in person, stabbed herself to death, and Chauragarh, her capital, was taken. A far more formidable task now awaited him. Many of the Rājpūt chiefs had refused to respond to Akbar's attempt to win them over, and had deeply resented the action of Rājā Bihār Māl of Āmber in giving his daughter in marriage to a foreigner. The centre of resistance was Chitor, the capital of the Rānās of Mewar, the leading Rājpūt clan. Rānā Sanga of Mewar had been Bābur's opponent at Pānipat. Udai Singh, the present ruler, had given shelter to the fugitive Bāz Bahādur, and refused to present himself at Court. In 1567, Akbar determined to strike terror into Rājputāna by the capture of its leading fortress. The task was no light one. The first reconnaissance of the position was a failure, as the rains were so heavy that it was shrouded in mist, but when he again approached it in October he saw the great fort, crowning a hill which rose sheer out of the level plain, surrounded by battlements whose circumference was nearly eight miles. It was well supplied with water and provisions. Akbar's artillery made no impression on the walls, and an attempt to blow up a bastion by means of mines proved unsuccessful. Many of the storming party were overwhelmed in the explosion, and the remainder were driven back with loss. Akbar now constructed penthouses which overlooked the walls and enabled their occupants to fire upon the garrison from above, and it was from one of these that the Emperor himself, by a lucky shot, picked off Jaimāl, the "valiant unbeliever" who had been the heart and soul of the defence. Then the garrison lost heart. Smoke began to appear, rolling in dense clouds over the fortress, and the Moguls knew that the site of Jauhār and begun.

"The flames of the Jauhār and the lull in the fighting showed the besiegers that the garrison was in extremities, and they began to enter the fort in parties. Some of the boldest of the garrison who had no families to burn stood to their posts ready to sell their lives in defence. From the top of the panthouse the Emperor watched the combats, and ordered three elephants to be ridden into the town. One of them killed many of the enemy and though often wounded never turned tail; another was surrounded and killed with spears and swords. In the last watch of the night the besiegers forced their way into the fortress and fell to slaughter and pillage. At early dawn the Emperor rode in on an elephant, attended on foot by his nobles and chiefs. A general massacre was ordered. There were at least eight thousand fighting Rājpūts in the fort. Some took their stand in the temple and fought to the last. In every street and lane and bazaar there was desperate fighting. Now and again a band of Rājpūts, throwing away hope of life, rushed from the temple and were despatched in detail. By mid-day some two thousand were slain. Those who escaped were made prisoners and their property confiscated."

Akbar departed from his usual clemency to the fallen after the capture of Chitor, and 30,000 of the inhabitants, regardless of age or sex, were barbarously put to the sword. Apparently he thought it necessary to make an example. The town was ruthlessly plundered. The great drum which stood outside the palace door and summoned the clansmen to battle, the candelabra from the shrine of the Goddess and other spoils were carried off to Agra, and Chitor became a ruin, haunted only by the wild beasts. "From that day," says the historian of the Rājpūts, "Chitor has been held accursed; no successor of Udai Singh has entered it, and 'thesin of the slaughter of Chitor,' like the 'curse of Cromwell,' has become proverbial." But Mewar never submitted. A handful of suvivors escaped to the fortress of the Aravalli hills, where their heroic leader Pratāp Singh "single-handed for a quarter of a century withstood the combined efforts of the Empire, at one time carrying destruction into the plans.... at another fleeing from rock to rock, feeding his family from the fruits of his native hills, and rearing the nursling their Amar amidst savage beasts and scarcely less savage men, a fit heir to his prowess and revenge."* In 1576 he was defeated by the Imperial troops under Mān Singh, but made good his escape. He died in 1597, leaving his son Amar Singh to carry on the implacable struggle. After the fall of Chitor, Akbar proceeded to reduce the two great remaining strongholds of Ranthambor and Kalinjār. It is said that he entered Ranthambor disguised as a mace-bearer in Rājā Mān Singh's retinue. Sarjan Singh, and Bundi chief, who commanded the fortress, recognised his royal visitor, and almost instinctively seated him on the throne. Sarjan Singh agreed to surrender to condition that the Bundi rājās should never be called upon to give their daughters to the royal harem, that they should have the privilege of entering the Hall of Audience fully armed and not prostrate themselves before the Emperor, that their temples should be respected, that they should not be compelled to forfeit caste by serving beyond the Indus, that they should

* Tod, *Rājasthān* (1914 edn.) I, 265. The story of the siege of Chitor is related in Chapter X of the same work.

be exempted from humiliating impositions such as the payment of the poll-tax and having their chargers branded by the state, and that their historic capital should never be changed. In 1670 Akbar further cemented his ties with the Rājpūts by marrying princesses from the families of Bikanīr and Jaisalmīr. By this consummate stroke of policy, he converted the Rājpūts, hitherto the bulwark of opposition to Muslim rule, into his staunchest supporters; they were secured in their privileges and given a place at Court on an equal footing with the Muhammadan nobles, with prospects of an official career and honourable military service under the Crown.

After the campaign in Rājputāna, Akbar had a short breathing space to devote to domestic affairs. He had been deeply distressed by the fact that both of his children had died in infancy, and at the end of 1568 had gone to consult a hermit, Shaikh Salīm, who dwelt in a rocky cell near the tomb of the celebrated saint, Muinud-dīn of Chisht, at the village of Sīkrī, about 25 miles from Agra. The Emperor's prayers were abundantly answered. His Rājpūt wife bore him a son, Salīm, named after the saint, in August, 1569. Another son, Murād, was born in June, 1570, and a third, Daniyāl, in September 1572, both of different mothers. Akbar was convinced by this that Sīkrī was an auspicious spot, and he determined to take up his residence there. He built a noble mosque and tomb for the saint, and gradually surrounded it with buildings, public and private, for himself and his court. Akbar worked with his usual volcanic energy at this new scheme under his personal direction. Palaces, halls of audience, gardens and baths, sprang up as if by magic. A great lake six miles long provided the water, and the city was surrounded by a battlemented wall of red sandstone.

Akbar could never remain inactive for very long. As soon as the building of this new city was well in hand, his restless mind turned to fresh schemes of conquest. One of his "happy sayings" recorded by his faithful servant, Abul Fazl, is to the effect that a monarch should "ever be intent on conquest, otherwise his enemies rise in arms against him." To the west lay the fertile province of Gujarāt, a tempting prey owing to internal dissensions, and particularly valuable because it would give him a much-needed access to the sea. It had originally been part of the Sultanate of Delhi, and had been annexed for a short time by Humāyūn. Akbar set out for Gujarāt in July 1572. He occupied Ahmadābād without difficulty and the Sultan Muzaffar Shāh surrendered to him. He then marched southwards to Cambay, where he saw the sea for the first time, and encountered the Portuguese, the hereditary enemies of the Sultans of Gujarāt, and was greatly impressed by their ships and merchandise, their artillery, and their religious observances. He concluded an agreement with the Portuguese commander, whereby the pilgrim ships going to Mecca should not be molested. He then proceeded to lay siege to the fortified town of Surat at the north of the Tapti and captured it in due course. The commandant, who had formerly been in the service of Humāyūn, had his tongue torn out. Among Akbar's opponents in Gujarāt were his cousins, the Mirzas, who raised a considerable force to contest his intrusion into what they considered to be their domains. In an encounter with these troops, Akbar, who had rashly ridden ahead of his troops with his personal staff, was attacked in a narrow lane, and had to cut his way out in a hand to hand encounter.

Akbar returned to Sīkrī in 1573 and had resumed the interrupted work of building and adorning his new capital when news arrived that Gujarāt was in rebellion, and the Governor whom he had left in Ahmadābād was being besieged. It was August; the rivers were in flood, and the Mirzas had thought that no one could cross the deadly Rājputāna Desert, the 'Abode of Death', at the height of the hot season. But they had reckoned without their host. Akbar, with 3,000 picked cavalrymen, at once set out, and performed the almost incredible feat of covering the whole distance, nearly 600 miles, in eleven days. The first tidings which the rebels had of his approach was the sound of his trumpets, blown to reassure the beleaguered force. Before they had recovered, Akbar charged them furisouly at the head of his men and completely routed them. It is said that the enemy were so panic-stricken that the Moguls plucked the arrows out of their quivers on their backs as they fled, and used them against their owners. Fortythree days from his departure, Akbar re-entered Sīkrī in triumph, after the most brilliant of his campaigns. In honour of it he named the new city Fathpur Sīkrī, or Sīkrī the City of Victory, and erected that magnificent triumphal arch, the Buland Darawāzā, or Lofty Portal. In 1601, after the conquest of the Deccan, he adorned it with its famous inscription:

> Jesus, Son of Mary (on whom be peace) said: *The World is a bridge: pass over it, but build no house upon it.* Who hopes for an hour, hopes for Eternity. The world is an hour: spend it in prayer, for what follows is unseen.*

In 1574 Akbar completed the conquest of Northern India by the annexation of Bengal. The young Afghan ruler, Dāud by name, refused to acknowledge the Mogul Emperor as his suzerain; but Akbar moved to Bengal by river in the height of the rainy season, when fighting was generally at a standstill. Dāud was taken completely by surprise: the important town of Patna was captured, and in 1576 he was defeated and killed.

The year 1576 was the turning point in Akbar's life. He was now thirty-four, and the master of the whole of northern India from the Indus to the mouth of the Ganges, and from the Himālayas to the Vindhya mountains. His campaigning days were behind him; henceforth he devoted himself to the government of his dominions, leaving the comman of his armies to his generals. His first object was the organisation

* It is not known why Akbar attributes this saying to Jesus, but he was strongly influenced by Christianity at this time. It has been traced to old Muslim sources, and occurs on a ryal tomb at Burhānpur in Khāndesh.

of the vast empire which he had so amazingly acquired. The system introduced by Akbar, and elaborated with the help of his able Hindu Minister, Rājā Todar Mal, was bureaucratic. At the head of the State was the Emperor, who ruled by Divine Right, and was only morally bound by the precepts of the Koran. He was assisted by the Vakīl or Prime Minister, the Diwān or Finance Minister, the Bakshi or Paymaster and the Sadr, who controlled religious and ecclesiastical affairs. The Empire was divided into twelve Subas or Provinces, later increased to fifteen, each of which was ruled by a great noble or member of the Royal Family, the Subadar or Governor, who maintained a court at his provincial capital, modelled on the Imperial Court at Agra or Delhi. Each Suba was divided into districts, and the districts again into smaller units for administrative purposes. The executive officials were known as Mansabdars or Commanders, and were classified upon a military scale, according to the number of horsemen that they were supposed to provide for the use of the government. At one end were the commanders of 10,000, at the other commanders of ten. About seventy per cent of Akbar's officials were foreigners, that is, members of families who had originally accompanied Bābur or Humāyūn from beyond the border; the remainder were Hindus or Indian Muhammadans. During the whole of his reign, twenty-one Hindus held Mansabs of 5,000 and over, the thirty-seven lower appointments. Most of these were Rājpūts. Akbar discouraged the granting of jāgīrs of fiefs to officers by way of payment, at this weekened the central authority and made the holders too independent; it also led to corruption and oppression. Higher officials received their salaries from the Imperial Treasury every month and were highly paid, but a mansabdar had to provide out of his salary the number of horsemen required by government, and strenuous efforts were made, by means of muster rolls and branding of horses, a prevent evasions of this obligation. Even then a 'commander of 1,000' drew 5,000 rupees a month. The purchasing power of money being about six times what it is to-day, this is roughly the equivalent of thrice the salary of a Lieutenant-Governor under British rule. It is small wonder that these magnificent prizes drew to the Imperial Court the ablest and most ambitious men from all over Asia. All the higher appointments were made by the Emperor himself.*

In the villages the headman was responsible for the maintenance of Law and Order; in cities this devolved upon an officer named the Kotwal, who had to undertake the most multifarious duties, such as the water supply, sanitation and lighting of the town. the maintenance of roads, the supervision of the markets, the arrest of thieves and the recovery of stolen property. In country districts, an official named the Faujdar was in charge of the policing of the highways and the protection of travellers from robbers. Criminal cases, such as dacoity, murder and rebellion were tried by the executive officers. Torture could be employed to extract evidence, and, as in

* W. H. Moreland, *India at the Death of Akbar* (1923), Chapter III.

contemporary Europe, punishments were summary and barbarous and designed to inflict terror on evil doers. They included impalement, dragging to death at the feet of elephants and amputation of limbs. Civil cases were decided by the Kāzi, who was the repository of Muhammadan Law; there was no written code. Akbar was anxious that all should receive justice. "If I were guilty of an unjust act," he said, "I would rise up in judgment against myself," but it is doubtful whether the central government had any effective control over what happened in distant provinces, and the corruptness of the Kāzi was proverbial. All persons, however, had the right of personal appeal, irrespective of rank, to the Emperor himself. The system of revenue collection was organised by Todar Mal upon the lines laid down by Sher Shāh. In India the bulk of the revenue has always come from the soil. Akbar claimed as 'the King's Share' one third of the average annual yield over a period of ten years. The historian Badaoni, describing the new systems, tells us: "In the year 982 (A.D. 1575) an order was promulgated for improving the cultivation of the country and the condition of the peasants. All the parganas (districts) were to be measured, and every space of land which under cultivation would produce a crore of tankas (250,000 rupees) was to be divied off and placed under an officer called the Krori, selected for his trutworthiness, so that in three years all uncultivated land might be brought into cultivation and the Treasury replenished."

Badaoni, who, as an orthodox Mussalman of the old school, had no sympathy with these new-fangled ideas for the protection of the peasant from his masters, complains, rather comically, that dishonest officials were brought to account by Rājā Todar Mal, "and many a good man died from severe beatings and the torture of rack and pincers." Other sources of revenue were the salt-tax, excise and customs dues, and the total amount raised annually has been estimated as equivalent to about 38 millions sterling. Much of it was expended upon the Imperial Court, with its enormous retinue which followed the Emperor wherever he went, the salaries of the nobles, the sumptuous buildings erected at the capitals and the army. There was a small but prosperous middle class composed of officials and merchants, the latter residing chiefly in the ports on the West Coast which were beginning to drive a lucrative trade with the European nations. Artists and skilled artisans found ready employment; unskilled labour, on the other hand, was poorly paid, and much of the menial work was performed by slaves. The majority of the people lived, as they do now, in the innumerable villages scattered over the face of the land; the standard of living was low and their wants were few. They were no doubt happier and more contented under Akbar than at any time since the Muhammadan conquest. Amongst the many improvements introduced by Akbar was an excellent system of coinage, which for purity of metal, fullness of weight and artistic workmanship excelled anything in the West. It is probably no exaggeration to say that the Mogul Empire at the beginning of the 17th century was the best organised and most prosperous in the world.

In May 1578 Akbar had another of those strange spiritual crises which had first come to him as a boy of fourteen in the Punjab. A Royal Hunt had been organised at Nandāna, on the banks of the Jhelum river. These battues were carried out on an enormous scale; the army turned out to act as beaters, and the birds and beasts within a circumference of fifty miles were enclosed in an ever contracting ring, to be slaughtered by the members of the Court. Akbar was sitting under a tree waiting for the driven game, when suddenly a "strange and strong frenzy came upon the Emperor." He gave orders for the hunt to be discontinued forthwith; "not the feather of a finch was to be touched." After his return to Fathpur Sikri he appeared to be a changed man, and began to ponder deeply upon religious matters. "He spent whole nights meditating upon God and modes of addressing Him. Reverence for the Great Giver filled his heart, and in gratitude he would sit many a morning alone in prayer and mortification upon the stone bench of an old cell in a lonely spot near the palace." He sought the company of Shaikh Mubārak, a learned theologian of extremely unorthodox views who had been at various times a Sunni, a Shiah, a Mahdist (one who believes in the approach of the millennium) and a Sūfi. The Shaikh's two sons, Abul Fazl and Faizi, were his constant associates. The former, 'the King's Jonathan,' to use the picturesque phrase of the Jesuits, became his confidential secretary and adviser; according to orthodox Muhammadans these two led the King's mind from God and His Prophet. Abul Fazl was the most learned man of his age and the author of that vast encyclopedic work, the *Ain-i-Akbari* or Institutes of Akbar, which took seven years to compile and is our chief authority for the events of the reign and the organisation of the Empire. To assist him in his quest for the truth, Akbar arranged every Thursday a series of religious debates, which were held in the Ibādat Khāna or Hall of Worship, specialy built for the purpose, and often lasted till dawn. At first these were confined to Muslim theologians, but their narrow bigotry disgusted the Emperor, and he began to invite outsiders, Brahmins, Jains and Zoroastrians. "From early childhood," says Abul Fazl, "he had passed through the most diverse phases of religious practices and beliefs and had collected with a peculiar talent in selection all books that can teach, and thus there gradually grew in his mind the conviction that there were sensible men in all religions, and austere thinkers and men with miraculous gifts in all nations. If some truth were thus found everywhere, why should Truth be restricted to one religion or to a comparatively new creed like Islam, scarcely a thousand years old?" Akbar's beliefs at this stage are finely expressed in a verse written by Abul Fazl:

> O God, in every temple I see those who seek Thee.
> And in every tongue that is spoken, Thou art praised.
> Polytheism and Islam grope after Thee.
> Each religion says, 'Thou art One, without equal'.
> Be in mosque, men murmur holy prayers; or church,

The bells ring for the love of Thee.
Awhile I frequent the Christian cloister, anon the mosque,
But Thee only I seek from fane to fane.
Thine elect know naught of heresy or orthodoxy, whereof
Neither stands behind the screen of Thy truth.
Heresy to the heretic; dogma to the orthodox;
But the dust of the rose-petal belongs to the heart of the perfume-seller.*

Akbar was doubtless prompted by a mixture of motives, religious and political. Besides his impatience at the narrowness of orthodox Muhammadanism there was a desire to find a formula which would satisfy men of all various creeds in his Empire and bring them together. As he said himself, "Although I am master of so vast a kingdom, yet, since true greatness consists in doing the will of God, my mind is not at ease in this diversity of sects and creeds, and apart from the outward pomp of circumstance, with what satisfaction in my despondency can I undertake the sway of Empire?" His contemporary, Elizabeth of England, was making a somewhat similar effort. In 1579, in order to invest himself with the power to make religious reforms, he compelled the theologians to subscribe to an Infallibility Decree which he drew up with the assistance of Shaikh Mubārak. It ran as follows :

"We declare that the King of Islām, Amīr of the Faithful, Shadow of God in the World—Abul-fath Jalāl-ud-dīn Muhammad Akbar Pādshāh Ghāzi—whose Kingdom God perpetuate!—is a most just, a most wise, and a most god-fearing king. Should, therefore, in future, a religious question come up, regarding which the opinions of the *mujtahids* (theologians) are at variance, and His Majesty, in his penetrating understanding and clear vision, be inclined to adopt, for the benefit of the nation, and as a political expedient, any of the conflicting opinions existing on that point, and issue a decree to that effect, we do thereby agree that such decree shall be binding on us and on the whole nation. Further, we declare that should His Majesty think fit to issue a new order, we and the nation shall likewise be bound by it, provided that such order be not only in accordance with some verse of the Koran, but also of real benefit to the nation; and further that any opposition on the part of his subjects to such an order passed by His Majesty shall involve damnation in the world to come, and loss of property and religious privileges in this."

In June of the same year, in his new capacity of Head of the Church, he ascended the pulpit of the Mosque at Sīkrī, and recited the Bidding Prayer composed for him by the poet Faizi:

The Lord to me the Kingdom grave;

* That is, we should extract the essence from all creeds, as the perfume-seller extracts the essence from the rose.

He made me prudent, strong and brave;
He guided me with right and ruth,
Filling my heart with love of truth.
No tongue of man can sum His State,
Allahu Akbar! God is great!

It is said that he was so overcome by emotion that he was unable to finish the words. As time went on, Akbar became more and more hostile or orthodox Muhammadanism. He stopped the use of the name of the Prophet in public worship, and began to adopt Parsee and Hindu religious customs. He ordered Sanskrit religious books to be translated into Persian, and appeared with a Hindu sectarian mark on his forehead. He prostrated himself before the Sun and the Sacred Fire. He forbade the slaughter of animals for food, and proclaimed universal toleration in a country where the persecution of Hinduism had been the rule for centuries. His own words were: "Men fancy that outward profession to the mere letter of Islam, without a heartfelt conviction, can profit them. I have forced many Hindus by fear of my power to adopt the religion of my ancestors, but now that my mind has been enlightened by the beams of Truth, I have become convinced that in this distressful place of contrarieties where the dark clouds of conceit and the mists of self-opinion have gathered round you, not a step can be made without the torch of proof. That belief can only be beneficial which we select with clear judgment. To repeat the words of the Creed, to perform circumcision, or to lie prostrate on the ground from dread of kingly power is not seeking God:

Obedience is not in prostration on the dust;
Practice Truth, for sincerity is not borne on the brow."

Akbar, however, was still unsatisfied. He had no more than one occasion come into contact with Christian, and he wondered whether he would not find in Christianity the ideal religion for which he sought. He therefore despatched an envoy to the Viceroy of Goa, requesting him to send to the Court "two learned priests who should bring with them the chief books of the Law and the Gospel, for I wish to study and learn the law and what is best and most perfect in it."* In response to this invitation three Jesuit Fathers, Ridolfo Aquaviva, Anthony Monserrate and Francis Henrique went to Sīkrī. The latter was a Persian convert and acted as interpreter. After a long and arduous journey, the mission reached Fathpur Sīkrī at the end of February 1580 and was kindly received. The Fathers made an excellent impression. They were learned and pious men, and shone in the religious debates which the Emperor so greatly enjoyed. Abul Fazl gives a graphic description of one of these debates which ended in the complete dicomfiture of the mullahs :

* Sir E. Maclagan, *The Jesuits and the Great Mogul* (1932).

"One night the Hall of Worship was brightened by the presence of Padre Ridolfo, unrivalled among Christian doctors for intellect and wisdom. Several carping and bigoted men attacked him, and this afforded an opportunity for display of the calm judgement and justice of the assembly. These men brought forward the old received assertions and did not attempt to arrive at the truth by reasoning. Their statements were torn to pieces and they were nearly put to shame; and then they began to attack the contradictions in the Gospel, but they could not silence their opponent by proving their assertions. With perfect calmness and earnest conviction, the Padre replied to their arguments, and then said: 'If these men have such an opinion of our Book, and if they believe the Koran to be the true Word of God, then let a fire be lighted and let us with the Gospel in our hand, and the *ulama* with their Holy Book in theirs, walk into that testing-place of Truth, and the right will be manifest.' The black-hearted, mean-spirited disputants shrank from this proposal, and answered only with angry words."

For a time the efforts of the Fathers to convert the Emperor and his court seemed about to be crowned with success. The Padres were allowed to build a chapel; they translated the Gospel into Persian, and Akbar attended Mass, and was even disappointed that he was not given Communion. He wore a medallion bearing effigies of the Virgin and the Angus Dei, and visited the Crib erected at Christmas. He walked in public with his arm round Father Ridolfo's neck, and appointed Father Monserrate as Prince Murād's turor. But Akbar gradually lost interest in this, as in his other religious experiments. He had the profoundest admiration for the teaching and person of Jesus Christ ('He had the Spirit of God, and neither man nor Angel spoke as He spake'), but he found in the doctrines of the Trinity and Incarnation insurmountable stumbling-blocks, and for political reasons he refused even to entertain the idea of disbanding his harem. Reluctantly the Fathers came to the conclusion that "the Emperor is not a Muhammadan, but is doubtful as to all forms of faith and holds firmly that there is no divinely accredited form of faith, because he finds in all something to offend his reason and intelligence, for he thinks everything can be grasped by reason."

Akbar's heretical views, and the favour shown to the "Padres," aroused wide-spread alarm in Muhammadan circles. A dangerous rebellion broke out in Bengal in 1581, and a movement was afoot to call in from Kābul Muhammad Hakīm, another son of Humāyūn, who held strictly orthodox views. Akbar suppressed the trouble in Bengal with great severity, and publicly hanged one of his Ministers, Shāh Mansur, for complicity in the conspiracy. He then led an expedition to Kābul. Father Monserrate accompanied him, and gives a vivid picture of the Imperial Army in the field. It was like a moving town; an immense number of followers and attendants accompanied it, and wherever a halt was made, the camp was laid out in an orderly fashion, the Imperial Headquarters being marked by a light on a lofty pole at night. There were bazaars in which food and other commodities could be purchased at fixed rates, and hunts on a large scale took place on the line of march. The expedition reached Kābul by way of Lahore and the Khyber, and returned to Sīkrī after a bloodless campaign. On the way Father Monserrate had many religious conversations with Akbar, as the result of which the Fathers finally decided that further efforts were useless, and they returned to Goa in 1582. Akbar parted with them with real grief. They never met again. Father Aquaviva received the crown of martyrdom at the hands of a Hindu mob in 1583; Father Monserrate was captured by the Arabs and sent to the galleys but survived to die at Goa in 1600. Other Jesuit missions visited the Court in this and the succeeding reign, but more in the capacity of informal ambassadors, and were a regular feature until the expulsion of the Order from Portuguese territory in 1759. But under Shāh Jahān and Aurangzeb their privileges were greatly curtailed; the latter ruler looked on them with suspicion owing to their friendliness with the rebel, Dārā Shikoh.

After the departure of the first Jesuit mission, Akbar proceeded to promulgate a new creed of his own, which he termed the Divine Faith (Dīn Ilāhi). Its inauguration was marked by the commencement of a new era.* The details are obscure, but it is described by Abul Fazl as an eclectic creed, 'with the great advantage of not losing what is good in one religion while gaining whatever is better in the other. In that way honour would be rendered to God; peace would be given to the peoples and security to the Empire.' Its observances were to a great extent borrowed from the Jains and Hindus. Cows were to be regarded as sacred, and worship was paid to the Sun. There appears to have been an inner circle of disciples at the Court, who prostrated themselves before Akbar as their Pontiff, received a secret pass-word, abstained from meat, shaved their beards, and practised other mystic observances. The Divine Faith, however, made few converts, and dissolved at the death of its founder.

In 1585, there arrived at Fathpur, almost unnoticed, three Englishmen named William Leedes, Ralph Fitch and John Newbery, bearing a letter from Queen Elizabeth, in which she requested that they might be 'honestly intreated and received,' and granted 'liberty and security of voyage,' in order to start trading opertions 'by which means the mutual and friendly trafique of merchandise on both sides may come.' They were the survivors of a party of four which had set out for the East on the ship *Tyger* two years previously. Disembarking at Tripolis, they had made their way to Aleppo: had there joined a caravan which took them to Bagdad. From Bagdad they went on to Ormuz, where they were arrested and sent to Goa as suspected

* The date of the commencement of the *Ilāhī era* is February 19th, 1556. It was discontinued by Shāh Jahān.

heretics. They escaped the attention of the Inquisition by 'behaving themselves very catholikly and devout, everic day hearing Mass with beades in their hands,' but they were put on parole. One of their number married and settled in Goa; the others broke their parole, and finally found their way to Agra, which was 'much greater than London and very populous.' In the bazaars were 'a great resort of merchandise from Persia and out of India, and very much merchandise of silk and cloth and of precious stones, both rubies, diamonds and pearls.' All the way along the road from Agra to Sīkrī was 'a market of victuals and other things, as full as though a man were still in a town, and so many people as if a man were in a market.' They had an interview with the Emperor, who was attired in 'a white *cabie* (or tunic), made like a shirt tied with strings on one side, and a little cloth on his head, coloured often times with red and yellow,' but apparently Elizabeth's letter received no reply. Leedes obtained a post as a jeweller at the Court, and Newbery resolved to return home by the overland route through Lahore. Here they disappear from the page of history. Fitch, however, after travelling down the Ganges to its mouth and visiting Bassein, Pegu and Ṃalacca, managed to make his way home by way of Ceylon, Ormuz and Aleppo. He reached England after an absence of eight years, and his report of his experiences led to the foundation of the East India Company.

In 1588, Akbar was compelled by menacing conditions of affairs in the North West to leave Fathpur Sīkrī and take up his abode at Lahore. He never returned save for a brief visit in 1601, and the beautiful city became a deserted ruin. From Lahore he despatched forces which undertook the reduction of Sind and Kashmir; Baluchistan and Kandahār were also annexed, and in the far east his armies overran Orissa. But these years were saddened by domestic tragedies. The wise and witty Birbal, his constant companion, was killed on the frontier, and Bhagwan Dās and Todar Mal both passed away. His sons were a constant source of anxiety: Murād and Daniyāl had taken to drink, of which the former died in 1599 and the latter in 1604; Salīm, his favourite, was wayward and idle. In 1593, Akbar, whose ambitions only increased as his conquests extended, resolved upon the annexation of the Deccan. This was a most unfortunate decision, and ultimately led to the ruin of the Mogul Empire. The natural boundary of Hindustan is the Vindhya range, and any additions beyond this point were bound to be a source of weakness rather than of strenght. In 1593, however, an excuse was found to intervene in the affairs of Ahmadnagar and an army was sent under Prince Murād. But the city was stoutly defended by the heroic Chānd Bībī, and Murād was unsuccessful. On his death in 1599, Abul Fazl took command, and Chānd Bībī having been murdered, Ahmadnagar was taken in 1600. Meanwhile Akbar had captured the strong fortress of Asīrgarh by bribery and had annexed Khāndesh, but his triumph was marred by the outbreak of a terrible famine, with which the resources of the administration were quite unable to cope. A worse blow was to come. His son Salīm started a rebellion against his father during his absence, and had the incredible baseness to arrange for the great minister, Abul Fazl, to be ambushed and murdered on his return journey from the Deccan in 1602.

Akbar did not long survive the death of his oldest friend and the shock of Salīm's base ingratitude. He fell ill with dysentery and passed away at Agra, October 27th, 1605. His body was hastily interred, with little pomp or ceremony, in a noble mausoleum of his own devising, at Sikandra. "Thus," writes one of the Jesuit onlookers, "does the world treat those from whom no good is to be hoped, and no evil feared." Even so, he was not allowed to sleep in peace. In 1691 a band of rebellious Jāt peasants plundered his tomb and scattered his remains to the four winds.

Two portraits of Akbar have come down to us from contemporaries. One is from the pen of his old friend, Fathr Monserrate:

> "One could easily recognise even at the first glance that he is King. He has broad shoulders, somewhat bandy legs well-suited for horsemanship, and a light brown complexion. He carries his head bent towards the right shoulder. His forehead is broad and open, his eyes so bright and flashing that they seem like a sea shimmering in the sunlight. His eyelashes are very long. His eyebrows are not strongly marked. His nose is straight and small though not insignificant. His nostrils are widely open as though in derision. Between the left nostril and the upper lip there is a mole. He shaves his beard but wears a moustache. He limps in his left leg though he has never received an injury there. His body is exceedingly well built and is neither too thin nor too stout. He is sturdy, hearty and robust. When he laughs his face becomes almost distorted. His expression is tranquil, serene and open, full also of dignity, and when he is angry awful majesty."*

The other is by his son Salīm, afterwards the Emperor Jahāngīr:

> "My father always associated with the learned of every creed and religion: especially the Pundits and the learned of India, and, although he was illiterate, so much became clear to him through constant intercourse with the learned and the wise, in his conversations with them, that no one knew him to be illiterate, and he was so well acquainted with the niceties of verse and prose compositions that his deficiency was not thought of. In his august personal appearance he was of middle height, but inclining to be tall; he was of the hue of wheat; his eyes and eyebrows were black, and his complexion rather dark than fair; he was lion-bodied with a broad chest, and his hands and arms long. On the left side of his nose he had a fleshy mole, very agreeable in appearance, of the size of half a pea. Those skilled in the science of physiognomy considered this mole a sign of great prosperity and exceeding good fortune. His august voice was very loud, and in speaking and explaining, had a peculiar richness. In his actions and

* Monserrate's *Commentary,* trans. J. S. Hoyland (1922), pp. 196-7.

movements he was not like the people of the world, and the Glory of God manifested itself in him. Notwithstanding his Kingship, his treasures and his buried wealth past computation, his fighting elephants and Arab horses, he never by a hair's breadth placed his foot beyond the base of humility before the Throne of God, and never for one moment forgot Him. He associated with the good of every race and creed and persuasion, and was gracious to all in accordance with their condition and understanding. He passed his nights in wakefulness, and slept little in the day; the length of his sleep during a whole night and day was not more than a watch and a half. He counted his wakefulness at night as so much added to his life. His courage and boldness were such that he could mount raging, rutting elephants, and subdue to obedience murderous elephants which would not allow their own females near them. Of the austerities practised by my revered father one was not eating the flesh of animals. During three months of the year he ate meat, and for the remaining nine, contented himself with Sūfi food and was in no way pleased with the slaughter of animals. On many days and in many months this was forbidden to the people."*

Akbar lived in an age of great monarchs. His contemporaries were Elizabeth of England, Henry IV of France and Shāh Abbās of Persia, but he towers head and shoulders above them all. He was no pacifist. His ambition was to create for himself a mighty empire, and he carried out his purpose ruthlessly. Terrible in his wrath, he inflicted punishments on those who opposed him which shock modern humanitarian sentiment. But he was not a mere conqueror. The justification of imperialism is that the conquered benefit by the exchange, and Akbar at once set himself to establish throughout his kingdom the rule of justice and law, to ascertain that the peasant was fairly taxed, and that all men should receive a fair hearing and a fair trial. The greatness of his work is shown by the fact that his administrative system is the basis of that which is in vogue in India to-day. His sayings, preserved by Abul Fazl, testify to his earnest desire to do what was right, and his recognition of the enormous responsibilities of his position. "If I could but find anyone capable of governing the kingdom, I should not once place this burden on his shoulders and withdraw therefrom." He was the first of his race to be inspired with the visions of a united India, where everyone, Mussalman, Brahmin and Jain, Christian and Parsee, could live side by side on terms of perfect equality before the law. His enforcement of religious toleration at the time when the rack and the state were the accepted weapons of religious controversy in Europe places him centuries in advance of his age. At the same time, he did his best to repress barbarous customs practised in the name of religion, such as child-marriage, Suttee and animal sacrifices. "Formerly I persecuted men in conformity with my faith," he said, "and deemed it Islam. As I grew in

* Jahāngīr's *Memoirs,* trans. Rogers and Beveridge, pp. 33-4.

knowledge, I was overwhelmed with shame. What constancy is to be expected from proselytes on compulsion?..." "If men walk in the way of God's will, interference with them would be in itself reprehensible: if otherwise, they are under the malady of ignorance and deserve my compassion...." "Miracles occur in the temples of every creed...." "Each person according to his condition gives the Supreme Being a name, but in reality to name the Unknowable is vain."

Akbar was a man of violent passions, and he had the craving for strong drink and opium, which was a family failing; but he subdued his body by an iron self-discipline, amounting almost to asceticism. He was a fond parent and a great lover of little children. "Children are the young saplings in the garden of life; to love them is to turn our minds to the Bountiful Creator," is one of his most beautiful sayings. In his manner he was every inch a king, 'great with the great, and lowly with the lowly.' Specially characteristic of the man were his flashing eyes, 'vibrant like the sea in sunshine,' as one of the Jesuit Fathers notes. It is difficult to write without hyperbole of this great and very human monarch, one of the noblest, surely, in all history.

LEADING DATES

A.D. 1556	Second battle of Pānipat, accession of Akbar.
1560	Akbar assumes full powers.
1565	Abolition of the poll-tax.
1567-8	Siege of Chitor.
1569	Building of Fathpur Sīkrī.
1572-3	War in Gujarāt.
1574	Abul Fazl comes to Court.
1574-6	Wars in Rājputāna and Bengal.
1579	Infallibility Decree.
1580	Arrival of the Jesuit Mission.
1585	Akbar shifts his capital to Lahore.
1586-90	Conquest of Kashmir and Sind.
1591-1600	Wars in the Deccan. Conquest of Ahmadnagar and death of Chānd Bībī.
1601	Capture of Asīrgarh.
1602	Rebellion of Prince Salīm and murder of Abul Fazl.
1605	Death of Akbar.

Chapter XIX

The Climax of the Mogul Empire

On the death of Akbar, Prince Salīm was enthroned at Agra on October 24th, 1605, with the title of Jahāngir or World Holder. He was thirty-eight years of age, and had four sons, Khusru, Parvīz, Khurram and Shahriyār. Jahāngīr on his accession tried to win over popular sentiment by promising a number of reforms, the principal ones being the protection of the Muhammadan religion, the abolition of barbarous punishments such as mutilation, the suppression of highway robbery, the confirmation of the nobles and of religious bodies in their estates, the prohibition of the sale of intoxicating liquors, the provision of public hospitals, and a general amnesty for political prisoners. It is doubtful, however, whether these promises were ever kept; they certainly did not prevent a rising in favour of Khusru, the Emperor's eldest son, who was a popular hero. Khusru possessed a singularly attractive personality. Terry, the chaplain of Sir Thomas Roe, the English Ambassador, describes him as "a gentleman of a very lovely presence and fine carriage, exceedingly beloved of the common people.... He was a man who contented himself with one wife, which with all love and care accompanied him in all his streights, and therefore he never would take any wife but herself, though the liberty of religion did admit of plurality." Roe is equally admiring. He speaks of Khusru as "favouring learning, valour and the discipline of war, abhorring all covetousness, and discerning the base customs of taking used by his ancestors and the nobility." Khusru fled to the Punjab and raised the standard of rebellion, but the governor of Lahore refused to open the gates to him. His army, which was composed of raw levies, was easily dispersed, and he was defeated and captured. Jahāngīr stamped out the rising with revolting barbarity. Two of the prince's chief supporters were sewn up in raw hides which contracted on exposure to the sun. Arjun, the Sikh pontiff who had blessed the undertaking, was seized and put to death. Three hundred rebels were impaled on stakes on either side of the road, and Khusru, trembling and weeping and loaded with chains, was paraded on an elephant, between the lines of writhing victims and forced to witness their death agonies. He was then blinded with a hot iron, but did not lose his sight entirely. Till his murder in 1622, he was a state prisoner. He was buried in a garden at Allahābād, and was popularly regarded as a martyr.

At the beginning of his reign, Jahāngīr, in cynical disregard for his promises to protect Muhammadanism, began to renew his father's favours to the Jesuits. Catholic processions were constantly seen in the streets of Agra, and Christian pictures were hung on the palace walls. Religious discussions were resumed, in which the name of the Prophet was openly reviled. At one time it was even thought probable that the Emperor would be received into the Catholic Church, and this caused a great scandal among Muhammadans of all classes. But early in 1609, there arrived in Agra an English captain of the name of William Hawkins, who had been sent by the newly formed East India Company in order to try and obtain permission to set up a trading factory at the port of Surat. Hawkins had learnt to speak Turkish while in the Levant; the mother-tongue of the Emperor was Turki, and for this reason they were able to converse without an interpreter. Hawkins became the Emperor's boon companion, and was admitted to his drinking-bouts, which often lasted till far into the night. Hawkins gives a vivid picture of Jahāngīr's private life:

> "First in the morning about the break of day he is at his beads with his face turned to the westward. The manner of his praying when he is in Agra is in a private fair room, upon a goodly jet stone, having only a Persian lamb-skin under him; having also some eight chains of beads, every one containing four hundred. At the upper end of this jet stone the pictures of Our Lady and Christ are placed, graven in stone; so he turneth over his beads and saith 3,200 words, according to the number of his beads, and then his prayer is ended. After he hath done, he showeth himself to the people, receiving their salaams or good-morrows; unto whom multitudes resort every morning for this purpose. This done, he sleepeth two hours more, and then dineth, and passeth his time with his women; and at noon he showeth himself to the people again, sitting till three of the clock, viewing and seeing his pastimes and sports made by men and fighting of many sorts of beasts, every day sundry kinds of pastimes.
>
> "Then at three of the clock all the nobles in general (that be in Agra and are well), resort unto the Court, the King coming forth in open audience sitting in his seat royal, and every man standing in this degree before him, his chiefest sort of nobles standing within the red rail, and the rest without. They are all placed by his lieutenant-general. This red rail is three steps higher than the place where the rest stand; and within this red rail I was placed, amongst the chiefest of them all. The rest are placed by officers, and they likewise be within another very spacious place railed; and without that rail stand all sorts of horsemen and soldiers that belong unto his captains and all other comers. At these rails there are many doors kept by many porters, who have white rods to keep men in order. In the midst of the place, right before the King, standeth one of his sheriffs, together with the master hangman, who is accompanied by forty hangmen,

wearing on their heads a certain quilted cap different from all others, with a hatchet on their shoulders; and others with all sorts of whips being there ready to do what the King commandeth. The King heareth all causes in this place and stayeth some two hours every day.

"Then he departeth towards his private place of prayer; his prayer being ended, four or five sorts of very well dressed and roasted meats are brought him, of which as he pleaseth he eateth a bit to stay his stomach, drinking once of his strong drink. Then he cometh forth into a private room, where none can come but such as himself nominateth (for two years 1 was one of his attendants there). In this place he drinketh other three capfuls, which is the portion that the physicians allot him. This done, he eateth opium, and then he ariseth, and being in the height of his drink, he layeth him down to sleep, every man departing to his own home. And after he hath slept two hours they awake him and bring his supper to him; at which time he is not able to feed himself; but it is thrust into his mouth by others; and this is about one of the clock; and then he sleepeth the rest of the night."*

Hawkins rose into high favour, and was made a "commander of 400" with a salary equivalent to £3,000 a year in English money. This deeply alarmed the Jesuits, who, as he says, became 'like madde dogges,' and tried to poison him, but Jahāngīr gave him an Armenian girl from the royal harem as his wife, to cook his food and look after him. After two and a half years at Court, Hawkins fell into disfavour; Jahāngīr grew tired of him, and he took ship for England in 1612, but died within sight of home. From this time, Portuguese influence at the Mogul Court steadily declined. They lost a great deal of prestige when an attack on some English merchantmen lying in the roadstead off the mouth of the Tapti was repulsed with loss in full view of the native population, and they made the mistake of capturing and holding to ransom a pilgrim ship bound for Mecca, in violation of treaties on the subject.

In 1611, Jahāngīr married a lady of the name of the Mihr-un-Nisa, on whom he bestowed the title of Nūr Jahān, or Light of the World. The story resembles that of David and Bathsheba. Nūr Jahān was originally the wife of a Persian nobleman named Ali Kuli Beg, who had been given an estate in Bengal by Akbar. Apparently Akbar made this arrangement to get her away from the Court, as his son was already in love with her. Be this as it may, in 1607 Jahāngīr sent a force to arrest Ali Kuli Beg, who was killed in the scuffle which ensued. His widow was brought to Agra, but was not united to her royal lover until four years later. She was then thirty-four, an age when Oriental women are usually long past their prime, but she was a person of

* W. Foster, *Early Travellers in India* (Oxford 1921), p. 114-5.

singular beauty and intelligence. With her she brought her father, who received the title of Itimād-ud-daulah, her brother Āsaf Khān, and a host of relatives, whom she installed in high offices. She married her daughter to Prince Shahriyār. She was a fearless horsewoman and an excellent shot, and on one occasion, as Jahāngīr notes in his Memoirs, she killed four tigers in quick succession. She sat in the Hall of Audience and received petitions; coins were issued in her name and she put her signature beside her husband's on the royal *firmans*. Jahāngīr, now sodden with drink and opium, was completely under her influence. He candidly admits that 'Nūr Jahān was wise enough to conduct the business of state, while he only wanted a bottle wine and a piece of meat to make merry.' Nūr Jahān used her power well. She was 'an asylum to all sufferers,' helped needy suppliants, and provided dowries for hundreds of orphan Muslim girls. But for her, the government might well have collapsed altogether. The older nobles, though intensely jealous, were afraid to interfere.

In 1615, an ambassador from James I of England arrived at Agra, in the person of Sir Thomas Roe. Roe was a man of great dignity, and very different from the low-born and uproarious Hawkins. His dairy of his Embassy is a most valuable document, and is supplemented by an amusing narrative written by his chaplain, Edward Terry.* Roe's account of his reception gives an interesting description of the daily routine of the Court:

> "Jan. 10. I went to Court at 4 in the evening to the Durbar, which is the place where the Mogul sits out daily to entertain strangers, to receive petitions, to give commands, to see and to be seen. To digress a little from my reception and to declare the customs of the Court will enlighten the future discourse. The King hath no man but eunuchs that comes within the lodgings or retiring rooms of his house. His women watch within and guard him with manly weapons. They do justice one upon another for offences. He comes every morning to a window called the *Jharokha* (Window of Audience) looking into a plain before his gate, and shows himself to the common people. At noon he returns thither and sits some hours to see the fight of elephants and wild beasts; under him within a rail attend the men of rank; from whence he retires to sleep among his women. At afternoon he returns to the Durbar before mentioned. At eight after supper he comes down to the *Ghuzlkhana* (private apartments), a fair court where in the midst is a throne erected of freestone, wherein he sits, but sometimes below in a chair; to which are none admitted but of great quality, and few of those without leave; where he discourses of all matters with great affability. There is no business done with him concerning the state, government, disposition of war or peace, but at one of these

* Roe's *Embassy* has been edited by Sir W. Foster, Hakluyt Society, 1899. Terry's *Voyage to East India* is in the same authority's *Early Travellers in India,* p. 388 ff.

two last places, where it is publicly propounded and resolved and so registered, which if it were worth the curiosity might be seen for two shillings, but the common base people know as much as the council, and the news every day is the King's new resolutions tossed and censured by every rascal. This course is unchangeable, except sickness or drink prevent it; which must be known, for as all his subjects are slaves, so is he in a kind of reciprocal bondage, for he is tied to observe these hours and customs so precisely that if he were unseen one day, and no sufficient reason rendered, the people would mutiny; two days no reason can excuse, but that he must consent to open his doors and be seen by some to satisfy others. On Tuesday at the *Jharokha* he sits in judgment, never refusing the poorest man's complaint, where he hears with patience both parts; and sometimes sees with too much delight in blood the execution done by his elephants.

"At the Durbar I was led right before him at the entrance of an outer rail, where met we two principal noble slaves to conduct me nearer. I had required before my going leave to use the customs of my country, which was freely granted, so that I would perform them punctually. When I entered within the first rail I made an obeisance; entering in the inward rail another; and when I came under the King a third. The place is a great court, whither resort all sorts of people. The King sits in a little gallery overhead; ambassadors, the great men, and strangers of quality within the inmost rail under him, raised from the ground, covered with canopies of velvet and silk, under foot laid with good carpets; the meaner men representing gentry within the first rail, the people without in a base court, but so that all may see the King. This sitting out hath so much affinity with a theatre—the manner of the King in his gallery, the great men lifted on a stage as actors; the vulgar below gazing on—that an easy description will inform of the place and fashion."

Roe was not greatly impressed by what he saw. Jahāngīr's drunken orgies disgusted him. He "never imagined that a Prince so famed would live so meanly." The Hall of Audience was richly decorated, "but of so divers pieces and so unsuitable that it was rather patched than glorious, as if it seemed to strive to show all, like a lady that with her plate set on a cupboard her embroidered slippers."

Roe returned home in 1619, having obtained substantial trading concessions. The English now established a regular factory at the port of Surat, in a building hired from the local governor. It was organised on the collegiate model usually followed in similar establishments in Europe and the Near East: the members were controlled by a president, attended daily chapel, and dined together at mid-day. Discipline was strictly maintained. The English factors lived in considerable pomp and state, but life between the departure and arrival of the annual trading fleets was dull and lonely. The climate was unhealthy and they were entirely cut off from the world, at the mercy of corrupt and rapacious local officials. Now almost the sole extant relic of the cardle of British rule at Surat is the graveyard, where the early factors sleep beneath gigantic piles of masonry, erected apparently in rivalry of the tombs of the Mogul noblemen. These grotesque monuments were greatly admired in their day. The chief exports were printed cotton goods, silk, indigo, spices of all sorts, saltpetre, sugar and opium. Against these, the East India Company's ships imported European broadcloths, velvets and brocades, clocks and mechanical toys, metals such as copper, zinc, lead and quicksilver, and bullion. There was a great demand for English clothes, pictures, jewellery and other luxuries at the Imperial Court.*

From the point of view of conquest, the reign of Jahāngīr was inglorious, as he was too indolent to take the field. But his generals forced the Rānā of Mewār to conclude an honourable peace; they subdued Ahmadnagar in the Deccan, and the strong fortress of Kāngra on the Himalayan border. On the other hand, the Persian armies of Shāh Abbās succeeded in taking the important town of Kandahār, which they held until 1638, when the gates were opened by its treacherous governor.

Jahāngīr's closing years were distracted by disturbances and rebellions on the part of his sons, whom he was too feeble to control. In 1622, Prince Khurram, and orthodox and bigoted Muhammadan, obtained the custody of his unfortunate brother, the half-blind Khusru, and had him strangled. He then openly rebelled, but being defeated, retired to Bengal and the Deccan for the remainder of his father's reign. In 1626, Mahābat Khān, one of the great nobles, made an abortive attempt to seize the person of the Emperor and the Empress. In the following year, Jahāngīr died on his way of Kashmir, and was buried in a magnificent Mausoleum at Shāhdāra, on the banks of the Rāvī river near Lahore. (Plate XIX.)

Jahāngīr's character, says Terry, was "composed at extremes; for sometimes he was barbarously cruel, and at other times he seemed to be exceeding fair and gentle." He was a very accomplished man. His Memoirs are written in elegant Persian. He inherited his father's admiration of music, poetry and the fine arts. He was a connoisseur of painting. He erected a number of sumptuous buildings, and he had a genuine love of nature. He went into raptures over the scenery of Kashmir, and writes with real feeling of the birds and flowers he observed there.

> "Its pleasant meads and enchanting cascades are beyond all description. There are running streams and fountains beyond count. Wherever the eye reaches, there are verdure and running water. The red rose, the violet and the narcissus grow of themselves; in the fields, there are all kinds of flowers and all sorts of sweet-scented herbs more than can be calculated. In the soul-enchanting spring the hills and plains are filled with blossoms; the gates, the walls, the courts, the roofs, are lighted up by the torches of the banquet-adorning tulips. What shall we say of these things or the wide meadows and the fragrant trefoil?

* H. G. Rawlinson, *British Beginnings in Western India* (1920), Chapter IX.

"The garden-nymphs were brilliant,
Their cheeks shone like lamps;
There were fragrant buds on their stems,
Like dark amulets on the arms of the beloved;
The wakeful, ode-rehearsing nightingales
Whetted the desires of wine-drinkers;
At each fountain the duck dipped his beak
Like golden scissors cutting silk;
There were flower-carpets and fresh rosebuds,
The wind fanned the lamps of the roses,
The violet braided her locks,
The buds tied a knot in the heart."*

Jahāngīr's religious views are difficult to ascertain. They were probably those of his father. In early life he showed a passing interest in Christianity. At other times he shocked the Court by his eccentric display of affection towards a dirty and ragged Hindu ascetic. He shared Akbar's views about the sanctity of animal life, and in 1618, when his grandson Shūja was seriously ill, he made a vow to give up hunting if the child were spared. On the other hand, he inflicted the most atrocious punishments, such as impalement and flaying alive and having men torn to pieces by elephants, and loved to gloat over his victim's sufferings. He killed a clumsy huntsman who spoilt his shot at a wild bull, and when men were seriously injured at elephant fights, they were thrown into the river without compunction, as useless for further service. He was weak, indolent, capricious, and easily led. In later life he fell more and more under the influence of alcohol until at the end he was little more than a confirmed drunkard, incapable of any kind of exertion or public transaction.

On the death of Jahāngīr's disputes for the succession immediately broke out. There were two candidates: Prince Khurram, the elder son, to whom his father had given the title of Shāh Jahān, 'King of the World,' and Shahriyār, the younger, a worthless fellow, but married to the daughter of the dowager Empress Nūr Jahān by her first husband. Shāh Jahān on the other hand was married to Mumtāz Mahāl, the 'Ornament of the Palace,' daughter of the Empress's brother, Āsaf Khān. Brother and sister at once started intriguing to annex the throne for their respective sons-in-law. Shāh Jahān was far away in the Deccan at the time, but Āsaf Khān sent express messengers to recall him; meanwhile he defeated Shahriyār, threw him into prison and blinded him. Shāh Jahān on his return ordered the whole of his male relations to be put away, and all perished except one, who found asylum in Persia. Nūr Jahān was banished from the court with a handsome allowance. Revolts which broke out in Bundelkhand and the Deccan were easily stamped out, and Shāh Jahān was

* *Memoirs,* trans. Rogers and Beveridge (Royal Asiatic Society, 1914), II, 114.

proclaimed Emperor at Agra in 1628. In 1631, the Empress Mumtāz Mahāl, to whom he had been married for nearly twenty years, died in childbirth. She had been the mother of fourteen out of his sixteen children. Mogul princes, despite polygamy, were usually devoted husbands. Shāh Jahān was prostrated with grief and never married again. The body of Mumtāz Mahāl was taken to Agra for burial, and the sorrowing Emperor erected over her tomb one of the most beautiful monuments in the world, the famous Tāj Mahal, where they now sleep side by side.

Despite his Rājpūt mother, Shāh Jahān shared none of his father's and grandfather's liberal views on religion. He was no doubt influenced by the Empress, who was a devout Muslim. Sir Thomas Roe speaks of him as "earnest in his superstitions, a hater of all Christians, proud, subtile, false, and barbarously tyrannous." In 1632, he issued an order that all Hindu temples, recently erected or in course of erection, were to be razed to the ground. In Benares alone, seventy-two were destroyed, and no doubt local governors freely availed themselves of the opportunity in other places. The Jesuits were too firmly established to be expelled, but Christian churches at Agra and Lahore were demolished.

In the same year, a pretext was found to attack the flourishing Portuguese settlement at Hugli, about thirty miles from the present city of Calcutta. The Portuguese were accused of kidnapping the inhabitants, infecting them with Nazarene doctrines, and shipping them as slaves to Europe; but the real reason for their unpopularity was the face that they were monopolising the sea-borne trade of Bengal. Hugli was a large, open town, surrounded by nothing more formidable than a moat, and its regular garrison consisted of only three hundred European regular soldiers and seven hundred trained natives; yet such was the military reputation of the Portuguese, that an army of 150,000 was sent against it. The siege lasted for three months, but in the end the moat was drained and the flimsy defences were mined. The inhabitants tried to slip away down-stream, but a ship containing 2,000 women and children was sunk, and a mere remnant reached Saugor island at the mouth of the Ganges, only to die of fever and starvation. Of the remainder, 10,000 were 'blown up with powder, drowned in the water or burnt by fire,' and 4,000 were taken as captives to Agra, where they were treated with abominable cruelty in order to force them to embrace Islam. But only a handful, terrified at the prospet of being trampled to death by elephants, accepted release on these terms; the remainder, in the words of the official historian, 'passed from prison to hell.' The traveller Bernier says that the misery they endured was unparalleled in modern times. Women, children and priests suffered alike; boys beame pages in the Imperial household, and the younger women went to the harems. The Jesuit Fathers and others did their utmost to alleviate the miseries of these poor people, but without much effect.*

* F. Bernier, *Travels in the Mogul Empire* (1914 edn.), p. 177.

In 1630, Shāh Jahān had resumed his grandfather's plans for the reduction of the Deccan. The territory of Bijāpur was ravaged, and Fath Khān, the treacherous minister of Ahmadnagar, who had taken possession of the person of the last Sultan, opened the gates of the city to the enemy. The Sultan was sent off as a prisoner to Gwalior,* and the State of Ahmadnagar ceased to exist. (1632). One of the features of the operations against Ahmadnagar was the guerilla campaign carried on by Shāhjī, the father of the famous Marāthā chieftain Sivājī. From 1631 to 1635, Shāh Jahān was detained by pressing affairs at the capital, but in 1635 he returned to the Deccan. The Sultan of Golkonda humbly submitted, but the Sultan of Bijāpur was less complaisant. After fierce fighting, he was forced to submit and pay a fine of twenty lakhs of rupees. The Deccan was divied into four provinces, but put under the charge of Prince Aurangzeb as viceroy. Aurangzeb held charge of the Deccan from 1636 to 1644, when he was recalled for operations on the North-West Frontier. In 1653 he returned to the Deccan and found the country stricken with famine and in a deplorable state of disorder. He endeavoured to put matters upon a better financial basis with the assistance of his able minister Murshid Kuli Khān, who introduced the lana-revenue system of Todar Mal. Aurangzeb, who was an orthodox Sunni by religion, hated the Shiah Sultans of Bijāpur and Golkonda and seized every opportunity for attacking them. In this he was aided by an able but unscrupulous soldier of fortune named Mir Jumla. Mir Jumla was originally in the service of the state of Golkonda. He had the unique advantage of possessing a park of artillery served by European gunners, and was always willing to sell his services to the highest bidder. Fortunately for them, the kingdoms of the Deccan received a respite of thirty years owing to the illness of Shāh Jahān in 1657 and the War of Succession which ensued.

In the north-west, the Imperial armies were less successful. An attempt in 1647 to annex the ancestral possessions of Bābur, Badakshān and Balkh, ended in failure. In 1649 the Persians once more captured Kandahār, the great fortress commanding the Central Asian trade routes, which had long been a bone of contention. Prince Aurangzeb was ordered to re-take it, but three attempts to do so, commanded first by himself, and then by Dārā Shikoh, in 1649, 1652 and 1653, failed disastrously; the Moguls were notoriously inefficient in siege operations. An immense amount of revenue was expended on these campaigns.

Shāh Jahān had four sons—Dārā Shikoh,† his father's favourite, who was viceroy of the Punjab and usually remained at the capital, Shūjā, viceroy of Bengal and Orissa; Aurangzeb, viceroy of the Deccan; and Murād Baksh, viceroy of Gujarāt. Each of the sons was virtually an independent ruler, with vast estates, revenues and armies.

---

* The stronghold of Gwalior, now the capital of H. H. Mahārājā Sindia in Central India, was used by the Moguls as their state prison.

† This was his title, and means 'equal in splendour to Darius.' His name was Muhammad.

In 1657 Shāh Jahān's health began to fail. He no longer appeared at the palace window to give public audience, and his sons immediately began to take steps to seize the throne. The contest really resolved itself into a duel between Dārā Shikoh and Aurangzeb, the other two being mere pawns in the game. The protagonists were in striking contrast. Dārā Shikoh was an amiable and enlightened man, and almost universally popular. Manucci, the Italian traveller, who had been in his service, describes him as a person of "dignified manners, a comely countenance, joyous and polite in conversation, ready and gracious of speech, of most extraordinary liberality, kindly and compassionate, but over-confident in his opinion of himself."* He shared the broad religious views of his great-grandfather, was on excellent terms with the Rājpūt princes and the Jesuit Fathers, and was deeply interested in Hinduism. He had a Persian translation made of the Upanishads, which he declared to be a revelation far older than the Koran. In his wife, Nādira Begum, 'his nearest and dearest friend,' he had a devoted and worthy helpmate. Had he succeeded to the throne, the subsequent history of the Mogul Empire would have been very different. Aurangzeb, on the other hand, was cold and crafty, and an unscrupulous intriguer. A bigoted Sunni, he detested his brother as a heretic, and left nothing undone to compass his destruction. "There is only one of my brothers I fear, the Prayer-monger," Dārā Shikoh is reported to have remarked. He first of all won over the foolish and trusting Murād Baksh with lavish promises, and the two brothers advanced upon Agra. Dārā Shikoh went to meet him with a force composed principally of Rājpūt levies. After a skirmish near Ujjain, battle was joined at Samugarh, outside Agra, on May 29th, 1658. The Rājpūts fought gallantly, and for a time the issue was in doubt, but when Dārā Shikoh got down from his elephant to mount his war horse in order to lead a charge in person, a cry went up that he was dead, and his army broke in panic. Aurangzeb entered Agra on June 8th, and annexed the vast sums of money in the vaults of the Imperial Treasury. The old Emperor was made a captive in the fort, where he remained until his death in 1666, tended by his faithful daugther Jahānāra, and gazing, it is said, upon the distant view of his fairest creation, the Tāj Mahal, where he was laid to rest beside his beloved consort.

Meanwhile, Aurangzeb was busy disposing of his rivals. The unfortunate Murād Baksh received an unexpected reward for his co-operation. He was invited to a banquet and arrested while under the influence of drink. He was sent to Gwalior, where he was executed for having put to death a Muhammadan in Gujarāt. Aurangzeb preferred to rid himself of his rivals by legal forms. Meanwhile, Dārā Shikoh was forced to

* Niccolao Manucci, the Venetian, landed at Surat and took service as an artilleryman under Dārā Shikoh. After this he served under Rājā Jaisingh. He lived for a time in Bandra near Bombay and Goa, and then settled in Madras, where he died in 1717. His *Storia do Mogor* has been translated by W. Irvine under the title of *A Pepys of Mogul India* (London, 1908).

fly to Multān, but at a critical moment Aurangzeb was recalled from the pursuit in order to meet an invasion from Bengal by Shāh Shūjā. Shāh Shūjā was defeated and followed up so vigorously that he took refuge in the jungles of Arakan, where, apparently, he and his followers were murdered by the tribesmen. They were never heard of again. Dārā Shikoh in the meantime made his way down the Indus and through Sind and Kāthiāwār to Gujarāt, where he was hospitably received by the governor of Ahmadābād. He might well have escaped to the Deccan, where he would have found a warm welcome, but in an evil day he accepted the overtures of Jaswant Singh of Mārwār. The Rājpūt, corrupted by Aurangzeb, betrayed his ally, and Dārā was defeated by the Imperial troops near Ājmīr (April 14th, 1659). The unhappy prince took to his heels; his followers were deserting him one by one, and the ever-dwindling body of fugitives was attacked and plundered by the Bhils, Kols and other wild tribes. Dārā once more appeared before Ahmadābād; but this time the governor, fearing the vengeance of Aurangzeb, refused to open his gates to him. The French traveller Bernier, who happened by chance to be present, vividly describes the consternation with which the news was received.* Behind the *purdah,* the women could be heard piteously weeping and wailing, while the unhappy Dārā, despair written on his face, went from man to man, asking even the common soldiers for their advice. The only course left was to escape across the Persian border to safety. It was the height of the summer, and the heat in the Sind desert at that time of the year is almost unbearable. The party became split up, and one day a foot-messenger arrived to say that the faithful Nādira was no more. "She had died of heat and thirst, not being able to find a drop of water in the country to assuage her thirst. The Prince was so affected by the news that he fell as though he were dead." Dārā Shikoh now seems to have become quite indifferent about his fate. He accepted the offer of an Afghan chief named Jiwān Khān to escort him through the Bolān Pass. He had once saved Jiwān Khān from execution, but the ungrateful wretch handed him over to his pursuers. The final act in this unutterably pitiful tragedy is recoutned by Bernier:

> "Dārā was now seen seated on a miserable and worn out elephant covered with filth; he no longer wore the necklace of large pearls which distinguished the princes of Hindustan, nor the rich turban and embroidered coat; he and his son were not habited in dirty cloth of the coarsest texture, and his sorry turban was wrapped round with a Kashmir shawl or scarf resembling that worn by the meanest of the people. Such was the appearance of Dārā when led through the

* François Bernier, the French physician and traveller, landed at Surat at the end of 1658, and like Manucci, accompanied Dārā Shikoh for a time. He was afterwards with Aurangzeb in Delhi, Lahore and Kashmir. He accompanied another French traveller, Jean Baptiste Tavernier, to Bengal and Golkonda, and returned home in 1668. His *Travels in the Mogul Empire* was published in 1670. The edition here quoted is by V. A. Smith (Oxford, 1914).

bazaars and every quarter of the city. I could not divest myself of the idea that some dreadful execution was about to take place.... The crowd assembled upon this disgraceful occasion was immense; and everywhere I observed the people weeping and lamenting the fate of Dārā in the most touching language. I took my station in one of the most conspicuous parts of the city, in the midst of the largest bazaar; I was mounted on a good horse and accompanied by two servants and two intimate friends. From every side I heard piercing and distressing shrieks, for the Indian people have a very tender heart; men, women and children wailing as if some mighty calamity had happened to themselves.

"Aurangzeb was immediately made acquainted with the impression which this spectacle produced upon the public mind. A second council was consequently convened and the question discussed whether it was more expedient to conduct Dārā to Gwalior, agreeably to the original intention, or to put him to death without further delay.... The charge of this atrocious murder was entrusted to a slave of the name of Nazar, who had been educated by Shāh Jahān, but experienced some ill-treatment from Dārā. The Prince, apprehensive that poison would be administered to him, was employed with Sipihr Shikoh in boiling lentils, when Nazar and four other ruffians entered his apartment. 'My dear son,' he cried out, 'these men are come to murder us!' He then seized a small kitchen knife, the only weapon in his possession. One of the murderers having secured Sipihr Shikoh, the rest fell upon Dārā, threw him down and while three of the assassins held him, Nazar decapitated his wretched victim. The head was instantly carried to Aurangzeb, who commanded that it should be placed in a dish and that water should be brought. The blood was then washed from the face, and when it could no longer be doubted that it was indeed the head of Dārā, he shed tears and said, '*Ai badbakht!* Ah, wretched man! Let this shocking sight no more offend my eyes; but take away the head and let it be buried in Humāyūn's tomb' "*

The execution was sanctioned by the obsequious theologians of the Court on the ground that Dārā Shikoh was guilty of heresy. It is some satisfaction to learn that the villain who betrayed him was stoned to death by the enraged populace. Dārā's eldest son, Sulaimān Shikoh, fled to the Rājpūts, and was not captured till 1660. He was brought in chains before his uncle and then sent to the state-dungeon at Gwalior, where two years later he died of slow poisoning.† Aurangzeb was now king in all but name. He had rid himself of all his rivals. In justification it may perhaps be said that, had he fallen into the hands of his brothers, his fate would probably have been like theirs.

* *Travels in the Mogul Empire,* p. 103.

† *Post,* a decoction of opium, was administered to state-prisoners. It had the effect of slowly depriving them of their reason and finally of killing them.

The reign of Shāh Jahān is usually spoken of as the Golden Age of the Mogul Empire. The wealth stored in the strong-rooms of the Imperial Treasury at Agra was enormous, and has been estimated as worth 340 million pounds sterling. Buildings of almost incredible splendour sprang up at Agra, Delhi, Lahore and other places. At Shāh Jahān's new capital at Delhi, the plain red sandstone of Akbar's time was replaced by marble, inlaid with precious stones; ceilings were of solid gold and silver,

Fig. 41 : Dārā Shikoh and his son Sipihr Shikoh.
(After the drawing in Valentyn's *Beschriving.*)

and the Peacock Throne, encrusted with gems, was alone valued at ten millions of rupees. The official historian paints a glowing picture of the state of the Empire under Shāh Jahān:

"The means employed by the King in these happy times to protect and ncurish his people, his knowledge of what made for their welfare, his administration by honest and intelligent officers, the auditing of accounts, his care of the crown lands and their tenants, and encouragement of agriculture and the collection of revenue, together with his punishment and admonition of evil-doers, oppressors, and malcontents, all tended to the prosperity of the empire. The pargana which had brought in three lakhs in Akbar's reign now yielded ten, though some fell short, and those who increased the revenue by careful agriculture were rewarded, and *vice versa.* The expenditure of former reigns was not a fourth of the cost of this reign, and yet the King quickly amassed a treasure which would have taken years to accumulate under his predecessors. Notwithstanding the extent of the country, plaints were so rare that only one day a week was assigned to the administration of justice, and seldom did even twenty plaintiffs appear on that day, to his Majesty's disappointment. But if offenders were discovered, the local authorities generally tried them on the spot, with right of appeal to the governor or Diwān or Kāzi (Finance Minister and Chief Justice) when the cause was reviewed and judgment given with great care and discrimination, least it should come to the King's ears that justice had not been done."*

The panegyrics of obsequious court-annalists are not borne out by the numerous European travellers who now began to visit India in increasing numbers. Their accounts reveal beneath the glittering facade a vast amount of human poverty and misery. In 1630, Gujarāt was visited by a terrible famine, due to the failure of the seasonal, rains, which lasted for two years. The most horrifying accounts of this great calamity have come down to us, and there is no reason to suppose that it was an isolated occurrence. "As the famine increased," says the Dutch merchant, Van Twist, "men abandoned towns and villages and wandered helplessly. It was easy to recognise their condition: eyes sunk deep in the head, lips pale and covered with slime, the skin hard, with the bones showing through, the belly nothing but a pouch hanging down empty, knuckles and knee-caps showing prominently. One would cry and howl for hunger, while another lay stretched on the ground dying in misery; wherever you went, you saw nothing but corpses."† Further details are almost too horrifying for repetition. It was impossible to approach the villages owing to the stench of the piled up bodies; whole families drowned themselves in the rivers, and cannibalism was openly practised. It was dangerous for travellers to appear on the roads, which were haunted by bands of desperate men, reduced to savagery. A pestilence was a natural result of these conditions, and swept away numbers of the survivors. The local administration was helpless. About one and a half lakhs of rupees were spent on relief works, and revenue was remitted: but the real causes of the heavy mortality were over-taxation and the rapacity of the officials, which left the peasant no reserves on which to fall back, and the huge Mogul armies, which absorbed the bulk of the supplies of grain which should have gone to the stricken districts. Bernier says that the jāgīrdārs or fief-holds had an almost despotic authority over not only the peasants in their domains, but the merchants and artisans; and nothing could be more cruel and oppressive than the manner in which it was exercised.‡ The grandiose building-schemes of the Mogul Emperors included few works of public utility, except a certain number of roads, caravanserais and canals; buildings were often, as in the case of the city of Fathpur Sīkrī, abandoned after erection, and the country was strewn with these costly and useless monuments of the caprice and

---

* S. Lane-Poole, *Medieval India*, p. 110.

† W. H. Moreland, *From Akbar to Aurangzeb* (1920), p. 212.

‡ Travels in the *Mogul Empire*, p. 225.

extravagance of departed rulers. While they were in progress, the peasants' carts were impressed, and work in the fields was at a standstill. Francisco Pelsaert, the chief of the Dutch factory at Agra, gives a vivid picture of the utter subjection and poverty of the common folk. "There are three classes of people who are indeed nominally free, but whose status differs little from voluntary slavery—workmen, peons or servants and shopkeers. For the workmen there are two scourges: low wages and oppression. Workmen in all crafts, which are very numerous (for a job which one man would do in Holland here passes through four men's hands before it is finished), can earn by working from morning till night only five or six *tackas,* that is four or five stivers.* The second scourge is the oppression of governor, nobles, Diwān, Kotwāl, Bakshi, and other Imperıal officers. If one of these wants a workman, the man is not asked whether he is wiling to come, but is seized in his house or in the street, well beaten if he should dare to raise any objection, and in the evening paid half his wages, or perhaps nothing at all."† Bernier has a similar tale to tell. "The country is ruined by the necessity of defraying the enormous charges required to maintain the splendour of a numerous court, and to pay a large army maintained for the purpose of keeping the people in subjection. No adequate idea can be conveyed of the sufferings of that people. The cudgel and the whip compel them to excessive labour for the benefit of others; and driven to despair by every kind of cruel treatment, their revolt or their flight is only prevented by the presence of a military force."‡

Such, says the leading authority on the subject, was the economic system, which was drawing towards collapse. "Weavers, naked themselves, toiled to clothe others. peasants, themselves hungry, toiled to feed the towns and cities. India, taken as a unit, parted with useful commodities in exchange for gold and silver, or in other words gave bread for stones. Men and women, living from season to season on the verge of hunger, could be contented as long as the supply of food held out; when it failed, as it so often did, their hope of salvation was the slave-trader, and the alternatives were cannibalism, suicide or starvation. The only way of escape from that system lay through an increase in production, coupled with a rising standard of life, but this road was barred by the administrative methods in vogue, which penalized production and regarded every indicating of increased consumption as a signal for fresh extortion.§

---

* There were twenty-four stivers to the rupee, then valued at *2s. 3d.*

† Quoted in W. H. Moreland, *From Akbar to Aurangzeb,* p. 199.

‡ *Travels in the Mogul Empire,* p. 230.

§ W. H. Moreland, *From Akbar to Aurangzeb,* p. 304-5.

LEADING DATES

A.D. 1605	Coronation of Jahāngīr.
1606	Rebellion of Khusru.
1608-11	William Hawkins at the Imperial Court.
1611	Marriage of Jahāngīr and Nūr Jahān.
1615-18	Embassy of Sir Thos. Roe.
1622	Loss of Kandahār.
1622-5	Rebellion of Prince Khurram.
1627	Death of Jahāngīr.
1628	Enthronement of Prince Khurram as Shāh Jahān.
1631	Death of the Empress Mumtāz Mahāl.
1632	Siege of Hugli. Destruction of Hindu temples. End of Ahmadnagar.
1636	Prince Aurangzeb, Viceroy of the Deccan.
1638	Kandahār retaken.
1639	Foundation of the English settlement of Madras.
1649	Second loss of Kandahār.
1653	Aurangzeb returns to the Deccan. War against Golkonda and Bijāpur.
1657	War of Succession.
1666	Death of Shāh Jahān.

Chapter XX

The Decline and Fall of the Mogul Empire

Aurangzeb, having waded through blood to the throne, was proclaimed Emperor in June 1659, with the title of Ālamgīr, or Holder of the Universe. He was now forty, and as viceroy of the Deccan had received a thorough training in the art of government. The first twenty years of his reign were comparatively peaceful. Distant campaigns in Assam and Arakan on the one hand, and against rebellious tribes on the North-West Frontier on the other, were scarcely felt in Hindustan. He began his reign with a number of useful edicts intended to curb rapacity and dishonesty on the part of tax collectors, and to encourage agriculture. At the same time, he received numerous embassies from Persia, Basra, the Sharīf of Mecca, the Emperor of Abyssinia, and the Dutch, congratulating him on his accession. The reception of the envoy from Shān Abbās II of Persia was in particular a scene of great brilliance, and is described by an eye-witness. "Soldiers were posted on both sides of the street, a league in length, through which the ambassador would pass. The principal streets were decorated with rich stuffs, both in the shops and also at the windows, and the ambassador was brought through them, escorted by a number of officers, with music, drums, pipes and trumpets. On his entering the fort or royal palace, he was saluted by all the artillery.... It was a fine sight to see the ambassador followed by his 500 horsemen, large-limbed and handsome men with huge moustaches, riding excellent and well-equipped horses." Delhi was assuming the position of the political centre of Muhammadan world.

Aurangzeb, with grim and fanatical earnestness, now set about his task of purifying the land of vice and wickedness, and restoring it to the pristine purity, piety and simplicity of the early Caliphs. The extravagances of the Court were curtailed; drinking, gambling and other vices were suppressed; musicians, painters and architects no longer enjoyed the royal patronage; and apostates from Islam were arrested and put to death after due trial. A contemporary, writing from the view-point of orthodox Muhammadanism, vividly describes the Emperor's sweeping reforms:

"The Emperor, a great worshipper of God by temperament, is noted for his rigid attachment of religion. In his great piety he passes whole nights in the palace mosque and keeps the company of devout men. In privacy he never sits on a throne. Before his accession he gave in alms part of his food and clothing and still devotes to alms the income of some villages near Delhi and of some salt tracts assigned to his privy purse. He keeps fast throughout Ramazān and reads the holy Koran in the assembly of religious men with whom he sits for six or even nine hours of the night. From his youth he abstained from forbidden food and practices, and from his great holiness does nothing that is not pure and lawful. Though at the beginning of his reign he used to hear the exquisite voices of ravishing singers and brilliant instrumental performances, and himself understands music well, yet now for several years past, in his great restraint and self-denial, he entirely abstains from this joyous entertainment. He never wears clothes prohibited by religion, now uses vessels of silver and gold. No unseemly talk, no word of backbiting or falsefood, is permitted at his Court. He appears twice or thrice daily in his audience chamber with a mild and pleasing countenance, to dispense justice to petitioners, who come in numbers without hindrance and obtain redress. In any of them talks too much or acts improperly he is not displeased and never knits his brows. By hearing their words and watching their gestures he says that he acquires a habit of forbearance and toleration. Under the dictates of anger and passion he never passes sentence of death."*

Unfortunately, Aurangzeb did not stop there. He conceived it to be his duty to take active measures to put and end to the religious toleration which had been the keyňote of the policy of Akbar and Jahāngīr. Shāh Jahān had stopped the building of fresh temples, but in 1669 Aurangzeb issued an order "to demolish all the schools and temples of the infidels, and to put down their religious teaching and practices." The Visvānāth temple at Benares was destroyed, and a mosque erected in its place, in the very heart of the most sacred of all Hindu cities. In the following year, the great temple of Keshava Deva at Mathurā, erected in the reign of Jahāngīr at the cost of £350,000, was razed to the ground, and the richly-jewelled idols taken to Agra, where they were placed on the threshold of a mosque, to be trodden under foot by true believers. The very name of the town, associated for centuries with the worship of Krishna, was changed to Islāmābād. Thousands of places of worship were thus destroyed, to the consternation of pious Hindus all over India, and special officers were appointed to see that The Emperor's orders were strictly carried out.

Aurangzeb now proceeded to further measures which inflicted great economic hardship upon his Hindu subjects. In 1671 he dismissed the Hindu clerks in his service, but this order had to be partially rescinded, as it was found impossible to carry on the administration without them. An octroi duty of five per cent was levied on goods imported by Hindus, while Muhammadan traders were exempted. But the

* Elliot and Dowson, VII, 15.

most impolitic act of all was the re-imposition in 1680 of the poll-tax on unbelievers. This tax was universally unpopular, as it was regarded as badge of servitude. It is true that certain exceptions were made in the case of government officials and the very poor, but the general results were disastrous, and many Hindus who were unable to pay were forced to turn Muhammadan in order to escape from the insults of the collectors.

The Muhammadan historian Khāfi Khān gives a vivid picture of the consternation among the Hindu population of the capital when the news spread abroad of the renewal of the hated tax. "The Hindus round Delhi assembled in multitudes under the *jharokha* of the Emperor on the river-front of the palace, declaring that they were unable to pay, and praying for the revocation of the edict. But the Emperor would not listen to their complaints. One Sabbath, as he went to prayers at the great mosque, a vast crowd of Hindus thronged from palace to mosque. Every moment the crowd swelled, and his equipage was brought to a standstill. Then the elephants were brought out and charged the mob, and many people were trodden to death. For days the Hindus went on assembling and complaining, but in the end they had to pay the *jizya*."*

An anonymous but nobly-worded protest, sent to Aurangzeb about this time from one of his Hindu feudatories, gives a vivid picture of the outraged feelings of loyal subjects at the treatment to which they were subjected.† The writer points out that under the great Akbar, all sects, Christians, Jews, Muslims, Hidus, Jains and even atheists lived together in perfect harmony. "The aim of his liberal heart was to cherish and protect all the people." He and his successors had the power to collect the poll-tax, but refrained because they did not give place to bigotry in their hearts, and considered all men, high and low, to be created alike by God. "Such were the benevolent intentions of your ancestors. Whilst they pursued these great and generous principles, wheresoever they directed their steps, conquest and prosperity went before them; and then they reduced many countries and fortresses to their obedience. During your Majesty's reign, many have been alienated from the Empire, and further loss of territory must necessarily follow, since devastation and rapine now universally follow without restraint. Your subjects are trampled underfoot; every province of your Empire is impoverished; depopulation spreads, and difficulties accumulate.... If your Majesty places any faith in those books by distinction called divine, you will be there instructed God is the God of all mankind, not the God of Mussalmans alone. Pagan and Mussalman are alike in His Presence. Distinctions of colour are His ordination. In your mosques, to His name the voice is raised in prayer; in a house of images,

* Elliot and Dowson, VII, 296.

† The authorship of this letter is disputed. Tod ascribed it to Rānā Rāj Singh, while sir J. Sarkar has adduced reasons to attribute it to Shivājī the Marāthā, the actual writer being his secretary. Nīl Prabhu Munshi. (*History of Aurangzeb,* Book III, Chap. 34. Appendix).

when the bell is shaken, still He is the object of adoration. To vilify the religion or customs of other men is to set at naught the pleasure of the Almighty. When we deface a picture we naturally incur the resentment of the painter and justly the poet has said, 'Presume not to arraign or scrutinise the works of Power Divine.' "

Unhappily, this remarkable protest fell upon deaf ears. To Aurangzeb, toleration in any form was an offence against Islam, and soon the Empire was ablaze with rebellion. The Jāt peasantry round Mathurā, enraged at the violation of their temples, killed their governor and plundered Akbar's tomb at Sikandra. They were only put down after a pitched battle in which the Imperial troops lost four thousand men. In 1672 a sect of low-caste Hindus, known as the Satnāmis, started a rising in the Punjab, which was only suppressed after severe fighting. In 1675 Aurangzeb committed the incredible folly of attempting to force Teg Bahādur, the Sikh Guru, to embrace Islam, and, when he refused, he put him to death with prolonged tortures. But Aurangzeb's most serious blunder was the alienation of the Rājpūts, whom Akbar had rightly looked upon as the pillars of his Empire. Aurangzeb had no words too bad for the "beast-faced, beat-hearted Rājpūts, Satans in human form," and an opportunity of humiliating them soon presented itself. In 1678 Mahārājā Jaswant Singh of Mārwār died while serving the Empire on the North West Frontier, and the Emperor had the incredible baseness to annex the State while its defenders were far away fighting his battles. Muslim officials were placed in charge of the administration, the poll-tax was imposed, temples were demolished and idols broken, and the young rājā was taken off to Delhi to be brought up as a Muhammadan noble. From this fate he was rescued by a devoted band of his followers, who carried off the boy and his mother, and cut their way out with their swords. The Imperial troops sent after them were attacked so fiercely that they were forced to abandon the pursuit. Aurangzeb had also given dire offence by demanding a princess of the family for the royal harem, but the Rājpūt lady expressed her determination to commit suicide rather than yield to the embraces of the "monkeyfaced barbarian." The whole of Rājputāna was now in revolt. The rebels were led by the Rānā Rāj Singh of Udaipur, and when Aurangzeb took the field and occupied their principal towns, they fled to the hills and defied him to attack them. Prince Akbar, the Emperor's favourite son, who was left to carry on the war, protested in impassioned language to his father against the suicidal folly of his policy. "Blessings be on this race's fidelity to salt," he wrote, "who, without hesitation in giving up their lives for their master's sons, have done such deeds of heroism that for three years the Emperor of India, his mighty sons, famous ministers and high grandees have been moving in distraction against them, although this is only the beginning of the contest." When Aurangzeb refused to listen, Prince Akbar joined the enemy, and attempted to seize the throne with the help of his Hindu allies. But the wily Emperor contrived that a letter should fall into the hands of Rājā Durgā Dās, in which it was proposed that the Rājpūt troops should be placed in the forefront of the battle and left to their fate. He also enticed one of Akbar's ministers, Tahavvur Khān, into his camp and murdered him. The Rājpūts, scenting treachery, deserted *en masse,* and Prince Akbar was compelled to flee for his life. He eventually reached the Deccan, where he was hospitably received by the Marāthā chief Sambhājī. When Aurangzeb entered the Deccan in pursuit of him, he escaped to Bombay, and took ship to Persia, where he tried in vain to collect an army to reinstate himself. He died in 1704.

When Prince Akbar fled to the Deccan in 1681, the Emperor determined to put into execution his long deferred plan for the conquest of the South. The continued existence of the heretical states of Bijāpur and Golkonda, in spite of the fact that they had made a formal submission, was a deep offence to him, and he resolved to make an end of them altogether. Another object which he had in view was the reduction of the Marāthās. The history of the Marāthā State will be described in a later chapter; it is sufficient to mention here that the great Sivājī (1627-1680) had broken away from Bijāpur, set up a Hindu state, and had defeated all attempts of the Bijāpur and Mogul armies to bring him to book. Sivājī died in 1680, but his son Sambhājī succeeded him and carried on his father's policy. Prince Muazzam, Aurangzeb's eldest son, protested against the impolicy of destroying Bijāpur and Golkonda, which served as bulwarks against the rising Hindu power, but the Emperor was implacable. The Imperial army moved slowly and ponderously into the Deccan and it did not reach Sholapur, the base of operations, until 1685. Gemelli Careri, and Italian traveller who visited the Emperor in 1695, gives a vivid account of this huge city, thirty miles in circumference, with its 250 bazaars, 500,000 camp followers, merchants and artificers, and 50,000 camels and 30,000 baggage elephants. The royal tents alone, including the accommodation for the harem, covered three square miles of ground, and were defended by palisades and ditches, with guns mounted at regular intervals. Such an unwieldy host was entirely as the mercy of the nimble Marāthās, who were experts at guerilla warfare. "The enemy cut down the grass, which was a cause of distress to man and beast, and they had no food but coconuts and a grain called *kudun,* which acted like poison upon them. Great numbers of men and horses died. Grain was so scarce and dear that wheat flour sometimes could not be obtained for less than three or four rupees. The men who escaped death dragged on a half existence, with crying and groaning as if every breath they drew was their last. There was not a noble who had a horse in his stable fit for use."*

Foiled in his attempt to subdue the Marāthās, the Emperor withdrew to Ahmadnagar, and in 1685 he advanced to attack Bijāpur. Bijāpur surrendered in October 1686, the young king was made prisoner and died in captivity fifteen years later. This was the end of the great and flourishing city which had been the centre

* Elliot and Dowson, VII, 314.

of art and culture in the Deccan for over two centuries. The turn of Golkonda came next. Abdul Hasan, the Sultan, had been guilty of unspeakable abominations. "The evil deeds of this wicked man," writes Aurangzeb,* "pass beyond the bounds of writing.... First, placing the reins of authority and government in the hands of vile, tyrannical infidels; oppressing and afflicting *saiyids, shaikhs* and other holy men; openly giving himself up to excessive debauchery and depravity; indulging in drunkenness and wickedness night and day; making no distinction between infidelity and Islam, tyranny and justice, depravity and devotion; waging obstinate war in defence of infields; want of obedience to the Divine commands and prohibitions, especially to that command which forbids assistance to an enemy's country, the disregarding of which had cast a censure upon the Holy Book in the eyes of God and man." The siege of Golkonda was opened in January 1687, but the inefficient Mogul artillery made no impression on the walls, and at last Aurangzeb had to have recourse to bribery. The gates were opened, but one gallant officer, Abdur Razzāk, with a handful of men, attacked the Mogul columns as they entered and fought until at last he fell from his horse, with no less than seventy wounds. He was carefully tended by Aurangzeb's surgeons, and eventually entered the Imperial service. The Sultan Abdul Hasan was sent to Daulatābād, where he was placed in honourable confinement. In 1689 Aurangzeb achieved his last success by the capture of the Marāthā Rājā Sambhājī and his family. Sambhājī was offered his freedom if he would embrace Islam, but he derisively refused and, having blasphemed against the Prophet, he was put to death with torture. His son Shāhu was sent to the Court, to be brought up as a Muhammadan nobleman.

In 1690 the tide of Mogul conquest had reached its highwater-mark. The last independent kingdoms of the Deccan had been subdued. Aurangzeb was Emperor of India from Cape Comorin to Kābul, and he would have been wise to return to Delhi, leaving Prince Azam Shāh in the Deccan as viceroy. But, in reality, his triumph was a hollow one. The mighty empire was actually on the verge of collapse. The Deccan campaign was a continual drain upon the Imperial treasury, and the stored-up wealth of Aurangzeb's ancestors was poured out like water in maintaining the huge army in the field. India was far too vast to be governed by a single man, and the Emperor was too suspicious to delegate power to another. He had now been absent for twenty years from his capital, from which he was entirely cut off, and had lost all control over the central government. Corruption and oppression flourished unchecked, and in the Punjab the Sikhs and Jāts were in open revolt. Nor were the Marāthās by any means subdued. Their ranks were swelled by numbers of masterless men and professional soldiers, whom the fall of Bijāpur and Golkonda had left without employment. Led by Rājārām, the younger brother of Sambhājī, they fell back upon

* *Ibid.*, p. 325.

Jinji, the almost inaccessible stronghold in the far South. From 1694 to 1698 the Mogul generals tried in vain to take Jinji, and when at last they succeeded, Rājārām and his followers slipped away to carry on the contest. Gemelli Careri's account of his interview with Aurangzeb in 1695 is full of interest. He found him encamped on the banks of the Kistna river. The old man entered slowly, leaning on a staff; he was in white muslin, with a single enormous emerald in his turban. He received his visitor courteously, and enquired about the reasons which brought him to India and the war then being waged between Turkey and Hungary. Careri says that he was of low stature, with a large nose, slender and stopping with age. The whiteness of his round beard was the more conspicuous over his olive-coloured skin. Careri noticed that, in spite of his advanced age, he was able to read petitions presented to him without spectacles, "and by his cheerful, smiling countenance seemed to be pleased with the employment."* The never-ending war with the Marāthās dragged on interminably. In 1700 the Imperial army laid siege to Sātārā, the Marāthā capital, and compelled it to surrender, but what the Moguls won one day the Marāthās recovered on the next. In 1704 another European travellers, Niccolao Manucci, visited the royal camp; he gives a pathetic description of the aged Emperor. "Most of the time he sits doubled up, his head drooping. When his officers submit a petition, or make report to him of any occurrence, he raises his head and straightens his back. He gives them such an answer as leaves no opening for reply, and still looks after his army in the minutest particulars. But those who are at a distance pay very little attention to his orders. They make excuses, they raise difficulties: and under cover of these pretexts, and by giving large sums to the officials at Court, they do just what they like. If only he would abandon his mock sainthood and behead a few of those in his Empire, there would not be so much disorder, and he would be better obeyed." In 1705 Aurangzeb was attacked by fever. He was now eighty-eight, and at last the indomitable old man was forced to give the order to retire. He was persuaded to fall back upon Ahmadnagar, fro which twenty-four years earlier he had set out so full of hopes of conquest and glory; the rearguards of the retreating army were continually harried by the exultant Marāthās, and it seemed to the weary and dispirited troops as though "not a soul would escape from that land of mountains and raging infidels." For two years Aurangzeb lingered on, clinging desperately to life, but daily becoming weaker. His letters written during this period are full of pathos. To his son Kambaksh he writes:

> "My fears for the camp and followers are great; but alas! I know not myself. My back is bent with weakness, and I have lost the power of motion. The breath which rose has gone and has left even hope behind it. I have committed numerous crimes and know not with what punishments I may be seized. Though the

* *A Collection of Voyages and Travels,* by A. & J. Churchill (1707-1747), IV, p. 222 ff.

Protector of Mankind will guard the camp, yet care is incumbent also on the Faithful and on my sons. When I was alive, no care was taken, and now I am gone, the consequences may be guessed. The guardianship of a people is a trust by God committed to my sons. Be cautious that none of the Faithful are slain or that their miseries fall upon my head.... The domestic and courtiers, however deceitful, yet must not be ill-treated. It is necessary to gain your views by gentleness and art. The complaints of the unpaid troops are as before. Dārā Shikoh, though of much judgment and good understanding, settled large pensions on the people, but paid them ill, and they were ever discontented. I am going. Whatever good or evil I have done, it was for you. Take not amiss nor remember the offences I have done unto yourself, that account may not be demanded of me hereafter."*

On February 21st, 1707, after he had finished his prayers and was absorbed in meditation, an attack of faintness came on, but "still the fingers of the dying King continued mechanically to tell the beads of the rosary, and a quarter of the day later he breathed his last." So passed "the crowned saint of Islam." His personal life had been of the simplest; he habitually practised fasting and austerities; at one time he had seriously considered the question of giving up the world and joining an ascetic order. He had devoted himself to the task of purging the land of heresy and idolatry, and his declining years had been passed in the field in an ineffectual crusade against the infidel. It is one of the tragedies of history that all his efforts only led to the ruin of the greatest Empire that India had witnessed.

No gorgeous mausoleum marks the last resting-place of the Great Puritan of India. By his own directions he was wrapped in a shroud of coarse canvas, bought from the proceeds of the sale of caps which he had quilted with his own hand. Three hundred rupees, the proceeds of copies of the Koran which he had himself made, were distributed to the poor, and he was laid in a humble tomb of plastered masonry among the Muslim saints who are buried in the village of Rauza near Daulatābād.

The death of Aurangzeb was followed by the usual scramble for power between the three surviving sons. In the end, Prince Muazzam seized Agra and the Imperial treasury, and was enthroned with the title of Bahādur Shāh. Bahādur Shāh was an elderly man, pious and amiable, but little fitted for the control of affairs of State. He managed, however, to patch up a truce with the Rājpūts, and tried to conciliate the Marāthās by sending back Rājā Shāhu to govern the Deccan as a feudatory of the Mogul Empire. He had to deal with an insurrection of the Sikhs, under Bāndah, the 'false Guru,' who was captured and executed. Bahādur Shāh died in 1712, and disorders at once broke out in Delhi. The story of the next fifty years is one of the

* Sarkar, *History of Aurangzeb* (Calcutta, 1912), V, 259.

most piteous in all history, anarchy and bloodshed stalked unchecked through the unhappy capital. "Many persons of no party, and followers of the camp, unmindful of what fate had in store for them, were greatly alarmed, and went off to the city with their families. Ruffians and vagabonds began to lay hands on the goods of many. Several persons were to be seen seeking refuge in one little shop. Friends and relations were unable to answer the calls made upon them. Great disturbances arose in the armies of the princes, and none of the great men had any hopes of saving their lives." The streets were filled with mutinous soldiers, clamouring for their pay, and the scene, in the words of the chronicler, "was like the Day of Judgment." The power fell into the hands of two brothers, Abdullah and Hussain Ali, known as "The King-Makers," who set up puppet Emperors at their will, and when they had no further use for them, threw them into dungeons, blinded and murdered them. The Empire now began to break up. Asaf Jāh, the Nizām-ul-Mulk, the foremost of the Mogul nobles, disgusted at the degeneracy of the Court, with its buffoons and dancing girls, shook the dust of Delhi from his feet, and went off to the Deccan, where he carved out for himself the great state of Hyderabad. In a similar fashion another great noble, Saādat Khān, the Nawāb Vazīr, set himself up in Oudh, and Allavardi Khān, the Governor of Bengal, also ceased to pay tribute and became virtually independent. The Marāthā horsemen had long overrun the fertile territories of Central India, and in 1737 they appeared before the gates of Delhi; after cutting to pieces a force sent to meet them, they vanished as suddenly as they came. Their mere appearance, however, spread panic in the city. In 1739 a fresh terror arose, Nādir Shāh, one of the mightiest warriors that Persia had produced, proclaimed himself King, and finding the gateway of India unbolted and unguarded, advanced almost unopposed to the capital, brushing aside with ease the wretched levies which tried to bar his path. The Emperor Muhammad Shāh went trembling to meet him; the two rulers entered Delhi side by side and exchanged visits of courtesy and presents. "Strange are the freaks of fortune," writes an Indian historian. "All the resources of the Mogul Emperor and his nobles at the disposal of the Persian Red Caps! The Mogul monarchy seemed to all to be over." All, however, went well until some of the Persian soldiery were murdered in the byeways by the city rabble. Then the order was given for a general massacre. For half a day the slaughter went on, while Nādir Shāh, seated in the Golden Mosque, watched the scene. The gutters ran with blood. "The streets were strewn with corpses like a garden with dead leaves. The city was reduced to ashes and looked like a burnt plain." The Chāndni Chowk, the famous street of the merchants, was gutted. Never since the days of Timūr had Delhi seen such a visitation; the ruin of its beautiful buildings was such that only the labour of years could restore the capital to its former grandeur. At length the Shāh yielded to the piteous entreaties of the Emperor and called off his men. The conquerors then departed, laden with loot of fabulous worth. All the Imperial gold plate and jewels, to the value of many millions of rupees, elephants, horses, costly stuffs, and, lastly, the famous Peacock Throne itself, were carried off to Persia. Even the wretched inhabitants were held up to ransom, and many committed suicide, rather than face the same and misery which had befallen them.

The sack of Delhi in 1739 sounded the death-knell of the Mogul Empire, though plantom Emperors continued to occupy the throne, sitting in their ruined halls under tattered canopies. Yet, so powerful was the magic of the name of the Great Mogul, that he was still regarded as almost sacred throughout the country, and rival powers contended for the control over his person, "Notwithstanding His Majesty's total deprivation of real power," writes Arthur Wellesley, "almost every state and every class of people continue to acknowledge his nominal sovereignty. The current coin of every established power is struck in the name of Shāh Ālam. Princes and persons of the highest rank and family still bear the titles and display the insignia of rank which they their ancestors derived from the throne of Delhi under the acknowledged authority of Shāh Ālam, and His Majesty is still considered to be the only fountain of similar honours. The pride of numerous classes of Mussalmans in India is gratified by a recognition of the nominal authority of the illustrious representative of the House of Timūr over the territories which once constituted the extensive and powerful Empire of the Mogul, and the Mussalmans are still disposed to acknowledge the legitimacy of the pretensions and demands ostensibly proceeding from the authorty of the Imperial Mandate."*

In 1765 Clive wrung from the titular ruler the grant of the Diwāni of Bengal, Bihār and Orissa, that is, the right to collect and administer the revenue of those province for the East India Company; later on the Emperor bestowed upon him a similar grant for the 'Northern Circars,' a large district in the north-east of the present Madras Presidency. Shāh Ālam was now residing at Allahābād, virtually a pensioner of the English. Later he returned to Delhi and become the tool of the Marāthās; in 1788 he was seized by a ruffian named Ghulām Kādir, who flogged the royal princesses and blinded the Emperor in an attempt to force him to disclose the whereabouts of his treasures. The Marāthā chieftain, Māhādjī Sindia, seized this unspeakable brute, cut off his hands, nose and ears and sent him in a cage to his victim. In 1804 Lord Lake, after beating the Marāthās outside Delhi, took the poor, blind old man under his protection. In 1827 Lord Amherst insisted on meeting Shāh Ālam's successor as an equal, the Emperor seated on his throne in the Hall of Private Audience, and the Governor General by his side on a chair, but the Imperial titles still appeared on the Company's rupees.

On that fatal Sunday, May 10th, 1857, when the Indian Mutiny broke out, the

* Wellesley's Despatches (ed. M. Martin, 1840), IV, 154-5.

sepoys from Meerut rushed into Delhi, proclaiming as their leader the Emperor the aged Bahādur Shāh, who was still regarded by millions of pious Muslims as the rightful ruler of India. After the fall of Delhi, Bahādur Shāh was, with doubtful legality, put on trial for rebellion against the East India Company. He was deposed and ended his days as a state-prisoner in Rangoon. Such was the ignominious end of the greatest and most powerful of all the Indian dynasties which had ever occupied the throne of Delhi.

The causes of the downfall of the Mogul Empire are many and complex. The first was that the Moguls were essentially foreigners, and had no roots in the soil. They were aliens both by race and religion from the vast majority of their subjects. The far-sighted attempt of Akbar, the only one of his line with a vision transcending the necessities of the moment, to unite the peoples of India under a truly national government, found no sympathy with his successors. The religous policy of Aurangzeb, which resulted in the alienation of the Rājpūts, deprived the Empire of its strongest supporters, and provoked widespread risings among the Hindus from the Punjab to the Deccan, while his attempts to check the lax morality and general corruption of the age ended in failure. His simple way of life found no imitators among his officers. The presence of the Emperor at the capital was essential in order to maintain the government; Aurangzeb's absence for a quarter of a century, during which time he was cut off in the inaccessible wilds of the Deccan, was fatal to good government. The incessant wars which broke out on the occasion of each fresh occupant of the throne resulted in the extermination of the old Mogul nobility. New blood from Central Asia no longer flowed into the country, and it is a commonplace that a foreign race rapidly degenerates under tropical conditions unless it is constantly recruited from without. The descendants of the hardy followers of Bābur, who braved snowstorms and mountains on their way to India, had become pale, languid and effeminate persons, clad in voluminous muslin petticoats, who took the field in palanquins, accompanied by hordes of camp-followrs, luxurious tents and immense trains of baggage. "Great empires," says Bacon, "do enervate and destroy the forces of the natives which they have subdued, resting upon their own protective forces; and then, when they fail also, all goes to ruin, and they become a prey.... When a warlike state grows soft and effeminate, they may be sure of war; for commonly such states are grown rich in the time of their degeneracy, and so the prey inviteth, and their decay in valour encourageth a war."

Another cause of the downfall of the Mogul state was its military weakness. Its vast, unwieldly armies were nothing more than an armed rabble. Bernier compares them to a herd of animals, and says that 25,000 French veterans under Condé or Turenne, could rout them with ease.* The French, and later the English, discovered

---

* *Travels in the Mogul Empire,* p. 55.

that a handful of Indian sepoys, drilled and disciplined in European fashion, could rout an Indian lost. At Plassey (June 23rd, 1757), Clive had only 3,000 men, including 950 Europeans. With these he put to flight the huge army of the Nawāb of Bengal, consisting of 50,000 infantry, 18,000 cavalry and fifty-three guns: his own losses amounted to twenty-two killed and forty-nine wounded! The Nawāb's were over five hundred. Against the Marāthās, with their guerilla tactics, the Moguls were equally helpless. Their artillery was crude and badly served; fortresses which later on surrendered in a few days to the English held out indefinitely and could only be reduced by bribery.

Of the economic causes at work—the corruption of the officials, the extravagance of the nobility, the waste of money on costly and useless buildings, and the oppression of the peasantry, which was driving large sections of the country out of cultivation, mention has already been made. The country was torn to pieces by civil wars, and groaned under every species of domestic confusion. Villainy was practised in every form; all law and religion were trodden underfoot; the bonds of private friendship and connections, as well as of society and government, were broken; and every individual, as if amidst a forest of wild beasts, could rely on nothing but the strength of his own arm.*

The Mogul Emperors

From Bābur to Aurangzeb.
(Principal names only).

TIMŪR (d. 1404).

(I) BĀBUR (1526-30).

(II) HUMĀYŪN (1530-1556). | Kamrān | Hindāl | Askari

(III) AKBAR (1556-1605) | Muh. Hakīm

(IV) JAHĀNGĪR (1605-1627) | Murād | Daniyāl

Khusru | Parviz | (V) SHĀH JAHĀN (1627-58) | Shahryār

Dārā Shikoh | Shāh Shūjā | (VI) AURANGZEB ĀLAMGĪR (1658-1707) | Murād

* Alexander Dow, *History of Hindostan* (1778), II, 96.

LEADING DATES

A.D. 1659	Enthronement of Aurangzeb.
1669	Destruction of Hindu Temples. Jāt Rebellion.
1672	Satnāmi rebellion.
1679	Reimposition of the poll-tax.
1680	Rebellion of Prince Akbar. Rājpūt war.
1681	Aurangzeb goes to the Deccan.
1686	Annexation of Bijāpur.
1688	Annexation of Golkonda.
1706	Retreat of the Imperial Armies from the Deccan.
1707	Death of Aurangzeb. Accession of Bahādur Shāh.
1712	Accession of Farrukhsiyar.
1724	Commencement of the break-up of the Empire. Secession of Oudh and the Deccan.
1739	Sack fo Delhi by Nādīr Shāh.
1740	Secession of Bengal.
1756	Sack of Delhi by Ahmad Shāh Durrāni.
1804	The Emperor places himself under British protection.
1857-8	Sepoy Mutiny. Trial and deposition of the last Mogul Emperor. Assumption of the Government of India by the Crown.

Chapter XXI

Mogul Art and Culture

With the advent of the Moguls, Indian architecture enters upon a new phase, in which the rugged austerity of the work of the earlier sultans is softened and beautified by Persian influence. The chief characteristics of Mogul buildings are the bulbous dome, the cupolas at the corners standing on slender pillars, and the lofty vaulted gateway. Bābur's disgust at the lack of the amenities to which he had been accustomed in his new capital at Agra has already been recorded, and he at once sent for architects from Constantinople and other centres of Islamic culture, and employed large numbers of skilled Indian stonemasons to remedy these defects. Unfortunately, most of Babur's work has been cleared away to make room for later buildings. Mogul architecture, as we know it, for all practical purposes begins with Akbar. Akbar had a passion for building. In the words of Abul Fazl, "His Majesty plans splendid edifices, and dresses the work of his mind and heart in the garment of stone and clay." His earliest erection, the tomb of his father Humāyūn, has many novel characteristics. The main body of the building is of red sandstone, inlaid with marble, and surmounted by the characteristic cupolas. The dome is of white marble. It was clearly a tentative essay in a new style, and Fergusson remarks on the poverty of the general design and the absence of the picturesque boldness of the tombs of the earlier dynasties. The most characteristic product of Akbar's genius is the city of Fathpur Sīkrī, happily preserved almost intact. The central feature is the great mosque built round the tomb of Salīm Chishti (Plate XVIII). The tomb, which stands in the midst of the courtyard, is of marble inlaid with mother of pearl. The windows contain marble tracery of fine workmanship. The cornice is supported by brackets of elaborate and almost fantastic character, clearly Hindu in style, and the glittering white building, seen in the bright light of an Indian winter morning, contrasts vividly with the red sandstone of the mosque itself. On the south side is the gigantic gateway, the Buland Darawāza, or Lofty Portal, erected to commemorate the conquest of Khāndesh in 1601. This has been described as the most perfect architectural achievement in the whole of India. The whole edifice has an almost indescribable dignity and impressiveness, and the sandstone has weathered to a beautiful rose colour. There are numerous other public and private buildings in Fathpur Sīkri, all of which present features of great interest, but mention can only be made here of the Diwān-i-Khās, or Hall of Private Audience. A single carved column of red sandstone, surmounted by a gigantic capital, stands in the midst of the chamber. From the capital radiate four railed balconies. Akbar, 'like a god in the cup of a lotus flower,' seated himself in the middle, with his ministers at the four corners, while the nobles and others admitted to the audience stood below. This singular erection is a striking illustration of the originality of the Emperor's genius; indeed, as Fergusson justly remarks, the whole city is a romance in stone, such as very few are to be found anywhere, it is a reflex of the mind of the great man who built it, more distinct than can be obtained from any other source. "In the empty palaces, the glorious mosque, the pure white tomb, the baths, the lake, at every turn we realise some memory of the greatest of Indian Emperors. We may even enter his bedroom, the Khwābghar or House of Dreams, and see the very screens of beautiful stone tracery, the same Persian couplets, the identic ornament in gold and ultramarine on which Akbar feasted his eyes in the long sultry afternoons."* Another characteristic work is Agra Fort, a vast structure of red sandstone, with walls seventy feet high and lofty gateways.

The reign of Jahāngīr was not remarkable for any public buildings on a large scale. The chief architectural remains of this period are Akbar's mausoleum at Sikandra, completed in 1612, and the tomb of Itimād-ud-daulah, the father of the Empress Nūr Jahān, erected in 1628. Akbar's tomb, with its four diminishing storeys or terraces, is a most interesting structure, and was no doubt planned by the great Emperor himself. It has been suggested that the design was a reminiscence, on the part of Hindu craftsmen, of the ancient Buddhist vihāra. Others have maintained that it was the work of Cambodian visitors from the Far East. At the summit is the 'false tomb,' which consists of a block of solid marble carved with flowers and bearing the formulae of the Divine Faith, *Allah-u-Akbar,* 'God is Great,' and *Jalli Jalālun*, 'Magnificent in his Glory'. Originally it was intended that it should be covered with a domed marbe canopy, 'to be ceiled all within with pure sheet-gold, richly inwrought'. The Emperor's body reposed below, in a high vaulted chamber dimly lighted from above, beneath a white marble sacrophagus. The elegant tomb of Itimād-ud-daulah calls for little comment. It is wholly of white marble, elaborately carved, and is decorated with the dainty *pietra dura* work which is such a feature of the succeeding reign.

Under Shāh Jahān, Mogul architecture reached its climax. Nothing can be more striking than the contract between the manly simplicity of Akbar's sandstone buildings and the lavishly ornamented and elaborately inlaid marble work of his grandson. It is significant of the decadence which was already about to set in. In Shāh Jahān's

* S. Lane-Poole, *Medieval Indian Under Muhammadan Rule,* p. 271.

buildings, the Hindu influence, so strong under Akbar, entirely disappears. The most famous of all Shāh Jahān's works is the incomparable Tāj Mahal, begun in 1632, the year after the death of his beloved Empress, and not completed until 1647, though 20,000 workmen were employed on it daily. Its total cost was stated to have been just over 411 lakhs of rupees, or four and a half million pounds sterling; fortunately, perhaps, for the resources of the unhappy and overtaxed peasantry, the Emperor's dream of a replica on the opposite side of the Jumna, linked by a flying bridge, was never realised. As unsupported statement of Father Manrique, that the architect was a Venetian named Jerome Veroneo, may safely be disregarded. The design is purely eastern in conception, and Persian authorities ascribe it to a certain Ustād Isa (Master Jesus), a Turk from Constantinople, who had previously worked in Shirāz and Samarkand. The Tāj Mahal is a great complex of buildings, surrounded by a massive wall, with mosques on two sides. In the centre the marble mausoleum rises lotus-like from the midst of the formal gardens and fountains which surround it. "At the end of a long terrace, its gracious outline, partly mirrored in the still water of a wide canal, a fairy vision of silver white—like the spirit of purity—seems to rest so lightly, so tenderly, on the earth, as if in a moment it would soar into the sky".* At the corners of the raised platform stand, sentinel-like, four lofty minarets. The spandrels and other architectural details are picked out in *pietra dura* work, the stones employed being agate, carnelian, jasper and turquoise. "They are combined in wreathes, scrolls and frets, as exquisite in design as beautiful in colour, and relieved by the pure white marble in which they are laid, they form the most beautiful and precious style of ornament ever adopted in architecture."† Descending, we find ourselves in the room where the royal lovers sleep side by side. "No words can express the chastened beauty of that central chamber, seen in the soft gloom of the subdued light which reaches it through the distant and half-closed openings that surround it." The Tāj Mahal is, indeed, 'the miracle of miracles, the final wonder of the world' (Plate XX). Of Shāh Jahān's buildings in Agra Fort, the most attractive is the little Pearl Mosque, built of delicately veined marble, and entirely unadorned.

In 1638, Shāh Jahān commenced to build for himself a new capitla at Delhi, which he named Shāhjahānābād. The palace is surrounded by a wall of red sandstone. On entering, the visitor finds himself in a valuted hall like the nave of a gigantic Gothic cathedral. Passing through the Naubat Khānā, or Music Chamber, where the drums announced the approach of the Imperial cortège, he arrives at the Dīwan-ī-Ām, or Hall of Public Audience. Beyond this lies the Diwān-ī-Khās, or Hall of Private Audience. This is a marble pavilion, the fretted pillars richly inlaid with *pietra dura* work. The ceiling was originally of crimson, overlaid with gold and silver foliage,

* E. B. Havell, *Handbook to Agra and the Taj*, p. 80.

† Fergusson, *History of Indian and Eastern Architecture*, p. 598.

and here the Great Mogul, on his Peacock Throne, gave audience in private to princes of the blood, nobles and foreign ambassadors. On the cornices at either end of this superb chamber is the couplet:—

Agar firdaus bar ruyi zamin ast,
..umin ast, hamin ast, hamin ast!

If on earth be an Eden of bliss,
It is this, it is this, it is this!

Behind is a maze of buildings which comprise the private apartments of the Emperor and his seraglio. These rooms included the painted Chamber (Rang Mahāl), the House of Dreams (Khwābgha.), and many others. An outstanding feature of these rooms is the pierced marble screens between them. One doorway, which bears above it the Scales of Justice inlaid in gold, is especially famous. It is somewhat of a relief after the dazzling and voluptuous splendours of the palace to turn to Shāh Jahān's two other great buildings, the Jama Masjid or Cathedral Mosque at Delhi, and Jahāngīr's tomb outside Lahore (Plate XIX). The Jama Masjid, intended as a centre of public worship for the populace of the capital, is a dignified and nobly-proportioned structure, admirably suited for its purpose.

The Mogul love of nature has already been commented on; Babūr and his descendants revelled in trees and flowers and landscape-gardening as a favourite diversion. A Muhammadan nobleman was wont to plan for himself a Bārādārī or summerhouse where he could take his ease after the heat of the day, and which would become his resting-place at death. It usually stood in the midst of a formal garden, laid out in geometrical patterns. In a hot, dry country such as India, water is essential, and the garden was well supplied with fountains, artificial cascades, and marble channels and basins. It was planted with shade and fruit trees. But the Mogul garden was not invariably associated with the tomb. Jahāngīr and his consort, the Empress Nūr Jahān, laid out gardens wherever they stayed. Jahāngīr in his *Memoirs* constantly reverts to the subject and records the intense pleasure which he derived from them. The Shālimār, Nishāt and other gardens in Kashmir are perhaps the best examples of the Mogul gardener's art. Above the gate of the Shālimār Garden in Lahore is the famous couplet:

Sweet is this garden, through envy of which the tulip is spotted,
The rose of the sun and moon forms its beautiful lamp.

Painting was no novelty in India when Humāyūn brought Persian draughtsmen back with him on his return from exile. The Hindus had long adapted the ancient art of Ajanta to the illumination of religious manuscripts, and there were flourishing schools of painting in Jammu, Kāngra and Rājputāna. In Rājputāna the artists enjoyed the patronage of the wealthy Hindu princes, and their work, like that of Agra and

Delhi, tended to become a Court art. The subjects chosen by these painters are usually mythological; the favourite themes are episodes from the *Mahābhārata* and *Rāmāyana*, and from the life of Krishna; his amours with the Gopīs or Divine Milkmaids afford almost inexhaustible scope for the imagination (Plate XXI). Others were the Hindu musical modes, (*Rāg*), allegorically represented. By appropriating a different mode to each of the seasons, the artists of India connected certain strains with certain ideas. Albums of pictures depicting these went by the name of *Rāgmālā* or 'Garlands of Modes'. Scenes from Hindu daily life—girls worshipping at a shrine, ascetics plunged in meditation under a banyan tree, elephants, cattle and deer—are very common. (Fig. 42). Night scenes, with their startling chiaroscuro effects, were also extremely popular. "In these works, Nature is represented with a simple and decorative directness, expressive of all forms but rigorously excluding the complex and immaterial; an art that is true to nature, to the artist's ideals and to the time and country he lived in; without effort, without falseness and without prevarication."*

Humāyūn's chief artists were Mir Sayyid Ali and Khwājā Abdus Samad. Mīr Sayyid Ali was a pupil of the famous Bihzād of Herat, 'the Raphael of the East', and early Mogul art bears pronounced traces of its Persian origin. But with Akbar began the fusion of the Hindu and Persian styles from which Mogul art was evolved. Abul Fazl records Akbar's remarkable dictum on the subject of painting, which was regarded by strictly orthodox Muhammadans as idolatrous. "There are many," he said, "who hate painting, but such men I dislike. It appears to me as if a painter had quite peculiar means of recognising God; for a painter, in sketching anything that has life, and in devising the limbs one after another, must come to feel that he cannot bestow personality upon his work, and is thus forced to thank God, the Giver of Life, and will thus increase his knowledge."† Akbar especially admired Hindu Art. "Their pictures," he was wont to say, "surpass our conception of things; few in the whole world are found equal to them." Among the Hindu artists who caught Akbar's attention, one of the most remarkable was Daswānāth. Daswānāth was the son of a poor palanquin-bearer, who used to amuse himself by drawing on walls. The Emperor recognised his talent, and sent him to Khwājā Abdus Samad's studio for training, but unfortunately he became insane and committed suicide. An even greater genius was another Hindus, Basāwan. "In background," says Abul Fazl, "drawing of features, distribution of colours, portrait-painting and several other branches, he excels, so that many critics prefer him to Daswānāth." Akbar used to pay regular visits to the studios, and reward the artists according to their proficiency. The studios, with their staff of painters, calligraphists, grinders of colours and gilders, were busy hives of industry. Among the tasks undertaken in the Royal ateliers were

* L. Heath, *Examples of Indian Art*, p. 16.

† *Ain-i-Akbari*, trans. Blochmann and Jarrett (Calcutta, 1873-1891), I, 107.

Fig. 42 : Portrait of a Hindu Lay (Rajput School).

an album containing portraits of His Majesty and the great nobles of the Court, and illustrations for the *Akbar Nāmā*, the *Rāz Nāmā* (a Persian version of the *Mahābhārata*), his grandfather's Memoirs, and other works.

Jahāngīr was a great connoisseur of painting. He speaks of two artists, Abul Hasan and Mansur, whom he specially admired. The former was commissioned to paint the frontispiece to his Memoirs, and Jahāngīr recognised his talent by raising him to the rank of a Grandee (Khān) of the Empire. Speaking of himself, Jahāngīr says, "when any work is brought before me, either of deceased artists or of the present day, without the names being told me, I say on the spur of the moment that it is the work of such and such a man. And if there be a picture containing many portraits, and each face be the work of a different master, I can discover which face is the work of each of them. If any other person has put in the eye and eyebrow of a face, I can discover whose work the original face is, and who has painted the eye and eyebrows."* During the reign of Jahāngīr, Mogul painting began to be affected by

* *Memoirs,* trans. Rogers and Beveridge, I, 20.

European contact; Western influence is chiefly seen in greater naturalism, and the use of perspective and shading. The Jesuit Fathers brought with them numerous religious pictures, mostly reproductions of works by famous Italian artists, which were immensely admired. The court painters were adepts at copying. Sir Thomas Roe tells an amusing story of a wager which he had with Jahāngīr about a picture which he brought as a present. He said he would give a "painter's reward"—fifty rupees—to anyone who could imitate it with absolute accuracy. The same evening, six copies were laid in front of the English ambassador, who confessed himself unable to pick out the original. The Emperor was so merry and joyful at his artists' success that he 'craked like a Northern man.' Bernier's remarks on Indian painting are interesting. He says that all artists were in the pay of the Court or some nobleman, and could not exist apart from patronage. He admired the beauty, softness and delicacy of their paintings and miniatures, though he thought them deficient in 'just proportions and in the expression of the face.' He mentions a shield displaying the exploits of Akbar by a celebrated artist, which took seven years to complete.*

Fig. 43 : Calligraphic Drawing composed of the names of the Twelve Imāms.

Mogul painting may be said to have reached its zenith under Jahāngīr. The Court artists now appear to have emancipated themselves from the Persian conventions which

* *Travels in the Mogul Empire,* p. 255.

make the work of Akbar's time appear stiff and formal, and the best art of the period is delightfully fresh and natural—a happy blending of Iranian, Indian and European influences, while maintaining a character peculiarly its own. (Plate XXI). A saying attributed to Prince Daniyāl happily sums up the prevailing sentiment. "We are tired of the old wearisome tales of Laila Majnun, the moth and the nightingale. Let the poets the artists take for their subjects what we have ourselves seen and heard."* And this is what they did. Instead of illustrations for Persian manuscripts, we have striking portraits, animated hunting scenes, and charming studies of animals, birds and flowers. Mansur in particular excelled in the latter, and examples survive in all the great collections. Their fidelity to nature is striking, and their flower studies should be compared to those in the *pietra dura* work on the palace walls.

Shāh Jahān was more interested in architecture than painting and during his reign the number of Court artists was reduced. Their work shows signs of approaching decadence in the lavish use of gold and other ornamentation. Most Mogul pictures are on paper, and the technique is generally the same. The surface is treated with a pigment and afterwards burnished. The outline is then drawn and the body-colours laid on in successive layers. The brush employed was of squirrel's hair, and a one-haired brush was used for finest work. There are remains of mural paintings at Fathpur Sīkrī, and also at Bijāpur in the Deccan, but only fragments have survived. A single picture was often the work of a number of collaborators, one being responsible for the outline, a second for the colour and a third for the back-ground, while a calligraphist executed the floral border and superscription.

Closely allied with the art of painting was that of calligraphy. Calligraphy was the only form of art permitted by extreme Islamic orthodoxy, and was cultivated as assiduously in Muhammadan countries as in China and Japan. (Fig. 43). Connoisseurs gave large sums for the work of celebrated calligraphists. Calligraphy also entered largely into the decoration of the mosque; the ninety-nine Divine names the Koranic texts are inscribed round the portal and on the walls, and appear in the tracery of the windows. There are various types of lettering, from the stiff upright Kufic to the flowing Nastālik beloved of Akbar. The Imperial palaces contained immense libraries. The library of Agra, according to Father Manrique, who was there in 1641, contained 24,000 volumes, and was valued at six and a half million rupees, or nearly three-quarters of a million sterling. Most of these were dispersed or destroyed in the troubled times which followed on the death of Aurangzeb. Many albums of pictures found their way to Europe, where they found warm admires. Rembrândt and Sir Joshua Reynolds are among European artists who keenly appreciated the beauty and delicacy of Indian painting. Many fine collections exist in England and in various parts of

* Quoted in N. C. Mehta, *Studies in Indian Painting* (Bombay, 1926), p. 75.

Europe and may be seen at the Victoria and Albert Museum, the British Museum and the India Office. A pathetic interest attaches to a particularly beautiful album in the latter place. It belonged to the gifted and ill-fated Dārā Shikoh, and bears the inscription: "This album was presented to his nearest and dearest friend, the lady Nādira Begam, by Prince Muhammad Dārā Shikoh, son of the Emperor Shāh Jahān, in the year 1051" (A.D. 1641-2).

Brief mention must be made of the other arts. Sculpture was cultivated to some extent, in spite of the Koranic prohibition, but no specimens have escaped the iconoclastic fury of Aurangzeb. The figures of two Rājās, said to be Jaimal and Patta, the defenders of Chitor in 1568, originally stood outside the gates of the fort at Delhi, and there were statues of Amar Singh the Rānā of Chitor and his son beneath the audience window at Agra. Jewelry reached a high degree of perfection: the crowning triumph of the jeweller's art was the famous Peacock Throne, the enamelled canopy of which was supported by twelve golden pillars inlaid with emeralds. Between the pillars were pairs of peacocks, encrusted with diamonds, rubies, emeralds and pearls. It was supported by six massive feet of solid gold. It was the work of the Court jeweller, Bebadal Khān, and took seven years to construct. There was a great demand for inlaid work, damascening and enamelling, and for the goldsmith's and silversmith's art. The Royal Mints turned out a fine series of gold, silver and copper coins. These were usually stamped with calligraphic devices, though Jahāngīr shocked orthodox sentiment by representing himself holding a wine-cup. Everyone wore gold and silver ornaments, and the amount of precious metal consumed in this way was incredible. The looms turned out fine carpets, brocades and silks. Indian muslins, shawls, and chintzes were famous all over the world. The bare, deserted halls of Agra and Delhi presented a very different appearance in 1659, when the Great Mogul, seated on his 'throne of royal state,' gave audience to his court. Here is Bernier's vivid description of the scene in 1659:

> "At the foot of the throne were assembled all the Omrahs in splendid apparel, upon a platform surrounded by a silver railing and covered by a spacious canopy of brocade with deep fringes of gold. The pillars of the hall were hung with brocades of a gold ground, and flowered silken canopies were raised over the whole expanse of the extensive apartment, fastened with red silken cords from which were suspended large tassels of silk and gold. The floor was covered entirely with carpets of the richest silk, of immense length and breadth. A tent was pitched outside, larger than the hall, to which it was joined by the top. It spread over half the court, and was completely enclosed by a great balustrade covered with plates of silver. Its supporters were pillars overlaid with silver, three of which were as thick and as high as the mast of a barque, the other smaller. The outside of this magnificent tent was red, and the inside lined with elegant Masulipatam

chintzes, figured expressly for that very purpose with flowers so natural and colours so vivid that the tent seemed to be encompassed with real parterres."*

Literature flourished under the patronage of the Mogul Emperors, two of whom, Bābur and Jahāngīr, composed their own memoirs. Those of Bābur were written in his native Turki, but were translated into Persian in the reign of Akbar. At Akbar's court was gathered a galaxy of poets, musicians and men of letters. Of the poets enumerated by Abul Fazl, the best was his brother Faizi, extracts from whose compositions are given in the *Ain-i-Akbari*, or Institutions of Akbar. Of the historians of the age incomparably the greatest is Abul Fazl himself. His vast *Akbar Nāma* or Life of Akbar, of which the *Ain-i-Akbari* is a part, is the most important historical work which India was produced. The first part contains a history of the House of Timūr down to the forty-sixth year of the Emperor; the remainder is a Gazetteer. It deals with the Imperial Household and Court; the military and civil services; the judicial and executive departments, including finance and land revenue; the social, religious and literary characteristics of the Hindu population; and lastly, the sayings and observations of Akbar himself. Written in a spirit of frank hero-worship, it has earned for its another the title of the Mogul Boswell. No details, from the revenues of a province of the price of a pine-apple, are beyond his microscopic and patient investigation, but his annals have none of the pregnant meaning and point that in a few master-strokes exalt or brand a name to all time, and flash the actors of the drama across the living page in scenes that dwell for ever in the memory.† Some of the most important undertakings of the men of letters of the Mogul Court were the translation into Persian of standard Sanskrit works. A deep interest was taken in Hindu philosophy, and Faizi, the Poet Laureate, rendered the *Bhagavad Gītā* into Persian verse. Dārā Shikoh was a student of the Vedānta and the Upanishads. Persian abridgements of the Hindu Epics, the Purānas, and the *Lilāvati* (a treatise on mathematics) were made.

With the accession of Aurangzeb, a deadly blight fell upon the arts. The Court musicians, artists and historians were dismissed, and no important buildings were erected save a few mosques on the site of Hindu temples which had been demolished. Though an accomplished poet, Aurangzeb discouraged poetry on the ground that poets dealt in falsehood. History was banned, because it gave rise to feelings of undue pride. "After the expiration of ten years, authors were forbidden to write the events of this just and righteous Emperor's name." Paintings on the walls of Fathpur Sīkrī and Bijāpur were defaced as idolatrous, and Aurangzeb even gave up showing himself at the audience-window because his subjects gave him worship only due to the Creator.

---

* *Travels in the Mogul Empire,* pp. 268-70.

† *Ain-i-Akbari,* trans. Blochmann and Jarret (Calcutta, 1873, 1891), Vol. II, Preface.

A well known story relates how one day he heard a funeral procession passing the palace. On asking whose funeral it was, he was told that the mourners were bearing the corpse of music to his grave. "Bury him deep," replied the Emperor, "that not a sound of him comes to my ears." Bernier gives a pathetic picture of the condition of the unfortunate court artists, only called in as occasion arose, grudgingly rewarded for their work, and lucky if they escaped without a flogging as part-payment.*

The Mogul Court at the height of its glory resembled in many respects that of Versailles. In both cases a fabulously wealthy and extravagant nobility were living a life of the utmost luxury, at the expense of an overtaxed and starving peasantry. In both cases, the art of the period was an art fostered by the Court, the art of the jeweller and miniature painter, with few roots in the life of the people. In neither instance did it survive the downfall of its patrons, and in India the decadence was rapid. The buildings erected by the royal family of Oudh, the chief centre of Muslim culture in the north after the decline of the Moguls, are tawdry abominations. But in Rājputāna and a few other Hindu states, the traditional arts have survived, and master-masons continue to work on the traditional lines. It is a matter of regret that the great opportunity to utilise their services in the building of the New Delhi in 1911 was allowed to slip.

Education under the Muhammadans

The high degree of culture in Mogul India was largely the result of the excellent system of education. Education was considered to be a religious duty; at the age of four, the boy, if he were the son of rich parents, was given a silver-mounted slate inscribed with a chapter of the Koran and was handed over to a tutor; if poor, he was sent to the Muktab or primary school kept by the Mullah, which was attached to every mosque. Here he learnt by heart the Kalima or creed and certain verses from the Koran which were necessary for his daily devotions. To this were added the *Hadis* or Traditions of the Prophet, the three R's and Persian. Elegant penmanship was cultivated, and if the boy wished to learn the arts and crafts, he was apprenticed to an Ustād or master. Catrou gives an interesting description of the education of the young Mogul princes: "Whilst they remain in the harem, under the eye of their father, a eunuch is charged with their education. They are brought to read, and sometimes to write, in Arabic and Persian. Their bodies are formed to military exercises, and they are instructed in the principles of equity. They are taught to decide rationally upon subjects of dispute which occur, or an supposititious suits at law. Finally, they are instructed in the Muhammadan religion and in the interests of the nation which they may be called one day to govern."† After leaving school, the morc

* *Travels in the Mogul Empire*, pp. 255-6.

† Catrou, *History of the Empire of the Great Mogul* (1709), p. 328,

advanced went to the Madrassah or College, where the curriculum was mainly religious. The chief subjects taught were theology, mathematics and physics, but Persian *belles letters* were added. But education in India was in very much the same state as in Medieval Europe. There had been no Indian Renaissance. Akbar had designs for making the curriculum more practical, but it is doubtful whether they were enforced, and Bernier comments on the lack of secular Universities of the European type, and he tells an amusing story of the reproaches which the Emperor Aurangzeb heaped on his tutor for wasting his time on the subtleties of Arabic metaphysics to the neglect of practical subjects such as geography and politics. "Forgetting how many important subjects ought to be embraced in the education of a prince, you acted as if it were chiefly necessary he should possess great skill in grammar!"

Women, owing to the purdah system, could not attend public institutions, but in nearly every nobleman's establishment a schoolmistress or governess was kept. Muhammadan noblemen demanded culture in their wives, and Akbar, always in advance of his age, built a girls' school at Fathpur Sīkrī. Many Muhammadan women were patrons of literature and themselves writers. The memoirs of Gulbādān Begam, Akbar's aunt, are well-known, and his foster-mother, Māham Anaga, endowed a college at Delhi. Akbar's wife, Salima Sultāna, the famous Empress Mumtāz Mahāl, and Aurangzeb's sister, the princess Jahanāra Begam, were poetesses of note. Muhammadam women, despite purdah, governed empires and led armies in the field: among these, the Sultana Razzayat of Delhi, Chānd Bībī, the heroic defender of Ahmadnagar, and the masterful Nūr Jahān, were the most distinguished.

Vernacular Literature

Mention must be made of the growth of vernacular literature during the Mogul period. Far away from the Imperial court, the Hindu peasant pursued his immemorial vocations, little influenced by the great world around. Mention has been made of the devotional movement, which centred round the worship of Vishnu in his various incarnations, especially as Krishna and Rāma. In Hindustan, a great leader had arisen in the person of Vallabha Āchārya (1479-1531), who had done much to spread the worship to Krishna among the masses; his teaching was carried by Chaitanya into Bengal, where it made a strong appeal. Chaitanya was deeply emotinal; he would sit with his disciples, chanting the praises of the Divine Name, until they became excited to the utmost pitch of religious ecstasy, and after this they would march through the Bengal towns and villages, with drums beating and flags flying, singing hymns in honour of Krishna and his consort Rādhā. (Fig. 44). Thanks to Chaitanya's teching, Bengal experienced a religious revival, and the worship of Krishna is immensely popular all over that part of the country to-day. It is a relief to turn from the erotic

Fig. 44 : Calligraphic Drawing : Krishna and the Gopīs.

and sensuous cult of Krishna to that of the hero-god Rāma. The greatest of the devotees of Rāma was Tulsi Dās, who was born near Delhi about A.D. 1532. Tulsi Dās was a Brahmin, but he determiend to compose a poem in praise of his god, not in Sanskrit but in the language of the people. "My lot," he says in his introduction, "is low, but my purpose high: I am confident of one thing: that the good will be gratified, though fools may laugh." He warns his readers to expect no sexual appeal in the "Lake of Rāma's Deeds," which was the title which he gave to his poem. "Here are no prurient and seductive stories, like snails or frogs or scum on the water, and therefore the lustful crow and the greedy crane, if they do come, are disappointed." The Rāmāyana of Tulsi Dās, as the poem is popularly called, is recited and read all over Northern India to-day. It retells the old story of Valmīki in simple, moving verse, but with the difference that Rāma is no longer a dead hero, but a living Saviour. The following quotation is from a passage of great beauty in which Rāma's mother soliloquises over the Divine Infant lying in her arms:

"With fingers locked in prayer she cries: 'How may I dare,
O Lord God immortal, Thy boundless praise to tell?
Far above the world's confusion and season's vain intrusion,
Whom all the Scriptures witness incomprehensible;
Whom saints and holy sages have hymned through all the ages,
the fountain of compassion, the source of every grace;
Why aye with Lakshmi reignest, Thou, even Thou, now
deignest to be my son and succour thy sore-tried chosen race.

Though we know by revelation, heaven and earth and all
    creation in each hair upon Thy body may be found,
In my arms Thou sweetly dreamest, O mystery supremast, far
    beyond the comprehension of a sage the most profount.' "*

It would be impossible to mention here the numerous poets who enriched the Hindi language at this period—Sūr Dās, the blind poet of Agra, Mīrā Bāi and a host of others. "Sūr is the sun, Tulsi the moon, Kesav Dās is a cluster of stars, but the poets of to-day are like so many glow-worms giving their light here and there."†

---

* Growse's translation, p. 96.

† F. E. Keay, *A History of Hindi Literature,* Heritage of India Series, Oxford, 1920.

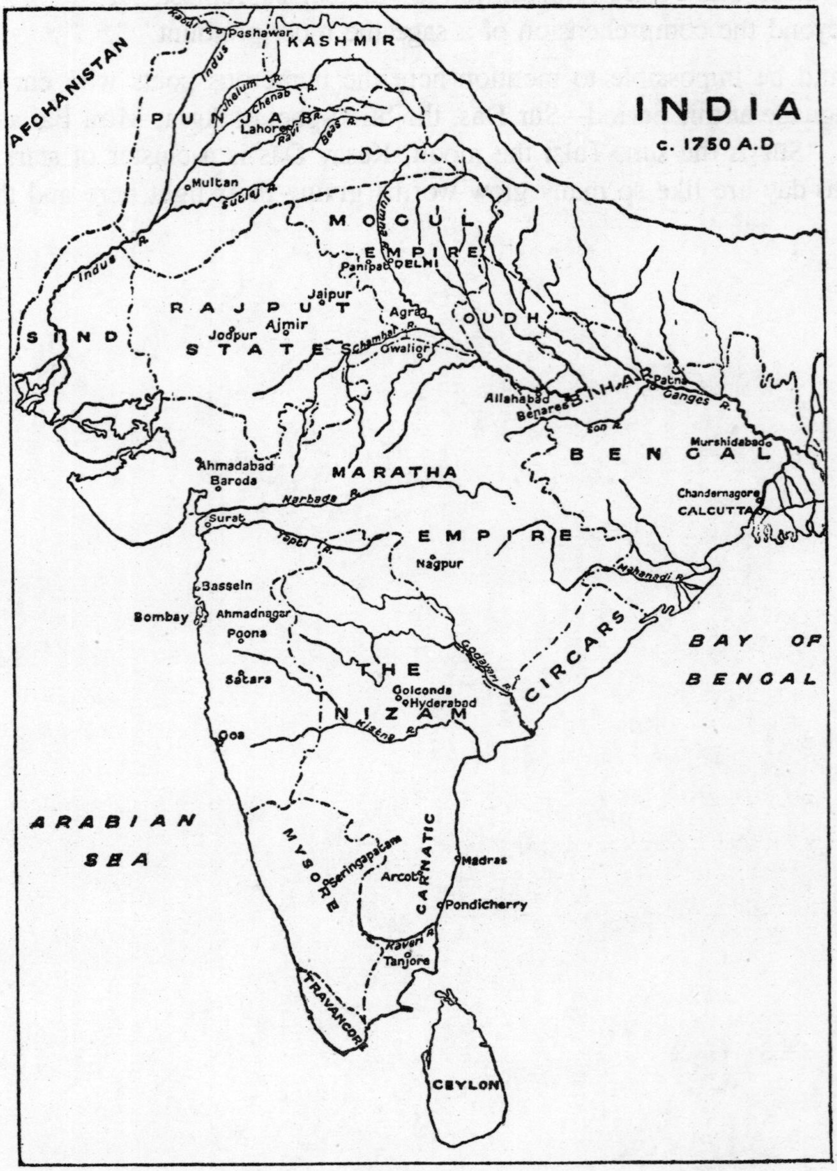

Map 12 : India A.D. 1750.

Chapter XXII

The Renascence of Hinduism – Sikhs and Marāthās and the End of Indian Rule

THE HINDU RENASCENCE

One of the most remarkable facts of Indian history is the vitality of Hinduism. Hindu India had suffered sorely at the hands of her Muhammadan conquerors. Many Hindus had been compelled by force, or for economic reasons, to accept Islam; priests had been killed, temples destroyed wholesale, and the schools of Sanskrit learning closed. But the torch had been kept alight and handed down, chiefly owing to the *bhakti* or devotional movement, which survived all persecution. In India, patriotism had always worn a religious aspect, and, as pointed out in the opening chapter of this work, 'cows and Brahmins' are the objects for which the Hindu is, first and foremost, willing to sacrifice everything. Had Akbar's wise policy towards his subjects been continued by his successors, the Hindu renascence would have doubtless followed purely religious lines: it was persecution which drove it into political channels. The *bhakti* movement, it is interesting to note, was a popular one. Its strength lay, not among the Brahmins or in the Rājpūt courts, but the common people. It was, indeed, strongly anti-Brahmanical. In the 17th century it centred chiefly round two nations, the Sikhs in the Punjab and the Marāthās in the Deccan.

THE SIKHS

In 1469, when the Sultans of the Lodi dynasty were clinging precariously to the throne of Delhi, Nānak, the founder of the Sikh sect, was born on the banks of the Rāvi near Lahore. He was the son of a corn-merchant. Nānak became a follower of Kabīr, who had died about half a century previously. Like Kabīr, Nānak tried to find a common bond between Hinduism and Islam. "God has said," he declared, "that man shall be saved by his works alone. God will not ask a man his tribe or sect, but what he has done." "In the beginning was the Real, in the beginning of the ages was the Real. The Real, O Nānak, is, and the Real will also be." "There is no Hindu and no Mussalman," was another of his sayings. When called upon to explain his attitude by the Muhammadan governor, he is said to have replied in a verse which has now been incorporated in the Sikh scriptures:

Make love thy mosque; sincerity thy prayer-carpet; justice the Koran;
Modesty the circumcision; courtesy thy Kaaba; truth thy Guru; charity thy creed and prayer;
The will of God thy rosary, and God will preserve thine honour, O Nānak.

Nānak went about the Punjab, preaching in mosques, Jain temples and Brahmanical shrines, and gathered a following of Sikhs or disciples. He retained the Hindu doctrines of karma and transmigration, but rejected the Vedas, caste, idolatry and the authority of the Brahmins. To those who rebuked him for breaking caste, he replied in another remarkable stanza, said to have been addressed to pilgrims assembled at the great annual bathing festival at Hardwār:

Evil-mindedness is the low-caste woman; cruelty is the butcher's wife; a slanderous heart the sweeper-woman; wrath the pariah woman.
What availeth it to have drawn lines round thy cooking-place, when these four sit ever with thee?
Make truth, self-restraint and good acts thy lines, and the utterance of the Name thine ablutions.
Nānak, in the next world, he is best, who walketh not in the way of sin.

It is even stated that Nānak performed the Hāj; on one occasion, when he was reproached with sleeping with "his feet towards God" (*i.e.* Mecca), he replied: "Show me a direction where God is not." The Guru or spiritual preceptor plays a leading part in Hinduism, and when Nānak felt death approaching in 1583, he appointed one of his disciples as his successor. There were in all ten such Gurus or Pontiffs. The first four were peaceful leaders of a small and struggling sect, which gathered adherents among the lower orders chiefly owing to its rejection of caste. Akbar, always liberal towards religious movements, granted Rām Dās, the fourth Guru, a piece of land near Lahore, on the banks of a tank which, on account of its healing properties, had acquired the name of the Pool of Immortality (Amritsar). Here the Guru built a shrine, the precursor of the famous Golden Temple (Plate XXIII) erected by Ranjit Singh, and Amritsar became the Mecca of the Sikhs. In 1604 the fifth Guru, Arjun, compiled from the inspired utterances of Kabīr and other teachers, and his own predecessors, the *Adi Granth* or Original Bible of the Sikhs. Arjun was the first of the Gurus to fall foul of the Mogul government. He helped Khusru, Jahāngīr's rebel son, and refused to pay the heavy fine imposed upon the sect for their contumacy. For this he was tortured and beheaded. But the blood of the martyrs is the seed of the church. His son Hargobind turned the Sikhs into a militant order. When his disciples wished to invest him with the turban and necklace, he replied, "My necklace shall be my sword-belt, and my turban shall be adorned with the royal aigrette."

After spending twelve years in a Mogul prison, he carried on a relentless war against the Imperial armies. Following a period of comparative peace during the reign of Shāh Jahān, the ninth Guru, Teg Bahādur, was haled to Delhi by the Emperor Aurangzeb. Before he left, he invested his son Gobind with his sword. At Delhi, Teg Bahādur was brought before Aurangzeb and charged with presuming to gaze from the roof of his abode upon the apartments of the ladies of the royal harem. According to a famous story, he replied; "Emperor Aurangzeb, I was on the top storey of my prison, but I was not looking at thy private apartment, or thy Queen's. I was looking in the direction of the Europeans who are coming from beyond the seas to tear down by *purdahs* and destroy thy Empire." Whether this legend is true or not, it was firmly believed, and was used by the Sikhs as their battle-cry when they marched under their English officers to the siege of Delhi in 1857.

Teg Bahādur received the crown of martyrdom in 1675, and his son Gobind, the tenth and last Guru, at once started to organise his followers into a great military fraternity, like the Knight Templars of Medieval Europe. They were to be known henceforth as the Khālsa or Elect, and the members adopted the surname of Singh or Lion. A ceremony of initiation known as the Baptism of the Sword was introduced, in which the initiates had to drink water stirred by a dagger, and partake of a sacramental meal of cakes prepared from consecrated flour. By this act they finally renounced caste, for sweeper and Brahmin sat down to eat side by side. The reversal of previous customs was striking and complete. "A scavenger or leather-dresser, the lowest of the low in Indian estimation, had only to leave his home and join the Guru, when in a short time he would return to his birthplace as its ruler." Members of the Khalsa swore to abjure wine and tobacco and to adopt five objects beginning with the letter *k*, –long hair, short drawers, comb, a dagger and an iron discus.* The Granth or Bible was revised and installed in the temple at Amritsar, where it was treated with extraordinary reverence. A copy is carried in front of Sikh regiments on the march to-day.

Gobind Singh was murdered by a Pathan in 1708, and with him the line of the Gurus came to an end. Their work was done; henceforth the Khālsa and the Granth were to be the guides of the members of the sect. But he appointed a military successor of the name of Bandah, known as the 'false Guru', and under him the Sikhs attacked and plundered Sirhind, slaying the Muhammadan inhabitants without pity, and defiling the mosques. They brought upon their heads condign punishment at the hands of the Imperial troops. The Sikhs had entrenched themselves in the town of Gurdāspur. This was captured after heavy fighting, and Bandah, his wife and son and a thousand survivors were sent to Delhi. The Sikhs were paraded round Delhi with blackened faces and put to death. Bandah was exhibited in an iron cage; his little son was slain

**Kes, Kaccha, Kankan, Kirpan, Kangha.*

before his eyes before he was executed. A story told by the historian Khāfī Khān shows the temper of the followers of the Khālsa. A mother had wrung from the Emperor a pardon for her son, and arrived on the ground with it in her hand, just as the executioner was raising his bloody sword. But the youth burst into reproaches, saying, "My mother tells a falsehood. I join with heart and soul my fellow-believers in devotion to the Guru. Send me quickly after my companions."

During the troubled times that befel the Punjab in the eighteenth century, the Sikhs suffered severely. Ahmad Shāh Durrāni, the Afghan invader, destroyed the Amritsar temple, having defiled it with cows' blood. With the retirement of the Afghans, the Sikhs slowly returned from the fastnesses in which they had taken refuge, and exacted a terrible vengeance on the Muhammadan population. But they had now greatly degenerated. They had become little more than a confederacy of independent robber chiefs, whose only law was the sword, and the teaching of the Gurus was well-nigh forgotten.

It was at this low ebb of their fortunes that Ranjit Singh, the greatest of the Sikh leaders, was born. He became head of his family in 1792, at the age of twelve, and very early he formed the desire to unite the Sikhs in a separate nation. He recovered Lahore and Amritsar, and at the latter place he built the famous Golden Temple on the site desecrated by the Afghans. He took the strong fortress of Multan, mainly by the help of the famous Zam Zam gun (the 'Luck' of the Sikhs), and occupied the frontier city of Peshawar. He imported two distinguished Napoleonic veterans, Ventura and Allard, to train his troops, and Court, Gardner, Van Courtland and Avaiabile and other Europeans occupied positions of trust in his state.

Ranjit Singh bore no love for the English, whose growing influence he distrusted and feared. It is related that, on being shown a map of India, he exclaimed in disgust, *"Sab lāl hojayega!"* "Soon it will *all* be red!" But he was far too prudent to challenge them, and in 1809 a 'treaty of amity'was signed, recognising the Sutlej as the boundary between the two powers. The English, on the other hand, were anxious to maintain the Sikhs as a buffer-state between themselves and Afghanistan in the event of a Russo-Afghan invasion of India, fear of which had become a bugbear with the British government. In 1831 a meeting was arranged between Ranjit Singh and Lord Amherst, the Governor-General at Rupar on the Sutlej. The scene was an Oriental Field of the Cloth of Gold. The flower of the Sikh army, barbaric horsemen in shining armour with heron's plumes in their helmets, was present. Sports and tourneys were held and for days the troops fraternised while the Mahārājā and Governor-General looked on.

In an evil hour, the Indian government, obsessed by its apprehensions of Russian influence in Afghanistan, was led into the folly of trying to depose Dost Muhammad, the king of Kābul, and to replace him by Shāh Shūjā, a weak and unpopular ruler who had been for some time a refugee in British territory. It was hoped that Shāh Shūjā, would rule Afghanistan as a puppet in British hands. Ranjit Singh, nothing loth to seize an opportunity for humiliating his ancient rivals, signed a 'tripartite treaty' with Shāh Shūjā and the British, by which he agreed to support the pretender. The tragic story of the first Afghan war happily falls outside the scope of the present work. The invaders reached Kābul in August 1838, and placed Shāh Shūjā on the throne. But the Afghans, who value their liberty above everything, rose *en masse* against the foreign army of occupation. The British envoy was murdered, and in January 1841, in the depth of winter, General Elphinstone, who was in command of the army of occupation, decided upon evacuation. On the 13th, a solitary horseman, badly wounded, appeared at the gates of the frontier fortress of Jalālābād. It was Dr. Brydon, a regimental surgeon. He announced that the whole of Elphinstone's army, "guns, standards, honour and all", had been annihilated by the tribesmen in the snow-bound passes of the Hindu Kush. So terrible a tragedy struck a fatal blow to the hitherto invincible prestige of the British arms, whose luck had been regarded as proverbial. Meanwhile, in 1839, Ranjit Singh passed away at the age of fifty-nine. He was altogether an extraordinary figure. He is described as small and partly paralysed, with the long beard prescribed by the Sikh religion. He had lost an eye through smallpox, and it is typical of the Mahārājā's awe-inspiring personality that when his minister was asked which eye it was, he replied, "such is the splendour of his face, that I have never dared to look close enough to discover." Four queens and seven slave-girls followed their lord to the pyre, for the Sikhs, in defiance of the teaching of the Gurus, had revived the dreadful rite of suttee.

Delhi was always an irresistible lure to the Sikhs, and the Afghan disaster had fatally lowered British prestige, which had only partially been restored by Sir Charles Napier's spectacular conquest of Sind from its Baluch rulers, the Talpur Amīrs, in 1843. Deprived of the restraining hand of Ranjit Singh, in December 1845, the army of the Khālsa, over 50,000 strong, with nearly five hundred guns, crossed the Sutlej and invaded British territory. A series of fierce battles ensued, and in February 1846 the Sikhs were bloodily defeated. The young Maharājā, Dhuleep Singh, was installed with Sir Henry Lawrence as Resident at Lahore, and a band of brilliant Englishmen, destined to become household words in Indian history – the Lawrence brothers, Edwardes, Nicholson, Abbott, Lumsden, Montgomery – took over the administration. Henry Lawrence sent his lieutenants to take charge of districts half as big as England, and their only orders were to "settle the country, make the people happy, and take care there are no rows!" Their presence was welcomed by the peasantry, who found the just if stern rule of the English a vast relief after General Avitabile, the monster who blew men from guns, flayed them alive and impaled them and inflicted other cruel punishments copied from the Moguls. But the proud Sikh aristocracy thought otherwise. They sorely chafed under the rule of the aliens who curtailed their ancient liberties and deprived them of their privileges, and in 1848 a rising of the soldiery took place at Multan, in which two British officers lost their lives. Dalhousie, now Governor-General, was nothing loth to take up the challenge. "The Sikh nation has called for war, and upon my word, Sirs, they shall have it with a vengeance!" The campaign was even more fiercely contested than the previous one, but at Sabraon the army of the Khālsa fought its last heroic fight (February 21st, 1849). On March 12th, thirty-five Sardars of rank laid down their swords, and the Sikh soldiers filed past, flinging their weapons upon the pile. Then, raising their hands to them in the Hindu form of salutation, they returned to their fields. "To-day Ranjit Singh is dead," a grizzled warrior was heard to exclaim. The Mahārāja's forebodings had come true. "It had all become red." England was mistress of India from Cape Comorin to the Khyber Pass.

THE MARĀTHĀS

The traveller from Bombay to Poona in the latter stages of his journey ascends the Western Ghauts and finds himself in a region of winding, forest-clad valleys and flat-topped hills, the latter often crowned with curtain and bastion, and forming ideal places of refuge. This is the Mahārāstra, 'hard, but a good nursing mother,' as was said aforetime of stony Ithaca. It is the home of the Marāthās, frugal, hardy peasants, who scrape a scanty living from the soil of their barren but beloved country. As a class, the Marāthās are manly and intelligent, independent and liberal, courteous, and, when kindly treated, trusting. Contrasting them with the Rājpūts, Mountstuart Elphinstone says: "If they have none of the pride and dignity of the Rājpūts, they have none of their indolence or want of worldly wisdom. A Rājpūt warrior, so long as he does not dishonour his race, seems almost indifferent to the result of any contest he is engaged in. A Marāthā thinks of nothing *but* the result, and cares little for the means, if he can attain his object. For this purpose, he will strain his wits, renounce his pleasures, and hazard his person; but he has not the conception of sacrificing his life, or even his interest, for a point of honour.... The Chiefs in those days were men of families who had for generations filled the old Hindu offices of heads of villages or functionaries of districts, and had often been employed as functionaries under the government of Ahmadnagar and Bijāpur. They were all Sūdras, of the same caste with their people, though some tried to raise their consequence by claiming an infusion of Rājpūt blood."

The Marāthās are profoundly pious. They were very early affected by the *bhakti* movement, which here centred round the shrine of a god named Vithoba, who dwelt at Pandharpur on the river Bhima in the heart of the Deccan. The name Vithoba appears to be a corruption of Vishnu and he is identified by his devotees with Krishna. Religion in the Deccan is, like the people themselves, homely and democratic.

Worshippers of Vithoba made a determined stand against the pretensions of the Brahmins, and, as has been already mentioned, one of the earliest works in the Marāthī language was a vernacular paraphrase of the *Bhagavad Gītā* by Jnānesvar at the end of the 13th century A.D. The Brahmins were deeply shocked by Jnānesvar's profanity in turning the scriptures into the vulgar tongue, and one legend relates that he confounded his opponents by causing a she-buffalo to recite the Veda! But the most popular of all the poet-saints of the Deccan was Tukārām. Tukārām was born in 1608. He was a humble grain-dealer by profession, but from boyhood he had been absorbed in the worship of Vithoba. Many stories are related of his unworldly and simple character. He gave away his goods to the poor and starving, and allowed unscrupulous men to cheat and rob him. The climax came in 1631. A terrible famine swept over the Deccan; his wife and child perished of hunger, and he determined to devote himself entirely to religion. He is said, like Saint Francis of Assisi, to have had a wonderful influence over beasts and birds. He betook himself to the temple at Pandharpur, and began to compose the lyric verses in honour of the god which are household words all over the Deccan to-day. Tukārām was overwhelmed by his passionate love for Vithoba, which he poured out in song after song. The following is a typical hymn:

> As the bride looks back to her mother's house,
> And goes, but with dragging feet,
> So my soul looks up unto Thee and longs
> That Thou and I may meet.
>
> As a child cries out and is sore distressed
> When its mother it cannot see:
> As a fish that is taken from out the wave,
> So 'tis, says Tuka, with me.*

The Brahmins, it is said, cruelly persecuted Tukārām. "How dares this Sūdra," they said, "enter the presence of God?" At one time he was dragged through a hedge of thorns: at another the manuscript in which he had written his inspired utterances was taken and thrown into the river, but by the miraculous intervention of the god, it was found floating unharmed. After this, the priests no longer barred his way to the shrine.

It was this admission to the sacred mysteries of men and women of all castes – Muhammadan converts, farmers, tailors, gardeners, potters, goldsmiths, repentant prostitutes and slave girls, and even the outcaste Mahārs or scavengers – which made the temple of Vithoba a national centre of worship. Thousands may still be seen at the time of the great annual festival, thronging the roads leading to

* N. MacNicol, *Psalms of the Marāthā Saints,* Heritage of India Series, Oxford, 1919, p. 56.

Pandharpur, carrying the orange flag which is the hall-mark of the pilgrim, often with their wives and families and their worldly goods packed upon bullock-carts, and chanting devotional verses from their favourite poets as marching-songs. As one watches the vast orderly multitude winding its way across the hills, and breaking into ecstatic cries as their goal comes into sight, the mind inevitably goes back to similar scenes which must have been enacted on the road to Canterbury in the days when England was still a religious country. At the shrine the vast crowds take part in the song-services, and listen for hours to recitations and expositions of the sacred text. In this manner was kept alive the national spirit during the dark days of Muhammadan rule which succeeded the overthrow of the last Hindu monarchy of the Deccan until a leader arose in the person of Sivājī.

Sivājī was born, according to most authorities, in the year 1627. His father Shāhjī, of the Bhonsle family, was a soldier of fortune who had enlisted in the service of the Muhammadan Kingdom of Ahmadnagar. For this purpose he had raised a troop of Marāthā horse, and even set up a puppet Sultan. In 1636, however, he was defeated by the Imperial army, and transferred his services to the state of Bijāpur. He had married a lady of the name of Jijābāī, of an old Marāthā family. While Shāhjī was away on his campaigns in the far south, Jijābāī retired to Junnar near Poona, and here, in the lofty hill-fortress of Sivner, overlooking the town, her son was born. He was brought up by his mother with the aid of a Brahmin tutor named Dādājī Kondeva. Jijābāī was a pious woman, devoted to the worship of the goddess Ambā Bhavāni. The boy was brought up on the stories of Rāma and the Pāndava princes, the heroes of the ancient Indian epics. He would listen for hours to the recitations and songs so popular in the Deccan. It is said that when Poona was in the hands of the Muhammadans, he risked his life in penetrating the enemy lines in order to be present at one of these recitals. Thus, though, like Akbar, Sivājī seems never to have learned to read or write, he was early imbued with an intense love of his country and religion, and a hatred of its foreign rulers, the oppressors, of "cows and Brahmins." During his boyhood, he was constantly in the company of the Mavalis, the hillmen of that part of the Deccan, who taught him to ride and shoot, and to find his way about the tangled maze of pathless jungle which then covered a great part of the country. It was an ideal training for his future career as soldier and liberator.

It was not until the death of his old tutor, however, that Sivājī, now twenty years old, profited by the wars going on in the far south to seize a number of hill-forts, some by surprise and others by bribery, in the Poona district. When the Bijāpur authorities heard of this, they arrested Sivājī's father; but Shāhjī explained that he had no control over his son, and was released. Meanwhile Sivājī was building up a small, independent state for himself; a rival chief was murdered, and Purandhar, a very powerful fortress, was occupied. Khāfī Khān, the Mogul historian, thus describes the rise of Sivājī:

"He was remarkable for courage and quick wits, and in craft and guile he was a clever son of the devil, the father of fraud. In that country, where all the hills rise to the sky, and jungles are dense with woods and bushes, he had an inaccessible lair. Like the landholders of those parts, he set about building forts. Adil Khān of Bijāpur fell sick and, in the ensuing confusion, Sivājī boldly and fraudulently seized the district with some of the neighbouring estates. This was the beginning of the system of tyranny which his descendants spread over the rest of the Konkan and all the Deccan.* Wherever he heard of a prosperous town or district inhabited by thriving farmers, he plundered it and seized it. He gathered a large force of Marāthā robbers and plunderers, and began reducing fortresses. Day by day he increased in strength, reduced all the forts and ravaged the country far and wide. He built some forts, until he had altogether forty, all well supplied with provisions and arms. Boldly raising the standard of rebellion, he became the most noted rebel of the Deccan." (Fig. 45).

Fig. 45. Sivājī
From Valentyn's Oud en Nieuw Ost Indien (1724)

In 1659 the Mogul forces had temporarily withdrawn from the Deccan, and the Bijāpur government sent a well equipped army of some 10,000 men, under Afzal Khān, a great noble, to chastise the rebel. Afzal Khān boasted that he would bring

* The Konkan is the country below, and the Deccan that above the Ghauts.

Sivājī back in chains without dismounting from his horse. On his way northwards, he entered the temple of Ambā Bhavāni, the tutelary guardian of the Bhonsle family, ground the idol to powder, and defiled it and other Hindu shrines. This impolitic action raised the Marāthās all over the countryside to join Sivājī in the defence of their religion. As the Bijāpur army advanced, Sivājī withdrew before it into the mountains country around the present hill-station of Mahābleshwar. Here he had built himself a veritable eagle's eyrie, which he named Pratāpgarh or the strong fortress, on the very edge of the Western Ghauts. He was in a desperate position; his back was to the wall, and he could retreat no farther. Nor was Afzal Khān's position very much happier. His troops were being drawn into wild, pathless country and he was unable to bring his wily adversary to action. Both, therefore, were ready to negotiate. Of the events which followed, accounts are conflicting. Afzal Khān and Sivājī agreed to meet in a cleared space beneath the fort. It may be that either hoped to seize by treachery the person of the other. What actually happened, however, was that Sivājī, pretending to embrace his opponent, stabbed him with the 'tiger claws', a terrible weapon consisting of sharp, steel hooks attached to the fingers, and cut him down. The Bijāpur army was then attacked by the Marāthās, who were lying in ambush. Taken by surprise, it was utterly routed, and its much needed horses, arms, stores and ammunition fell into Sivājī's hands. He chivalrously stopped the slaughter of the fugitives, and dismissed his prisoners after caring for them and tending to their wounds.

In 1660 the Emperor Aurangzeb left the task of restoring order in the Deccan to his maternal uncle, Shayista Khān. The Marāthās, however, were too wily to be drawn into an engagement, and retired to the mountains. The Khān took up his winter quarters in the town of Poona; Sivājī and a picked body of Marāthās entered the gates disguised as a wedding party, and in the middle of the night attacked the unfortunate noble as he lay asleep. Shayista Khān barely escaped with his life, and was so alarmed that he applied for a transfer to Bengal. In 1664 Sivājī brought off his most successful *coup*. On the coast of Gujarāt was the wealthy port of Surat, the great emporium of trade with the West, and the point of departure for pilgrims to Mecca. Secretly collecting a large force, the Marāthā leader swooded down upon Surat. The cowardly Mogul governor shut himself up in the castle, and left the inhabitants to the tender mercies of the invaders. For two days the town was plundered, and the rich Hindu traders were forced by torture to surrender their concealed wealth. The only resistance which the Marāthās encountered was from the English factors, who, under their President, Sir George Oxenden, put their factory into a state of defence, called up the sailors from the ships in the harbour, and threatened to open fire on anyone who molested them. The Marāthās, having utterly pillaged the city, disappeared as swiftly and silently as they had come, loaded with an immense booty.

Aurangzeb was so much impressed by the menace of this new danger that he sought to come to terms. Through Rājā Jai Singh of Jaipur, he sent Sivājī an invitation to visit Agra and make his submission. Sivājī agreed to do so, but on presenting himself at Court he found himself treated as a mere Commander of 5,000 and not as a ruling prince. He left the royal presence in a fit of rage. Aurangzeb's tortuous methods of dealing with political opponents were well-known, and Sivājī now found himself practically a prisoner in his apartments. Feigning sickness, however, he managed to escape, concealed in a sweetmeat basket, and at the end of 1665, after wandering in various disguises almost all over northern India, he once more returned to his people. In 1674. Sivājī was crowned king of the Marāthās amid great rejoicings at his fortress of Raigarh. An Englishman, Henry Oxenden, was present at the ceremony. In 1676 Sivājī made a great expedition to the Carnatic, as far south as Tanjore. His object was to claim his share of the territories which his father Shāhjī held as a feudatory of Bijāpur, and which had fallen to the lot of his brother Vyānkoji. Grant Duff, the historian of the Marāthās, says that this undertaking marks him as the foremost soldier of his age. "In the course of eighteen months, at a distance of 700 miles from his base, he had conquered a territory as large as his former kingdom. While a single reverse would have been fatal, he had not suffered a single check. Victory had succeeded victory; town had fallen after town. As he went, he organised his conquests, and when he returned to Raigarh, his new possessions were securely bound together from sea to sea by a line of fortified strongholds held by garrisons brave to the death and devoted to the cause." He was now at the zenith of his power. He had liberated the Marāthās, and set up once more a Hindu Rāj in the Deccan. Bijāpur and Golkonda were glad to make alliances with the erstwhile rebel. Even the Emperor Aurangzeb was constrained to admit that the "Mountain Rat" had proved too much for him. "My armies have been employed against him for nineteen years," he said, "and nevertheless his state has always been increasing." Sivājī was no mere conqueror. He excelled equally as an organiser. He broke up the power of the old feudal aristocracy by abolishing hereditary fiefs, and all castes, from the highest to the lowest, were allotted their places in the scheme of national defence. Sivājī was assisted in his government by a council of eight, each member of which had definite duties, civil or military, allotted to him. The peasants' lands were carefully assessed, and a tax of about thirty-three per cent was levied; in the case of foreign lands overrun by Marāthā troops, an officer was deputed to collect a tax of one-fourth the revenue, known as Chauth. The Deccan under Sivājī was far better governed than Bijāpur or the Imperial territories.

Sivājī died in 1680, at the age of fifty-three, leaving two sons, Sambhājī and Rājārām. He is described as short and slight, with long arms, an aquiline nose and a pointed beard. He had piercing eyes, and a frank, pleasing manner. He was a born leader, ruthless in war and a stern disciplinarian. No one on pain of death might bring a woman into camp. He was sincerely religious, and looked upon himself as inspired with a mission to be the deliverer of the country; he was devoted to his preceptor Rāmdās, by whose teaching he was guided. At one time, it is said, he laid his kingdom at the feet of his Guru and received it back as a 'gift of God', for which reason the national standard of the Marāthās was the orange-coloured robe of the ascetic. The nobility of Sivājī's character is exemplified by his conduct in the field. He studiously refrained from molesting the women and children of his opponents, and respected religious shrines. The historian Khāfī Khān, always ready to heap abuse upon his Hindu opponents, pays him a striking tribute:

> "He attacked the caravans which came from distant parts, and appropriated to himself the goods and the women. But he made it a rule, that wherever his followers went plundering they should do no harm to Mosques, the Book of God, or any one's women. Whenever a copy of the Holy Koran came into his hands, he treated it with respect, and gave it to some of his Mussalman followers. When the women of any Hindu or Muhammadan were taken prisoners by his men, and they had no friend to protect them, he watched over them till their relations came to buy them their liberty.... He laid down a rule, that whenever a place was plundered, the goods of the poor people, copper money, and vessels of brass and copper, should belong to the man who found them; but other articles, gold and silver, coined or uncoined, gems, valuable stuffs and jewels, were not to belong to the finder, but were to be given without the smallest deduction to the officers, and to be by them paid over to Sivājī's government."*

Such as eulogy, coming from a bitter opponent, is doubly significant. Modern historians have pointed out that some at least of his actions were open to the charge of cruelty and even treachery; but all Marāthās regard him as their national hero. To-day, rapt audiences listen spellbound in far-away villages of the Deccan hills while the Gondālis or wandering bards tell the thrice-told tales of the murder of Afzal Khān, the taking of the Lion Fort, and other episodes of the war of liberation.

Sivājī's successor Sambhājī was a worthless and dissolute man. It has already been related in Chapter XIX how he was captured by Aurangzeb and put to death by torture, while his son Shāhu was sent to Delhi to be brought up as a Muslim nobleman. The Mārāthā chiefs now elected his younger brother Rājārām as their king, and the struggle for freedom continued with unabated fierceness. Aurangzeb scored a great success by capturing Raigarh, the Marāthā stronghold, with all the government records and treasure. When Rājārām died in 1700, the war was carried on by his widow Tārābāī, and indomitable woman, to whose courage and tenacity the defeat of Aurangzeb was principally due.

* Elliot and Dowson, VII, 305.

The old Emperor passed away early in 1707, and his successors tried to solve the problem of the Deccan by sending back Shāhu to occupy the throne as a feudatory of the Mogul Empire. The return of Shāhu to the Deccan had the effect of throwing an apple of discord into the Marāthā midst. Shāhu's aunt Tārābāī coveted the throne for her own son, and the whole country was in a state of confusion. But Shāhu found assistance from an unexpected quarter in the person of a clever Brāhmin named Bālājī Visvānāth, who came from the Konkan, or country below the Ghauts. Shāhu, in gratitude, gave him the office of Peshwa or Prime Minister. One of Bālājī's first actions after restoring law and order was to obtain a decree from Delhi recognising his master as an independent ruler over all the districts owned by his grandfather Sivājī at the time of his death. Bālājī may be regarded as the second founder of the Marāthā Empire; Shāhu, a mild, pious man, was content to leave affairs of state to his minister, while he passed his time in hunting and fishing at his pleasant capital, Sātārā. The Marāthā nobles protested in vain against the growing power of the Brahmin; on his death in 1720, Shāhu invested his son Bājīrao with his father's robes of office. Bājīrao was an ambitious and far-seeing man, and conceived the bold plan of turning the tables upon the declining Mogul Empire and invading Hindustan. "Now is the time," he exclaimed, "to drive the strangers from the land of the Hindus! Let us strike at the trunk of the withering tree, and the branches will fall off themselves. By directing our efforts to Hindustan, the Marāthā flag shall fly from the Kistna to Attock." From that day, the faces of the Marāthās were turned northwards. Every Marāthā fortress has its 'Delhi Gate.'

The next period was one of the expansion. Marāthā soldiers of fortune carved out for themselves territories in Central India, and the Moguls were powerless to interfere. In this way arose the great states of Gwalior and Indore, ruled over by the houses of Sindia and Holkar, Baroda in Gujarāt, the seat of the Gaikwars, and many others. In 1739 the Marāthās descended on the Konkan, and took by storm the citadel of Bassein, the last Portuguese stronghold on that part of the coast. This brought them into uncomfortably close proximity to the English at Bombay. The island of Bombay had been acquired by Charles II as part of his wife's dowry from the Portuguese in 1660. It was let for a nominal rent to the East India Comany, who, on account of its fine harbour, had transferred thither their headquarters from Surat, which had proved to be no longer safe from Marāthā raids.

On Bājīrao's death in 1740, Shāhu once more bestowed the vacant office upon his son Bālājī Bājīrao, and when he himself passed away nine years later, the Peshwa, by a clever *coup d'état*, seized the government. Henceforth the descendants of the House of Sivājī were mere *rois fainéants*, and the Mayors of the Palace transferred the seat of government to Poona. The only rival to the Marāthā power was the Nizam of Hyderabad, but his troops were no match for their agile opponents.

By 1758 the Marāthā power was at its zenith. Even in distant Calcutta, the 'Marāthā ditch' was built to keep out the dreaded horsemen. The chiefs of the Sindia and Holkar families had advanced as far as Delhi, where they were taking an active part in the intrigues which rent the unhappy capital, and eventually they occupied Lahore. This brought them into conflict with the Afghan ruler, Ahmad Shāh Durrāni, who invaded the Punjab and defeated the Sindias and Holkars with great slaughter. When this news reached the Peshwa, he fitted out an army under his cousin, the Bhao Sāheb, to march to Delhi and drive out the intruders. The nominal commander was the Peshwa's son Visvāsrao, a hand-some boy of nineteen. As the troops moved slowly northwards, reinforcements poured in from every side. The expedition assumed the character of a national crusade. If the Marāthās were successful, a Hindu Empire would be restored at Delhi after over five centuries of Muslim rule. But the force presented a very different appearance from the hardy moss-troopers who had compassed the downfall of Aurangzeb, "like our ancient Britons", as a contemporary traveller puts it, "half-naked and as fierce." The great Sivājī had forbidden women to be brough into the camp, but now the Marāthā generals took the field in brilliant uniforms, accompanied by their wives and children, an immense horde of camp-followers and tents and baggage. The Bhao Sāheb placed especial reliance on a brigade of regular mercenary troops and artillery under Ibrāhīm Khān, who had been trained by the Marquis de Bussy, the Nizam's French General. Holkar, Sindia, and Suraj Mal, the Jāt chieftain, begged the Bhao Sāheb to place all his encumbrances in some strong fortress, and then to start operations in the traditional Marāthā fashion, by harassing the enemy's lines of communications. But the haughty Brahmin dismissed them with a sneer. "Who listens to the chatter of goatherds?" he exclaimed, with a contemptuous reference to Holkar's lowly origin. The Marāthā chiefs were deeply incensed. "If the Peshwa wins," they said, "he will annex our revenues, and compel us to wash his loin-cloths."

The Marāthās arrived outside Delhi in due course, and captured the capital without much difficulty. On October 19th, after celebrating the Dasara festival, which marks the end of the rains and the commencement of the campaigning season, they advanced to meet the Afghans, who were encamped about one hundred miles away, on the opposite bank of the Jumna. Unfortunately, the Bhao Sāheb allowed his opponents to cross the river and place themselves between him and his base. He then fell back upon the little town of Pānipat, where the fate of India has so often been decided. Here he dug himself in, and mounted his guns on the parapets, hoping that the Afghans would be tempted to attack him. But Ahmad Shāh Durrāni was too good a soldier to fall into the trap. The camp was closely invested, and soon the state of things in the vast host cooped up inside became almost indescribable. At last the chiefs came to the Bhao Sāheb and declared that the limit of endurance had been reached; they must either come out or starve. The next morning (January 13th, 1761), at dawn, the Marāthās issued forth and battle was joined. The conflict raged from dawn to midday with incredible fierceness, but early in the afternoon Visvāsrao was killed, and the Hindu army broke and fled. The fugitives were pursued to their entrenched camp, where they were butchered without mercy. Among the fallen was the Bhao Sāheb. A note couched in the enigmatic style of the day reached the Peshwa as he was advancing with a relief force. "Two pearls," it said, "have been dissolved, twenty-seven gold mohurs have been lost, and of silver and copper, the total cannot be counted up." Grief and consternation seized the whole Marāthā people as the news was received; every family had lost one or more of its members, and the Peshwa, returning to his capital, turned his face to the wall and died.

The Marāthā confederacy never wholly recovered from the defeat of Pānipaṭ. The centre of power pased from the Peshwa to Māhādjī Sindia, the able and far-sighted Marāthā chieftain whose capital was at Gwalior, but the mainstay of his army consisted mainy of Arab and other mercenaries trained in Western fashion by European officers. Politically, the chief result of the battle was to pave the way for the English conquest; it is doubtful whether the Company's forces could otherwise have made any headway. At Poona a period of disputed successions, action and intrigue supervened on the death of the fourth Peshwa in 1772. For a time, disaster was staved off by the astute policy of Nānā Farnavīs, 'the Indian Machiavelli', who was in control for thirty-eight years. But with this death in 1800, as the British Resident observed, departed all the wisdom and moderation of the Marāthā government. The declining fortunes of the Marāthās can only be traced in the briefest detail. In 1802, by the Treaty of Bassein, the last Peshwa, Bājīrao II, threatened by a coalition of his rivals, Sindia and Holkar, sacrificed his independence as the price of protection. He agreed to be restored to his throne by the East India Company, to pay a tribute of 26 lakhs of rupees, and to accept a British Resident and a subsidiary force at his capital of Poona. The arrangement did not last long. In November 1817 he tried to shake off his masters, but was defeated on the plain of Kirkee; a few months later he surrendered to the British cavalry, and was sent off to exile at Bithur near Cawnpore with a princely pension. The descendant of the house of Sivājī was restored to the throne of Sātārā as a British feudatory.

Meanwhile, the other members of the Marāthā confederacy had been also disposed of. Daulatrao Sindia, who had succeeded the great Māhādjī in 1794, was defeated by Sir Authur Wellesley at Assaye near Aurangābād in 1803. Holkar was driven out of Northern India by Lord Lake, and both chieftains were compelled to accept subordinate alliances with the British. The Nāgpur rājā, another great Marāthā chief, was defeated at the same time as the Peshwa and the greater part of his territory was annexed. Thus the last independent Hindu state succumbed to the advance of the all-conquering British arms.

LEADING DATES

THE SIKHS

A.D.

1469-1539 Nānak, first Guru.
1577 Akbar grants the site of Amritsar to the Sikhs.
1604 First compilation of the Granth or Sikh Bible.
1606 Execution of Guru Arjun by Jahāngīr.
1606 Guru Hargobind forms the Sikhs into a brotherhood.
1675 Execution of Guru Teg Bahādur by Aurangzeb.
1675-1708 Guru Govind Singh, tenth and last Guru, organises the Khālsa.
1715 Execution of Bandah, the 'false Guru.'
1799 Rise of Mahārājā Ranjit Singh.
1809 Ranjit Singh signs a treaty of 'perpetual amity' with the British (Treaty of Amritsar).
1838-9 Tripartite treaty between Ranjit Singh, the British and Shāh Shūjā of Afghanistan. Death of Ranjit Singh.
1845 First Sikh War.
1846 Defeat of the Sikh army; treaty of Lahore.
1848 Rising at Multan; Second Sikh War.
1849 Annexation of the Punjab.

THE MARĀTHĀS

A.D. 1627 Birth of Sivājī.
1646 Sivājī commences to capture the hill-forts round Poona.
1659 Murder of Afzal Khān and defeat of Bijāpur army.
1664 Sivājī loots Surat.
1666 Sivājī goes to Agra.
1674 Coronation of Sivājī.
1676 Expedition to the Carnatic.
1680 Death of Sivājī. Sambhājī succeeds.
1689 Execution of Sambhājī. Rājārām succeeds.
1700 Death of Rājārām.
1707 Death of Aurangzeb.
1708 Shāhu sent back to the Deccan.
1714 Bālājī Visvanāth, first Peshwa.
1720 Bajirao I, Peshwa.
1737 Marāthās outside Delhi.
1740 Bālājīrao Peshwa.
1758 The Marāthās occupy the Punjab.
1761 Defeat of the Marāthās at Pānipat. Mādhurao Peshwa.
1794 Death of Māhādjī Sindia.
1796 Bājīrao II, Peshwa.
1800 Death of Nānā Farnavīs.
1802 Bājīrāo Peshwa signs the treaty of Bassein.
1803 Sindia defeated by Wellesley at Assaye.

1817 Last Marāthā War. Peshwa defeated at Kirkee.

1818 Banishment of the Peshwa to Bithur. Annexation of the Deccan by the British and restoration of the Kingdom of Sātārā.

1848 Annexation of Sātārā by the British.

THE PESHWAS OF POONA

- (I) Bālājī Visvanāth (1714-20)
  - (II) Bājīrao I (1720-40)
    - (III) Bālājī Bājīrao (1740-61)
      - Visvāsrao, killed at Panipat 1761
      - (IV) Mādhurao (1761-72)
      - (V) Narāyanrao (1772-3)
        - (VI) Mādhurao II (1774-95)
          - (VII) Bājīrao II (1796-1818)
            - Nānā Sāheb (died 1858)
    - Raghoba (Pretender) 1773-4
  - Chimājī Appa
    - Sadāshivrao (The Bhao Sāheb) killed at Pānipat 1761

Chapter XXIII

Modern India

The British were only one of the a number of European powers which tried to establish trading factories on the Indian coast. They had originally no thought of territorial conquest. In addition to their settlements at Surat and Bombay, the East India Company had been granted a site for a factory at Madras in 1639, and at Calcutta on the Hugli in 1690. The Portuguese, the pioneer European nation in the East, were already on the downgrade when the English arrived. The Dutch troubled themselves little about India: they had a factory at Surat, but their chief attention was focused upon the Spice Islands. The French were the latest comers. *La Compagnie des Indes* was formed in 1664, under the patronage of Louis XIV, and it acquired a settlement at Pondicherry on the Madras coast ten years later. A succession of wars were waged between the French and English for the control of Southern India in the eighteenth century. Both sides enlisted rival factions of the "country powers" to help them, and the success of the British was due, partly to the genius of Clive, but still more to the loss of the command of the sea by the French navy. The French never recovered from the capture of Pondicherry in 1761. Southern India passed under British control with the defeat of Tipu Sultan of Mysore in 1799. Meanwhile, the administration of Bengal had been ceded to Clive in 1765. The defeat of the last two independent Hindu powers, the Sikhs and the Marāthās, and the reduction of the remaining Indian rulers to the position of British feudatories, has already been described.

The condition of India in the 18th century was perhaps the unhappiest in the chequered history of the country. The break-up of the Mogul Empire caused widespread misery and disorder. The craftsmen who depended upon the Imperial Court lost their livelihood, and painting, architecture and the other arts declined. The gap was only partly filled by the growing demand for calico, printed cottons, silks, brocades and other goods for export to Europe, for the insecurity of the roads and of property in general made trade a precarious matter. The Marāthās, who were the dominant power, were purely predatory. Other Indian rulers took a pride in settling the country they conquered, building roads, resthouses and temples, and digging wells. The Marāthās did nothing of the kind. Like a swarm of locusts, their horsemen swept down upon a district when the crops were ripe and demanded blackmail. If this were not forthcoming, the village headman was tortured. If this, too, proved unsuccessful, the village was plundered and fired and the crops destroyed. After the defeat of the Peshwa, Central India was filled with a number of masterless men, popularly known as Pindāris, who carried on the evil tradition. Contemporary accounts are full of the terror with which the Pindāris inspired the peasantry. Women would throw themselves and their children into wells at their approach. They dragged bags of hot ashes over people's faces to force them to give up their money, and carried off young girls trussed up like calves on the backs of their pack-animals. On the approach of regular troops, the Pindāris, on their swift ponies, vanished from the spot. In Southern India things were no better. From 1761 to 1799 the state of Mysore was in the hands of two Muslim soldiers of fortune, Hyder Ali and his son Tipu. Hyder Ali's invasion of the Carnatic in 1780 has been described in impassioned language by Burke: "A storm of universal fire blasted every field, consumed every house, destroyed every temple. The miserable inhabitants, fleeing from their flaming villages, in part were slaughtered; others, without regard to sex, to age, to the respect of rank or the sacredness of function – fathers torn from children, husbands from wives – enveloped in a whirlwind of cavalry, and amongst the goading spears of drivers and the trampling of pursuing horses were swept into captivity in an unknown and hostile land. Those who were unable to escape this tempest fled to the walled cities; but escaping from fire, sword and exile, they fell into the jaws of famine." Tipu was an eccentric genius, with much literary and artistic taste; his state was, by contemporary standards, well governed and even prosperous, but he was ferociously cruel, and the forcible conversion of the Hindu peasantry was practised wholesale. The Christian population of the Malabar coast was nearly exterminated. The condition of the common people under the rule of the Nizam of Hyderabad was equally pitiable. A traveller describes a visit to a village where the people "were so far distracted with hunger, that many of them without distinction of sect devoured what was left by the European officer and sepoy from their dinner." Bengal under the East India Company, before the advent of the reforming genius of Warren Hastings, was little better off. "The dominions of Asia, like the distant Roman provinces during the decline of that Empire, had been abandoned, as lawful prey, to every species of peculators; insomuch that many servants of the Company, after exhibiting such scenes of barbarity as can scarcely be paralleled in the history of any country, returned to England loaded with wealth; where, intrenching themselves in borough or East India stock influence, they set justice at defiance, either in the cause of their country or oppressed innnocence."*

The earlier generation of officials of the East India Company were merchants, not administrators. They had come out to the East to make money, and it was only

* W. Bolts, *Considerations on Indian Affairs*, Preface, (1772).

after prolonged efforts that Warren Hastings was able to sweep clean the Augean stables and turn chaos into something resembling order. Hastings returned to England in 1785, to stand trial at the hands of his ungrateful countrymen for the very abuses which he had endeavoured to put down. His successors, Lord Cornwallis, continued the work of Hastings in purifying the administration; amongst other acts, he introduced the famous Permanent Settlement of Bengal, by which the amount of revenue to be recovered from the peasant-proprietors was fixed in perpetuity, the money being paid through the Zemindars, or hereditary rent-collectors, who were regarded as the actual landowners. The wisdom of this arrangement has been often questioned, and it subsequently entailed a considerable loss of revenue to the State; but it had the merit of fixing the sum to be collected, and putting an end to the worst forms of extortion. In British India, with the gradual introduction of settled government and a regular system of administration, there was a slow but distinct improvement in the peasants' lot.

By the beginning of the nineteenth century, however, only a fraction of the country was directly under British rule, and one of the most potent cause of misgovernment was the system of what were known as Subsidiary Alliances inaugurated by Cornwallis's successor, the Marquess of Wellesley (1798-1805). The Directors of the East India Company were averse from a policy of conquest, except where it was forced upon them, and, where possible, Indian princes were left in nominal control, their armies being replaced by British troops, who maintained them on their thrones. The result of the divorce between power and responsibility was disastrous. "The native prince, being guaranteed in the possession of his dominions but deprived of so many of the essential attributes of sovereignty, sinks in esteem and loses that stimulus to good government which is supplied by the fear of rebellion and deposition. He becomes a *roi fainéant,* a sensualist, an extortionate miser, or careless and lax ruler, which is equivalent in the East to an anarchist. The higher classes, coerced by external ascendancy, in turn lose their self-respect and degenerate like their master; the people groan under a complicated system of repression which is irremediable." The principal states thus brought under control were Hyderabad and Oudh. The Nizam of Hyderabad maintained a strong force commanded by French officers; troops were sent in 1799 to disarm and disband them, and the territory known as the Berārs was ceded in order to pay for the expenses of the army of occupation. The 'King of Oudh', as he was sometimes called, was coerced into a subsidiary alliance in 1801. The scenes enacted at the Court of Lucknow under its subsequent rulers surpass description. Lucknow during the first half of the nineteenth century, with its buffoons and parasites, its out-at-heels, European adventurers, its troopes of dancing-girls and its indescribable orgies, resembled a page from the Arabian Nights. This was the state of things which presented itself to Dalhousie, the greatest of the Governors General under the Company, when he arrived in India in 1848. Dalhousie was filled with the reformer's desire to sweep away abuses and among the foremost were the incurable Indian States. In some cases the method adopted was what was known as the Doctrine of Lapse. Few Indian rulers begot heirs of the body, and the permission to adopt was subject to the consent of the Paramount Power. In most cases this was refused, and the state in question lapsed to the British government. In this manner the Marāthā states of Sātārā, Nāgpur and Jhānsi lapsed to the Company, and the pension paid to the last Peshwa was discontinued in the case of his adopted son Dondhu Pant, afterwards notorious as the Nānā Sāheb. Oudh, after repeated warnings which passed unheeded, was annexed in 1856. There is no doubt, however, that Dalhousie's imperious policy, however beneficial in itself, was the predisposing cause of the Indian Mutiny. Orthodox people, Hindu and Mussalman alike, were uneasy at innovations such as railways and telegraphs, and at the teaching of Christian missionaries, which appeared to threaten caste, to lead astray the rising generation, and to undermine the very foundations of their ancient creeds. The abolition of Suttee and of the right of adoption seemed to show that no custom, however cherished, was safe. The English legal code, with its complications that no one save the lawyers understood, was universally feared and hated, and its introduction was intensely unpopular.

Muhammadans were, perhaps even more than Hindus, disquieted by the recent trend of events. The establishment of English rule meant the separation of Church and State, which was in itself repugnant to Islamic teaching, and with it came the substitution of the vernaculars, and even of English, for Persian, the classical language of their community. The annexation of Oudh, of the last of the great independent Muslim states in the North, outraged Muhammadan sentiment. The Tālukdārs of Oudh, the hereditary landholders, were deprived of many of their rights and liberties, and as Oudh was the recruiting-ground for the Bengal regiments. Feudal loyalty in India is very strong, and Hindus resented the discontinuation of the Peshwa's pension and the annexation of the Marāthā States as much as Muhammadans did the seizure of Oudh. Numbers of persons lost the positions which they had enjoyed at the native courts; there was now little left for an Indian, however able and ambitious, but a subordinate post under a none too sympathetic European official. Henry Lawrence and William Sleeman, both men with almost unparalleled knowledge of the Indian character, were fully alive to the dangers of the situation. Lawrence warned Dalhousie, but in vain. Writing to his wife in 1856, on the eve of the outbreak he had foreseen, and which was destined to cost him his life, he said: "We measure too much by English rules, and except, contrary to all experience, that the nergetic and aspiring, even where we are notorious imbeciles, should like our arrogating to ourselves all authroity and all emoluments. Until we treat natives, and especially soldiers, as having much the same ambitions and the same feelings as ourselves, we shall never be safe."*

* *Honoria Lawrence,* by Maud Diver, p. 471.

Sleeman was even more emphatic. "We have only that right to interpose in order to secure for the suffering people that better government which their sovereign pledged himself to secure for them but failed.... The Native States I consider to be breakwaters, and when they are all swept away we shall be at the mercy of our native army, which may not be always under control."*

The episode of the greased catridges served as a match to ignite the powder-barrel. On May 10th, 1857, the Bengal regiments at Meerut mutinied, and having killed their officers, rode off to Delhi and acclaimed the Emperor. The Government was caught unawares; the great arsenals at Delhi and Allahābād fell into the hands of the mutineers, and soon all the garrison-towns from Ambāla to Benares were ablaze. The massacres of non-combatants at Delhi and Cawnpore provoked stern reprisals. The garrison at Lucknow was besieged in the Residency, and not relieved till November. All the available resources were concentrated on the capture of Delhi, the rebel stronghold, and when it was taken by storm on September 14th, the back of the mutiny was broken. Meanwhile, what was really a separate rebellion, with the object of reinstating the Peshwa, had been started by the Rānī of Jhansi, the widow of one of the Marāthā chiefs whose state had lapsed. She seized Gwalior, but was finally defeated by a contingent from Bombay, and died fighting at the head of her troops. Her principal lieutenant, Tantia Topi, was caught and hanged; Nānā Sāheb fled to the jungles of Nepal, and was never heard of again. The Emperor was deposed and banished to Rangoon, and on November Ist 1858, the transfer of the government of India from the East India Company to the Crown was announced at Allahābād. Queen Victoria's proclamation, issued at the time, was a remarkable document; it announced a general amnesty, guaranteed the Indian princes against further encroachments, promised complete religious freedom, and reiterated that public offices should be thrown open to all, irrespective of race or creed.

The Mutiny was not a national movement. To call it a War of Independence is a misnomer. The mutineers were divided in their aims: their foremost leader, the Rānī of Jhānsi was fighting for the restoration of the Marāthā Rāj, while the Muhammadan soldiery aimed at the resuscitation of the Empire of Delhi. The princes who had escaped Dalhousie's axe remained loyal. The Nizam of Hyderabad, whose defection might well have meant the loss of India, cast in his lot with the British. Most important of all, the Sikhs, oblivious of the fact that eight years before they had been defeated with slaughter, cheerfully joined the side of their new masters, and marched to the siege of the Mogul capital. The Indian peasant knows little and cares less who are his rulers. *Dilli dur ast*—'It's a far cry to Delhi.' All he demands is justice, light taxation and non-interference, and outside Oudh there was no popular rising in support of the rebels. Afghanistan remained neutral, and Nepal sent her Gurkha troops to

* *A Journey through the Kingdom of Oudh in 1849-1850* (1858 edn.) II, 393.

support the English. The Mutiny was a painful episode, but it swept the sky clear of many clouds. It was the revolt of the old against the new, and was bound to come sooner or later. It abolished a pampered and ill-disciplined army and an out-of-date and unprogressive system of administration, and paved the way for the introduction of a uniform system of government, which provided security of tenure, regular taxation, protection of life and property and equal justice to high and low throughout the country.* How great these blessings were may be gathered from the study of Indian history of the preceding century and a half.

Social and Religious Movements in the Nineteenth Century

One of the first acts of Warren Hastings in order to establish a system of government in Bengal in consonance with the traditions of the people, was to institute an enquiry into the ancient language and literature and the legal system of the Hindus. In this he was following the precedent of enlightened princes like Akbar and Dārā Shikoh, who had caused Persian translations of the Hindu scriptures to be made. The result was that European scholars were encouraged to take up the study of Sanskrit. In 1785 Charles Wilkins published a translation of the *Bhagavad Gītā*, and five years later, Sir William Jones translated Kālidāsa's great drama, *Sakuntalā*. In 1802 an Englishman named William Hamilton, who was detailed in France owing to the Napoleonic Wars, beguiled his time by teaching Sanskrit to his fellow-prisoners. Among them was the German poet William Schlegel. The effect upon Europe of the discovery of Sanskrit literature and philosophy and electrifying, and may not unfairly be compared to the discovery of Greek at the Renaissance. To Schopenhauer, the Upanishads came as a new Gnosis or revelation. "That incomparable book," he exclaimed, "stirs the spirit to the very depths of my soul.... In the whole world there is no study, except that of the original, so beneficial and exhilarating. It has been the solace of my life: it will be the solace of my death!" Goethe's verse in praise of *Sakuntalā* is well-known:

Would'st thou the young year's blossoms, and the fruits of its decline,
And all by which the soul is charmed, enraptured, feasted, fed,
Would'st thou the earth or Heaven itself in one sole name combine?
I name thee, O Sakuntalā! and all at once is said.

Indian thought deeply influenced the German transcendentalists and, through them, Coleridge, Carlyle, Emerson, and the other pioneers of the Romantic Movement in England and America.

India benefited in her turn by contact with European minds. The application of western methods of study of Oriental literature had an intensely stimulating effect.

* V. A. Smith, *Oxford History of India,* p. 725, quoting Sir Lepel Griffin.

The Vedas were no longer part of a mysterious ritual, the very meaning of which was forgotten, but living works, to be interpreted and studied like the Greeks and Latin classics. Until the coming of the British, the history of the pre-Muhammadan period in India did not exist, and the very name of the great Emperor Asoka was forgotten. But in 1834 James Prinsep dicovered the clue to the Brāhmī and Kharoshthī alphabets, and this enabled him to undertake the reading of the ancient Hindu inscriptions. Since then generations of scholars—Indian and European—have been engaged in the laborious task of reconstructing, line upon line, the early history of India. Buddhism as well as Hinduism has been investigated, and now the western world can read in reliable translations the authentic words of the greatest of India's religious teachers. One of the pioneers in this direction was the Oxford scholar, Professor Max Müller, who, after thirty years of unremitting labour, published the first complete text of the Rig Veda in 1875. He followed this up by editing *The Sacred Books of the East,* in fifty volumes, which for the first time enabled the western world to have a first-hand acquaintance with the Hindu, Buddhist, Islamic and Chinese scriptures. The early European officials in India were often excellent connoisseurs of Indian art, and brought home to England collections of Mogul and Rājput pictures. One of the most important is that made by Mr. R. Johnson, the banker of Warren Hastings, which is now in the India Office.

The earlier Englishmen in India adapted themselves to the customs and habits of the country. Colonel Kirkpatrick, Resident at Hyderabad, "married a Muslim lady of rank, spoke Persian like a gentleman, and in manners and costume could hardly be distinguished from a Muslim noble." The "nabobs", as the Anglo-Indians were familiarly called in the eighteenth century, were thoroughly Oriental in their outlook, with their queer Easern habits, their hookahs and curries and native servants, and above all their inexplicable habit of taking a daily bath. Thackeray has immortalised the Civil Servant of the old type in Jos Sedley. It was part of the Company's policy not to interfere with the religion or customs of the people. The money spent on education was devoted to the encouragement of the indigenous learnign of the country. Warren Hastings endowed a Madrasah or Muhammadan College at Calcutta: Jonathan Duncan, the 'Brahmanised Englishman', founded at Benares, where he was Resident, a Hindu College for teaching Sanskrit. Customs such as suttee, infanticide, and slavery were tolerated. Government acted as trustees for temples; they derived a handsome income from the pilgrim-tax, and Indian regiments formed guards of nonour and fired salutes at Hindu religious processions. Protestant missionaries were not admitted into British India, though a small body established itself at the Danish colony of Serampore near Calcutta outside the Company's jurisdiction. In the South, Catholics had in many instances adopted the prevailing attitude towards Hinduism. The Jesuit Robert de Nobili and his followers adopted the saffron robe and sacred thread of the

Brahmins, lived on vegetarian food, and studied Sanskrit; they allowed their converts to retain the caste-system, and the Pariahs had separate arrangements made for them in their churches. Father Beschi, another Jesuit, wrote a Christian poem in Tamil which has become a classic. The Abbé Dubois vividly describes a Christian religious procession in the eighteenth century. "Accompanied with hundreds of tom-toms, trumpets and all the discordant music of the country; with numberless torches and fire-works; the statue of the saint is placed on a car which is charged with garlands of flowers and other gaudy ornaments according to the taste of the country—the car slowly dragged along by a multitude shouting all along the march—the congregation surrounding the car all in confusion, several among them dancing or playing with small sticks or native swords; some wrestling, some playing the fool; all shouting or conversing with each other, without anyone exhibiting the least sign of respect or devotion."

But with the beginning of the nineteenth century, a change set in. In 1813, when the Company's Charter was renewed, a sum of £10,000 was ear-marked or "the revival and improvement of literature and the encouragement of the learned natives of India, and for the introduction and promotion of a knowledge of the sciences among the inhabitants of British territories in India." A demand for western education was rapidly growing up among better class Indians who had come into contact with Europeans. This was encouraged by the Baptist mission at Serampore. The missionaries started a printing-press, and gave a great impetus to the vernaculars by printing the first Bengali newspaper in 1818, and translations of the Bible in Bengali, Tamil and Marāthī. Numerous institutions to promote western literature and science sprang up in Calcutta; the first was the Hindu College, afterwards the Presidency College, founded in 1816. Four years later the Bishop's College was established.

In 1825, Lord William Bentinck, the most enlightened of the Governors General, arrived in India. A bitter controversy had been raging for some time whether the sum of money to be devoted to education was to be spent on subsidising the traditional institutions of the country, the old *tol* and *math* and madrassahs, or upon western learning. The demand for the latter was becoming more and more pressing, especially as, by the provisions of the renewed Charter of 1833, Indians were to be admitted to the higher branches of the civil service. The matter was finally clinched by Thomas Babington Macaulay, who had come out to India as Bentinck's Law Member. Macaulay ridiculed the venerable literature of the Hindus as "false history, false astronomy, false metaphysics, which attended their false religion," and concluded by pointing out that "the languages of Western Europe civilised Russia; I cannot doubt they will do for the Hindu what they have done for the Tartar." However much we may deplore the tone of Macaulay's minute, there is little doubt that the change was inevitable. It certainly convinced the other members of the Governor General's

Council, and Lord Bentinck issued his famous resolution that "all the funds appropriated for education would be best employed on English education alone."

The pioneer in the changes which have revolutionised modern India was undoubtedly Rām Mohun Roy. He was born in 1772 and belonged to a good Brahmin family, whose members had held office for generations under the Muhammadan rulers. His parents were orthodox Hindus, and he was married while he was still a child. He studied Persian, Arabic and Sanskrit while at school, and when he was about twenty, he learnt English and started to read the Bible. Not satisfied with a translation, he acquired enough Hebrew and Greek to study the original. In 1804, disgusted with the corruption of the Hindu religion practised around him, he wrote a pamphlet in Persian denouncing idolatry. In 1811, his desire for reform was brought to a point by witnessing the immolation of his sister-in-law on her husband's funeral pyre; this terrible sight altered his whole life, and soon after, he gave up a lucrative government appointment to devote himself to the religious and social betterment of his countrymen. He found in the Vedas and the Upanishads a pure and noble creed which had long been overlaid with superstition and idol-worship. Still higher teaching, however, he discovered in the first three Gospels, and in 1820, he published a remarkable book entitled *The Precepts of Jesus, The Guide to Peace and Happiness*. It recorded the moral precepts of Jesus Christ in the words of the Gospels, but explicitly omitted all mention of miracles or of Christ's Divinity. This deeply offended the Serampore missionaries, hitherto friendly to him, but gained him friends in David Hare, a Unitarian watchmaker, and William Adam, both devoted to the cause of bringing western enlightenment to India. Orthodox Hindus were deeply suspicious of the new education and Mussalmans stood entirely aloof. Rām Mohun Roy's courageous and outspoken views "raised such a feeling against him, that at the last he was deserted by every person except two or three Scotch friends." He addressed a remarkable letter on the subject to the Governor General, Lord Amherst, in which he asserted that "if it had been intended to keep the British nation in ignorance of real knowledge, the Baconian philosophy would not have been allowed to displace the system of the Schoolmen, which was best calculated to perpetuate ignorance. In the same manner, the Sanskrit system of education would be the best calculated to perpetuate ignorance, if such had been the policy of the British Legislature. But as the improvement of the native population is the object of government, it will consequently promote a more liberal and enlightened policy of instruction."

In 1828, Rām Mohun Roy brought to fruition one of the great objects of his life, the establishment of the Brahma Samāj, a Church open to all sorts and conditions of men for "the worship and adoration of the Eternal, Unsearchable and Immortal Being Who is the Author and Preserver of the Universe." The offering of sacrifices, the taking of life, and the use of any kind of image, painting or portrait were forbidden.

In the following year, Lord Bentinck, supported by Rām Mohun Roy, took the courageous step, in the face of his more conservative advisers, of declaring Suttee illegal; those aiding and abetting it were liable to be prosecuted for murder. Other cruel practices, the murder of female babies at birth, and thugee, the ritual strangling of travellers by assassins who were devotees of the goddess Kālī, were also suppressed. The Hindu College and other institutions for imparting English education were now in full swing, and Rām Mohun Roy proceeded to do what was then practically unheard-of for a high-caste Hindu. He accepted an invitation from the Emperor of Delhi to go to England in order to represent certain grievances to the Board of Directors. Rām Mohun's English visit was an unqualified success. He was given a banquet by the Directors; he was presented to King William IV and was accorded a seat of honour at the Coronation; he was a constant visitor at the House of Commons, and heard the debates on the Reform Bill, the Factory Act and the Act for the abolition of Slavery. He impressed on the Court of Directors the necessity of codifying the Indian criminal code, substituting English for Persian as the official language, and admitting Indians to the highest posts, freely and impartially, without distinction of race, religion or colour. The momentous Charter Act of 1833, which put an end to the commercial character of the Company, was largely due to his inspiration. Soon after it was passed, he died at Bristol at the age of sixty-one.

Rām Mohun Roy was the greatest Indian of his age. He was indeed the prophet of the new India. It is untrue to say that he wished to denationalise his country. He was a fine Oriental scholar, and deeply read in Persian and Sanskrit. But he recognised, years before any of his countrymen, that the education which had been fostered by the pandits and maulvis was too vague and unpractical to influence the people at large; western knowledge would not only enable India to fight against the abuses and corruptions which disfigured her social life, but would lead to a truer understanding of her own immemorial culture.

The Brahma Samāj received considerable development from its third leader, Keshab Chandra Sen. A reformed church arose, which, while mainly Hindu in its outlook, anticipated the more modern Theosophical movement in recognising the inspiration of the Scriptures of all creeds. The Samāj movement has done an immense amount of good in Bengal, in purifying the popular religion, putting down social evils like child-marriage, developing the vernacular and popularising education. Nearly all the leading writers and thinkers of Bengal in the last century have been Samajists, and many of them have come from the Tagore family, which was produced a galaxy of philosophers, artists, musicians, dramatists and poets. The best known is Rabindranāth, born in 1861, whose *Gītānjali*, or Handful of Songs, published just before the War, gained for him the Nobel Prize, and an international reputation enjoyed by no other Indian writer. His poems breathe the passionate love of God which is familiar to students of Kabīr and Chaitanya:

Thus it is that thy joy in me is so full. Thus it is that thou hast come down to me.

O thou Lord of all heavens,
Where would be thy love if I were not?

Thou hast taken me as thy partner of all this wealth.
In my heart is the endless play of thy delight.
In my life thy will is every taking shape.

And for this, thou who art King of kings hast decked thyself in beauty to captivate my heart.

And for this thy love loses itself in the love of thy lover,
And there art thou seen in the perfect union of the two.*

Dr. J. N. Farquhar, speaking of *Gītānjali*, says: "There is no Karma, no transmigration, no inaction, no pessimism in this lofty verse; but there is the perception that Nature is the revelation of God; there is everywhere the joy of meeting Him in sun and shower; there is the dignity and wroth of toil, deliverance won by going down where God is, among the poorest, lowliest and lost, the duty of serivce, the core of religion found in righteousness, life won by dying to self, sin recognised as shame and thraldom, and death as God's messenger and man's friend!"

Rabindranāth Tagore combines in his person the old and the new, and his work is the product of the union of the Eastern and Western culture to a unique degree. He is an ardent lover of his country, and mourns for her lost greatness, but he recognises her indebtedness to the West. "It is only by knowing the Europe that is great and good that we can effectively guard ourselves against the Europe that is base and greedy." He has a deep desire for union with God; but union comes not from Yoga and asceticism, but from mixing in the world and helping others. "God is the great playfellow who creates flowers of beauty for His children, and death is a momentary interruption of the *līlā*".† At Bolpur, Rabindranāth Tagore has established a school where the teaching is carried out in the traditional Indian manner. The pupils study beneath the trees in the open air; they are responsible for their own discipline, and they begin and end the day with prayers to "the Deity who is in fire and water, nay, who pervades the universe through the through, and makes His abode in tiny plants and towering forests."‡

The Samāj movement spread to Bombay, where the Prārthanā Samāj or Society of Prayer was inaugurated. As in Bengal, its followers tried to evolve a pure and

---

* *Gītānjali,* p. 32.

† E. J. Thompson, *Rabindranath Tagore,* p. 100. *Līlā* is the 'Sport' of the Creator with His creatures.

‡ E. J. Thompson, *op. cit.*, p. 97.

simple theism, purged of idolatry and superstition and evil social customs. Its members adjured child-marriage and caste restrictions. The most enlightened writers and politicians of Western India, Rāmkrishna Bhāndārkar, M. G. Rānade and G. K. Gokhale, supported it, and from it sprang the Society of the Servants of India, which has taken a leading part in promoting educational and social reform.

The Brahma movement was regarded by pious Hindus as unduly rationalistic in its outlook, and it led to a number of attempts to purify orthodox Hinduism. The most remarkable of these reformers was Dayānand Sarasvatī, who was born in Kāthiāwār in 1824. In his autobiography he describes his conversion. He was keeping vigil as part of the ceremony of initiation in the temple of Siva, when doubts suddenly assailed him. "I feel it impossible," he told his father, "to reconcile the idea of an omnipotent, living God, with this idol, which allows the mice to run upon its body, and thus suffers its image to be polluted on the slightest provocation." After this, like the Buddha, he wandered about India as a mendicant ascetic, seeking the truth. He practised Yoga, but found it a fraud. In 1860, however, he met his Master, a blind Brahmin, who instructed him in the Vedas. After a further period of study, Dayānand started his public career in 1868, and founded the Ārya Samāj. Like Luther, Dayānand aimed at stripping religion of all its later accretions, and going back to the primeval simplicity of the Vedic hymns and Upanishads. The Vedas are the source, not only of all religious truth, but moreover, of all knowledge. They contain implicity every thing worth knowing, even the most recent inventions of modern science, steam-engines, railways and aeroplanes. Dayānand threw open the study of the Vedas to both men and women, regardless of caste; idolatry is forbidden, but members of the Ārya Samāj believe in Karma and rebirth. The Ārya Samāj has many followers in the Punjab, and maintains a College in Lahore. The Ārya Samāj represents militant Hinduism; it adapts a polemical attitude towards Christianity and Islam, and vigorously condemns cow-killing.*

An equally interesting personality is Rāmkrishna Paramahamsa, who was born near Hooghly in Bengal in 1834. He was a Brahmin by caste, but in 1871, when he forsook the world and donned the ascetics' robes, he worked in a temple as a scavenger, performing the most menial offices and joining in the meals of outcasts. At one time he shared the humble abode of a Muhammadan fakir. He had visions of Krishna and Jesus, and came to the conclusion that all creeds are only facets of the same Truth. "Every man should follow his own religion. A Christian should follow Christianity, a Muhammadan should follow Muhammadanism. For Hindus, the ancient path, the path of the Aryan Rishis, is the best." Rām Mohun appealed to the head, Rāmkrishna to the heart. The saintliness of his life and the simplicity of his teaching

* Max Müller, *Biographical Essays,* p. 170. J. N. Farquhar, *Modern Religious Movements in India* (1915), p. 101.

won him a large following. Among these was Swāmi Vivekānanda, a highly educated man, and a staunch defender of Hinduism. To him, everything in Hinduism is right; the West is degraded and materialistic. His creed was based on the Vedānta, and was an attempt to graft Hindu beliefs on modern thought. He was a powerful orator, and in 1893, when he attended the Parliament of Religions in Chicago, he created a profound impression. He made numbers of American converts, and in San Francisco is a picturesque Hindu temple, the headquarters of the Rāmkrishna Mission. One of his European followers was Margaret Noble (Sister Nivedita), whose charming work, *The Web of Indian Life,* presents a highly idealised view of the Hindu religion.

One result of these movements was to check the conversion of the educated classes to Christianity which seemed almost inevitable in Macaulay's time. Another was to encourage the growth of the Indian vernaculars. When Macaulay advocated the adoption of English for purposes of higher education, the choice lay between it and Sanskrit or Persian. Sanskrit, like Latin in medieval Europe, was the *lingua franca* of the learned. Educated men regarded the vernaculars, as a literary medium, with contempt. Thanks first to the Christian missionaries and then to the various Hindu reformers, the various Indian vernaculars have now developed an extensive prose literature.

At first, in their desire to enlarge the vocabulary, Sanskrit words were freely introduced, and early vernacular prose literature was as alien from the language of the people as, say, Dr. Johnson's English from the common English speech of his day. But now there is a return to a simpler and less affected style. Almost all the vernaculars have now a flourishing literature. The chief literary forms are the novel, the essay, the drama and lyric poetry. The novelists and dramatists usually select as their themes the glories of India's past and social reform. Several of the early novelists—Bankim Chandra Chatterji in Bengal, Nanda Shankar in Gujarāt, Hari Narāyan Āpte in the Deccan and others, were imitators of Sir Walter Scott. Bankim Chandra Chatterji's chief claim to fame lies in his poem *Bande Mātaram* (I salute the Motherland) which has been adopted as the Indian national anthem. It has been translated into English by Aurobindo Ghose, the great Indian philosopher and nationalist:

Mother, I bow to thee!
Rice with thy hurrying streams,
Bright with thy orchard gleams,
Cool with the winds of delight,
Dark fields waving, Mother of might,
Mother free.

Who hath said thou art weak in thy lands,
When the swords flash out in seventy million hands,

And seventy million voices roar
Thy dreadful name from shore to shore?
With many strengths who art mighty and strong,
To thee I call, Mother and Lord,
Thou who savest, arise and save!
To her I cry, who ever her foemen drave
Back from plain and sea,
And shook her country free.

"Bankim Chandra Chatterji," says Mr. R. W. Frazer, "is the first creative genius modern India has produced. For the western reader his novels are a revelation of the inward spirit of Indian life and thought."* The modern vernacular drama, in Marāthī, Gujarātī and Bengali, is chiefly a comedy of manners. Social reform, caste, the lot of the widow, and the anomalies rising from the clash of East and West, are the usual themes, treated often with an almost Shavian humour.

We must now turn to the Muhammadans. Urdu, the Muhammadan *lingua franca,* flourished chiefly at the courts of the local rulers, and was considerably developed in the eighteenth century, after the downfall of the Mogul Empire. In the Mogul Court, which was essentially foreign, Persian was alone patronised, but now people began to realise the absurdity of writing one language and speaking another. The Nawābs of Oudh were great patrons of Urdu poetry, and it is claimed that the purest Urdu is still spoken at Lucknow. With the coming of the English, the need for prose literature in Urdu as in other Indian languages was felt. In 1800 a College was founded at Fort William in Calcutta for training the cadets who came out to the Company's service; its learned Principal, Dr. J. B. Gilchrist, found that it was necessary to translate books into Urdu, and for this purpose a number of learned Indian scholars were employed. From translation, the Fort William writers went on to original prose works; the chief difficulty was to persuade them to adopt a simple style and avoid Persian embellishments. After the Mutiny, the Muhammadan community remained in a state of deep depression; less adaptable and more conservative than the Hindus, they were outstripped by their more nimble-witted competitors, and this led to a recrudescence of the latent bitterness always subsisting between the two communities. From this parlous condition they were retrieved chiefly by the work of Sir Sayyid Ahmad Khān, the great Muslim reformer who did for his co-religionists what Rām Mohun Roy had done for the Hindus. Sir Sayyid was a pioneer of simple Urdu; he was indefatigable in his efforts to bring modern knowledge to his fellow-countrymen by means of magazines, books, societies and schools. In 1869, at the age of fifty-two, he visited England and met Thomas Carlyle and other famous people. His liberal

* *Literary History of India,* p. 420.

views on religious and social matters earned him the hatred of the orthodox, and at one time his life was in danger; but in 1877 he realised the dream of his life in the foundation of the Muhammadan College at Aligarh, now the Muslim University. To-day, the most distinguished Muhammadan writer is Sir Muhammad Iqbal, poet and mystic. His *Secrets of the Self,* published in 1915, created a great stir. Iqbal was greeted as a Messiah who stirred the dead bones of Islam to fresh life. Iqbal, who wrote in Urdu and Persian, is the apostle of militant Muhammadan nationalism. His philosophy is coloured by his studies of Nietzsche and Bergson, but at heart he remains a mystic with ideas attuned to those of the Persian Sufis, and his dominant note is abhorrence of the materialism of the West.

> The glitter of modern civilisation dazzles the sight,
> But it is only a clever piecing together of false gems.
> The wisdom or science in which the wise ones of West took such pride.
> Is but a warring sword in the bloody hand of greed and ambition.

The Osmania University in Hyderabad State, under the patronage of H.H. the Nizam, employs Urdu as its language. Hyderabad, the premier Indian State, is now the leading centre of Urdu culture.

English, however, is the medium in which educated men and women from different parts of India communicate with one another; it is the language of the courts, the universities and the press. Toru Dutt in the past generation, and Sarojini Naidu in the present, have written English verse of great charm and distinction.

It is now over forty years since Sir Edmund Gosse exhorted the young Deccani poetess to vouchsafe to her readers 'some revelation of the heart of India, and of such mysterious intimations as stirred the soul of the East long before the West began to realise that it had a soul':

> What longer need hath she of loveliness,
> Whom Death hath parted from her lord's caress?
> Of glimmering robes liek rainbow-tangled mist,
> Of gleaming glass or jewels on her wrist,
> Blossoms or fillet-pearls to deck her head,
> Or jasmine garlands to adorn her bed?

In the realm of fiction, the most significant writer is Mulk Rāj Ānand, whose studies of Indian peasant life have been described as the most important and promising books ever written in English by an Indian. Indians have won for themselves a place among the world's scientists: Sir Jagadish Bose in botany, Sir P. C. Roy in chemistry, and Sir C. V. Raman in physics have secure niches in the temple of Fame. Indian statesmen have taken a large part in the political mvoements of the day. Of the past generation, perhaps the most distinguished was G. K. Gokhale; the most inspiring figure of to-day is Mr. M. K. Gandhi. The Mahātmā, as he is affectionately called, combines India's traditional asceticism with a very modern outlook. Deeply imbued with the teachings of Tolstoi, Ruskin and the Sermon on the Mount, he believes that the remedy for the social and political evils of to-day lies in simplification. He has told India to abandon her mills and railways and other capitalistic machinery and return to the spinning-wheel. He has imported into politics the old principle of *ahimsā* or non-violence, stressed by Asoka 2,000 years ago. Mr. Gandhi's great hold on the peasant is partly due to his power of writing plain, unadorned, nervous Gujarāthī; he is one of the great masters of prose in his own tongue as in English, and his recent autobiography is a classic of its kind.

One of the most helpful signs of to-day is the revival of interest in Indian art. The old traditional arts and crafts of India have never died; masons and sculptors may be found to-day in the Indian States, who work according to the rules laid down in the ancient manuals. Lord Curzon's zeal for the preservation of historic monuments of the country did much to rescue them from the oblivion into which they had fallen; but educated India had almost forgotten her ancient heritage in these matters, until two notable pioneers, E. B. Havell and Ananda Coomaraswamy, succeeded in arousing the national conscience. A school of painting has arisen in Bengal, chiefly under the inspiration of Abanindro Nāth Tagore and his followers Nanda Lāl Bose and Surendra Nāth Ganguly, which has inaugurated a new era. Their work, which draws its inspiration from Ajantā, has not the strength or vigour of the old indigenous schools, but has great charm and grace. The Bombay school, on the other hand, seeks to free itself from the shackles of tradition, and to apply modern methods to express Indian themes.

The Tagores have done much to rescue Indian music, the most characteristic and ancient of the Indian arts, from oblivion. Indian music has close affinities with painting, drama and dancing. In Calcutta, Bombay, Poona and Baroda there are academies of music, and one of the latest developments has been the application of western music science to traditional Indian forms. Indian dancing, based on classical traditions and borrowing some of its technique from the European ballet, has attracted much attention in Western countries.

At present India stands on the threshold of a new era. Political and social changes have followed in bewildering succession. The nationalist movement has created a revulsion against the indiscriminate imitation of the West which was the fashion in the Victorian era. When, however, occidental influence has been assimilated, we may look forward to the emergence of a new eclectic culture combining what is best in both; the future of India, in art and literature, seems to lie in the amalgamation of Western thought with her own immemorial civilisation.

"Men such as Ram Mohun Roy, Keshav Chandra Sen, Michael Madhusadhan

Datta, Bankim Chandra Chatterji, Kasinath Trimbak Telang," says R. W. Frazer, "are no bastard bantlings of Western civilisation; they were creative geniuses worthy to be reckoned in the history of India with such men of old as Kālidāsa, Chaitanya, Jayadeva, Tulsī Dās and Sankarāchārya, and destined in the future to shine clear as the first glowing sparks sent out in the fiery furnace where new and old were fusing."*

* *Literary History of India*, p. 446.

Bibliography

I : General History

*The Cambridge History of India,** six volumes (vol. II and IV in press). Cambridge.

*The Oxford History of India,** by V. A. Smith. Oxford, 1921.

The Imperial Gazetteer of India (vol. I and II deal with Indian History). Oxford, 1927-9.

The Cambridge Shorter History of India, ed. H. H. Dodwell. 1934.

A Short History of India, by W. H. Moreland and A. C. Chatterjee. 1936.

Chronology of India. C.M. Duff. 1899.

II : Hindu Religion and Cuture

Hastings's *Encyclopedia of Religion and Ethics.*

Antiquities of India. By L. D. Barnett. 1913.

*Ancient India and Indian Civilization.** By P. Masson-Oursel. 1934.

*India's Past.** By A. A. Macdonell. Oxford, 1927.

Buddhist India. By T. W. Rhys Davids. 1903.

The Life of Buddha. By E. J. Thomas.

The History of Buddhist Thought. By E. J. Thomas.

A Primer of Hinduism. By J. N. Farquhar. Oxford, 1912.

Indian Thought and Its Development. By Albert Schweitzer. 1935.

The Heart of India. By Dr. Lionel Barnett. 1913.

Alberuni's India, trans. By E. Sachau. (Trübner's Oriental Series). 1879.

III : Hindu Literature

The Sacred Books of the East, edited by F. Max Müller. Brahmanism, 22 volumes, Buddhism and Jainism, 12 volumes. (Translations of the classical religious literature). Oxford.

The Heritage of India. (A series of popular volumes on the Indian vernaculars, philosophy, art and music). Oxford.

A History of Sanskrit Literature, By A. A. Macdonell. 1899.

Indian Wit and Wisdom. By E. Monier Williams. 1892.

IV : History : Hindu Period

Mohenjo-Daro and the Indus Civilization. By Sir J. Marshall. 3 vols. 1931.

*The Early History of India**. 4th edition (1924). By V. A. Smith.

*Ancient India.** By E. J. Rapson. Cambridge, 1914.

Asoka. By V. A. Smith (Rulers of India). Oxford, 1920.

Harsha. By R. Mookerji (Ditto). Oxford , 1926.

Commerce between the Roman Empire and India. By E. H. Warmington.

Buddhist Records of the Western Wrold. By S. Beal. (Trübner's Oriental Series). 1865.

On Yuang Chang. By E. Watters. 1905.

Ancient India as described in Classical Literature. J. W. McCrindle. 1901.

V : Indian Art and Architecture

The History of Indian and Eastern Architecture. By J. Fergusson. 2nd edition. Revised by J. Burgess. 1910.

Indian Sculpture. By Stella Kramrisch. (Heritage of India Series). 1933.

Buddhist Art in India, Ceylon and Java. by J. Ph. Vogel. Oxford, 1936.

A History of Fine Art in India and Ceylon. By V. A. Smith. Second edition. Revised by K. de. B. Codrington. 1930.

A History of Indian and Indonesian Art. By A. K. Coomaraswamy. 1927.

Ancient India. By K. de B. Codrington. 1926.

Indian Scultpure and Painting. By E. B. Havell. 1908.

The Court Painters of the Grand Moguls. By L. Binyon and T. W. Arnold. 1921.

The Ajanta Frescoes. By Lady Herringham. 1915.

The Beginnings of Buddhist Art. By A. Foucher. (Trans L. A. & F. W. Thomas). 1917.

VI : The Muhammadan Period

(a) Sources

The History of India as told by its own Historians. By H. M. Elliot and J. Dowson. 8 vols. (A complete source-book for the period). 1867-1877.

The Memoirs of Babur. Trans.Leyden and Erskine and edited by Sir Lucan King. Oxford, 1921.

Abul Fazl's Ain-i-Akbari. Trans. Blochmann and Jarrett. Calcutta, 1875-1891.

Memoirs of Jahangir. Trans. Rogers and Beveridge. 2 vols. Royal Asiatic Society, 1909-1914.

(b) European Travellers

European Travellers in India. By E. F. Oaten, 1909.

Travels in the Mogul Empire. A.D. 1656-1668. By François Bernier. Trans. Constable and edited V. A. Smith. Oxford, 1914.

Travels in India. By Jean Baptiste Tavernier. Ed. by V. A. Ball and revised by W. Crookee. 1899.

Storia do Mogor. By Niccolao Manucci. Trans. W. Irvine. 1907-8.

(c) Modern Histories : Muhammadan Period

Medieval India under Muhammadan Rule. By Stanley Lane-Poole.

Akbar, the Great Mogul. By V. A. Smith. 1919.

Akbar. By Laurence Binyon. 1932.

History of Aurangzeb. Sir Jadunath Sarkar. 5 vols. Calcutta, 1912-1924.

The Jesuits and the Great Mogul. Sir E. D. Maclagan. 1932.

Lives of Babur, Akbar and Aurangzeb in *Rulers of India Series.* Oxford 1892, etc.

Mughal Rule in India. By S. M. Edwardes and H. L. O. Garrett. 1930.

India at the Death of Akbar. By W. H. Moreland. 1920.

From Akbar to Aurangzeb. By W. H. Moreland. 1923.

(d) Hindu Dynasties in the Muhammadan Period

The story of a Forgotten Empire. (Vijayanagar). By R. Sewell. 1904.

Annals and Antiquities of Rajasthan. By James Tod. Ed. W. Crooke.

History of the Sikhs. By J. D. Cunningham. Ed. H. L. O. Garrett. 1918.

The Sikh Religion. By M. A. Macauliffe. 3 vols. Oxford, 1909.

A History of the Mahrattas. By J. C. Grant Duff. Ed. S. M. Edwardes. 1921.

Shivaji. By Sir Jadunath Sarkar. Calcutta, 1929.

A History of the Maratha People. By C. A. Kincaid and D. B. Parasnis Oxford, 1931.

VII : Modern India

The Making of British India. By Ramsay Muir. 1915.

India (Modern States Series). By H. H. Dodwell. 1936.

The Rise and Fulfilment of British Rule in India. By E. Thompson and G. T. Garratt. 1934.

Short biographies of British statesmen and governors in the *Rulers of India Series*. Oxford, 1892, etc.

Indian History of the end of the East India Company. By P. E. Roberts, Oxford, 1916.

Modern Religious Movements in India. By J. N. Farquhar. 1915.

Index

PLATE III

PLATE IV

PLATE V

PLATE VI

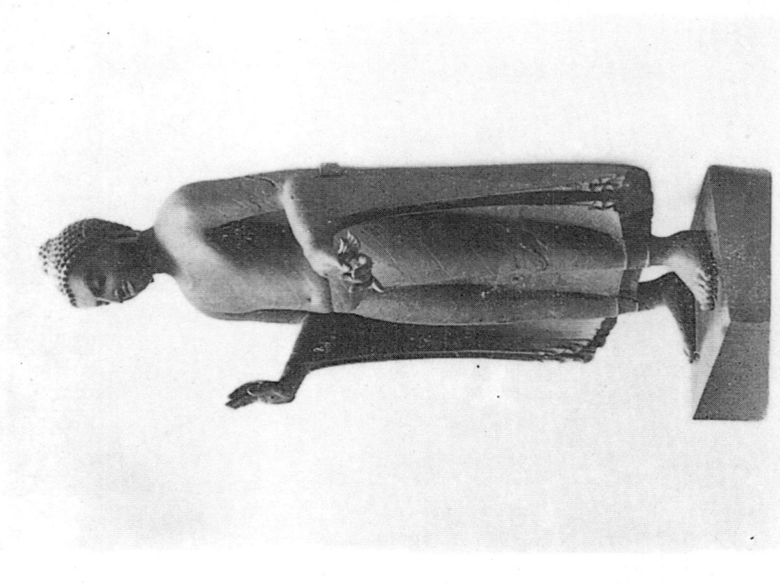

PLATE VII

PLATE VIII

PLATE IX

PLATE X

PLATE XI

PLATE XII

PLATE XIII

PLATE XIV

PLATE XVI

PLATE XVII

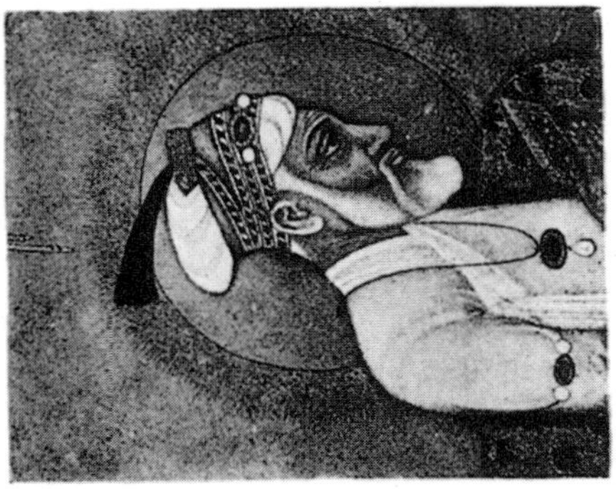

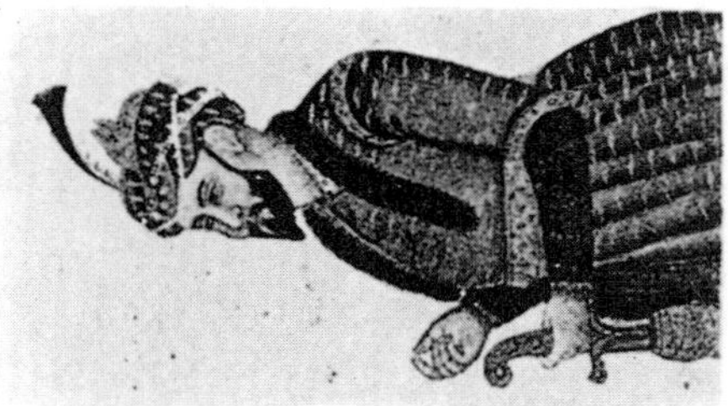

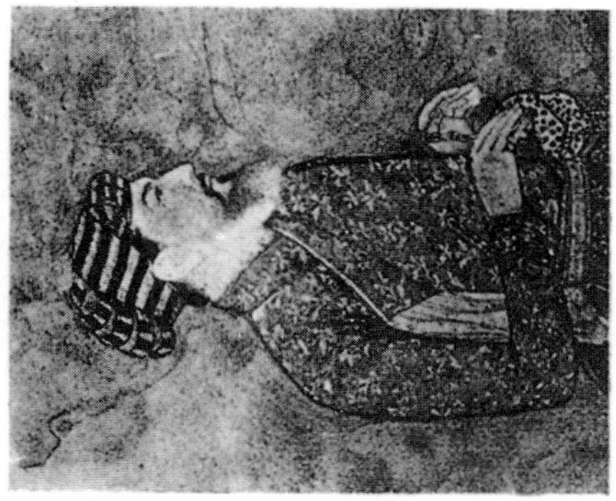

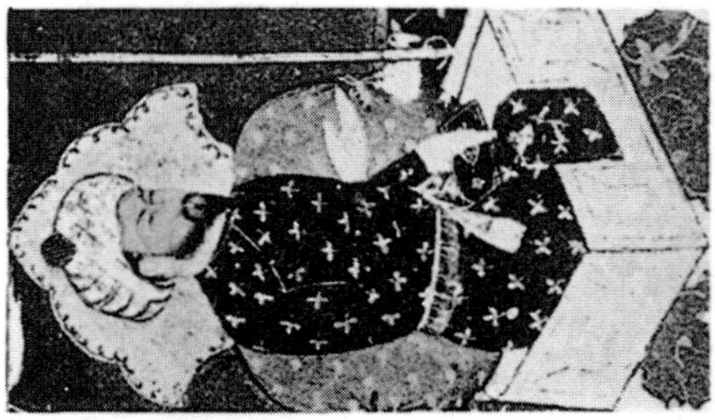

PLATE XVIII

PLATE XIX

PLATE XX

PLATE XXI

PLATE XXII

PLATE XXIII